Confucian Constitutionalism in East Asia

Western liberal constitutionalism has expanded recently, with, in East Asia, the constitutional systems of Japan, South Korea, and Taiwan based on western principles, and with even the socialist polities of China and Vietnam having some regard to such principles. Despite the alleged universal applicability of western constitutionalism, however, the success of any constitutional system depends in part on the cultural values, customs, and traditions of the country into which the constitutional system is planted. This book explains how the values, customs, and traditions of East Asian countries are Confucian, and discusses how this is relevant to constitutional practice in the region. The book outlines how constitutionalism has developed in East Asia over a long period, considers different scholarly work on the ease or difficulty of integrating western constitutionalism into countries with a Confucian outlook, and examines the prospects for such integration going forward. Throughout, the book covers detailed aspects of Confucianism and the workings of constitutions in practice.

Bui Ngoc Son is a Research Fellow in the Centre for Asian Legal Studies of the Faculty of Law at the National University of Singapore.

Routledge Law in Asia
Series editors:
Randall Peerenboom
Pip Nicholson

1 **Asian Discourses of Rule of Law**
Theories and implementation of rule of law in twelve Asian countries, France and the U.S.
Edited by Randall Peerenboom

2 **Human Rights in Asia**
A comparative legal study of twelve Asian jurisdictions, France and the USA
Edited by Randall Peerenboom, Carole J. Petersen and Albert H.Y. Chen

3 **Support for Victims of Crime in Asia**
Edited by Wing-Cheong Chan

4 **Administrative Law and Governance in Asia**
Comparative perspectives
Edited by Tom Ginsburg and Albert H.Y. Chen

5 **Regulation in Asia**
Edited by John Gillespie and Randall Peerenboom

6 **New Courts in Asia**
Edited by Andrew Harding and Penelope (Pip) Nicholson

7 **Legal Education in Asia**
Edited by Stacey Steele and Kathryn Taylor

8 **Legal Reforms in China and Vietnam**
A comparison of Asian communist regimes
John Gillespie and Albert H.Y. Chen

9 **Public Interest Litigation in Asia**
Po Jen Yap and Holning Lau

10 **Freedom of Information Reform in China**
Information flow analysis
Weibing Xiao

11 **Law and Development in Asia**
Edited by Gerald Paul McAlinn and Caslav Pejovic

12 **The Judicialization of Politics in Asia**
Edited by Bjorn Dressel

13 **Juries in the Japanese Legal System**
The continuing struggle for citizen participation and democracy
Dimitri Vanoverbeke

14 **Confucian Constitutionalism in East Asia**
Bui Ngoc Son

Confucian Constitutionalism in East Asia

Bui Ngoc Son

Routledge
Taylor & Francis Group
LONDON AND NEW YORK

First published 2016
by Routledge

2 Park Square, Milton Park, Abingdon, Oxon OX14 4RN
711 Third Avenue, New York, NY 10017, USA

Routledge is an imprint of the Taylor & Francis Group, an informa business

First issued in paperback 2017

British Library Cataloguing in Publication Data
A catalogue record for this book is available from the British Library

Library of Congress Cataloging-in-Publication Data
Bui, Ngoc Son, author.
Confucian constitutionalism in East Asia / Bui Ngoc Son.
pages cm. – (Routledge law in Asia)
ISBN 978-1-138-85206-8 (hardback) – ISBN 978-1-315-72380-8 (e-book) 1. Constitutional law–East Asia–History. 2. Confucianism–East Asia. 3. Philosophy–East Asia. I. Title.
KNC527.B85 2016
342.5–dc23 2015034950

ISBN: 978-1-138-85206-8 (hbk)
ISBN: 978-1-138-09984-5 (pbk)

Typeset in Times New Roman
by Wearset Ltd, Boldon, Tyne and Wear

Contents

Acknowledgments

This book has been completed during my time as a postdoctoral fellow at the Centre for Asian Legal Studies, National University of Singapore Faculty of Law. I greatly appreciate the Centre, the university, and the faculty for offering me the opportunity to pursue my postdoctoral study at one of the finest academic environments in the world. I am deeply grateful to Professor Andrew Harding and Professor Wang Jiangyu for their instruction, encouragement, and support of my work here. I also would like to thank Ms. Regana Zara Mydin and Mr. Haikel Rino at the Centre for their excellent support and assistance.

I greatly appreciate the support, comments, and encouragement of the editors of *Routledge Law in Asia*, Professors Randall Peerenboom and Pip Nicholson. At Routledge, I also would like to thank Peter Sowden for providing excellent service and editorial guidance. Constructive comments by Routledge's anonymous reviewers are gratefully acknowledged.

This book is built on the base of my doctoral dissertation at the University of Hong Kong. I believe my work could not be accomplished without my supervisor at the University of Hong Kong, Professor Albert Chen. I express the deepest gratitude to him. His outstanding work on constitutional issues and Confucian issues and the "ritual propriety" in his behavior – as I observe – have greatly inspired me and enhanced my confidence in the possible contribution of Confucianism to the field of comparative constitutional law. He has been patient enough to read carefully every word I have written and provided me with productive comments. He has also been kind enough to introduce me to other scholars with similar research interests. In addition, his recommendations have helped secure my visiting and postdoctoral studies. In short, it has been my greatest fortune to study under his instruction. At the University of Hong Kong Faculty of Law, I would also like to thank Professors Richard Cullen, Zheng Ge, Fu Hualing, Robert Morris, and Simon Young, whose lectures, comments, and conversations enlightened and stimulated my mind.

At Harvard Law School, I am grateful to Professor William Alford for his sponsorship of my visiting study there. Thanks also have to be given to librarian Phan Thị Ngọc Chấn at Harvard-Yenching Library for assistance finding materials. I also deeply express my thanks to Professor Mark Sidel for his support of my work and for his exceptional studies of Vietnamese constitutional law, from which I have benefited greatly. I also thank Professors Tom Ginsburg and John Gillespie for their useful comments on my work.

I would like to acknowledge the following journals for publishing my earlier articles and for permitting me to incorporate this material in this book: Bui Ngoc Son, "Confucian Constitutionalism: Classical Foundations," *Australian Journal of Legal Philosophy* 37 (2012): 61–98; Bui Ngoc Son, "The Introduction of Constitutionalism in East Asian Confucian Context: The Case of Vietnam in the Early Twentieth Century," *National Taiwan University Law Review* 7(2) (2012): 425–465; Bui Ngoc Son, "Confucian Constitutionalism in Imperial Vietnam," *National Taiwan University Law Review* 8(2) (2013): 373–435; and Bui Ngoc Son, "Beyond Judicial Review: The Proposal of the Constitutional Academy," *Chinese Journal of Comparative Law* 2 (1) (2013): 43–77.

Most of all, I thank my virtuous wife, Nguyễn Thị Phượng, and our lovely daughter, Bùi Tố Nguyên (Fifi), who have humanized my meaningful life in ineffable ways. I dedicate this book to them.

Bui Ngoc Son
July 2015

Introduction

In contrast to the negative view of Confucianism as the underpinning of "Oriental despotism," this book defends the thesis of the positive relations of Confucianism to constitutionalism – an antidote to despotism. This Introduction sets down the conceptual framework for the book, examining the epistemologies in comparative constitutional inquiry, and the theoretical approaches to the Confucianism–constitutionalism relationship.

Global constitutionalism and East Asia

Constitutionalism is now a global bellwether. Michel Rosenfeld observes: "Constitutionalism spread to all corners of the world."[1] This does not mean constitutional ideals always prevail over the siren song of power. Yet, when constitutionalism is universally recognized as the ideal model of political organization and practice of public power, even authoritarian rulers "feel compelled at least to pretend to be exercising their power within the constitutional framework."[2]

Modern constitutionalism is normally conceived as the political innovation of western modern civilization. Arguably, its substantial ideals, such as rule of law, human rights, democracy, and judicial review, are originated from the western world, largely associated with the Enlightenment liberalism.[3] Modern constitutionalism, therefore, is virtually comprehended as analogous to western liberal constitutionalism. So, the global trend of constitutionalism is the extension of western liberal constitutionalism to non-western contexts. East Asia[4] has also been swept along by that global wave. South Korea, Japan, and Taiwan have developed new democracies in line with western liberal constitutionalist standards.[5] Even constitutional discourse in socialist East Asia (China and Vietnam) has been influenced by the language of western liberal constitutionalism.[6]

The phenomenon of global constitutionalism is epistemologically connected to normative universalism and functionalism in comparative constitutional law.[7] Normative universalism operates with the assumption that constitutionalism itself entails everywhere some fundamental normative principles which involve both human rights and governmental structures.[8] It is closely associated with the studies of international human rights.[9] In addition, normative universalism is underpinned by American political philosopher John Rawls' hypothetical social contract undertaken behind "a veil of ignorance"[10] and German political philosopher Jurgen Habermas' consensus-based discourse theory,[11] which "combine a proceduralist approach with a deontological one and maintain that questions of justice and of the right can be answered independently of questions of the good."[12] According to these theoretical underpinnings,

> whatever differences regarding what constitutes the good may exist within a polity, constitutional essentials, to borrow Rawls's term, consistent with the ideal of constitutionalism may be derived from universally applicable criteria of justice and of the right. Accordingly, [...] there is a constant availability of a justice-based universal means for the achievement of constitutional unity above all actual differences.[13]

Habermas' theory of "constitutional patriotism" exemplifies universalist constitutional thinking, which argues that: "One can rise above all particular differences, be they sectarian, cultural, national, or ethnic, to commit to a common project of forging a unified polity resting on universally shared constitutional values."[14] Another paradigmatic example of universalism is T.R.S. Allan's ratiocination of "common elements" of a liberal constitutional order, which includes the rule of law, separation of powers, freedoms of speech and conscience, civil disobedience, procedural fairness, administrative justice, the right of silence, and equal protection or equality before the law.[15]

Like normative universalism, functionalism tries to search for common things that happen in every constitutional system. Functionalists assume that there are ubiquitous governmental tasks, e.g., going to war or coping with domestic emergences.[16] A body of literature on global constitutionalism, constitutional borrowings, migration of constitutional ideas, and constitutional convergence has been produced under the influence of normative universalism and functionalism with different levels.[17]

Mark Tushnet argues that universalism and functionalism are both flawed as they "operate on too high a level of abstraction"[18] and do not "pay adequate attention to the extent to which constitutional problems are informed by politics and culture."[19] To illustrate, he states:

> We can assume that there are universal principles of liberty and justice, for example, but we can be reasonably confident that such principles are not fully captured in general terms such as *free speech* or *equality*. The free speech principle, for example, whatever it is, is likely to be extremely complex, sensitive to the circumstances presented by particular problems.[20]

Contextualism

Another constitutional epistemology, endorsed by this study, is called contextualism, which

> emphasizes the fact that constitutional law is deeply embedded in the institutional, doctrinal, social, and cultural contexts of each nation, and that we are likely to go wrong if we try to think about any specific doctrine or institution without appreciating the way it is tightly linked to all the contexts within which it exists.[21]

Tushnet contends that human rights principles as well as governmental structures are "sensitive to the circumstances presented by particular problems."[22] Similarly, Vicki C. Jackson also opines that: "Constitutions are made and then interpreted in complex and distinctive historical contexts,"[23] and that constitutions are "particularly situated to express, or help constitute, or (possibly even) influence national identity."[24] Jackson and Tushnet's seminal textbook *Comparative Constitutional Law*[25] typically presents the combination of functionalism with contextualism. It is organized around common constitutional themes facing every constitutional system, such as constitutional change, constitutional review, structure of government, and human rights, but at the same time takes contextual factors seriously. As Teitel aptly remarks, "Jackson and Tushnet seek to account for historical and political context and more particularly, for the politics of democratic transformation."[26] In the same vein, Hart Publishing's series of national constitutional systems in the world, edited by Peter Leyland, Andrew Harding and Benjamin Berger, adopts the contextualist approach.[27]

Contextualism can be tracked back to French legal philosopher Charles-Louis de Secondat, Baron de Montesquieu. He opines: "The political and civil laws of each nation ... should be so appropriate to the people for whom they are made that it is very unlikely that the laws of one nation can suit another."[28] Contextualist thinking is also evident in G.W.F. Hegel's "immanent" approach to constitutional questions.[29] The Hegelian approach is "immanent" in the sense that "it does not impose normative criteria for evaluating constitutional law from the outside, as it were; but rather develops these normative standards from the concepts which constitutional law itself uses but fails to fully honour."[30] Within a Hegelian constitutional order, "the validity of the immanent ideals of constitutional law requires a *fusion* of a conceptual *form* (which is universalistic) with its social *contents* (that are particular)."[31] The ultimate goal of the immanent constitutional theory is "to bring the empirical reality of constitutional practice into line with the highest requirements of human reason, with the latter understood concretely as embodied with the immanent development of particular social and historical movements."[32]

Hegel's immanent theory of constitutional law, therefore, replaces "the abstract and merely formal conceptions of freedom which are rooted in spurious de-contextualized and ideologically predetermined 'freedom of choice' with a historical contextualized account of the unfolding of the idea of substantive freedom."[33] In contrast to normative universalism, Hegel introduces the alternative immanent theory which "develops constitutional justice as a social theory of communally evolving, enacted, and self-determined modes of freedom, such that the will is liberated in order to act upon itself."[34] He puts that in this way:

> Spirit is actual only as that which it knows itself to be, and the state, as the spirit of a people, is both the law which *permeates all relations within the state* and at the same time the customs and consciousness of its citizens. It follows, therefore, the constitution of any given people depend in general on the character and development of its self-consciousness. In its self-consciousness, its subjective freedom is rooted and so, therefore, is the actuality of its constitution.[35]

As "the state in its constitution must permeate all relationships within the state," "every people has the constitution appropriate to it and suitable for it."[36] Therefore, "A people's constitution must embody its feeling for its rights and its condition; otherwise, there may be a constitution there in an external way, but it is meaningless and valueless."[37] To verify this argument, Hegel invoked the case of the abortive imposition by Napoleon of an alien constitution upon Spain.[38]

Robert Cover's theory on *nomos* and narrative similarly reflects contextualist legal thinking. Cover contends that "no set of legal institutions or prescriptions exists apart from the narratives that locate it and give it meaning."[39] He names such narratives which provide meaning to legal institutions as *nomos*, a normative universe we inhabit.[40] Because *nomos* is something that determines the meaning of law and legal actions, the same law and the same legal actions may carry different meanings depending on people inhabiting the *nomos*. Cover asserts that

> if there existed two legal orders with identical legal precepts and identical, predictable patterns of public force, they would nonetheless differ essentially in meaning if, in one of the orders, the precepts were universally venerated while in the other they were regarded by many as fundamentally unjust.[41]

Cover's theory on *nomos* may challenge the claim that "in all directions of the globe, now have similar constitutions."[42] Constitutional texts may include identical concepts, principles, and institutions, but would be differently understood and practiced in different narratives. Cheryl Saunders argues that under the influence of the recent hegemonic processes of globalization of constitutional law, together with the more traditional factors of admiration and colonization, a certain degree of constitutional convergence is inevitable, but "convergence in form does not necessarily mean convergence in understanding, in values and priorities, or in the operation of constitutional arrangements in practice in the face of a plethora of local contextual factors."[43] Therefore, constitutional convergence should not bind contextualist thinking. As Saunders elaborates:

> No constitution is exactly the same in form or operation. Constitutional concepts have different meanings in different systems. In any event, constitutions are complex organisms. To some degree at least, every constitution is affected by its history, including the circumstances of its making; the

> context in which it operates; the often unarticulated assumptions on which it is based; the priority accorded to particular values; and a tendency to develop organic characteristics over time. The significance of these features may be mitigated, but it is unlikely to be eliminated, by the forces for constitutional convergence.[44]

Contextualism, however, does not pose a fatal challenge to constitutional borrowings, transplants, or migrations. The actual challenge is that these comparative constitutional enterprises must be carried out with great caution. Constitutional institutions and notions may be borrowed, transplanted, or migrate, but to be successful, they at the same time must experience a process of contextualization, through their adoption, adaption, and transformation in local contexts.[45]

Expressivism and constitutional culture

There are two forms of contextualism, namely institutional and expressivist contextualism. The former emphasizes the institutional and doctrinal contexts, while the latter focuses on the social and cultural milieus by taking constitutional ideas as the expressions of a particular nation's self-understanding.[46] For the purpose of this study, expressivism is more relevant.

Expressivism perceives the constitutional order as the embodiments of a particular nation's self-understanding. Yet, expressivism should be understood in a dynamic way. It does not imply that constitutional arrangements and ideas are merely the passive expression of a firmly established self-understanding. Rather, constitutional order is both shaped by and shapes constitutional self-understanding. Constitutional self-understanding may change as a response to a variety of contextual factors which may include the dynamic and contextual functioning of the constitutional order. In addition, constitutional self-understanding must not always be generated from autochthonous sources; rather, it may also involve polity's self-conscious adoption and adaption of extraneous sources. Therefore, expressivists need not be the opponents of globalization of constitutional law. Moreover, as Tushnet notes, a polity's self-understanding is not necessarily a single one, as those who constitute the polity are often contestable and actively contested.[47] In the same vein, Gary Feffrey Jacobsohn argues that constitutional identity "emerges *dialogically* and presents a mix of political aspirations and commitments that are the expression of a nation's past."[48] The dialogical interactions among contestable actors of the polity who may support alternative constitutional understandings and the dialogical engagements of the local actors in global discourse animate the dynamics of expressivist constitutional identity.

In term of its substantial concern, expressivism focuses on the social and cultural contexts. While self-understanding embodied in the constitutional order may contain various visions, concepts, and beliefs, the one involving constitutionalism presents the "constitutional culture" of the polity, "a series of expectations and understandings about the constitutional order, how it is and how it ought to be."[49]

Some scholars broadly define constitutional culture as inclusive of "the ideas, values, attitudes, and opinions people in a given polity hold with respect to law and the constitution."[50] This broad definition may include things that could be pertinent to the *constitution* but not necessarily be *constitutional* (for example, an attitude favoring a totalitarian regime), and therefore, may not be qualified as "constitutional culture." Constitutionalism is different from constitution. Likewise, an understanding about the constitution which people in a given polity accept may be anti-constitutionalist, and hence does not necessarily constitute a constitutional culture. As constitutionalism is substantially associated with constraints on public power, constitutional culture must include things relevant to constitutional constraints. In this narrow sense, Jason Mazzone defines constitutional culture as including:

> Such things as the disposition of regular citizens to recognize and accept that they are governed by a written document, one that creates institutions of government and sets limits on what the government may do; the accepted belief that the governing charter is created by the citizenry; the knowledge that the charter is not timeless, but rather that the citizens may change it or revoke it under certain circumstances; and the understanding that until the charter is changed we are bound by it and required to go along with its ultimate results even though we are free to disagree with them.[51]

In a rather similar vein, Nikolai Wenzel defines constitutional culture as encompassing "the norms, attitudes, and beliefs, explicit and implicit, that individuals (and preponderant groups within a country) hold about the nature, scope, and function of constitutional constraints."[52] But, in Wenzel's understanding, constitutional culture includes culture that both accepts and rejects constitutional constraints.[53] The latter component seems to turn constitutional culture into an oxymoron. Despite its various definitions, "culture" etymologically implies something "good" or valuable, with its Latin origin "*cultura animi*" (cultivation of the soul). So, it seems self-contradictory to refer to "bad culture" or "bad constitutional culture." A disposition or understanding that fails to *cultivate* a better constitutional soul is not a constitutional *culture*. A "culture" that "can reject constitutionalism outright" when "expediency is valued more than principle"[54] is not a constitutional culture at all. Therefore, it is more proper to narrow the scope of constitutional culture which only includes legal-political understanding, beliefs, attitudes, and disposition that accept constitutional constraints or are supportive of constitutionalism.

An important attribute of constitutional culture, namely its traditional quality, should be noted. Constitutional culture "is passed from generation to generation."[55] This, however, by no means implies that constitutional culture is unchangeable. Constitutional culture is a "complex phenomenon," "the ongoing dynamic process of millions of interactions" among individuals, groups, governments, and the rest of the world.[56] Therefore, constitutional culture is not static but in flux.[57] It can be changed as a response to internal (such as cultural, social, economic, and political self-renovation) and external (such as globalization of constitutional law) dynamics.

Having defined constitutional culture, we are now in a position to consider its relevance to constitutionalism. Constitutionalism does not merely mean the formal existence of constitutional ideals, which are in the modern sense mostly articulated in a written constitution. Constitutionalism essentially requires the real actions rather than merely ideal words. Constitutionalism requires "normative constitution" in Karl Loewenstein's theory,[58] which both embodies constitutional ideals and in reality constrains the practice of the public power. The real constraint of the formal constitutional norms requires, among other things, the support of the underlying political tradition. In other words, successful constitutionalism entails the support of a particular constitutional culture.

As Wenzel submits, Hayek's theory of "sensory order" as a mental model through which people make sense of the physical world can be heuristic in understanding the intimate connection between successful constitutionalism and constitutional culture. In the legal sphere, Hayek highlights the connection between the articulated rules or formal law and the unarticulated rules or underlying cultural norms: "The whole process of development, change and interpretation of law would become wholly unintelligible if we closed our eyes to the existence of a framework of such unarticulated rules from which the articulated law receives its meaning."[59]

The viability of constitutionalism requires the understanding of the meanings of formally articulated constitutional rules. Meanwhile, constitutional culture is a shared system of symbols or signs or the "mental model" in Hayekian sense[60] by which people give meanings to constitutional formality and provide critical judgments on constitutional actions. Therefore, without the support of a particular constitutional culture, formal constitutional rules may merely exist ostentatiously, and constitutionalism may fail. Wenzel points out, "If a critical mass of individuals refuses to be bound, if it rejects constitutionalism generally or the constitution specifically, if it does not accept the deferral of current power for long run stability, the entire constitutional undertaking will fail."[61]

The premise that the success of constitutionalism must be underpinned by political culture and tradition receives a consensus among constitutional law scholars.[62] To illustrate, Lutz asserts that: "Without this underlying political culture, the formal institutions of constitutionalism are moribund."[63] He recalls that even Montesquieu did not treat the separation of powers as a dogma because formal institutions are not the exclusive solution to arbitrary power. Lutz concludes that unless the people have a culture that allows the creation of constitutionalism, it will not occur; likewise, unless the people are ready to organize their polity in the way allowed by the separation of powers, constitutionalism will not last.[64]

Ruth Gordon's theory of "growing constitutions" as the bottom-up process equally underlines the importance of political culture. He argues that any constitution grows at the bottom of a culture where the complex norms and relationships tie the people together as a society. He then concludes:

> Constitutions can flourish and succeed only if they are firmly planted in the cultural soil from which they gain legitimacy.... Constitutions that are not firmly grounded in the cultural mores of the society in which they operate are destined to fail, become irrelevant, or be reshaped and adapted to meet the needs of the culture and society in which they are situated.[65]

There are ample empirical constitutional studies verifying the thesis that successful constitutionalism relies on the support of the local constitutional culture. Christopher Tiedemann, an American luminary in constitutional theory, asserts that: "Constitutions are effective only so far as their principles have their roots imbedded in the national character, and consequently constitute a faithful reflection of the national will."[66] He reminds us that: "history furnishes numerous examples of fruitless attempts to impose constitutions upon people whose principles are not in harmony with the popular political sentiment."[67] He recalls the cases in which Locke prepared a written constitution for the Carolinas whose principles are not in harmony with popular instinct and that Napoleon Bonaparte prepared paper constitutions for the nation he conquered.[68] Tiedeman, then, attributes the success of American and English constitutions to the underlying political culture of the respective countries:

> English and American constitutions work well, and challenge the admiration of political students, not because of their inherent and abstract excellences – for it would be no arduous or insuperable task to point out several glaring defects, but because they are in complete correspondence with the political sentiment of the respective nations, and they are themselves the natural products of Anglo-American civilization. It is not so much what is found in the written constitution, as the conservative, law-abiding, and yet liberal-loving character of the Anglo-Saxon, which guarantees a permanent free government to England and to the United States of America.[69]

Daniel P. Franklin and Michael J. Baun's 1992 research project on the relationship between political culture and constitutionalism provides further empirical evidence. Case studies in ten selected countries – namely Britain, the United States, Canada, Germany, Japan, Mexico, Turkey, India, Egypt, and Nigeria – help conclude that apart from institutional design, strong cultural commitment to constitutionalism is an important prerequisite for a stable and successful constitutional government.[70] In the same vein, focusing on constitutional law in the Asia-Pacific, Craham Hassall and Cheryl Saunders contend that "failure to identify the values that accompany a set of laws renders those laws ineffective," and point out that "in Asia Pacific, legal systems continue to draw on the other religious traditions, notably Hindu, Buddhist and Islamic, and similarly, the Chinese legal systems continue to reflect the ethical systems of Confucian thought."[71]

Wenzel's recent studies offer additional empirical justifications. To begin with, he discloses that three major systems of constitutional review (American,

Commonwealth, and Kelsen) meaningfully reflect the respective underlying constitutional culture.[72] The American system which allows ordinary courts to set aside unconstitutional legislations reflects the American attitude that the legislature is not a collective organ of the people but just one among government's bodies created as "necessary evils." The Commonwealth nations' weak form of judicial review stems from a different disposition which views the Parliament as the expression of the popular will, with complete sovereignty. The Commonwealth culture supports legislative supremacy, rejects the strong American model of judicial review, and only allows courts to practice weak or advisory judicial review.[73] The Kelsen model, first created in Austria in 1920, occupies the middle position, which allows a specialist constitutional court to review and void legislative and executive actions. The Kelsenian constitutional court also has its root in the tradition of Parliament sovereignty, for which it has institutional connections with the Parliament. For example, some of its members are selected by the Parliament. Wenzel concludes that the Kelsenian constitutional review model reflects a constitutional culture "that is distrustful of a wholly unfettered legislator, yet simultaneously weary of 'undemocratic' institutions that might attempt to thwart the will of the people."[74]

In regard to the constitutional system as a whole, Wenzel offers four case studies which help verify the thesis that whether constitutionalism is successful depends on whether constitutional parchment matches with constitutional culture. Two cases come from Asia: Japan and the Philippines.[75] Post-war constitution-making in these two nations were under the same external influence – the United States Constitution – but resulted in different outcomes: Japan succeeded while the Philippines failed. Wenzel attributes successful constitutionalism in Japan to the congruence of formal constitutional parchment with the underlying constitutional culture. According to him, Japan's 1946 Constitution, rather than parroting the US Constitution, drew on sufficient indigenous political, cultural sources (such as the communitarian orientations and the Shinto-Taoist tradition), which is instrumental to the half-century of constitutional stability, democracy, and economic development in Japan. In contrast, Wenzel states, the post-war Filipino Constitution failed to appreciate the local political tradition, which led to a generation of martial law and dictatorship. He explains that several Anglo-Saxon liberal ideas, such as human rights, limited government, and rule of law, adopted in the Constitution are alien to the Filipino *caudillo* strongmen tradition and Spanish and Filipino traditions of family/communal rights and *raison d'état*.[76]

Two other cases are drawn from post-colonial constitution-making in Latin America, Mexico, and Argentina.[77] The 1917 Constitution of Mexico demonstrates the consistence with the local political tradition – the consistent movement toward mature limited access order which helps maintain constitutional stability – while Argentina's Constitution matches the US Constitution virtually verbatim and at the same time mismatches with the local Spanish-infused authoritarian-centralized tradition, which generates military coups and dictatorships.[78]

In sum, an underlying legal-political disposition which accepts constitutional restraints and makes constitutional parchment meaningful is crucial to workable constitutionalism. Yet, the emphasis on constitutional culture should not lead to a form of "cultural determinism" which devalues formal constitutional arrangement. Constitutional texts provide transparent platforms for political discourse and formal organization of political power. Constitutional culture gives meanings to constitutional texts and helps to sustain the constitutional endurance, which is instrumental to viable constitutionalism. Also, the importance of constitutional culture should not lead to a radical form of "cultural relativism" which denies learning from others. As mentioned above, contextualism claims that exogenous constitutional ideas or institutions can be adopted, adapted, and transformed in the indigenous context.

Approaching Confucianism and constitutionalism

In the East Asian context, Confucianism has played a crucial role for centuries. In pre-modern East Asia, Confucianism, as a philosophy, constituted a major school of thought. As a political ideology, it served as the formal foundation of the imperial governments and laws, and, as living mores, it inculcated in the popular mind. More importantly, in contemporary East Asia, despite the abrasives posed by modernization, the influence of Confucianism is continuous. Scholars have demonstrated the Confucian influences in various dimensions of the contemporary societies in mainland China, Hong Kong, Japan, Singapore, South Korea, Taiwan, and Vietnam.[79] As Chaihark Hahm observes,

> Many of the idioms and vocabularies used by East Asians for making sense of the world and rendering normative judgments are derived from Confucian tradition. The way an East Asian interprets another person's actions and makes normative judgments is still powerfully informed by Confucian teaching. This is true even in the political sphere.[80]

The continuous influence of Confucianism in contemporary East Asia results in the academic concern for its relation to several political ideas and practices putatively originated in the western world, such as human rights, democracy, and constitutionalism. The relevance of Confucian tradition to human rights[81] and democracy[82] has been studied by historians, philosophers, and political scientists for several decades, especially after the third wave of democratization spread to East Asia in the late twentieth century. In the early twenty-first century, the Confucian relevance to constitutionalism has drawn the attention of some constitutional law scholars, such as Albert Chen, Chaihark Halm, Tom Ginsburg, and others. The scholarship on this era is creditable but rather parsimonious for comprehensible reasons. Epistemologically, to many constitutional law scholars, Confucianism is a shibboleth which mobilizes for submission, absolute monarchism, moral obligations, and hierarchal order. This antediluvian tradition seems inconsequential to the zeitgeist of constitutional inquiries which are preoccupied by modern, "cutting-edge," and global issues of constitutionalism. Methodologically, to embroil in the Confucian intellectual conversation, a constitutional law scholar who is mainly concerned with modern constitutional issues may be discombobulated by the labyrinthine gnomic aphorisms and esoteric statements in Confucian classics. This explains the neglect of Confucianism in comparative constitutional studies. To be sure, the literature on the relations of Confucianism to human rights and democracy is relevant to this study, given the complex interplay of constitutionalism to human rights[83] and democracy.[84] However, constitutionalism involves the constitutionalization of human rights and democracy, which does not often fall within the purview of historians, philosophers, and political scientists. An inquiry into the relation of Confucianism to constitutionalism, therefore, requires an examination of its relation to distinctive constitutional issues, such as limited power, constitution (written and unwritten), constitutional rights and goods, the separation of powers, and constitutional review and other forms of constitutional restraints.

The existing scholarship indicates that there are three theorizing models on the relationship between Confucianism and constitutionalism, which can be labeled as conflictivism, compatibilism, and indigenism.

Conflictivism

Those who adopt this view argue that Confucianism basically conflicts with constitutionalism. While constitutionalism is negatively defined as limited government, Confucianism is normally caricatured as associated with despotism. It seems logical to conclude on their antagonism. To illustrate, Edward Shils remarks that Confucius knew nothing of rule of law; constitution; elections; competing political parties; representative institutions; the separation of legislature, executive, and judiciary; public discussion and public opinion; freedom of expression and the press; freedom of association, assembly, and petition or representation; and individual rights.[85] In similar vein, Yu Chen in his article entitled "Confucianism versus Constitutionalism" comprehensively contrasts constitutionalism with Confucianism, arguing that constitutionalism focuses on rule of law, individualism, people's rights, and pursuit of justice via legal litigation, whereas Confucianism places emphasis on rule of men, collectivism, people's obligations, and discrimination against lawsuit.[86] If the conflictivist argument were valid, then Confucian legacy would be an impediment for the development of modern constitutionalism in the contemporary East Asia. From this perspective, to uphold constitutionalism in the modern East Asia, Confucianism must be downplayed.

In this study, I reject the conflictivist thesis because of its problematic theoretical underpinnings. Conflictivism confuses both constitutionalism and Confucianism. Conflictivists fail to distinguish different versions and forms of both constitutionalism and Confucianism. As far as constitutionalism is concerned, they tend to merely perceive it in a liberal sense. As Li-ann Thio states, since liberal constitutionalism is the dominant form, it is normally referred to as constitutionalism itself, but this is actually misleading.[87] The conflictivist vision occludes the fact that constitutionalism is indeed a polymorphic phenomenon.

Liberal constitutionalism is defined by liberalism, pivoting liberal rights as the end, and employing institutional arrangements such as the separation of powers and judicial review as a means. Other forms of constitutionalism, however, have different theoretical underpinnings, different ends, and different means. For example, ancient constitutionalism and medieval constitutionalism do not accentuate liberal rights; non-liberal constitutionalism pursues public moral values other than individual rights; communitarian constitutionalism is more concerned with citizen's duties.[88] In short, conflictivists fail to appreciate the plurality of constitutionalism.

Regarding Confucianism, it seems that conflictivists are confused by various forms and versions of Confucianism. Sor-Hoon Tan distinguishes two versions of Confucianism; first, a philosophical tradition based on Confucius' teachings; and second, a state orthodoxy.[89] Tu Weiming calls the latter "politicized Confucianism."[90] Conflictivists fail to distinguish philosophical Confucianism from the politicized one. Some imperial dogmas and practices, which stemmed from the egoistic politicization of political principles in Confucian philosophy, may conflict with constitutionalist aspirations, but whether Confucian philosophy itself is an antithesis of constitutionalism is another story. For example, in classical Confucianism, the ministry/ruler relationship is mutual: both have the obligation to adhere to what is right. The so-called "three bonds and five relationships" of politicized Confucianism, however, distorted this relationship (and others), mobilizing for the ministers' kowtowing to the ruler.[91] This practice may lead to the conclusion that Confucianism supports despotism. Similarly, the discrimination against litigation was the practical outcome of mandarin administration of later imperial governments in the history of China. It should be remembered that Confucius is reported to say that he could hear litigation well.[92] In addition, *The Book of Changes* or *I Ching*, one of five Confucian classics, has the *song* (訟, conflict) hexagram, which gives guidance to hear litigation.[93]

Compatibilism

This theorizing model juxtaposes Confucianism with constitutionalism (more precisely, western liberal constitutionalism) and seeks for notions and practices in the Confucian tradition which are said to be consistent with ideas and institutions of western liberal constitutionalism. Compatibilism is epistemologically connected to universalism in comparative constitutional law. Compatibilists adopt the universalist view that western liberal constitutionalism can be extended to different societies, including Confucian East Asian societies.

Michael C. Davis, for example, argues that in Japan, Taiwan, and South Korea there is emerging commitment to requirements of western liberal constitutionalism, such as periodic elections allowing opposition government to take power, human rights and freedom of press and association, and judicial review of government action.[94] According to him, authoritarian practices in North Korea, China, and Vietnam would be explained by Marxist state ideology rather than Confucianism. To illustrate, citing Asian scholars, Davis concedes that the principles of compassion and mutual respect, and *minben* (people as basis) make Confucianism compatible with human rights and against authoritarian power.[95]

Tom Ginsburg characteristically highlights the compatibility of Confucian tradition to judicial review. In imperial China, Ginsburg argues, the Confucian mandarins who drafted the law for imperial promulgation would *ex ante* substantially check the consistence of the laws with the *li*, and hence the external *ex post* constraints on the law-making did not exist. But in the modern law-making system based on the democratically elected legislature, positive law becomes the threat to the *li* as it now is no longer "the expression of universal and shared traditional norms, but an expression of particular policy goals identified by temporal individuals in the legislature."[96] How, then, can a polity prevent the *li* from being violated by positive statutes? The solution would be "to establish a supreme Confucian council of wise men who served only as authoritative interpreters of the *li* with the power to strike legislation incompatible therewith."[97] Ginsburg also contends that

> this Confucian model of judicial review is also consistent with the long Chinese traditions of rationalism and rule by the learned.... By providing for a constraint on democratic assemblies by a small group of elite experts in interpretation, judicial review of legislation actually serves the traditional function of control by the learned.[98]

On that ground, particularly concerning the possibility of judicial review in future China, Ginsburg believes that "although judicial review of legislation did not and could not develop within the Confucian tradition, there are elements of imperial Chinese legal institutions that make judicial review attractive, once it is on the menu of constitutional design."[99]

It can be seen that unlike the conflictivists, the compatibilists are more optimistic about the role of Confucianism in the development of constitutionalism. From this perspective, Confucianism is not a handicap to the development of constitutionalism. In contrast, Confucian tradition is explained as consisting of some ideas and practice consistent with constitutionalism, and hence can be explored and re-interpreted to justify and support the practice of constitutionalism, enabling the practice to proceed more smoothly and naturally. The compatibilist thesis is empirically supported by the emergence of constitutionalism in Japan, South Korea, and Taiwan.

However, compatibilism is far from an appropriate approach to fully explore the relevance of Confucianism to constitutionalism. The first reason is related to its western exceptionalism. To compatibilists, constitutionalism is comprehended as a distinctively western innovation. Compatibilists fail to appreciate the existence of non-western forms of constitutionalism.[100] Second, they analogize constitutionalism with western liberal constitutionalism,[101] and hence fail to acknowledge the non-liberal forms and more generally the plurality of constitutionalism. For these two reasons, compatibilists tend to cling on to the western hegemony in the bailiwick of comparative constitutional law. Third, compatibilism implies a kind of what can be called "constitutional Orientalism." As Jiunn-Rong Yeh and Wen-chen Chang remark, "this body of scholarship tends to imply an orientalist view that relegates East Asia to an exotic category that may or may not be comparable to modern constitutional democracies in the West."[102] A more serious implication may be that values of western constitutionalism are universal standards and Confucian East Asia is the passive region receiving the "superior" values. Confucianism may be regarded as an inferior legacy to legitimize the transplantation of the allegedly superior institutions and notions of western constitutionalism in East Asian soil. The specious compatibilist thesis fails to appreciate the equilibratory and dialogical discourse on Confucianism and western constitutionalism.

Indigenism

In the existing scholarship, indigenism is the dominant model for theorizing about the relationship between Confucianism and constitutionalism. Unlike compatibilists, indigenists do not collate Confucianism with western constitutionalism to seek for a match between them, but expound some Confucian concepts and practices as constitutionalist. They argue that the Confucian tradition self-generates the indigenous model of constitutionalism, named as "Confucian constitutionalism." However, there are variants within this model of indigenous thinking. Some scholars pay more attention to the philosophical foundation of Confucian constitutionalism, while other are more concerned with its practice. Some arguments about Confucian constitutionalism are descriptive, while others are prescriptive. Different scholars focus on different aspects of Confucian tradition. Indigenous accounts of Confucian constitutionalism can be categorized as ritual, virtual, institutional, and religious.[103]

Ritual Confucian constitutionalism, deeply expounded by Hahm Chaihark,[104] emphasizes the importance of the Confucian *li* (ritual). Borrowing Michel Foucault's concept of "discipline," Hahm defines constitutionalism as a set of institutional and discursive practices designed to discipline political power. He then suggests that the Confucian *li* can be conceptualized as a kind of "constitutional norms" used to discipline imperial rulers. In fact, the idea that *li* can be used to legitimize power is affirmed by many scholars, but even so, *li* is understood in its non-legal meaning. Hahm's idiosyncrasy is to reveal the legal content of *li*. Running counter to the customary understanding of Confucian endorsement of rule of *li* contrary to the rule of law, Hahm explained that *li* in Confucian philosophy (and practice) is inclusive enough to encompass the laws. He explains that: "The idea of *li*, when used to refer to the norms applicable to the state and its ruler, can become indistinguishable from codified rules and regulations."[105] After giving examples in Confucian classical texts which indicate that infringement of *li* resulted in legal sanction, he concludes: "the term *li* was certainly capacious enough to include what we nowadays would call legal institutions and norms, including constitutions."[106]

On that ground, Hahm moves on to discuss the constitutionalist significance of *li*. According to his explanation, *li* provides the basis for judgments on the legitimacy of political power. *Li* confers "legitimacy and dignity on power" and by that it can be deployed in "resisting and questioning the legitimacy of power."[107] Hahm finally concludes: "Just as modern constitutions can be invoked by political leaders to justify their policies and actions, while their critics also advance arguments based on the same constitution to criticize them, so Confucian ritual could be used to legitimize the power of the ruler as well as to censure and discipline the ruler."[108]

After interpreting the philosophical foundations of Confucian constitutionalism, Hahm explains the political discourse of the Choson dynasty of Korea as a model of Confucian constitutionalism. In his treatment, various Confucian constitutional norms included "the way of the former kings," political norms in the Confucian Classics, and the ancestral precedents. In addition, Hahm points out various institutionalized forums enabling the Confucian scholar-officials to use the *li* – the constitutional norms – to discipline and restrain their ruler, consisting of the institution of prime minster, the imperial lecture, the Censorate (the remonstrating institution), and the historian office.[109] Hahm also reveals the real function of the ritual Confucian constitutionalism in seventeenth-century Korea by demonstrating how *li* was practically employed to dispute the ruler's legitimacy.[110]

Virtual Confucian constitutionalism is more concerned with the importance of virtue. Sungmoon Kim disagrees with the understanding of Confucian constitutionalism exclusively in the term of *li* and suggests another dimension of Confucian constitutionalism which stresses the ruler's moral virtue. He argues that there are two competing versions of Confucian constitutionalism in classical Confucianism, namely the "rule by virtue" (*dezhi* 德治) version and "rule by ritual" (*lizhi* 禮治) version developed by Mencius and Xunxi, respectively.[111] In Kim's interpretation, the main idea of Mencius' *dezhi* constitutionalism is that "the Mandate of Heaven is relegated to the will of the Son of Heaven, and the will of the Son of Heaven is placed, albeit tacitly, over the royal candidate's moral virtue and the people's approval."[112] Pierre-Étienne Will has explored the practice of "virtual constitutionalism" in the late Ming dynasty of China.[113]

Institutional Confucian constitutionalism pays more attention to the role of institution. Jaeyoon Song has discovered the institutional theory of Confucian constitutionalism developed by neo-Confucian thinkers of Southern Song (1127–1279) dynasty like Ye Shi and Zheng Boqian on the ground of their fundamental reinterpretation of the Confucian classic called the *Zhou Li* (Rites of Zhou). Song argues that the *Zhou Li* may have functioned as "a meta-constitution" in Southern Song political discourse. In his explanation, the structure and organization of the classic enabled Southern Song neo-Confucian thinkers to develop systematic constitutional theories. Like modern constitution, *Zhou Li* begins with a general preamble defining the people as the ultimate purpose of government, lays down the structure of the six-part government, and regulates the functions of each office. On the ground of the classic, Southern Song neo-Confucian thinkers advanced a theory of institutional checks and balances by articulating the separation of powers between kingship and ministership, which were meant to superimpose constitutional restraints on both ministerial tyranny and monarchical autocracy. Song points out that the primary concern of Southern Song neo-Confucians' discourse on the *Zhou Li* was "how to constrain the coercive power of the state by preventing the abuse of power by government authority, both in both institutional and theoretical aspects."[114] Song eventually concludes that Southern Song thinkers like Ye Shi and Zheng Boqian promoted an "indigenous constitutionalism" in the Chinese tradition.[115]

Another version of institutional Confucian constitutionalism can be found in American sinologist Wm. Theodore de Bary's deconstruction of seventeenth-century Chinese neo-Confucian Huang Zongxi's *Plan for the Prince*.[116] Huang rejected the legitimacy of dynastic laws, which he regarded as "unlawful laws" – "unlawful" in the sense that they were enacted for the private interests of the ruler and his family rather than for the public interest. In replacing the dynastic laws, Huang turned to "the paradigmatic institutions of the sage-kings." "The paradigmatic institutions of the sage-kings," as de Bary pointed out, "in the canonical literature had always been classified as Rites (*Li*)" but Huang "incorporated them under the general heading of Law, while referring to the rites as just one subset among them."[117] "The paradigmatic institutions of the sage-kings" in Huang's plan were the fundamental laws – the "lawful laws" higher than the government created for the welfare of the people. Huang's distinction between unlawful law and lawful law "asserts a new concept of Law as higher than the state, challenging the sacredness of dynasty law.... Law, properly speaking, should at minimum protect the self-interest of the many from the selfishness of the powerful few."[118]

Based on the new concept of fundamental laws, Huang went further to impose constitutional constraints on imperial power. De Bary writes:

> By the new conception of law as higher than the state, and by his subjecting of the ruler to this higher law, Huang attempts to impose constitutional limitation on the ruler's power (legally defined and structurally incorporated in the organization of the government), rather than continuing to put faith in the ruler's capacity for self-restraint.[119]

To search for the countervailing force of the imperial power, Huang accentuates the institutionalized position of the scholar-official:

> Huang calls repeatedly for strengthening the status and the identity of the scholar-official (*shi*) and expanding both their numbers and functions – giving them an increased role in civil government in general, but especially an enhanced status as ministers – with the prime minister, as leader of the *shi*, in an executive position strong enough to balance the power of the emperor.[120]

Huang's Confucian constitutionalism was "Confucian" in the sense that it depends on the personal vocation of Noble Man and the spirit de corps of the *shi* (scholar-official) and "constitutionalist" in the sense that Huang will no longer rely simply on the good intentions and exemplary character of the ruler, but insists on imposing institutionalized limits to the exercise of the ruler's power.[121]

Religious Confucian constitutionalism is not an empirical exploration of constitutionalist elements in Confucian tradition as in the above models of indigenous thinking, but is a normative proposal of an indigenous model of constitutionalism for future China, comprehensively based on Confucianism promoted as a state religion. This model of thinking features the scholarship of Jiang Qing.[122] Jiang's Confucian constitutionalism is religious in nature for two things. First, it calls for restoration of Confucianism as a state religion. Second, it suggests that the ultimate source of sovereignty lies with heaven.[123]

Jiang rejects the western constitutional principle of secular sovereignty of people because he believes that "the people are secularized, limited, and narrow collection of human desires."[124] He then proposes the alternative principle of sacred sovereignty of heaven, stating that: "The sovereignty of the heaven means that the origin of the legitimacy of the highest political authority comes from heaven, not from the people. Heaven is the higher legal background of Confucian constitutionalism or its transcendental value."[125]

On that ground, Jiang advances the theory of tri-legitimacy. Jiang deprecates western constitutional legitimacy for its uniqueness of the legitimacy of the popular will, extreme secularization, contractualism, utilitarianism, selfishness, commercialism, and the like.[126] Then, drawing from the *Gongyang Commentary* of the *Spring and Autumn Annals*, one of the five Confucian Classics, Jiang enunciates an alternative model of trinity of legitimacy: legitimacy of heaven whose source comes from the ecological values; legitimacy of earth whose source comes from history and culture; and legitimacy of human whose source comes from the will of the people.[127]

On the ground of the theory of tri-legitimacy, Jiang moves further to propose a tri-cameral Parliament consisting of the House of *Ru* (the house of Confucian scholars) representing legitimacy of heaven, the House of the Nation representing legitimacy of earth, and the House of the People representing legitimacy of humans. Jiang's Confucian constitutional order additionally comprises a symbolic monarch who must be the direct heir of Confucius,[128] and a supervisory body called the Academy.[129]

I concur with the descriptive indigenous accounts of constitutionalism within the Confucian tradition. The conflictivists and the compatibilists, regardless of treating Confucianism as a friend or an enemy of constitutionalism, all argue from the western-centric perspective, and assume that Confucianism must give way to or converge with western liberal constitutionalism. Confucian constitutionalists transcend the domination of the liberal understanding of constitutionalism. Their exploration of Confucian constitutionalism is consistent with the pluralist reality of constitutionalism. Confucian constitutionalism is a distinctive form of pre-modern constitutionalism in East Asia. Furthermore, descriptive accounts of Confucian constitutionalism aptly distinguish between philosophical Confucianism and the politicized version.

However, there are some problems associated with the descriptive studies of Confucian constitutionalism. First, they seem to be sporadic. Different scholars choose to focus on different dimensions of Confucian tradition to interpret them as constitutionalist. Moreover, although efforts in shedding constitutionalist light on Confucian political concepts are momentous, scholars ignore the constitutionalist importance of other Confucian concepts. I therefore propose a more systematic and integrative exploration of constitutionalism in Confucian philosophy (Chapter 1) and practice (Chapter 2).

Another problem is that indigenists fail to relate their atavistic excavations of traditional Confucian constitutionalism to the development of modern constitutionalism in contemporary East Asia. It seems to me that Confucian constitutionalists are inclined to a better understanding of pre-modern Confucian polities and that they demur about the possible role of Confucianism in the development of modern constitutionalism in contemporary East Asia. To be sure, one may think that Confucian constitutionalist tradition can serve as the cultural soil in support of the present development of constitutionalism. However, this alone does not considerably distinguish the indigenists' contributions from compatibilists'. Alternatively, I submit a grave consideration of the relevance of traditional Confucian constitutionalism to modern constitutionalism in East Asia.

To be sure, Jiang's normative proposal of religious Confucian constitutionalism has related Confucianism to contemporary constitutional issues. However, this proposal is untenable from both Confucian and constitutional perspectives.[130] My own objection is elaborated in detail in Chapter 4.

Toward a mixed approach

I propose an alternative approach to explore the relevance of Confucianism to modern constitutionalism in East Asia, which can be called the mixed approach. This approach serves to explore descriptively and normatively the existential and potential integration of Confucianism with western modern constitutionalism. A descriptive constitutional mixture examines how modern Confucian intellectuals in East Asia have combined elements of Confucian tradition with elements of western modern constitutionalism to produce their distinctive Confucian constitutional vision. Normative constitutional mixture moves a further step to develop a new theory of mixed constitutionalism, which aims to marry traditional Confucian constitutionalism with western modern constitutionalism to produce a distinctive model of East Asian constitutionalism. I will elaborate in detail the descriptive and normative constitutional mixture in Chapters 3 and 4.

The argument of this book

This book argues for the intellectual sources and the practices of Confucian constitutionalism in traditional East Asia and its positive relevance to the development of constitutionalism in modern East Asia.

Chapter 1, *Classical Confucian Constitutionalism*, systematically explores the intellectual sources of constitutionalism in classical Confucian philosophy. This chapter argues that *zheng ming* (rectification of names) government is a Confucian model of constitutional government, an antithesis of despotic government, a government responsible for the people's public good (*minben*) functioning in accordance with the parameter of traditional norms and institutions (*li*) protected by internal moral cultivation of the ruler and external education, remonstrance, and discourse by scholars.

Chapter 2, *Imperial Confucian Constitutionalism*, considers how Confucian constitutionalist ideas were practiced in imperial East Asia. This chapter argues that there were numerous norms as the embodiment of *li* used to rectify the royal authority, namely the models of ancient kings, the political norms in the classics, the ancestral precedents, and the institutions of the precedent dynasties; and that there were institutions enabling the scholar-officials to use the norms to rectify the royal power, including the royal examination system, the deliberative institutions, the educative institution, the remonstrative institution, and the historical institution. This argument is developed based on the consideration of the experiences in Choson dynasty Korea, Ming dynasty China, and Nguyễn dynasty Vietnam. This chapter, however, focuses more on the case of Vietnam.

Chapter 3, *Modern Confucian Constitutionalism*, turns to examine the relevance of Confucian tradition to modern Constitutionalism in early twentieth-century East Asia. It argues that modern Confucian intellectuals (such as Sun Yat-sen and Liang Quichao in China, and Phan Bội Châu and Phan Châu Trinh in Vietnam) have adopted some elements of western constitutionalism and integrated them with the Confucian tradition to produce their distinctive modern Confucian constitutional vision. This argument is exemplified by the two Vietnamese Confucianists.

Chapter 4, *Toward East Asian Constitutionalism*, turns to consider the normative constitutional mixture. It proposes a normative theory of mixed constitutionalism in the East Asian context. It argues that empirically there is no distinctive model of constitutionalism that can be found in East Asia, but normatively it is possible for East Asia to develop a distinctive model of constitutionalism by considering the relevance of Confucian moral and political ideas and values. East Asian constitutionalism as a type of mixed constitutionalism is defined by the axiological, ideational mixtures of ingredients of Confucianism and ingredients of western liberal constitutionalism.

All in all, the general implication of this book is that there is a cornucopia of human constitutional experiences and possibilities. Pluralizing the conceptions of constitutionalism is subservient to our discovery of humans' projects of constitutionalism.

Notes

1 Michel Rosenfeld, "Is Global Constitutionalism Meaningful or Desirable?" *The European Journal of International Law* 25(1) (2014): 178.

2 Dieter Grimm, "The Achievement of Constitutionalism and its Prospects in a Changed World," in *The Twilight of Constitutionalism?* ed. Petra Dobner and Martin Loughlin (Oxford: Oxford University Press, 2010), 3.

3 See generally, Alan S. Rosenbaum, ed., *Constitutionalism: The Philosophical Dimension* (New York: Greenwood Press, 1988); Larry Alexander, ed., *Constitutionalism: Philosophical Foundations* (New York: Cambridge University Press, 1998).

4 The definition of "East Asia" is relatively ambiguous. This study adopts a geographical and cultural definition of East Asia, which includes China, Taiwan, Japan, Korea, and Vietnam. Whether Vietnam belongs to East Asia is debatable. Geographically, Vietnam is a part of Southeast Asia, but culturally it is a part of East Asia. Particularly, Vietnam shares the Confucian culture with China, Taiwan, Japan, and Korea.

5 Jiunn-Rong Yeh and Wen-chen Chang, "The Emergence of Asian Constitutionalism: Features in Comparison," *American Journal of Comparative Law* 59(3) (2011): 805–839; Albert H. Chen, "Pathways of Western Liberal Constitutional Development in Asia: A Comparative Study of Five Major Nations," *International Journal of Constitutional Law* 8 (2010): 849–850.

6 Rogier Creemers, "China's Constitutionalism Debate: Content, Context and Implications," *The China Journal* 74 (2015): 91–109; Nguyen Thi Huong, "Pursuing Constitutional Dialogue within Socialist Vietnam: The 2010 Debate," *Australian Journal of Asian Law* 13(1) (2012): 1–18; Thiem Hai Bui, "Liberal Constitutionalism and the Socialist State in an Era of Globalisation: An Inquiry into Vietnam's Constitutional Discourse and Power Structures," *The Global Studies Journal* 5 (2013).

7 On normative universalism and functionalism in comparative constitutional law, see Mark Tushnet, "Some Reflections on Method in Comparative Constitutional Law," in *The Migration of Constitutional Ideas*, ed. Sujit Choudhry (New York: Cambridge University Press, 2007), 67–83.

8 Ibid., 69.

9 Ibid.

10 John Rawls, *A Theory of Justice* (Cambridge, MA: Belknap Press of Harvard University Press, 1971).

11 Jurgen Habermas, *Between Facts and Norms: Contributions to a Discourse Theory of Law and Democracy.*, trans. William Rehg (Cambridge, MA: MIT Press, 1998).

12 Rosenfeld, "Global Constitutionalism," 183.

13 Ibid.

14 Ibid.

15 T.R.S. Allan, *Constitutional Justice: A Liberal Theory of the Rule of Law* (Oxford: Oxford University Press, 2003).

16 Tushnet, "Method in Comparative Constitutional Law," 72.

17 "Symposium: Global Constitutionalism," *Indiana Journal of Global Legal Studies* 16 (2009); "Symposium: Constitutional Borrowings," *International Journal of Constitutional Law* 1 (2003); Sujit Choudhry, ed., *The Migration of Constitutional Ideas* (New York: Cambridge University Press, 2007); Zachary Elkins, Tom Ginsburg, and Beth Simmons, *Getting to Rights: Treaty Ratification, Constitutional Convergence, and Human Rights Practice, Harvard Journal of International Law* 54(64) (2013); David S. Law and Mila Versteeg, "The Evolution and Ideology of Global Constitutionalism," *California Law Review* 99 (2011): 1163.

18 Tushnet, "Method in Comparative Constitutional Law," 74.

19 Ruti Teitel, "Comparative Constitutional Law in a Global Age," *Harvard Law Review* 115 (2004): 2578.

20 Tushnet, "Method in Comparative Constitutional Law," 74 (italic in original).

21 Ibid., 76.

22 Ibid.

23 Vicki C. Jackson, "Methodological Challenges in Comparative Constitutional Law," *Penn State International Law Review* 28 (2010): 324.
24 Ibid., 325.
25 Vicki C. Jackson and Mark Tushnet, *Comparative Constitutional Law* (New York: Foundation Press; St. Paul, MN: Thomson/West, 2006).
26 Teitel, "Comparative Constitutional Law," 2581.
27 For information about this series, see www.hartpub.co.uk/SeriesDetails.aspx?SeriesName=Constitutional+Systems+of+the+World.
28 Montesquieu, *The Spirit of the Laws*, trans. and ed. Anne M. Cohler *et al.* (Cambridge and New York: Cambridge University Press, 1989), 8.
29 Hegel's immanent perspective of constitutional law is well analyzed in Michael Salter and Julia J.A. Shaw, "Towards a Critical Theory of Constitutional Law: Hegel's Contribution," *Journal of Law and Society* 21(4) (1994): 464–486.
30 Ibid., 465.
31 Ibid., 466 (italic in original).
32 Ibid.
33 Ibid., 467.
34 Ibid.
35 G.W.F. Hegel, *Outlines of the Philosophy of Right*, trans. T.M. Knox, ed. Stephen Houlgate (Oxford: Oxford University Press, 2008), 263.
36 Ibid.
37 Ibid.
38 Ibid.
39 Robert Cover, "Nomos and Narrative" in *Narrative, Violence, and the Law: The Essays of Robert Cover*, ed. Artha Minow *et al.* (Ann Arbor, MI: University of Michigan Press, 1992), 95–96.
40 Ibid.
41 Ibid., 99.
42 Jiunn-Rong Yeh and Wen-Chen Chang, "The Emergence of Transnational Constitutionalism: Its Features, Challenges and Solutions," *Penn State International Law Review* 27 (2008): 97.
43 Cheryl Saunders, "Towards a Global Constitutional Gene Pool," *National Taiwan University Law Review* 4(3) (2009): 12.
44 Ibid., 28.
45 South Africa and Japan are typical examples of successful stories. See D. Davis, "Constitutional Borrowing: The Influence of Legal Culture and Local History in the Reconstitution of Comparative Influence – The South African Experience," *International Journal of Constitutional Law* 1 (2003): 181; Christopher A. Ford, "The Indigenization of Constitutionalism in Japanese Experience," *Case Western Reserve Journal of International Law* 28 (1996): 3. Scholars also point to the failure of constitutional borrowings; see L. Epstein and J. Knight, "Constitutional Borrowing and Nonborrowing," *International Journal of Constitutional Law* 1 (2003): 196; Y. Hasebe, "Constitutional Borrowing and Political Theory," *International Journal of Constitutional Law* 1 (2003): 224; W. Osiatynski, "Paradoxes of Constitutional Borrowing," *International Journal of Constitutional Law* 1 (2003): 244; C. Rosenkrantz, "Against Borrowings and Other Nonauthoritative Uses of Foreign Law," *International Journal of Constitutional Law* 1 (2003): 269; K. Lane Scheppele, "Aspirational and Aversive Constitutionalism: The Case for Studying Cross-constitutional Influence Through Negative Models," *International Journal of Constitutional Law* 1 (2003): 296.
46 Tushnet, "Method in Comparative Constitutional Law," 76–80.
47 Ibid., 82.
48 Gary Feffrey Jacobsohn, *Constitutional Identity* (Cambridge, MA: Harvard University Press, 2010), 7 (italic in original).

49 Nikolai Wenzel, "From Contract to Mental Model: Constitutional Culture as a Fact of the Social Sciences," *The Review of Austrian Economics* 23(1) (2010): 65.
50 Wen-Chen Chang *et al.*, *Constitutionalism in Asia: Cases and Materials* (Oxford and Portland, OR: Hart, 2014), 68.
51 Jason Mazzone, "The Creation of a Constitutional Culture," *Tulsa Law Review* 40(4) (2004): 672.
52 Wenzel, "Constitutional Culture," 65.
53 Ibid., 61.
54 Ibid.
55 Donald S. Lutz, "Thinking About Constitutionalism," *Publius: The Journal of Federalism* 30(4) (2000): 128.
56 Wenzel, "Constitutional Culture," 59.
57 Chang *et al.*, *Constitutionalism in Asia*, 66.
58 Karl Loewenstein, *Political Power and the Government Process* (Chicago, IL: University of Chicago Press, 1957).
59 F.A. Hayek, *The Market and Other Orders*, ed. Bruce Caldwell (Chicago, IL and London: University of Chicago Press, 2014), 299.
60 Wenzel, "Constitutional Culture," 65.
61 Ibid., 56–57.
62 Ibid.; J. David Greenstone, "Against Simplicity: The Cultural Dimensions of the Constitution," *University of Chicago Law Review* 55 (1988): 428–449; W.O. Okoth-Ogendo, "Constitutions without Constitutionalism: Reflections on an African Political Paradox," in *Constitutionalism and Democracy: Transitions in the Contemporary World*, ed. Greenberg *et al.* (New York: Oxford University Press, 1993), 65–84; Michel Rosenfeld, ed., *Constitutionalism, Identity, Difference, and Legitimacy: Theoretical Perspectives* (Durham, NC and London: Duke University Press, 1994); Ruth Gordon, "Growing Constitutions," *University of Pennsylvania Journal of Constitutional Law* 1 (1999): 530.
63 Lutz, "Thinking About Constitutionalism," 133.
64 Ibid.
65 Ruth Gordon, "Growing Constitutions," 530–531.
66 Christopher Tiedeman, *The Unwritten Constitution of the United States: A Philosophical Inquiry into the Fundamentals of American Constitutional Law* (New York: William S. Hein & Co., Inc, 1974), 18.
67 Ibid., 19.
68 Ibid.
69 Ibid., 20.
70 Daniel P. Franklin and Michael J. Baun, eds., *Political Culture and Constitutionalism: A Comparative Approach* (Armonk, NY and London: M.E. Sharpe, Inc., 1995).
71 Graham Hassall and Cheryl Saunders, *Asia-Pacific Constitutional Systems* (Cambridge, New York and Melbourne: Cambridge University Press, 2002), 42–43.
72 Wenzel, "Constitutional Culture," 66–68.
73 For more detail on the Commonwealth model of constitutionalism, see: Stephen Gardbaum, *The New Commonwealth Model of Constitutionalism: Theory and Practice* (Cambridge and New York: Cambridge University Press, 2013); Mark Tushnet, *Weak Courts, Strong Rights: Judicial Review and Social Welfare Rights in Comparative Constitutional Law* (Princeton, NJ: Princeton University Press, 2007).
74 Wenzel, "Constitutional Culture," 68.
75 Nikolai G. Wenzel, "Constitutional Culture in Japan and the Philippines: Success and Failure in Post-War Constitutional Choice," *Pacific Focus: Inha Journal of International Studies* 15 (2010): 396.
76 Ibid., see also: Nikolai G. Wenzel, "Lessons from Constitutional Culture and the History of Constitutional Transfer: A Hope for Constitutionally Limited Government?" *International Advances in Economic Research*, published online: March 20, 2014.

77 Nikolai G. Wenzel, "Matching Constitutional Culture and Parchment: Post-Colonial Constitutional Adoption in Mexico and Argentina," *Historia Constitucional* 11 (2010): 321.

78 Ibid.; see also Wenzel, "Lessons from Constitutional Culture."

79 Wonsuk Chang and Leah Kalmanson, eds., *Confucianism in Context: Classic Philosophy and Contemporary Issues, East Asia and Beyond* (Albany, NY: State University of New York Press, 2010); Zhengxu Wang, *Democratization in Confucian East Asia: Citizen Politics in China, Japan, Singapore, South Korea, Taiwan, and Vietnam* (Youngstown, NY: Cambria Press, 2008); Daniel A. Bell, *China's New Confucianism: Politics and Everyday Life in a Changing Society* (Princeton, NJ: Princeton University Press, 2008); Benjamin A. Elman, John B. Duncan, and Herman Ooms, eds., *Rethinking Confucianism: Past and Present in China, Japan, Korea, and Vietnam* (Los Angeles, CA: UCLA Asian Pacific Monograph Series, 2002); Martin Lu, *Confucianism: Its Relevance to Modern Society* (Singapore: Federal Publications, 1983); Lim Aik, "Confucianism in Singapore: Ethics and Politics of a Global City-State" (PhD Dissertation, National University of Singapore, 2010); Pi-chien Peter Kung, *Confucianism and Economic Dynamism of Singapore, Hong Kong, South Korea, and Taiwan, R.O.C.* (Ann Arbor, MI: University Microfilms International, 1997).

80 Chaihark Hahm, "Constitutionalism, Confucian Civic Culture, and Ritual Propriety," in *Confucianism for the Modern World*, ed. Daniel A. Bell and Hahm Chaibong (Cambridge and New York: Cambridge University Press, 2003), 42.

81 Justin Tiwald, "Confucianism and Human Rights," in *Handbook of Human Rights*, ed. Thomas Cushman (New York: Routledge, 2012), 244–254; Craig Williams, "International Human Rights and Confucianism," *Asia-Pacific Journal on Human Rights and the Law* 1 (2006): 38–66; Joseph Chan, "A Confucian Perspective on Human Rights for Contemporary China," in *The East Asian Change for Human Right*, ed. Joanne R. Bauer and Daniel A. Bell (Cambridge: Cambridge University Press, 1999), 212–237; Wm. Theodore de Bary, *Asia Values and Human Rights: A Confucian Communitarian Perspective* (Cambridge, MA and London: Harvard University Press, 1998); Wm. Theodore De Bary and Tu Weiming, eds., *Confucianism and Human rights* (New York: Colombia University Press, 1998); Du Gangjian and Song Gang, "Relating Human Rights to Chinese Culture: The Four Paths of the Confucian Analects and the Four Principles of a New Theory of Benevolence," in *Human Rights and Chinese Values: Legal, Philosophical, and Political Perspectives*, ed. Michael C. Davis (Hong Kong: Oxford University Press, 1995), 34–56.

82 Sungmoon Kim, *Confucian Democracy in East Asia: Theory and Practice* (New York: Cambridge University Press, 2014); Joseph Chan, *Confucian Perfectionism: A Political Philosophy for Modern Times* (Princeton, NJ: Princeton University Press, 2013); Doh Chull Shin, *Confucianism and Democratization in East Asia* (Cambridge: Cambridge University Press, 2011); Daniel A. Bell, *Beyond Liberal Democracy: Political Thinking for an East Asian Context* (Princeton, NJ: Princeton University Press, 2006); Sor-hoon Tan, *Confucian Democracy: A Deweyan Reconstruction* (Albany, NY: State University of New York Press, 2004); Daniel A. Bell and Hahm Chaibong, eds., *Confucianism for the Modern World* (New York: Cambridge University Press, 2003); David L. Hall and Roger T. Ames, *The Democracy of the Dead: Dewey, Confucius and the Hope for Democracy in China* (Chicago and Lasalle, IL: Open Court Publishing Company, 1999); Lee Teng-Hui, "Confucian Democracy: Modernization, Culture, and the State in East Asia," *Harvard International Review* 21(4) (1999): 16. The *Journal of Chinese Philosophy* published a special theme on Confucianism and democracy in Volume 34, Issue 2, 151–319.

83 Lawrence W. Beer, *Human Rights Constitutionalism in Japan and Asia* (Folkestone: Global Oriental, 2009).

84 Jon Elster and Rune Slagstad, ed., *Constitutionalism and Democracy* (Cambridge: Cambridge University Press, 1988).
85 Edward Shils, "Reflections on Civil Society and Civility in the Chinese Intellectual Tradition," in *Confucian Traditions in East Asian Modernity*, ed. Tu Wei-ming (Cambridge, MA: Harvard University Press, 1996), 53–71.
86 Yu Chen, "Confucianism versus Constitutionalism," *Journal of Cambridge Studies* 2(2) (2007): 32–33.
87 Li-ann Thio, "Constitutionalism in Illiberal Polities" in *The Oxford Handbook of Comparative Constitutional Law*, ed. Michel Rosefeld and András Sajó (Oxford: Oxford University Press, 2012), 133.
88 See Chapter 1.
89 Sor-Hoon Tan, *Confucian Democracy*, 132.
90 Wei-ming Tu, "Probing the 'Three Bonds' and 'Five Relationships' in Confucian Humanism," in *Confucianism and the Family*, ed. Walter H. Slote and George A. DeVos (Albany, NY: SUNY Press, 1998).
91 Bary, *Asian Values and Human Rights*, 19.
92 James Legge, *The Chinese Classics with Translations, Critical and Exegetical Notes, Prolegomena, and Copious Indexes, Volume I., Confucian Analects, The Great Learning, The Doctrine of the Mean* (Hong Kong: Hong Kong University Press, 1960), 257.
93 James Legge, trans., *I Ching: The Book of Changes* (New York: University Books, 1964), 69. For more discussions on the Confucian view on meditation and litigation, see Albert H.Y. Chen, "Mediation, Litigation, and Justice: Confucian Reflections in a Modern Liberal Society," in *Confucianism for the Modern World*, ed. Daniel A. Bell and Hahm Chaibong (New York: Cambridge University Press, 2003), 257–287.
94 Michael C. Davis, "Constitutionalism and Political Culture: The Debate Over Human Rights and Asian Values," *Harvard Human Rights Journal* 11 (1998): 113.
95 Ibid.
96 Tom Ginsburg, "Confucian Constitutionalism? Globalization and Judicial Review in Korea and Taiwan," *Law and Social Inquiry* 27 (2002): 794.
97 Ibid., 795.
98 Ibid.
99 Ibid., 795–796.
100 In a more recent article, Tom Ginsburg adopts the view that there are East Asian antecedents of constitutionalism. See Tom Ginsburg, "Constitutionalism: East Asian Antecedents," *Chicago-Kent Law Review* 88 (2012): 11
101 Davis notes: "In this essay, the term 'constitutionalism' will be used interchangeably with the term 'liberal constitutionalism.'" Davis, "Constitutionalism and Political Culture," 110.
102 Jiunn-Rong Yeh and Wen-chen Chang "The Emergence of Asian Constitutionalism," 810.
103 Peng Chengyi identifies three approaches to Confucian constitutionalism, namely ritualist, institutional, and religious. Peng Chengyi, "Traditional Confucian Constitutionalism: Current Explorations and Prospects," *Frontier of Philosophy in China* 8 (2013): 76. I would suggest incorporating another approach which particularly underlines the importance of virtue. Note that this category is relative. There are sometimes mixtures among these theories. For example, those who focus on the ritualist aspect of Confucian constitutionalism also consider its institutional and virtual aspects.
104 Chaihark Hahm, "Confucian Constitutionalism" (SJD dissertation, Harvard Law School, 2000); Chaihark Hahm, "Conceptualizing Korean Constitutionalism: Foreign Transplant or Indigenous Tradition?" *Journal of Korean Law* 1(2) (2001): 151; Chaihark Hahm, "Ritual and Constitutionalism: Disputing the Ruler's Legitimacy in a Confucian Polity," *The American Journal of Comparative Law* 57 (2009): 135.

105 Hahm, "Ritual and Constitutionalism," 148.
106 Ibid., 148–149.
107 Ibid., 150.
108 Ibid.
109 Hahm, "Confucian Constitutionalism"; Hahm, "Conceptualizing Korean Constitutionalism," 151–169.
110 For his particular treatment on this, see Chaihark Hahm, "Ritual and Constitutionalism: Disputing the Ruler's Legitimacy in a Confucian Polity," *American Journal of Comparative Law* 57 (2009): 135–203.
111 Sungmoon Kim, "Confucian Constitutionalism: Mencius and Xunzi on Virtual, Ritual, and Royal Transmission," *The Review of Politics* 73(3) (2001): 347.
112 Ibid., 385.
113 Pierre-Étienne Will, "Virtual Constitutionalism in the Late Ming Dynasty," in *Building Constitutionalism in China*, ed. Stéphanie Balme and Michael W. Dowdle (New York: Palgrave Macmillan, 2009), 261.
114 Jaeyoon Song, "The *Zhou Li* and Constitutionalism: A Southern Song Political Theory," *Journal of Chinese Philosophy* 36(3) (2009), 436–437.
115 Ibid., 437.
116 Wm. Theodore de Bary, "Introduction" in Huang Zongxi, *Waiting for the Dawn: A Plan for the Prince*, trans. Wm. Theodore de Bary (New York: Columbia University Press, 1993).
117 Ibid., 22.
118 Ibid., 53.
119 Wm. Theodore de Bary, *Asia Values and Human Rights: A Confucian Communitarian Perspective* (Cambridge, MA: Harvard University Press, 1998), 101.
120 Ibid., 102.
121 Ibid., 104–105.
122 Jiang Qing, *A Confucian Constitutional Order: How China's Ancient Past Can Shape Its Political Future*, ed. Daniel A. Bell and Ruiping Fan, trans. Edmund Ryden (Princeton, NJ: Princeton University Press, 2013).
123 Peng Chengyi, "Traditional Confucian Constitutionalism," 91.
124 Jiang Qing, *A Confucian Constitutional Order*, 48.
125 Ibid.
126 Ibid., 33.
127 Ibid., 37–40.
128 Ibid., chapter 3, 71–98.
129 Ibid., 57.
130 See criticisms and Jiang's responses in Qing, *A Confucian Constitutional Order.*

1 Classical Confucian constitutionalism

Introduction

"Constitutionalism" is a modern term but the notion is traceable back to classical antiquity.[1] Some western constitutional theorists and historians have explored constitutionalist ideas in the writings of Hellenistic and Roman ancient intellectuals, such as Plato's *Republic*, Aristotle's *Politics*, Polybius' *The Histories*, and Cicero's works.[2] Western scholars, however, tend to consider the origins of constitutionalism to be endemic to the western cradle. Are there constitutionalist wisdoms in the repository of Oriental ancient lore? In particular, are there any ideas of constitutionalism in Confucian political philosophy? This question is important not only for a better understanding of Oriental legal-political thinking but also for the development of constitutionalism in contemporary East Asian nations (China, Japan, Korea, and Vietnam) where the influence of Confucianism has remained. If there exist Confucian constitutionalist ideas, Confucianism will not be a cultural impediment and can even be integrated into the modern projects for developing constitutionalism in East Asia.

There is no scantiness of people who believe that Confucianism is the proponent of despotism – the antithesis of constitutionalism. As Xinzhong Yao points out, modern critics of Confucianism tend to conclude that: "Confucianism has no positive role to play in modern life because it is related, as it always was, to political despotism."[3] Shaohua Hu also notes that "some regard Confucianism as the ideological underpinning of 'Oriental despotism.' "[4] The credence is traceable to the iconoclasts of the May Four Movement. In opposing Confucianism and expediting for human rights, science, and democracy, Chen Duxiu and his supporters connected Confucianism to despotism.[5]

In fact, those who believe that Confucianism underpins despotism fail to differentiate Confucianism as the tradition of philosophy from Confucianism as the orthodoxy of the imperial states. As noted by Sor-hoon Tan,

> since its establishment as the orthodoxy of the Chinese empire in the Han dynasty, Confucianism frequently has been misappropriated by those in power for their own selfish interests at the expense of those they ruled, so much so that many have viewed those distortions as constituting Confucianism itself.[6]

When Confucianism has been misused for the egoistic purposes of despots, people have been belied that Confucianism is supportive of despotic government.

Therefore, in order to answer the question of whether there are constitutionalist ideas in Confucianism, it is proper to return to consider classical Confucianism as a philosophy, or pre-Qin Confucianism established by Confucius (551–479 BC) and developed by Mencius (372–289 BC) and Xunzi (312–230 BC) during the late Spring and Autumn Period (770–476 BC) and Warring States Period (475–221 BC) in the history of China. This consideration relies on original work of Confucianism which includes the Four Books (*The Analects of Confucius*, *The Mencius*, *The Great Learning*, and *The Doctrine of the Mean*) and Five Classics (the *I Ching* or *Book of Changes*, the *Shu Ching* or *Book of History*, the *Shih Ching* or *Book of Poetry*), and the *Yi Li* or *Book of Rites* and the *Chunqiu* or *Spring and Autumn Annals*), in addition to Xunzi's writings.

In fact, Chaihark Hahm, Sungmoon Kim, and other scholars have investigated Confucian constitutionalism in classical philosophy.[7] Hahm accentuates the Confucian concept of *li* (ritual), while Kim is more concerned with the Mencian concept of virtue. These studies are creditable but incomplete, as they ignore the constitutionalist importance of other Confucian concepts, such as *minben*, the doctrine of rectification of names, and the concomitant *Spring and Autumn Annals*. I therefore propose a more systematic and integrative generalization of classical philosophical foundations of Confucian constitutionalism.

I agree with Hahm and other scholars that to understand Confucian constitutionalism, we must take the idea of *li* into account, but I do not think that *li* is the central concept of Confucian constitutionalism. From my point of view, *li* as well as virtue is just a practical continuation of another consequential doctrine in Confucianism, namely *zheng ming* (rectification of names). Hence, I alternatively suggest that to comprehend the philosophy of Confucian constitutionalism we must pay special attention to the doctrine of *zheng ming*. My argument runs as follows. Like any other intellectual projects of constitutionalism, Confucian constitutionalism is generated due to the apprehensiveness of despotic government. In searching for an antidote to despotic government, the classical Confucians suggest a *zheng ming* government which can be understood as a constitutional government. The purpose of this government is to ensure governmental responsibility for public good, which is encapsulated in the concept of *minben* (people as basis). The Confucians then propose articulation of standards for rectifying the governmental power, named as *li* – a variant of unwritten constitution. To enforce the *li*, they anticipate the practice of moral self-rectification by the ruler and the external rectification of the ruler by wise and virtuous scholars.

However, to understand classical philosophy of Confucian constitutionalism, it is important to clarify the meaning of constitutionalism because misconceptualizing constitutionalism will result in misunderstanding its relationship with Confucianism. This chapter is, therefore, structured as follows. The first section clarifies the concept of constitutionalism. On that ground, the second section systematically explores classical intellectual foundations of Confucian constitutionalism. The third section concludes the chapter with some further discussion.

Constitutionalism

Louis Henkin states that constitutionalism "is nowhere defined."[8] However, as Thomas C. Grey suggests,

> there is no reason to suppose that an adequate conceptual analysis of constitutionalism must produce a *definition*.... The group of ideas, institutions, and practices gathered under the terminological umbrella of the term "constitution" may bear "familiar resemblances" to each other without necessarily sharing any single quality or small group of quality as their common essence.[9]

So, rather than pursing an authoritative definition, I will elucidate a group of ideas that are instrumental to the recognition of whether a polity is a constitutionalism or not.

What is constitutionalism?

As it is commonly understood, constitutionalism is associated with the idea "that government can and should be legally limited in its powers, and that its authority or legitimacy depends on its observing these limitations."[10] This understanding was at an early stage developed by Harvard constitutional historian CH. McIlwain, who asserts that: "Constitutionalism has one essential quality: it is a legal limitation on government; it is the antithesis of arbitrary rule; its opposite is despotic government, the government of will instead of law."[11] Carl J. Friedrich, McIlwain's successor at Harvard, shares the view that constitutionalism is principally concerned with the limitation of government and is a contrast to arbitrary government. He defines constitutionalism as "an institutionalized system of effective restraints upon governmental action."[12] Put simply: in a constitutionalist polity, political leaders cannot act as they want but are bound by pre-established rules and principles. Constitutionalism subordinates political leaders to pre-established legal rules and principles which limit the public power.

I distinguish two dimensions of constitutional limitations, which are teleological and functional. *Teleological limitations* denote the idea that the public power is used for general public standards, not for private interests of power holders. *Functional limitations* concern certain political actions that power holders must do and must not do so as to ensure general public standards. So, functional limitations enable proper use of power and disable arbitrary use of power.

Teleological and functional limitations are articulated in constitutional norms. Constitutional norms can be written and unwritten and they can derive from formal enactment, reason and truth, and usage and acceptance.[13] While McIlwain conceptualizes constitutionalism as the government under law or legal limitation of the government, what he means by "law" or "legal" is not exclusively positive law but

> may be unwritten and entirely customary, as it has been for the greater part of its history; or it may be set forth in a single official document as in our state and federal constitutions, but in every case it is a law that puts bounds to arbitrary will.[14]

In similar vein, conceiving constitutionalism as the effective restraints of government action, Friedrich underlines that the effectiveness of the restraints does not depend on the legal formality: "It should be evident that the existence of formally legal restraints is in no wise an indication of the existence of a constitutional order in the political sense."[15] Rather, "a restraint may be very effective and thoroughly regularized, without necessarily being embodied in positive law unless law is very broadly defined as including all custom."[16]

Understood in that sense, constitutionalism must be distinguished from constitution, albeit the etymological genealogy. Craham Walker asserts: "Constitutionalism requires a certain kind of constitution: one that is self-limiting in character."[17] A "constitutionalist constitution" must be the one that comprises certain fundamental norms which not merely constitute but restrain governmental power. "Sham constitutions," for example, which fail to constrain the power, are irrelevant to constitutionalism.[18] Moreover, while a constitutional text may have multiple functions (restraining state power, organizing state, distributing the state power, and affirming certain social goals and values), the practice of constitutionalism is primarily concerned with its restraining function.[19] It is in this sense that Grey underlines: "The object of discourse in the study of constitutionalism should be constitutional *norms*, not entire constitutions."[20]

Constitutionalism should also be distinguished from ostensible constitutional implementation. According to Alec Stone Sweet, "constitutionalism denotes the commitment on the part of any given political community to be governed by constitutional rules and principles."[21] This is partially true. The phenomenon of "abusive constitutionalism" labeled by David Landau indicates that would-be autocrats can commit to being governed by constitutional rules but can undermine democracy and constitutionalism at the same time.[22] So, viable constitutionalism additionally requires that constitutional implementation is effective in constraining public power.

Moreover, constitutionalism should be differentiated from the legal limitations of the administrative authorities. Constitutionalism is principally meant to constrain the sovereign or the holder of the supreme power. The sovereign may enact legal norms to constrain agencies. However, the legal constraint of the agencies is a theme beyond the remit of the studies of constitutionalism, which scholars of administrative law may be concerned with.

Why constitutionalism?

Constitutionalism is "about its telos."[23] Why do we need to superimpose some legal limitations on government? What are the functions of constitutionalism? What problems do constitutional limitations aim to solve? What can constitutionalism do for rulers? What can it do for the public? In short, what is the goal of constitutionalism?

Certainly, to restrain the public power does not mean to enervate the government by eviscerating its governing devices. Leslie Lipson provides a useful metaphor: "Just as it is one thing to harness a horse and another to hobble it, so it is one thing to control a government and another to cripple it."[24] Since government cannot govern without power, constitutional limitations do not aim to hamstring government. Generally speaking, constitutionalism is meant to limit political leaders from doing what they want so as to benefit the public. Constitutionalism endeavors to achieve a legal-political matrix in which political leaders can hold proper communion with its subjects by warding off personal straining of public power for possible and effective government and public standards of a decent human life. Let me elaborate this idea in greater detail.

First, legal limitations of government, rather than handicap, make government possible and effective. The modern theory of "pre-commitment"[25] in constitutional law is instructive in this regard. It indicates that the rationale of political incumbents' willingness to be limited by pre-established constitutional norms lies in the fact that this enables, not disables, government.[26] The conventional metaphor is the story of Ulysses' having himself bounding to the mast of his ship so that he could enjoy the Sirens' song. "A constitutionally-bound government acquires capacity it would not otherwise have by effectively restraining itself, just as Ulysses empowered himself by inhibiting his own capacity to make certain decisions."[27] Equally invoking the Ulysses analogy, Stephen Holmes states:

> Limits do not necessarily weaken; they can also strengthen.... Constitutions, moreover, can be binding in a way that engenders unprecedented possibilities.... Most important of all, limited government can subserve self-government by helping create "self" (or national unity) which does the governing.[28]

Further illustrating the rationales of constitutional pre-commitments, Ginsburg reveals that the binding of pre-established constitutional rules and procedures helps resolve certain inter-temporal problems for a polity,[29] establishes on enduring institutional structure that makes government possible, diverts political resources from insoluble problems to soluble ones, and makes the promises of founding leaders believable.[30]

Second, constitutional restraints essay for the responsibility of government to "general public standards."[31] Walker states that: "the appeal of constitutionalism, now and in previous eras, seems precisely to lie in its capacity to ward off tyranny by structuring public life and institutions in a way that keep them accountable to general public standards."[32] Constitutionalism intends to preclude the lamentable potentiality of the rulers to pursue their selfish benefits to ensure their accountability to general public standards. By way of metaphor, an unbridled horse may become pugnacious, dangerous, and unserviceable; similarly, the power that slips the leash may easily become a Trojan horse for the general public standards. Public values are vulnerable to the mercurial whim which normally is the alter-ego of the procrustean ruler. Public values may be in peril if the political sways are free from restraints, which allows them to wield power by character of *ipse dixit* for their egoistic interests.

An important point is that protection of liberal rights is only the goal of modern liberal constitutionalism, not the exclusive goal of constitutionalism in general sense. Walker points out that: "constitutionalism predates the enlightenment. Liberalism does not."[33] He explains that theories of constitutionalism developed in the pre-Enlightenment period by Greek thinkers like Aristotle and Polybius, Cicero and other constitutional theorists of Republican Rome, medieval scholars, and social contract philosophers do not focus on liberty. Walker indicates that liberal definition of constitutionalism as to protect liberal rights is the outcome of the conflation of constitutionalism and liberalism, which is suitable for American constitutionalism.[34]

Walker asserts: "Constitutionalism in its essence is not individual rights but fettered power."[35] Threat to individual liberty is not the sole danger that requires the limitation of governmental power because "from the perspective of other places and other histories, there may well be other harms to avoid, and other goods to pursue publicly, besides individual freedom."[36] Therefore, defining constitutionalism as limitation of power holders to protect individual rights may be suitable for American constitutionalism or liberal constitutionalism where liberty is conceived as the predominant value but may not be proper for understanding constitutionalism in a general sense. A fortiori, in America, individual liberty is predominant, but it is not the sole goal of constitutionalism. Richard S. Kay demonstrates that the freedom to associate and act collectively is also the consequential object of the US Constitution. He opines: "the Constitution must, then, be understood as a protection for every potential subject of state authority – individual, families, groups."[37]

Individual rights may be the goal of liberal constitutionalism in societies dominated by Christian tradition[38] but cannot be conceived as the exclusive standards that constitutionalism in general aims at. In non-Christian traditions, people may commit to alternative general values. In short, with regard to the telos of constitutionalism, it should be epistemologically self-emancipated from the parameter of individualism and liberalism.

How constitutionalism?

Walker argues that to practice constitutionalism, it is paramount to publicly articulate a polity's normative architecture, and formal promulgation of a written constitution is just one means for that articulation: "Defining quality of constitutionalism is not having definite texts; it is the public articulation of (at least some of) a polity's normative architecture."[39] The constitutionalist significance of the public articulation is that:

> To articulate a polity's normative architecture is to objectify it. It is to confer upon it a kind of separate existence – the separate, especially, from the immediate holders of power, even if those holders of power are ones doing the articulating. Public articulation means that the shape and the purposes of the polity are no longer hostage to vagaries of their subjectivity.[40]

The public articulation of a polity's normative architecture can be practiced "via all forms of influential public discourse," and making a written constitution is just one of them. In a similar vein, Richard S. Kay states that constitutionalism necessarily entails the creation of prior rules to define and limit state power and this is in turn needed to invoke some fixed verbal formulation of those rules.[41] He then notes that "the medium by which the formulation is preserved and communicated is not crucial. It could be oral or electronic, but for the founders of the United States Constitution, of course, it was written."[42]

A careful consideration of modern constitutionalist states can further enhance the thesis that constitutionalism cannot be analogized to the formal enactment of a written constitution. Let us illustrate by the cases of the United Kingdom and the United States. As far as the United Kingdom is concerned, A.V. Dicey long ago stated that constitutional rules of the nation consisted of both formal legal rules and conventional rules.[43] Similarly, Giovanni Sartori asserts that the English Constitution derives from a tortuous sedimentation of common law, acts, and conventional usage, partly legal and partly extra-legal.[44] Vernon Bogdanor notes that "the term 'unconstitutional' cannot in British mean contrast to law; instead it means contrast to convention, contrast to some understanding of what it is appropriate to do."[45]

Similarly, in the United States, what reins in the governmental power is not merely the single document codified in Philadelphia in 1787 together with its 27 formal amendments. There have been discussions on "unwritten constitution" in the United States by American scholars.[46] The discussions suggest that, apart from the written constitutional text, American constitutionalist norms also include the understandings of liberty and equality brought by the Supreme Court in effectuating its judicial review power which have been, in turn, shaped by "unwritten social text."[47] These "unwritten higher law principles" as C. Grey affirms, "had constitutional status."[48] Akhil Reed Amar's recent book entitled *America's Unwritten Constitution*[49] further reveals that a number of rules, principles, rights that actually govern the constitutional life of the United States cannot be found in the Philadelphia Constitution and the formal amendments but are unwritten in nature – for example, the rule of law, the principle of separation of powers, and the right of privacy. In short, the studies of America's unwritten constitution suggest that written and unwritten constitutionalist norms work together to form the working constitutionalist regime of the United States.

Why does constitutionalism need both written and unwritten constitutional norms? Robert Lowry Clinton is instructive in this regard. He differentiates the written constitution with "underlying constitution" or "real constitution" which virtually means the actual existence of a polity. He states: "since any written constitution may be conceived as representative of an underlying constitution in the wider sense, the writtenness of a constitution cannot be its essence; its essence must be its function in constituting a polity."[50] He then goes further to claim that "no written constitution can articulate fully a polity's underlying constitutional principles."[51] Based on Etienne's metaphysical description of the constitution of Being as a composite of formal essence and actual existence, Clinton reasons:

> The constitution of any polity is a being that reflects the dominant underlying decisional predispositions of that polity's citizenry. The constitution of a polity is thus a composite of that polity's formal essence and its actual existence. Since the essence of any being is that which ensures that being's self-identity and lack of internal contradiction, the essence of a constitution, whether of a polity or of an individual, is that which ensures the self-identity and internal coherence of that polity or individual.[52]

Since "any truly viable constitutionalism presupposes the ideas of constitutional being as a composite of formal essence and actual existence,"[53] any truly viable constitutionalism encompasses both written and unwritten mediums of public articulation of polity's normative architecture.

Apart from public articulation, constitutionalism requires implementation of articulated constitutional norms. This involves the creation and practice of institutional, structural limits of the public power. Modern examples of such limits include the separation of powers, free elections, some forms of checks and balances, federalism, bicameralism, judicial review, and judicial independence. However, one should keep in mind that these are the structural limits of mature modern western constitutionalism. Other forms of constitutionalism may take other forms of structural institutions.

However, constitutionalism is not exclusively associated with structural limits. The implementation of constitutionalism also depends on social constitutional understanding and discourse. Michael W. Dowdle underlines that: "Historically, the true innovation that drove the advent of modern constitutionalism was epistemic, not structural. Modern constitutionalism was borne out of a new understanding that emerged in Europe in the eighteenth century that political morality – the questions of what constitutes good and bad, right and wrong, in the context of the state – was a form of knowledge, like rationality, that was understandable by all humans."[54]

Constitutional norms and institutions have authority not simply because they are the productions of positivist articulation. More than that, their authority stems from the fact that they are the embodiment of a particular understanding of justice. However, the perennial problem is that positive constitutional norms and institutions are not always the meaningful articulation of constitutionalist epistemology. To resolve this problem, constitutionalism requires both institutional constraints and intellectual constraints. It is in this sense that Dowdle conceptualizes the realization of constitutionalism as the necessary combination of both "intellectual authority" and "institutional authority."[55] The implementation of constitutionalism through social constitutional discourse or intellectual authority "appeals to norms and understandings that are presumed to be innate to the polis, independent of codification in constitutional text or sanctification by the formal pronouncements of judicial or other political institutions."[56] In short, constitutionalism involves both formal institutional, structural means and social, intellectual means for implementing articulated constitutional norms.

Classical Confucian constitutionalism

Ren *(humaneness)*

Before proceeding to examine the constitutionalist meaning of the different Confucian concepts, the fundamental idea of *ren* (variously translated into English as "love," "perfect virtue," benevolence," or "humaneness[57]) should be considered first, because, "whenever Confucians have spoken of ethics and of government, they have always taken *jen* [*ren*] as their basis."[58] Liang Qichao also states that "without comprehending the meaning of this word [*ren*] no understanding of Confucian philosophy is possible."[59]

While *ren* appears numerously in the *Analects*,[60] Confucius does not provide a definitive meaning of the term, which leads to diverse explanations in academia.[61] For our purpose, we should focus on the political meaning of the term instead of embarking on the indeterminate discourses on it. In Confucianism, as Donald J. Munro asserts, "*jen* [*ren*], more than any other tendency, was viewed as unique to man."[62] Confucius is reported in *The Doctrine of the Mean* to say that "humaneness is the characteristic element of humanity."[63] Similarly, Mencius states: "humaneness is the distinguishing characteristic of man."[64] It can be seen that humaneness or *ren* is conceptualized as the genuine nature of human, distinguishing the human being from other animate beings.

While the human being is distinguished from other sentient beings by various attributes such as biological constitution or physical appearance, in Confucianism the definitive attribute is social characteristic. Humaneness is the social characteristic endemic in human community. This is implied in the ideograph of the *ren* 仁, which is identified by the characters of "man" and "two." The implication is that *ren* only exists when a human lives with at least one other human. Put differently, humaneness is the distinctive characteristic of the socialized human.

If *ren* is the nature of the human, it follows that a human without *ren* is not a true human. Concomitantly, if *ren* only exists when a human lives with others, a human who does not live with others is equally not a true human. On this point, the renowned Confucian scholar Herbert Fingarette asserts that from the Confucian view, "to be most fully and perfectly a human being, to be a person, is inherently to live certain human relationships with other persons."[65] For Confucianism, a true man is a social man. Confucius says: "It is impossible to associate with birds and beasts, as if they are the same with us. If I associate not with these people, – with mankind, – with whom I shall associate."[66] In other words, in Confucian vision, to become a genuine human is to experience a process of humanization which is tantamount to a process of socialization.[67]

While there are various characteristics of a socialized human, the Confucian conviction is that the socialized human is differentiated by the moral quality characterized by the love or the concern among the members of the society. This is well illustrated by the fact that when a Confucian disciple inquired on *ren*, the master responded that it is "to love all men [*airen*]."[68] On the ground, Fung Yu-lan explains: "*ren* takes sympathy as its base. Therefore, it is love of others."[69] Analogously, Kung-chuan Hsiao construes *ren* as "an enlargement of self-respect, extended to become an attitude of love or concern for others."[70] James Legge, when translating *ren* as "benevolence" also captures this meaning of the term. In short, from the Confucian perspective, the love of others or the concern for others is the distinctive characteristic of the socialized human, distinguishing human being from other beings.

Ren is regarded as a revolutionary concept of Confucius. While the notion of concern for other people is not novel, Confucius' radical contribution is to enlarge the concern to all men (*airen*). Yongping Liu helpfully points out that Confucius' *ren* runs counter to the conventional dogma teaching people to love the members of their own *zu* or lineage, a consanguineous group of people descended from a common ancestor, the basic unit of society during the times of Shang and Zhou.[71]

Confucian humanism is more than the metaphysical conception of philanthropy. Beyond that, Confucius develops practical conceptions termed as *chung* (conscientiousness) and *shu* (altruism) to realize *ren*.[72] When Chung-kung asked about *ren*, the master answered: "not to do to others as you would not wish done to yourself."[73] These words express the core meaning of *shu*. The connation of *chung* is evinced in Confucius' response to Tsze-kung: "Now the man of humaneness, wishing to be established himself, seeks also to establish others; wishing to be enlarged himself, he seeks also to enlarge others."[74] According to the treatment of Fung Yu-lan, *shu* is the negative aspect of the practice of *ren* while *chung* is its positive aspect.[75] He concludes that: "the practice as a whole is called the principle of *chung* and *shu*, which is 'the way of practice *ren*.' "[76] The remark is well justified by the evidence in the Confucian scriptures. In the *Analects*, we find this passage:

> The Master said, "Shan, my doctrine is that of an all-pervading unity." The disciple Tsang replied, "Yes." The Master went out, and the other disciples asked, saying, "what do his words mean?" Tsang said, "the doctrine of our master is *chung* (conscientiousness) and *shu* (altruism) – this and nothing more."[77]

This does not mean that Tsang, the arguably most excellent disciple of Confucius, failed to descry *ren* as the leitmotif of his Master's doctrine. It can be conjectured that since he thought that the Delphic concept of *ren* may confuse the others, he chose to answer them by pointing out its binary practice: *chung* and *shu*.[78] *The Doctrine of the Mean* expresses the same idea: "*chung* and *shu* are not far from the path."[79] That is because *chung* and *shu* are the duplex realization of the path or the *ren*.

In Confucianism, the above general principles are by no means applicable to everyone in an egalitarian manner. It is my contention that the practice of Confucius' *ren* or *airen* is discriminative, differentiating it from Mohsism's *jian ai* which stresses universal love.[80] That is in part because "Confucius' *ren* accounted for different levels of allegiance."[81] Liu observes:

> The reason that Confucius advocated levels of allegiance was that he notes that there were differentiation and hierarchy among people. In practicing *ren*, it is not possible for every individual to achieve the highest state, that is, to extensively confer benefits on the people and to be able to assist all.[82]

That is a correct observation; however, Liu has just touched one facet of the discriminative character of Confucian humanism. Confucius possibly realizes that the social relations are diverse and the human's sentiment is varied according to the specific social situations. Hence, each relationship requires a corresponding way of love or concern. The way one concerns for his parents, for instance, is different from the way he concerns for his brother or his ruler. Therefore, on the ground of the central concept of *ren*, Confucianism develops different moral norms that will be applied to different social relationships. To illustrate, the way a person concerns for his parents is characterized by *xiao* (filial piety), *ti* (fraternal submission) for his brother, and *zhong* (loyalty) for his ruler. Consequently, various Confucian moral norms stem from, and are all the multifarious manifestations of, *ren*.

To recap briefly, *ren* or humaneness is a foundational concept of Confucianism whose basic meaning is the love or concern for all men practically embodied as to base on one's own self to negatively refrain from doing harmful things for others and to positively do beneficial things for them. It is on the ground of *ren* that various Confucian concepts are developed, including constitutionalist ideas that will be explored in the subsequent sections.

Confucianism vs. despotism

In McIlwain's negative definition, constitutionalism is opposite to despotism.[83] Given that, it is necessary to examine the Confucian stance toward arbitrary rule or despotism or tyranny,[84] which is the starting point of searching for constitutionalist origins in Confucian philosophy. I argue that classical Confucianism is an animadversion on despotism.

To begin with, the *Shu Jing* demonstrates a negative disposition towards despots. As indicated in the work, such revolutionists as the Tang of Shang and

King Wu, who were about to capsize the despots, tended to justify their conduct on the ground of the popular feeling against despotic rulers. For example, the Tang of Shang exculpated the last king of Xia:

> The King of Xia does nothing but exhaust the strength of his people, and exercise oppression in the cities of Xia. His people have all become idle in his service, and will not assist him. They are saying "When will this sun expire? We will all perish with thee." Such is the course of the Sovereign Xia, and now I must go and punish him.[85]

In the same manner, King Wu stigmatized the last king of Shang as the "solitary fellow" in the sense of his total alienation from the people.[86] He incriminated the enemy: "The ancient have said, 'He who soothes us is our sovereign; he who oppresses us is our enemy.' This solitary Zhou, having exercised great tyranny, is your perpetual enemy."[87]

In a well-known anecdote recorded in the *Book of Rites*, Confucius caustically excoriates oppressive government in this way:

> In passing by the side of Mount Tai, Confucius came on a woman who was wailing bitterly by a grave. The Master bowed forwarded to the cross-bar, and hastened to her; and then sent Tzu lu to question her. "Your wailing", said he, "is altogether like that of one who has suffered sorrow upon sorrow." She replied, "It is so. Formerly, my husband's father was killed here by a tiger. My husband was also killed (by another), and now my son has died in the same way!" The Master said, "Why do you not leave the place?" The answer was, "there is no oppressive government here." The Master then said (to the disciples), "Remember this, my little children. Oppressive government is more terrible than tigers."[88]

The *Analects* provides more evidence for Confucius' aversion toward arbitrary rule. This can be first corroborated by his formulation of "four bad things" pertaining to persons in authority:

> To put the people to death without having instructed them; – this is called cruelty. To require from them, suddenly, the full tale of work, without having given them warning; – this is called oppression. To issue orders as if without urgency, at first, and, when the time comes, to insist on them with severity; – this is called injury. And, generally, in the giving pay or rewards to men, to do it in a stingy way; – this is called acting the part of a mere official.[89]

The first three bad things are obviously linked to arbitrary rule. With respect to the first fault, Confucius' concern is that without public acknowledgment of ruling principles, public power can be arbitrarily practiced. The second fault, "oppression," is clearly related to unpredictable and mercurial execution of public power. The spirit of the third bad thing – injury – according to Leonard Shihlien Hsu, "resembles that of the *post facto* law which is made unconstitutional in practically all modern states."[90] In general, it can be deduced from the above language that arbitrary rule in Confucius' view is a "bad thing."

Equally significant, Confucius genuinely dreads uncontrolled power. One day, Duke Ting asked him: "Is there a single sentence which can ruin a country?" He replied,

> Such an effect as that cannot be expected from one sentence. There is, however, the saying which people have – "I have no pleasure in being a prince, but only in that no one can offer any opposition to what I say!" If a ruler's words be good, is it not also good that no one oppose them? But if they are not good, and no one opposes them, may there not be expected from this one sentence the ruin of his country?[91]

To explain Confucius' sally in constitutional parlance, the country can be destroyed by unchecked power.

In a more acrimonious tone, Mencius goes further to assert that the bad ruler should be dismissed. The following bandying indicates Mencius' mordant allusion that when the king drives his kingdom into a bad situation his power should be left in abeyance.

> Mencius said to King Hsuan of Chi: "Suppose that one of your Majesty's ministers were to entrust his wife and children to the care of his friend, while he himself went into Chu to travel, and that, on his return, he should find that the friend had let his wife and children suffer from cold and hunger; – how ought he to deal with him?" The king said, "He should cast him off." Mencius proceeded, "Suppose that the chief criminal judge could not regulate the officers under him, how would you deal with him?" The king said, "Dismiss him." Mencius again said, "If within the four borders of your kingdom there is not good government, what is to be done?" The king looked to the right and left, and spoke of other matters.[92]

More explicitly, in another audience with the king, in replying to the king's inquiry on the historical military events pertaining to the flagellations of King Tang and King Wu upon King Jie and King Zhou, respectively,[93] Mencius obviously supports the legitimacy of regicide in the case of executing despots or tyrants:

> He who outrages the benevolence proper to his nature, is called a robber; he who outrages righteousness is called a ruffian. The robber and ruffian we call a mere fellow. I have heard of the cutting off of the fellow Zhou, but I have not heard of the putting a sovereign to death, in his case.[94]

It can be seen that despotism, in Mencius' eyes, is an anathema.

In the same vein, Xunzi unequivocally asserts that a culpable tyrant is not a virtual ruler and deserved dethronement in favor of the worthy. He states:

> Since the world had come to have no real lord, were one of the feudal lords to have real ability, were he to make illustrious his moral power and gather up his majestic authority, none of the people within the sea would fail to long to gain him as their own lord and master. This being so, should he go on to seek out the isolated and extravagant tyrant for execution, it is certain that [this feudal lord] would have inflicted no injury nor done any harm, and that he would remain a blameless subject. For, to execute a tyrannical lord is like executing a "solitary individual."[95]

Xunzi, then, avers the legitimacy of King Tang's and King Wu's banishing the tyrant Jie and the tyrant Zhou, respectively, on the ground that "Tang and Wu were considered as the father and mother of the people" and Jie and Zhou Xin are not real rulers and deserved to be superseded because they "brought chaos to the divisions of social functions inherent in ritual and moral principles, behaved like wild beasts, gathered up their own ultimate catastrophe, completed their own evil, so that the world abandoned them" and consequently "Jie and Zhou Xin were hated as the predators of the people."[96] Unquestionably, like Mencius, Xunzi is of the view that the tyrants are not true rulers and should be dethroned.

It has been seen that there is ample evidence in the Confucian classical works indicating the antagonism to despotism or tyranny. If one returns to the central theory of *ren*, one may find that the fact that Confucianism opposes despotism is intelligible. By *ren*, Confucianism stresses the concern for other people. It is logically followed that despotism in which the interests and the uncontrolled powers of a single ruler are paramount is on the antipode. In more detail, Confucian antagonism to despotism is the natural consequence of *shu*, the negative practice of *ren*. Despotic government is something that a man who is *ren* should avoid. If the ruler himself never wishes to be the victim of despotism, he should not, in the spirit of *shu*, implement despotic governance of his subjects.

Given the numerous studies on the positive relations of Confucianism to democracy and human rights, the idea that Confucianism opposes despotism may not be novel. However, I would suggest approaching this idea in a constitutionalist light. If constitutionalism is negatively defined as the antithesis of despotic government, the Confucian antagonism of despotic government can be considered the gambit of Confucian philosophy in explicating constitutionalist postulates. The continuing odyssey entails a deeper consideration of whether the Confucians had any alternative to despotism in any constitutionalist sense.

Zheng ming *(rectification of names) as constitutionalism*

McIlwain states that: "the only alternative to despotism is constitutionalism."[97] While passing stricture upon tyranny or despotism, do the classical Confucians envisage any alternative in any constitutionalist sense? The doctrine of *zheng ming* government (variously translated into English as rectification of names, correctness of names, ordering of names) developed by Confucius and expounded by Mencius and Xunzi is the corollary of their dread of despotic power. Philosophical scholars have underlined the paramount importance of the doctrine of *zheng ming* in Confucian political philosophy. Chung-ying Cheng, for example, emphasizes: "It occupied an important, if not central, position in the political philosophy of Confucius."[98] Similarly, Chenyang Li states: "One of Confucius' most important political-ethic doctrines is the rectification of names."[99] However, what has been ignored is the constitutionalist importance of the doctrine. I suggest that Confucianism's doctrine of *zheng ming* can be comprehended in a constitutionalist sense and that in order to understand the philosophical foundations of Confucian constitutionalism we must seize this doctrine as the pivot. In a nutshell, I argue that *zheng ming* government is a Confucian alternative of constitutionalism.

What is zheng ming *(rectification of names)?*

To Confucius, *zheng ming* is the doctrine advanced mainly to deal with matters regarding government. This is well illuminated by the fact that he introduced the term "*zheng ming*" in his repartee to Zi Lu's inquiry on what he should do first if the Lord of Wei employs him to administer the government: "What is necessary is to rectify names."[100]

Because Confucius presented the term "*zheng ming*" in the situation related to the Lord of Wei, some are inclined to explain it on the ground of the historical context associated with the Wei state.[101] The historian Sima Qian of the early Han Dynasty, for example, believed that the name (*ming*) in Confucius' view of (*zheng ming*) refers to the two names: "father" and "son."[102] On the other hand, for some other Han commentators, Confucius' *zheng ming* is not restricted to the historical context of the relationship of father and son as the author of *Shi ji* believes. For example, Ma Rong (74–166) regards Confucius' *zheng ming* as "to correct the names of the one hundred affairs."[103]

It may be true that when introducing the doctrine of *zheng ming*, Confucius was aware of the imbroglio of Wei; however, it is unclear that the *ming* (name) in his *zheng ming* is restricted to "father" and "son." At the same time, the expansion of *ming* (name) to the names of all things appears to reach beyond his intention. When initiating the doctrine, Confucius may inadvertently give support to nominalists,[104] but he himself, by *zheng ming*, is not a nominalist who intends to correct linguistically the names of all things. My contention is that *zheng ming* is governmental rather than linguistic. Confucius introduces the doctrine for governmental purpose and to deal with governmental matters.

Why is *zheng ming* essential for government? What is it? To understand the doctrine, it is necessary to first explain what names (*ming*) means in *zheng ming*. Chenyang Li elucidates the etymology of the graph *ming* as follows:

> the Chinese word for name is "*ming* 名" which means "that by which something/someone is called," or "that for which something/someone is known."

> The character consists of two components, one for waning moon symbolizing night, the other for the mouth. The ancient Chinese lexicon *shue wen jie zi* explicates that "in the dark things cannot be seen, therefore use mouth (sound) to call them."[105]

However, to Confucius, "name" is more than a linguistic medium used to call things and persons. Fung Yu-lan defines "name" as the essence or concept of things. The name "ruler," for example, is the essence which makes a ruler a ruler.[106] From this point of view, the names of persons[107] are not merely linguistic labels but are more substantial, meaning their essences.

The continuing matter is what constitutes the essence of a person from Confucius' perspective. As previously mentioned, Confucian humaneness (*ren*) holds that human beings are by nature social beings. To a Confucian person, as Henry Rosemont writes,

> in order to be a friend, neighbour, or lover, for example, I must have a friend, neighbour, or lover. Other persons are not merely accidental or incidental to my goal of fully developing as a human being, they are essential to it.[108]

From Confucius' point of view, the relationships that people live are not something external to them; in the deepest sense, these relationships constitute the essence of their lives. Only through interpersonal relationships is one named as father, son, minister, or prince.

Hence, names like "father," "son," "minister," or "prince" are not only words to label people; rather, they encompass these relationships. For example, one is no longer called "prince" if one does not experience the corresponding relationship with ministers and subjects. Moreover, for Confucius, each relationship that a person is involved in normally suggests a possible virtue. It is on this ground that Chung-ying Cheng defines "names" as including "labels for relationships between individuals and the values inherent in those relationships."[109] He then explains:

> Names in this sense include specific terms indicating relationships between ruler and subject, parent and child, husband and wife, friend and friend, and younger and older siblings. These relationships suggest the possibilities of the virtues of loyalty and respect in the case of the ruler and the subject, kindness and filial piety in the case of the parent and child, mutual respect and performance of separate duties in the case of husband and wife, truthfulness and trustworthiness in the case of friends, and brotherly love and considerateness in the case of siblings.[110]

As names include the relationships, they indicate the roles of persons in which their duties and the functions are defined. The name "prince," for example, proposes what the named is supposed to do. It should be noted that as the prince's relationships are essential to him, he lives rather than plays the roles in those relationships: insofar as he lives these roles, he is named as "prince."[111] Furthermore, since the name implies positive moral virtue, it suggests certain ways of behavior. Therefore, the name "prince" points out not only what the named will do but also how he ought to do it. Chenyang Li helpfully generalizes names as being "both descriptive and prescriptive."[112]

Having defined the meaning of "names" (*ming*), we now proceed to clarify the meaning of *zheng ming*. In fact, the Confucian term *zheng* (正) has profound moral and political implications and we do not have an English word to sufficiently convey its meaning. It is translated into English as "correctness" or "ordering," but more popularly "rectification." I adopt the English term "rectification" to translate *zheng* but will understand "rectification" in Confucian political and moral connotations. According to Fung Yu-lan, *zheng ming* or rectification of names means that "the actual must in each case be made to correspond to the name, the thing's essence or concept."[113] The essential spirit of *zheng ming* is the correspondence between the names and the actuality. Consequently, rectifying the names involves various actions to maintain the correspondence between the names and the actualities. Since names indicate the relationships which define the roles together with their inherent virtues, it follows that to rectify the names is to rectify the relationships, which means to maintain the socio-political order by which those who carry certain names shall act in accordance with the roles and the virtues that the names or the relationships stand for. Consider this discourse for more illustration. When the duke Ching of Chi asked Confucius about government, he replied, "There is government, when the prince is the prince, and the minister is the minister; when the father is father, and the son is son."[114] In the sentence that "the prince is the prince," the first "prince" refers to a physical prince, while the second "prince" refers to the relationships which define the duties and functions together with moral values that the physical prince is supposed to follow.[115] "The prince is the prince" means to ensure the correspondence between the real actions of the physical prince with the roles and moral values that the term "prince" stands for.

In negative meaning, rectification of names is to avert the situation in which the acts of those who carry social titles do not correspond with the roles and the values that the titles stand for. It is on this ground that Confucius states that "he, who is not in particular office, has nothing to do with plans for the administration of its duties."[116]

It can be seen that the Confucian program of rectification of names is more than the precise nomenclature. According to Chung-ying Cheng's explanation,

> Rectifying names demands the correspondence of names to the natural facts as well as to the implementation of values. Thus, this doctrine does not just require definitional consistency, but implies a recognition of principles; that is, recognition of standards of action and that can be used to judge what is true, good, and right, on the one hand, and what is false, bad, and wrong, on the other. To rectify names therefore is to establish standards of the true, the

> good, and the right. But because moral knowledge of right and wrong in a normal situation carries a command for doing right, to rectify names therefore, is related to the program for carrying out the command for doing appropriate thing in accordance with the proper situation.[117]

Put another way, the Confucian program of rectification of names involves the articulation and execution of standards defining the functions and the values inherent in those functions. Governmentally speaking, rectification of names means to maintain the concordance between the real actions of the governors, like sovereigns and ministers, with the standards defining their duties, authority, and expected values. As the priority of the Confucian governmental program, rectification of names therefore involves the articulation and implementation of standards for the operation of public power.

Importantly, Confucius tends to define government as rectification. He states elsewhere in the *Analects*: "to govern means to rectify."[118] This statement is not simply meant to equate execution of governmental affairs to rectification of names. More substantially, it suggests that in the Confucian philosophy only a government practicing rectification of names or a rectified government is a true government.

Zheng ming *as constitutionalism*

So understood, I suggest that the Confucian doctrine of rectification of names can be considered a Confucian doctrine of constitutionalism. In a modern constitutionalist state, the primary concern is to ensure that physical political institutions, such as the congress, the president, and the prime minister, will function in accordance with metaphysical constitutional standards commonly articulated in a written constitution. Similarly, to practice the *zheng ming* government means to ensure the accordance between the real actions of the power holders with their names or the standards defining their authorities, duties, and expected virtues.

To be sure, constitutionalism is not simply about the formal correspondence of the material governmental institutions to the governmental standards or rules. The essential concern of constitutionalism is that that correspondence is meant to limit the public power to enable government to function efficiently and to keep the power holders responsible for general public standards. Even so understood, I believe that rectification of names also reflects constitutionalist sense. To rectify the names actually means to ensure the proper operation of public power and to prevent the arbitrary practice of the public power. In that sense, a rectified government tends to become a limited government.

The Confucian idea of rectification of names is similar to the modern western idea of "limitation" in that they pursue the same constitutionalist aspiration that political institutions must function in accordance with the defined boundaries so as to enable proper use of power and prevent misuse of power. However, the Confucian concept of "rectification" is different from the western liberal concept of "limitation" in several ways. First, the purpose of the Confucian rectifications is to guarantee the governmental responsibility for the public good rather than individual rights as the western limitations aim at. This is evident in the Confucian concept of *minben* (people-as-base). Second, the Confucian rectifications, like the western limitations, depend on the articulation of the established rules, but are distinctive in that the Confucian rules are a set of traditional norms and institutions – the *li* (ritual) – not being codified in a single document like modern written constitutions. Third, the Confucian rectifications are actually the limitations or restraints but are practiced by special means different from the western modern means of constitutional limitations or restraints. Let us consider the third difference in greater detail.

The liberal concern with constitutional limitations of public power is the natural consequence of the negative view of human nature. As noted by an American scholar, "by nature, the constitutionalist is pessimist."[119] This kind of pessimism is traceable back to the political thinkers of the Enlightenment age. Thomas Hobbes underlines "a general inclination of all mankind a perpetual and restless desire of power after power, that ceaseth only in death."[120] This perennial pathology of the human induces the need for constitutional restraints. C.S. Montesquieu states:

> Constant experience shows us that every man invested with power is apt to abuse it and to carry his authority as far as it will go.... To prevent this abuse, it is necessary from the very nature of things that power should be a check to power.[121]

So, the pessimist view of human nature of abusing power leads to a mechanistic or Newtonian approach of limitations by the separation of powers and other forms of checks and balances. This approach operates with the Jeffersonian assumption that: "In questions of power, then, let no more be heard of confidence in man, but bind him down from mischief by the chains of the Constitution."[122] Therefore, the constitution establishes mechanistic institutional means to "bind" the power holders "down from mischief." From the Newtonian perspective on constitutional limitations, power is viewed as a physical entity which has a weight and a size, and therefore can be divided into small parts so that it becomes less threatening or balanced with another power of equal weight and size so that it does not become larger and stronger.[123]

The Confucian concept of rectification of public power adopts a more positive view on human nature and hence proceeds to a more positive approach to means of limitations. To begin with, unlike the Western liberal concept of limitations, the Confucian concept of rectifications does not operate in a dark picture of the human being. The three classical Confucians – namely Confucius, Mencius, and Xunzi – in spite of their different perspectives on human nature, all believe in the educability of the human and hence heavily emphasize the importance of education. Confucius states that: "By nature, men are nearly alike; by practice, they get to be wide apart."[124] Even though this ambiguous statement does not provide a clear answer to the question of human nature, it indicates that "practices" differentiate "*great man*" (*chun-tzu*) and "small man" (*hsiao-jen*) and therefore, as Confucius routinely reminds us, to be the "great man" (*chun-tzu*), who is expected to administer governmental affairs, one should pay sober attention to learning and education to foster good practices.[125] Mencius particularly insists that human nature is good, but fragile to external influences, and therefore learning and education are imperative to restore the "lost heart" or the innate goodness.[126] Xunzi, despite his contradistinction to Mencius by his assertion that "human nature is evil,"[127] is not different from Mencius in that it is possible for everyone to become good by learning and education.[128] For Xunzi, "a man in the street (the common man) can become a Yu (a sage king)" if he can "engage in study, focus his mind on a single aim, unify his intentions, ponder these principles, accomplish them each day over a long period of time, and accumulate what is good without slacking off."[129]

With the assumption of the educable nature of the human, the Confucian theory of rectification of name develops a distinctive approach to limitations. To rectify the power is actually to limit or restraint it not by the Newtonian or negative forms, but by more constructive or positive forms through the ruler's self-cultivation and wise and virtue scholars' education, criticism, and remonstrance of the ruler.

To further understanding of *zheng ming* government as Confucian constitutionalism, its telos (the concept of *minben*), articulated norms and institutions (the concept of *li*), and distinctive positive means will be examined in greater detail in the subsequent sections.

Minben ***(people as basis): telos of Confucian constitutionalism***

Constitutionalism presupposes the idea of the existence of a proper relationship between the government and its subjects. The propriety of the relationship means that governmental power must be teleologically limited to general public standards. In this section, I shall argue that the Confucian concept of *minben* (people as basis) can be regarded as the source of constitutionalism in the Confucian intellectual legacy since it suggests that a *zheng ming* government must be responsible for general public standards.

The concept of minben

The concept of *minben* has been established in the *Shu Jing*. We find these verses in the classic: "The people should be cherished; they should not be down-trodden. The people are the root of the country; the root firm, the country is tranquil."[130] As people are the root or the base, the creation of government is for the people:

> The founding of the States, and setting up of capitals; the appointing of sovereign kings, of princes and dukes, with their great officers and heads of departments – were not designed to minister to the idleness and the pleasures of one, but for the good government of people.[131]

The happiness of the people is regarded as the end of government: "May you now succeed in making your prince a successor of my royal ancestor; and in securing the lasting happiness of the people."[132]

The Confucian concept of *minben* established in the *Shu Jing* originated from another concept, namely the "Mandate of Heaven" (*tianming*) established in the same classic. The *tianming* concept holds that the king receives the mandate from heaven to govern the kingdom and hence he is also called "the Son of Heaven." The Mandate of the Heaven is embodied in the will of the people, and therefore the "Son of Heaven" is required to govern his kingdom in accordance with the will of the people.[133]

Confucius goes further to develop the concept of *minben* on the foundation of his humanism (*ren*). While *ren* is understood as the love of all men, its incarnation in the political realm is the ruler's love of the people. In political meaning, to love the people means to work for their happiness. Consider this passage in the *Analects*:

> Tsze-kung said, "suppose the case of a man extensively conferring benefits on the people, and able to assist all, what would you say of him? May he be called perfectly virtuous?" The Master said, "why speak only of virtue in connexion with him? Must he not have the qualities of a sage?"[134]

Elsewhere in the *Analects*, Confucius is reported to respond to the Duke of Sheh's enquiry on government that "good government obtains, when those who are near are made happy, and those who are far off are attracted."[135]

From Confucius' perspective, the good government must be responsible for the welfare of the people, which includes both material and spiritual aspects. This can be well illustrated by this passage in the *Analects*:

> When the Master went to Wei, Zan Yu acted as the driver of his carriage. The Master observed, "How numerous are the people!" Yu said, "since they are thus numerous, what more shall be done for them?" "Enrich them," was the reply. "And when they have been enriched, what more shall be done?" The Master said, "teach them."[136]

It can be seen that in Confucius' thought, the responsibilities of the government are to first ensure prosperous conditions for the people and to subsequently educate them.

In line with the aforementioned precept that *shu* and *chung* are the dual practices of *ren*, in the political field, to love the people or to work for the benefit of the people means two things: first, not to do bad things to them (*shu*); second, to do good things for them (*chung*). This is demonstrated in Confucius' proclamation of four principles of bad government and five principles of good government. The four principles of bad government pertain to doing harmful things to the people that a person in authority should avoid, including: cruelty, oppression, injury, and meanness. Five principles of good government are related to doing beneficial things for the people that a person in authority should promote, including: to benefit the people without wasting great expenditure, to lay tasks on the people without their repining, to pursue desire without being covetous, to maintain a dignified ease without being proud, and to be majestic without being fierce.[137]

It can be seen that Confucius has humanized the traditional concept of *minben*. *Ren* is politically embodied as the love of the government of the people. Practically, in political meaning, *shu* becomes avoiding the principles of the bad government which is inimical to the people and *chung* means to execute the principles of the good government which is beneficial for the people. For the felicity of the people, the government must enrich and educate them.

Mencius expounds Confucius' concepts of *ren* and *minben* and goes further to develop them into his theories of "humane mind," "humane government," and "the importance of the people."[138] In his doctrine, the humane mind is the intrinsically good nature of the human,[139] politically embodied as the humane government which in turn induces the assertion on the importance of the people.

"Humane government," despite the fact that its idea has been introduced by Confucius, is the neology of Mencius, the production of his political expansion of Confucius' humaneness. Mencius believes that humaneness is the prerequisite of the government. He says: "It was by humaneness that the three dynasties[140] gained the throne, and by not being humane that they lost it."[141] Therefore, the humane government is vital for political order: "The principles of Yao and Shun, without a humane government, could not secure the tranquil order of the kingdom."[142] In Mencian theory, the way to practice the humane government is "the love and protection of people."[143] Vehemently, Mencius goes further to declare that "the people are the most important element in a nation; the spirits of the land and grain are the next; the sovereign is the lightest."[144]

In developing the concept of *minben*, Mencius particularly accentuates the responsibility of the government for the material benefits of the people.[145] Mencius considers nourishing the people as the foremost task of the humane government. His rationale lies in the conviction that the constancy of the material life is the precondition for the constancy of the spiritual life:

> As to the people, if they have not a certain livelihood, it follows that they will not have a fixed heart. And if they have not a fixed heart, there is nothing which they will not do, in the way of self-abandonment, of moral deflection, of depravity, and of wild license. When they thus have involved in crime, to follow them up and punish them; – this is to entrap the people. How can such a thing as entrapping the people be done under the rule of a humane man?[146]

Therefore, Mencius continues to suggest that

> an intelligent ruler will regulate the livelihood of the people, so as to make sure that, for those above them, they shall have sufficient wherewith to serve their parents, and, for those below them, sufficient wherewith to support

> their wives and children; that in good years they shall always be abundantly satisfied, and that in bad years they shall escape the danger of perishing.[147]

While underlining the responsibility of government for the material dimension of the people, Mencius by no means underestimates the importance of educating them. Also, it is far from true that Mencius usually treated the subject of teaching the people as something subsidiary to nourishing them, as Kung-chuan Hsiao asserted.[148] The readers of *The Works of Mencius* may have the feeling that Mencius is more emphatic on nourishing the people, but it should be recognized that he, as a Confucian, pursues the ultimate goal which is morally cultivated rather than affluent people. He asserts "if they [the people] are well fed, warmly clad, and comfortably lodged, without being taught at the same time, they become almost like the beasts."[149] Mencius even suggests that the government should establish educational institutions for the instruction of the people, namely *hsiang*, *hsü*, *hsüeh*, and *hsiao*.[150] While Mencius' goal was to morally educate people, he paid great attention to the livelihood of the people since he believed that economically decent conditions are required for the flowering of humane minds. Given that, material conditions are the instrument for spiritual life, and nourishing the people is contributory to educating them.

Different from Mencius, Xunzi plays his political theory on the ground of the conviction on the evil nature of the human. However, it seems that the discrepancy between Xunzi and Mencius tends to be exaggerated. Although their theories' starting points are different, some of their political conclusions are similar. Xunzi is by no means distant from Confucian humanism and *minben*.

Quite similar to the Hobbesian perspective, Xunzi gives credence to the inherently evil human nature, whose natural development will drive human life to the state of anarchism, chaos, and cruelty.[151] However, this does not necessarily lead him to the invocation of a Leviathan government, as Thomas Hobbes did, or draconian penal laws, as his unexpected student Han Fei did. Rather, he thinks that this inborn nature can be rectified by moral education and it is for this educational task that government is established.[152] He then describes the functions of the government as follows:

> In antiquity the sage kings took man's nature to be evil, to be inclined to prejudice and prone to error, to be perverse and rebellious, and not to be upright or orderly. For this reason they invented ritual principles and precepts of moral duty. They institute the regulations that are contained in laws and standards. Through these actions they intended to "straighten out" and develop man's essential nature and to set his inborn nature aright. They sought to tame and transform his essential nature and to guide his inborn nature with the Way. They caused both his essential and inborn natures to develop with good order and be consistent with the true Way.[153]

It is believed that Xunzi gives more credit to laws than either Confucius or Mencius.[154] However, the contents of the laws in Xunzi's theory are "ritual principles and precepts of moral duty" and hence the function of the laws is to rectify the people to the Way or moral principles. By this, Xunzi remains a bona fide Confucian rather than transforming to a legalist.

When emphasizing the responsibility of the government in educating the people, Xunzi does not depart from the Confucian concept of *minben*. He even asserts that the people are not created for the sake of the lord; conversely, the lord is established for the sake of the people.[155] Therefore, quite similar to Confucius and Mencius, Xunzi states that: "if the lord of men desires to be secure, no policy is as good as even-handed government and love of people."[156] To love the people or to work for the sake of the people, the government must both educate them and take care of their livelihood. Xunzi never ignores the responsibility of the government for the material life of the people. One of the ways of the ruler, he states, "lies in expertise in providing a living for people and in caring for them."[157] The law, apart from the educational function, is also designed for "nourishing the myriads of people."[158] It can be seen that Xunzi, albeit beginning with a negative outlook on human nature, has expounded the Confucian humanism and *minben*. In his theory, it behooves the government to take care of the people's spiritual and economical lives.

The Confucian concept of *minben* is teleologically linked to the doctrine of rectification of names. The welfare of the people is the *telos* of the *zheng ming* government. Insofar as the government serves for the benefit of its subjects it is qualified as a legitimate government. Conversely, if the government or the ruler betrays the benefit of the people, it is not a true government or a true ruler. It is on this ground that Mencius regards the tyrant Zhou as "a robber," "a ruffian" and "a mere follow" rather than a sovereign, and that Xunzi considers Tang and Wu true rulers as they "were considered the father and mother of the people" and Jie and Zhou Xin not as true rulers, who deserved to be superseded as they "were hated as the predators of the people." In short, a rectified government must be a government responsible for the people.

The Confucian concept of *minben* government is different from the western concept of democratic government. Unlike the concept of democracy, the concept of *minben* suggests a government *for* the people, not a government *of* the people. To early Confucians, the chief concern is the *results* of government rather than its forms to adopt. It is not completely clear that letting the people create the government and have the final voice in all public affairs is the best way of governing *for* themselves – for the purpose of their material well-being and ethical growth.[159]

Minben *as the telos of Confucian constitutionalism*

Clinton L. Rossiter states:

> Any system of government genuinely committed in theory and adhering in practice to constitutionalism of any form – and particularly to democracy – must involve the principle of responsibility in all of its meanings, including

> especially: answerability; duty; obligation; oversight; accountability; trusteeship; and causality.[160]

The *minben* concept is highly consonant with that essential spirit of constitutionalism. The Confucian theory of *minben* suggests that the ruler must be responsible in practicing his power. The ruler is obligated to work for the welfare of people, and this leads to prodigious responsibilities. He should preside over people with gravity, be final and kind to all, advance the good, and teach the incompetent.[161] He should honor the talented and virtuous, and bear with all, praise the good, and pity the incompetent.[162] He should love propriety, righteousness, and good faith.[163] He should pay reverent attention to business, be sincere, be economic in expenditure, love for men, and employ the people at the proper seasons.[164] One may want to further embellish this catalog, but these are sufficient to verify the profound Confucian concern for responsible government. In conclusion, as the *minben* concept necessarily leads to a responsible government, it can be counted as the idea of constitutionalism in the Confucian intellectual world.

Those who deny the constitutionalist implication of the *minben* concept may argue on the grounds of the *telos* of constitutionalism that *minben* does not include the notion of rights.[165] In fact, the absence of the concept of rights cannot be invoked to negate the constitutionalist meaning of *minben*. As previously illustrated, the conception that the ultimate goal of constitutionalism is to champion human rights is the consequence of the modern narrow combination of constitutionalism with the Enlightenment liberalism. Liberal rights of the individuals therefore can only be considered the *telos* of western liberal modern constitutionalism. Non-western and pre-modern constitutionalism need not be examined through a liberalistic and individualistic lens. Above all in the constitutionalist polity is the spirit of governmental responsibility for the "general public standards." The constitutional government is responsible for values other than rights. To that extent, the ruler in the *minben* government is teleologically limited to the public good rather than to be free to pursue his egoistic interests. In this sense, the Confucian concept of *minben* satisfies the requirement of teleological limitations of constitutionalism.

Li *(ritual): Confucian constitution*

Those who gainsay the constitutionalist meaning of *minben* may even state that the relationship between government and people in the *minben* scheme is paternalistic.[166] On the other hand, as Immanuel Kant asserts, under a paternalistic government,

> the subject, as immature children who cannot distinguish what is truly useful or harmful to themselves, would be obliged to behave purely passively and to rely upon the judgment of the head of state as to how they ought to be happy, and upon his kindness in willing their happiness at all.[167]

Such a government is the "greatest conceivable *despotism*."[168] It seems logical to follow that the *minben* government implies despotism or authoritarianism rather than constitutionalism.

It should be candidly noted that there is no lack of statements in the Confucian scriptures which compare the ruler to the parents of the people.[169] However, it would be a fallacy to, based on such evidence, reduce Confucian governmental inquiry to mere paternalism and hence to despotism or authoritarianism. While comparing the ruler to the parents of people, the classical Confucians by no means believe that the ruler can unilaterally and fecklessly superimpose his discretion upon the docile people. Rather, Confucian governmental theory proposes that the ruler, in governing the people, must be limited by articulated norms and institutions termed as *li* (ritual) in the Confucian nomenclature. In this section, I argue that *li* is a Confucian unwritten constitution.

Li *and the rule of* li

Li is rich in meaning and has no English equivalent.[170] According to Homer Dubs, there are 13 English words for translating the word *li*, namely: religion, ceremony, deportment, decorum, propriety, formality, politeness, courtesy, etiquette, good form, good behavior, good manners, and the rules of proper conducts.[171] Masayuki Sato notes that in the last two decades *li* is predominantly translated into English as "ritual."[172]

Li is a maneuverable concept which possesses various nuances of connotation in different periods of time. While the morphology of *li* 禮 pristinely refers to a religious ritual of libation,[173] the evolution of the concept leads to the inclusion of other things. Hahm notes:

> as Confucianism soon increasingly focused on social ethics, scholarly learning, and moral cultivation of the self rather than on salvation in the after-life or devotion to supernatural deities, the idea of *li* came to lose much of its religious overtones.[174]

In the Shang dynasty, *li* mainly indicated religious liturgy, but in the Zhou dynasty and especially when the Duke of Zhou systematically codified the *li* of Zhou, *li* was expanded to incorporate socio-political institutions and norms. At the same time, in the *Book of Poetry*, reportedly created during the Spring and Autumn Period prior to the birth of Confucius, *li* was conceptualized as manners and social norms. Confucius employs the precedent meanings of *li* and goes further to develop a novel sense, namely the moral norm. Following Confucius, Mencius views *li* as social norms, and in particular one of the four cardinal moral values.[175] Xunzi also pays special attention to *li*. His distinct contribution is to elevate *li* to the cosmic principle.[176] Benjamin Schwartz helpfully generalizes:

> The word *li* on the most concrete level refers to all those "objective" prescriptions of behaviour, whether involving rite, ceremony, manners, or

> general deportment, that bind human beings and the spirits together in networks of interacting roles within the family, within society, and within numinous realm beyond.... What makes *li* the cement of the entire normative sociopolitical order is that it largely involves the behaviour of persons related to each other in terms of role, status, rank, and position with a structured society.[177]

In short, *li* in Confucian philosophy is an extremely inclusive concept, which embraces comprehensively rituals, institutions, social and moral norms, which regulate all dimensions of people's lives, ranging from personal behavior and familial relationships to socio-political functions and structures.

In political meaning, the concept of *li* stemmed from the central doctrine of *zheng ming* government. Leonard Shihlien Hsu points out that: "*li* is an applied doctrine of rectification."[178] The *zheng ming* government requires political institutions to function in concordance with the established standards, which defines the limitations of their authorities and duties together with expected virtues. This depends on the presence of a set of established standards. *Li* is formulated as the articulation of such standards.

First, *li* defines the institutional framework of government. For the classical Confucians, as Qu Tongzu asserts, *li*, among other things, "are social and political institutions, including law and government."[179] The fact the Duke of Zhou composed the Confucian work entitled *Zhouli* (Rituals of Zhou) intentionally to describe the structure of the government of the Zhou dynasty demonstrates that *li* was conceived of as the institutional framework of government. It is for this reason that Kuo-Cheng Wu considers *Zhouli* as "the Constitution of Zhou"[180] and Jaeyoon Song renders it as a "meta- constitution."[181] In a similar vein, Hahm proposes that *li* can be referred to as "constitutional law" in a Confucian state.[182] It can be concluded that in Confucian philosophy, *li* establishes the institutional limitations of the government. It defines the scope of the authorities and duties of different governmental institutions. It is on the basis of the institutional limitations set up by the *li* that the rectification of government can be practiced.

Second, *li* defines the possible moral virtues which government individuals are supposed to possess. To classical Confucians, *li* connotes moral norms, apart from the governmental institutions. In this sense, *li* can be conceived of as a code of moral rules, which control the conduct of the political men. On the grounds of the code of conduct established by *li*, actions of government can be rectified.

The practice of the *zheng ming* government naturally leads to the Confucian concept of "the rule of *li*" whose locus classicus can be found in the *Analects*:

> If the people be led by laws, and uniformity sought to be given them by punishments, they will try to avoid the punishment, but have no sense of shame. If they be led by virtue, and uniformity sought to be given them by rules of propriety [*li*] they will have the sense of shame and moreover will become good.[183]

This well-known aphorism is frequently adduced to justify the view that Confucianism advocates rule of virtue instead of rule of law. However, little attention has been given to the affirmation of the rule of *li*.[184] The rule of *li* means that not only ordinary people but also the members of government including the sovereign must be under the rein of *li*. This assertion can be supported by a number of pieces of evidence in the *Analects:*

> If a prince is able to govern his kingdom with the complaisance proper to the rules of propriety (li), what difficulty will he have? If he cannot govern it with that complaisance, what has he to do with the rules of propriety (*li*)?[185]

> A prince should employ his minister according to the rules of propriety (*li*).[186]

> If a superior man loves propriety (*li*), the people will not dare not to be reverent.[187]

Unlike Confucius, Mencius does not frequently discuss *li* since he tends to focus more on *ren* (humaneness) and *yi* (righteousness). However, one may see Mencius' inclination toward the rule of *li* ensconced in his advocacy of implementing the *fa* of the ancient kings:

> There are now princes who have benevolent hearts and a reputation for benevolence, while yet the people do not receive any benefits from them, nor will they leave any example to future ages;– all because they do not put into practice the ways (*fa*) of the ancient kings. Hence we have the saying: "Virtue alone is not sufficient for the exercise of government; laws alone cannot carry themselves into practice."[188]

What does *fa* mean in this context? Is it the law fervently advocated by the legalists like Han Fei? On this point, Chung-ying Cheng provides excellent guidance: "The Chinese ancient word '*fa*' is an ancient word with many connotations. It stood for many things throughout the antiquity of early Zhou period (or perhaps early Shang) to the time of *fa-chia* (legalism)."[189] According to his exposition, "*fa*" is of three meanings, namely: the "method" or "model" for doing something; predetermined norms regarding institutional structure or administrative process; and a code of punishment.[190] Cheng goes further to demonstrate that Confucianism embraces to a large extent *fa* in the sense of predetermined norms as an essential element in the administration of the government while legalism (*fa-chia*) appropriates *fa* in the sense of a code of punishment.[191] Mencius, as a bona fide Confucian, while calling for practicing the *fa* of the ancient kings by no means understood *fa* as the criminal law. As de Bary pointed out:

> in his writings, Mencius used the term *fa* to designate the model institutions of the sage king.... At the same time, the actual institutions cited as

> representative of the humane rule of the sage-king, for example, the enfeoffment system, the land distribution system, the school system and the like, are all institutions identified with and included in the classical texts and rites.[192]

Given that, by "*fa* of the ancient kings" Mencius really means the traditional norms and institutions regulating the administration of government. Understood in this sense, *fa* is quite tantamount to *li*. It is logically followed that Mencius' advocacy of practice of the *fa* of the ancient kings is actually the endorsement of the rule of *li*.

The Confucian predicament on the rule of *li* is vehemently defended and developed by Xunzi. To him, *li*, among other things, is seen "as the essential element for the accomplishment of the social-political order."[193] Importantly, Xunzi considers rule of *li* the condition for the triumph of state:

> Rites [*li*] are the highest expression of order and discrimination, the root of strength in the state, the Way by which the majestic sway of authority is created, and the focus of merit and fame.... If they [kings and dukes] proceed in accordance with the Way of ritual principles [*li*], then they will succeed; if they do not, then they will fail.[194]

The Confucian principle of the rule of *li* was the natural corollary of the doctrine of rectification of names. A *zheng ming* government must be under the rule of *li*. In a *zheng ming* government, different political institutions are required to function in concordance with the institutional limitations and the moral norms articulated by *li*. A striking point of the Confucian principle of the rule of *li* is the requirement of the ruler's reverential observance of the *li*. When *li* in Confucian philosophy tended to depart from the pristine religious meaning and became increasingly associated with political, legal, and moral dimensions, its supernatural aspects may have become less prominent, but the principle of the rule of *li* "still retained the requirement of a reverential attitude in the correct performance of socially meaningful acts."[195] A true ruler or a rectified ruler, therefore, must show the constant, punctilious, and reverential observance of *li* or the institutions and moral norms regulating his public governance and his personal life.

With the above understanding in mind, I believe that Kim's dichotomy of Mencius' *dezhi* with Xunzi's *lizhi* is a mischaracterization. First, Mencius and Xunzi, like Confucius, are both supporters of the rule of *li*. The fact that Mencius stresses more humaneness and righteousness, and Xunzi devolves a separate chapter in his work to discuss *li* easily misleads one towards the contrary explanation of the competing political theories of these two early Confucians. In fact, as mentioned above, Mencius also advocates the rule of *li* in his calling for following the "*fa* of the ancient kings." More seriously, I contend that the conventional scholarly dichotomy of *dezhi* vs. *lizhi* in Confucian philosophy is rather misleading. In classical Confucianism, *li* and moral virtue are actually intertwined. To be sure, when *li* is solely understood as legal and political institutions, it is legitimate to speak of the distinction of *dezhi* and *lizhi*. But, as the meanings of *li* are extended, particularly by Confucius and Mencius, to incorporate moral norms, *dezhi* and *lizhi* are indistinguishable. After all, in classical Confucianism's governmental inquiry, the rule of *li* means the rule of both political-legal institutions and moral norms.

Li *as Confucian constitution*

Since *li* regulates all members of the polity, the rule of *li* implies the restraint of public power. It is because of this that *li* engrosses legal scholars, especially constitutional law scholars. Leonard Shihlien Hsu long ago examined the "constitutional significance of *li*," according to which *li* is described as a principle in accordance with the "natural law" and the will of the "God" that defines the limits of governmental authority.[196] Recently, Ginsburg also comprehended *li* as "a kind of higher natural law, constraining human positive law."[197]

In fact, as *li* presents reasonable principles, it is understandable that scholars compare it with the western concept of natural law. However, *li* is actually human-made institutions and norms. To illustrate, Xunzi asserts that *li* is the invention of the sage kings to prevent evil actions of humans.[198]

In addition, the dichotomy between natural law and positive law is improper to explain *li*. The Confucians do not require that positive law must be enacted in concordance with *li*, simply because they do not even endorse promulgation of positive law. The Confucian conviction is that positive law can only prevent people from doing bad deeds in concrete cases, but cannot cultivate people's morality and encourage good deeds in the long run. Therefore, in Confucian philosophy, the suggestion is not that positive law must be consistent with *li*, but that the enactment of positive law must be limited in favor of the practice of *li*. Thus, the Confucian dichotomy between *li* and law is not an analogy of the western dichotomy of natural law versus positive law.

Alternatively, I suggest that the constitutionalist significance of *li* lies not in the fact that *li* is a kind of natural law, but the fact that *li* is a set of traditional laws. In other words, the traditionalist nature of *li* results in its constitutionalist significance. *Li* consists of traditional institutions and norms which can be understood as constitutional norms.

However, it would be useful first to remember that the Confucians are traditionalists. Carl J. Friedrich, in his *Tradition and Authority*, notes that Confucians are "perhaps the most traditionalist."[199] Confucius, Mencius, and Xunzi are all admirers of the model of the ancient kings, especially the civilization of the early Zhou dynasty. Confucius himself declares that he is "a transmitter and not a maker" and that he believes in and loves "the ancients."[200] Particularly, the master is enamored of Zhou civilization: "Zhou had the advantages of viewing the two past dynasties. How complete and elegant are its regulations. I follow Zhou."[201] Mencius also supports the *fa* (model) of ancient kings. By that, Mencius in fact gives approval to the traditional cultural heritages, regulations and institutions of Zhou.[202] Xunzi is also an admirer of the "later kings" which are actually the early kings of Zhou.[203]

Li typically represents Confucian traditionalism. Herbert Fingarette points out that *li* is the medium for Confucius to "talk about the entire body of the *mores*, or more precisely, of the authentic tradition and reasonable convention of society."[204] William Alford points out that "thinking about … yesterday" is a prevalent tendency in all intellectual discourse of ancient China.[205] Particularly, he indicates that *li* "embodied and expressed the most profound insights and experience of the so-called Ancients who had established society and compiled the Classics."[206] Following Alford, Hahm has elucidated *li* as the traditionalist form of Confucian political discourse.[207]

It should be noted that the rule of traditionalist *li* is not a haphazard loyalty to past facts. For Confucius, as illustrated by Herbert Fingarette,

> the *li* and the *tao* represent deeply authenticated norms for conduct, rather than historically persistent forms of actual conduct. The significance of their origin in antiquity, in the golden age vouched for by their having been accepted in virtuous and wise regimes, regimes governed by men who (Confucius presumed) saw clearly and deeply into the meaning of human existence, and who live the truths they saw. On the other hand history was in reality a process of moral degeneration, and not at all a process of authentication by virtue of repetition.… Thus, the *substantive* wisdom that Confucius taught was not loyalty to tradition but, rather, the intrinsic wisdom of certain ways of living.[208]

Fingarette distinguished "social fact" and "social norms," according to which *li* (and *tao*) "do not refer primarily to past social fact but to social norms, i.e., rules or principles for guiding conduct."[209] For Xunzi, *li* is understood as the Ways of ancient kings recorded in the classics which indicate the "rightness" (*yi*) or "what is right."[210] *Li* is therefore the reflection of the general truth authenticated by the ancient sage kings. The spirit of *li* is its consonance with the common sense of rightness.[211] Xunzi says: "Ritual principles [*li*] use obedience to the true mind of man as their foundation."[212] In short, the genuine meaning of the rule of *li* is the rule of norms and institutions, which are the embodiments of the reasonable principles authenticated in the tradition.

We are now in the position to expound the constitutionalist implications of *li* stemmed from its traditionalist nature. As constitutionalism is the opposite of personal rule, which leads to the efforts of western constitutionalist projects to superimpose the popular will upon the will of the ruler, it is conventional to regard popular sovereignty as the fundamental principle of constitutionalism. Especially, the principle of the popular authorship of the written constitution, which originated in Rousseau's theory of social contract, is considered the hallmark of constitutional government. However, it is far from true that constitutionalism is equated to popular sovereignty and hence that a written constitution ratified by "we the people" is the sine qua non of a constitutionalist regime. The essential spirit of constitutionalism is the victory of the popular will against the personal will. Given that, popular sovereignty which leads to a contractual written constitution is not the exclusive path to constitutionalist polity. There are alternative paths to maintain a political order in which the sovereign's will is subjugated by the people's will.

The rule of tradition brings about such an alternative. Long ago, the English Christian thinker Gilbert Keith Chesterton underlined that tradition

> is trusting to a consensus of common human voices rather than to isolated or arbitrary record.... Tradition may be defined as an extension of the franchise. Tradition means giving votes to the most obscure of all classes, our ancestors.[213]

In a quite similar vein, constitutional theorists have underscored the role of tradition in constitutional theories. For instance, in the work of Carl Friedrich, tradition is of central importance.[214] To Friedrich, tradition is conceived not as a body of dogma to be followed unquestionably by succeeding generations, but as the expression of the vital core of truth which reflects the common reason and common deliberations of the best and wisest men.[215] Friedrich defines constitutionalism as regular restraints of the government and tradition, as a kind of higher moral law, knowable by right reason, as one with important roots in the idea of restraints.[216] Robert Lowry Clinton equally emphasizes the constitutionalist significance of tradition.[217] He particularly advocates the rule of tradition in a constitutionalist order because tradition presents the social consensus or "the tastes and values of most people."[218]

Returning to the case of *li*, it can be equally said that because *li* is the embodiment of tradition, it presents the social consensus. *Li* as a set of norms and institutions may originally present the social elites, but as *li*, by cultural osmosis, is handed from generation to generation as the embodiment of common truth, it becomes the expression of the popular voice. The rule of *li* is therefore designated to a political order in which the popular disposition is paramount. In a polity instilled with *li*, the popular will controls the polity. Consequently, the rule of *li* prevents the imposition of the will of a single ruler upon the society. In this sense, the ritualist norms can be regarded as constitutional norms.

That explains why early Confucians hold a negative attitude to the constant enactment of positive laws. In fact, they do not totally refute positive laws because *li* itself encompasses positive laws. As previously mentioned, the contents of *li* are extremely inclusive, and among other things, *li* includes both customary laws and positive laws. The positive law component of *li*, to the Confucians, is reasonable because it was a set of general institutions and norms created by the sage kings for the public interest, authenticated in the tradition, and presenting reasonable moral principles. In contrast, in the Confucians' view, the positive laws made by the contemporary kings are just for punitive purposes of the state, not for the people. Therefore, the Confucians require the contemporary kings to limit the promulgation of their own legislations and to follow the traditionalist *li*, the established norms and institutions, including the established laws. The Confucian dichotomy between *li* and law is the dichotomy of traditional law versus present law, not of natural law versus positive law.

At the same time, to be constitutionally meaningful, any form indicating the social consensus must be publicly articulated. The primary effort of the constitutionalist project is to publicly articulate rules that will control the future persons in authority. According to Craham Walker and then Beau Breslin, this public articulation is a prerequisite of constitutionalism due to its objectification.[219] Constitutionalism requires objectification of the structure and the rules within which the public power is practiced. That is because the objectification produces a limiting effect: once the governors are fenced out from manipulating the polity according to their vagaries, governmental discretion can be limited.

Now, let us consider whether Confucian *li* is objective to the government. Benjamin Schwartz defines *li* as "'*objective*' prescriptions of behaviour."[220] Similarly, Chung-ying Cheng describes *li* "as *objectified* principles, norms, or rule of human behaviour."[221] *Li* is objective to the government because of its traditionalist character. Since *li* comprises the norms and institutions agglomerated throughout generations and ingrained in tradition, it is rigidly anterior to the establishment of the contemporary government. Therefore, *li* averts narcissism of contemporary political figures. Consequently, once the dictates of *li* reign over the government, the destiny of the polity is not dependent on the ruler's subjective predilection. For this, the rule of *li* induces a limiting effect upon the government. It is because of this that the ritualist norms can be understood as constitutional norms.

Breslin, in going further to develop Walker's theory, submits that in order to secure objectification "a polity's organizing charter must subscribe to the principle of *externality*" in the sense that "for the conception of constitutionalism to be objective – and thus consequential – the limits impressed upon the will of the sovereign and its representative must in the first place exist separately from the political power centers."[222] However, Breslin believes that only the modern written constitution can be in concordance with the externalist demand of constitutionalist polity.[223] In fact, in the Confucian vision, *li* is equally external to the government. Since *li* presents the traditionalist sedimentations of norms and institutions, it is fixed "separately from the political power centers." When *li* is outside the government, rule of *li* actually means the operation of power in concordance with external orders. For this reason, the Confucian conception of rule of *li* is congruent to the spirit of constitutionalism, and, hence, ritualist norms can be referred to as constitutional norms.

Apart from the externality, Breslin posits that objectification in constitutionalism requires the "discernibility" of legal limitations:

> The society's population and its ruler alike must be as clear as possible as to the substantive and procedural message of the constitutional charter. Only that way will the text maintain the high standard of legitimacy needed to constitute the polity objectively.[224]

Once again, he contends that only through the modern constitutional text can the external legal limitations of governmental power become discernible.[225] Certainly, constitutionalism needs the transparency of legal restraints since nebulosity is the alter ego of despots. However, it is far from true that a codified constitutional charter is the sole medium for guaranteeing this discernibility. The classical Confucians equally conceptualize that *li* is the set of external limitation of the ruler that must be apparent to both the ruler and the common people.

Li in Confucian theory is intrinsically knowable, stemming from its traditionalist quality. On this regard, Alasdair MacIntyre's concept of tradition is instructive:

> For such a tradition, if it is to flourish at all ... has to be embodied in a set of texts which function as the authoritative point of departure for tradition-constituted inquiry and which remain as essential points of reference for enquiry and activity, for argument, debate and conflict within that tradition.[226]

In other words, a viable tradition indisputably necessitates textual manifestation which is subject to interpretation, argumentation, and debate. *Li* was a set of traditional norms and institutions, which the Confucians extol in their governmental inquiry, and was textually reified. *Li* was articulated under the format of the Confucian Classics. To illustrate, the conventional norms and institutions of the ancient kings that the Confucians eulogize were illustrated in *The Book of Historical Documents*, *The Book of Poetry* and the *Spring and Autumn Annals*, allegedly compiled by Confucius. Additionally, Confucius' particular emphasis on the rule of *li* galvanized the later Confucians in the Western Han dynasty who continually recorded the ancient *li*, which led to the advent of the *Li Ji* or *The Book of Rites*, one of five Confucian Classics. In this scripture, *li* establishes the basis of the polity and defines the sphere of government's authorities and functions, the limits of governmental power, principles of colonial administration and foundations for legal adjudications.[227]

Those who are familiar with the following dictum in the *Li Ji* may think that for the common people, the text of *li* must be esoteric: "the rules of ceremony (*li*) do not go down to the common people. The penal statutes do not go up to great officers."[228] In fact, as has been corroborated by Herrlee Glessner Creel, these words were intentionally written by some officials as the expression of their hope.[229] The apocryphal passage garbles the Confucian belief. In fact, for the classical Confucians, texts of *li* must be knowable to all. As mentioned above, Confucius considered that killing people without pre-instruction was an evil action of the government. The implication is that power should not operate in an opaque manner: the foundations for practicing public power should be apparent to the people. In other words, the people are required to be instructed about the *li*, which defines the scheme and the rules of the government. This leads to the Confucians' efforts in interpreting and imparting them to the public. Confucius established for the first time in Chinese history a private school to disseminate traditional textualized *li* to the plebeians with the educational philosophy that "in teaching there should be no distinction of classes."[230] Following Confucius, Mencius and Xunzi accepted ordinary students and educated them on the ancient *li*. In short, in the opinion of the Confucians, *li* must be discernible for everyone, and for this Confucianism particularly underlines the popular education of *li*.

While *li* defines the limits of the government, the public acknowledgment of *li* helps to ensure the operation of the government within parameters. Moreover, the commonly knowable *li* can restrict the ruler's dereliction of his responsibilities for the "general public standards." It is in this sense that the ritualist norms fit well with the requirement of discernability of constitutional norms.

Let us consider how *li* can be used for constitutionalist purposes. Along a different line to Hsu, Hahm refutes interpreting *li* as a form of morality or a Confucian analogue for natural law. Inspired by Michel Foucault's concept of discipline, Hahm particularly regards the disciplinary dimension of *li* as its constitutionalist significance: "Confucian constitutionalism in this sense refers to the application of *li* as a regularized restraint on the ruler through disciplining his body and mind."[231] When Hahm eulogized the disciplinary facet of *li*, he did think of Confucius' dictum in the *Analects 12:1*: "To subdue one's self and return to propriety [*li*], is perfect virtue [*ren*]." For Hahm, "to subdue one's self" (or "mastering oneself" as his preferable translation) can be rendered as "self-discipline."[232] I contend that the meaning of the *Analects 12:1* is essentially moral. To discipline oneself in consonance with *li* to become humane is inherently a moral action. To that extent, Hahm seems to fall to a non-sequitur while on the one hand refusing to discuss *li* under the form of morality and on the other hand signifying the disciplinary meaning of *li*.

I agree with Hahm that *li* can be used to discipline and hence restrain the ruler. However, I believe that *li*, among other things, is a form of morality. As previously mentioned, for classical Confucians, *li* includes moral norms. Hence, to discipline the ruler in accordance with the moral rules of *li* is actually a moral action. This, nonetheless, does not devalue the constitutionalist significance of *li* as the ruler is still restrained by established rules – the moral rules.

More importantly, while I agree on the disciplinary function of *li*, I do not think that the idea of "discipline" clearly indicates the constitutionalist aspiration of *li* and its relations to other Confucian constitutionalist concepts. When Hahm concentrates on the disciplinary function of *li*, he regarded the *li* as the central, if not the sole, concept to understand Confucian constitutionalism, and hence he tends to isolate the *li* from other Confucian constitutionalist ideas. From my point of view, *li* is the practical dimension of *zheng ming* or rectification of names government. Therefore, I propose to employ the idea of "rectification" rather than "discipline" for a better understanding of the constitutionalist functions of *li*. *Li* can be used to rectify the ruler, which means to cultivate, educate, criticize, and remonstrate the ruler to ensure the accordance of his political actions with certain norms and institutions defining his authorities, duties, and expected moral virtues so that the public power can be effectively restrained and properly used for public good. In the next section, I consider how *li* can be used to rectify the ruler.

Constitutional rectification

Once the standards for rectification of government are established by *li*, the next stage of the *zheng ming* program is to ensure the accordance of political institutions to the *li* or to implement functional limitations. This stage involves enforcement of the established standards or the *li*. The classical Confucians propose two mechanisms for implementation of the rule of *li*: internal rectification and external rectification, corresponding to the two components of *li* – moral norms and governmental institutions.

Moral self-rectification is the main means to implement the *zheng ming* government's requirement that those who carry certain governmental titles will act in concordance with the positive moral virtues of that title defined by the *li* (moral norms). Meanwhile, external rectification is the main means to safeguard the conformity of political institutions to the institutional limitations defined by the *li*. However, there may be a mixture of the two means. External rectification may be useful to the cultivation of the political morality, while internal rectification may self-restrict the power holders' violation of the institutional limitations.

Internal rectification: self-cultivation

In the imagination of Confucianism the sovereign should govern the country in concordance with *li* by immanent efforts. In the Confucian world, the ideal government relies not on coercion but on the self-discipline of political men.[233] Confucius considers self-discipline as the way to return to *li*, which is the *sine qua non* for any fully humanized person, including the sovereign.[234] The *Great Learning* expounds the central idea that from the Son of Heaven down to the mass of the people, all must consider self-cultivation the root of the peace and orderly polity,[235] and goes further to explain in this famous dictum:

> The ancients who wished to illustrate illustrious virtue throughout the kingdom, first ordered well their own States. Wishing to order well their States, they first regulated their families. Wishing to regulate their families, they first cultivated their persons. Wishing to cultivate their persons, they first rectified their hearts.[236]

Thus, the rectification of government first depends on the self-rectification of government's individuals. Moral self-rectification requires that those who hold certain positions shall act in concordance with the possible virtues of those positions. Moral self-rectification, to return to the *li*, therefore, becomes the essential step for realizing *zheng ming* government. Moral self-rectification is of constitutionalist importance in that it helps constrict misuse of power by the ruler. Internal efforts of the ruler to comply with the code of conduct are instrumental to limiting capricious power. In short, once the ruler constantly self-rectifies his personal morality, his practice of public power is regularly constrained.

External rectification: scholastic constitutionalism

The classical Confucians are never so naïve as to sacrifice the polity for the introspective rectification of the power holders. Beyond that, they propose that in order to enforce the *li*, political power must be checked by an external force. In classical Confucianism, the role of external rectification of the ruler in concordance with the institutional limitations established by the *li* is in particular the responsibility of the virtuous and wise scholars, an idea which can be labeled as "scholastic constitutionalism."

In Confucianism, as Daniel A. Bell points out, "only ethical and intellectual elites have a vocation to lead society.... Only those who acquire knowledge and virtue ought to participate in government, and the common people are not presumed to possess the capacities necessary for substantial political participation."[237] If Bell can read Confucian elitism so as to support democracy, can it equally be done to support a constitutionalist purpose? I believe that in the vision of Confucianism, the elites are conceived to play a constitutionalist role, since they are external forces to curb the arbitrary power of the sovereign.

To begin with, it should be underlined that the scholars occupy a special position in the Confucian governmental inquiry. The scholars, because of their virtue and wisdom, are viewed as even more valuable than the ruler. Mencius, as a Confucian scholar, provides excellent evidence. When Mencius was about to go to the court to meet with the king, the king sent an emissary with a message saying that he had wished to come to see Mencius but was unable to do so because of a cold, and that he wanted Mencius to go to the court to see him. Mencius replied that he was unable to go to the court because he too was unwell. For this act, a person called Dr. Chang reproved Mencius for his flouting imperial authority.[238] Mencius' apologia was that among three universal values, he possessed two – virtue and seniority – while the ruler had only one – nobility.

> In the kingdom there are three things universally acknowledged to be honourable. Nobility is one of them; age is one of them; virtue is one of them. In courts, nobility holds the first place of the three; in villages, age holds the first place; and for helping one's generation and presiding over the people, the other two are not equal to virtue. How can the possession of only one of these be presumed on to despise one who possesses the other two?[239]

As the scholars are of transcendent values in comparison with the possessions of the ruler, the ruler should respect them and govern the nation following their advice. The scholars therefore are not the servitors of the royalty; rather, they, on the ground of their sui generis merits, should be treated as the friends or even the teachers of the rulers.[240] Consequently, the scholars are not subjects to the ruler's arbitrary summons. "When he [the ruler] wishes to consult with them, he goes to them"[241] as a student. Moreover, if the ruler wishes to be served by the scholars he should show "the utmost respect and all polite observances" and agree to "carry their words into practice."[242]

Confucianism suggests that a virtue and talent scholar should be honored by the ruler so that "he is preserved from errors of judgment."[243] Hence, it can be said that the scholars are conceptualized as the sways that limit the misuse of power committed by the ruler. The savants of *li* are necessitated to advise the ruler to govern in accordance with the dictates of *li* and obviate him from its infringement. They can play this constitutionalist role via either structuralized institutions or free scholarship.

Scholars-officials: remonstrance

Confucian scholars are taught to serve in governmental institutions, typically as ministers.[244] However, a Confucian scholar engages in ministerial relationships not to sacrifice his life to royal whims, but to fully humanize his own life and to minister the others to humanize their life.[245] *Li* is the civilized guidance for these humanizing relations. It follows that the rule of *li* in all relationships is required for the process of humanization.[246] Hence, for the sake of humanization, it is the responsibility of the scholar-officials to implement the rule of *li*. This leads to the fact that the minister, insofar as he is a true Confucian scholar instead of a sycophant, should be loyal not to the ruler but substantially to the *li*. Consequently, if the ruler transgresses the *li*, the humanizing onus is upon the minister to remonstrate with him and if he, even in this case, fails to return to the *li*, the minister should end the relationship with the ruler.

Furthermore, the concept of scholars-officials' remonstrance is based on the Confucian conviction of the reciprocity of human relationships. Rosemount elucidated that, according to Confucianism, all of the relationships – spouses or lovers, neighbors, subjects, colleagues, friends, and more – are reciprocal.[247] So is the relationship between the prince and the minister.[248] It should be recalled that Confucius' dictum on rectification of names states that "there is government, when the prince is the prince, and the minister is the minister."[249] To say this in another way, if the prince is not the prince, then the minister is not the minster. The master holds that "a prince should employ his ministers according to the rules of propriety (*li*); ministers should serve their prince with faithfulness."[250] Given that, if the prince is devoid of *li* toward his ministers, then they are not obliged to be faithful.[251] In concordance with this spirit, Mencius acrimoniously asserts:

> When the prince regards his ministers as his hands and feet, his ministers regard their prince as their belly and heart; when he regards them as his dogs and horses, they regard him as another man; when he regards them as the ground or as grass, they regard him as a robber and an enemy.[252]

In short, the ruler–minister relationship is mutual rather than unilateral. The reciprocity of the relationship is the foundation for the possibility of the ministerial censure.

We now explore how the concept of remonstrance is elaborated in Confucian classics. It should be remembered that it is Confucius' position that it would be a tragedy for a nation in which no one dared oppose the wrong words of the ruler. Therefore, it is necessary for the ministers to censure the inappropriate policies and political skullduggeries. In fact, the relic of Confucius' concept of remonstrance can be found in his *Spring and Autumn Annals*. To be sure, the concept was not explicitly demonstrated, but ensconced in historical events on record. Investigating this classic, Hawkling L. Yen helpfully elicited the principle that:

> When a minister is convinced that what the king or prince is doing or is going to do is wrong or against the rules of established customs, it is his duty to expostulate with the ruler with a view of preventing his proceeding. If the ruler persists in his own way, after having been expostulated with three times, the minister is considered to have discharged his duty and may resign his position. There are five methods of expostulation, namely, postulation by hinting, by persuasion, by direct demonstration, by argumentation, and by mutilation or even suicide.[253]

Hence, it can be conjectured that the remonstrance was practiced during the Spring and Autumn Period, and even earlier. The contribution of Confucius is his theorizing the conventional practices and to clearly establish a constitutional principle of remonstrance in the *Analects*. Confucius differentiates "the great minister" from "the ordinary minister." Accordingly, the former is the one "who serves his prince according to what is right, and when he finds he cannot do so, retires," while the latter is no more than the minion who "will always follow their chief" except for the case of "parricide or regicide."[254] Confucius then goes further to suggest that preferably ministers should not dupe the ruler by having a veneer of loyalty, but should more importantly candidly remonstrate with him. When a Confucian disciple asked how a ruler should be served, the Master replied, "Do not impose on him, and, moreover, withstand him to his face."[255]

As a student of Confucius, Mencius vehemently advocates the ministerial restraints of the ruler. He says: "Is it a fault to restrain one's prince? He who restrains his prince loves his prince."[256] Mencius goes further to develop the principle of remonstrance. According to him, there are two kinds of high ministers: "There are the high ministers who are noble and relatives of the prince, and there are those who are of a different surname."[257] With regard to the high ministers who are noble and relatives of the prince, Mencius suggests: "If the prince has great faults, they ought to remonstrate with him, and if he do not listen to them after they have done so again and again, they ought to dethrone him."[258] As far as the ministers who are of a different surname are concerned, he states: "When the prince has faults, they ought to remonstrate with him; and if he do not listen to them after they have done this again and again, they ought to leave the State."[259] Mencius goes beyond Confucius to assert that in the case of the royal ministers, if the prince fails to follow their remonstrance, it is legitimate to dethrone him. In exceptional cases, Mencius even avers the legitimacy of ministers banishing their ruler. It is evident in the conversation between Mencius and Kung-sun Chau:

> Kung-sun Chau said, "I Yin said, 'I cannot be near and see him so disobedient to reason,'" and therewith he banished Ta-chia to Tung. The people were much pleased. When Ta-chia became virtuous, he brought him back, and the people were again much pleased. "When worthies are ministers, may they indeed banish their sovereigns in this way when they are not virtuous?" Mencius replied, "If they have the same purpose as Î Yin, they may. If they have not the same purpose, it would be usurpation."[260]

Like Confucius and Mencius, Xunzi also defends the remonstrance principle. He defined remonstrance as the capacity of a great officer or senior advisor to advance to the throne and address the lord concerning his transgression and leave if the advice is not implemented.[261] He contends that in the case of a sage lord, remonstrance is unnecessary but it is definitely needed in the case of a mediocre lord.[262] Moreover, Xunzi considers only men capable of remonstrance to be qualified as true ministers.[263]

There are concrete requirements for practicing ministerial remonstrance. First, only the worthy ministers can reprove the prince. To say this in a negative definition, they must not be mercenaries, careerists, or pedants. According to Confucius, they must be the "great ministers." Mencius also opines: "It is not enough to remonstrate with a sovereign on account of the mal-employment of ministers, nor to blame errors of government. It is only the great man who can rectify what is wrong in the sovereign's mind."[264] In fact, the "great ministers" in the Confucian vision are politicizing scholars prepossessed with moral principles and wisdom. Second, only the ministers who have obtained the confidence of the prince can admonish him. In the *Doctrine of the Means*, Confucius is reported to have said: "When those in inferior situations do not possess the confidence of the superior, they cannot retain the government of the people."[265] The *Analects* recorded a Confucian student saying that "having obtained the confidence of his prince, one may then remonstrate with him. If he has not gained his confidence, the prince will think that he is vilifying him."[266] Finally, remonstrance should be conducted with respect to important matters. The ministers should not officiously remonstrate against peccadilloes since "frequent remonstrance lead to disgrace."[267]

In short, remonstrance is the pivotal constitutional principle in Confucian governmental theory. The remonstrance by the ministerial clerisy is the external force that rectifies the ruler in accordance with the institutional limitations established by the *li*.

Free scholars: social intellectual authority

Confucian scholars, by their wisdom and virtue, may play the constitutional role without participating in the government. The ruler may "go to see them" as a student as Mencius suggests. Lectures given by cognoscenti of *li* are instrumental to the rectification of the ruler in consonance with *li*. However, even if the ruler refuses to "go to see them," the scholars can also restrain his power by their social intellectual authority. The constitutional importance of the *Spring and Autumn Annals* and the role of Confucius in this classic as a de facto constitutional judge should be understood in this light.

Spring and Autumn or *Chunqiu*, one of five Confucian Classics,[268] is a chronicle of Lu, which was arguably authorized by Confucius.[269] Confucius composed this writing after his fiasco of itinerant searching for a governmental position. Hence, he authorized the chronicle not as an official historiographer but as a free philosopher. To speak in constitutional language, Confucius composed the *Spring and Autumn* to deal with the problem of arbitrary power. Explaining the reason Confucius produced the work, Mencius says:

> Again the world fell into decay, and principles faded away. Perverse speaking and oppressive deeds waxed rife again. There were instances of ministers who murdered their sovereigns, and of sons who murdered their fathers. Confucius was afraid, and made the "*Spring and Autumn*." What the "*Spring and Autumn*" contains are matters proper to the sovereign. On this account Confucius said, "Yes! It is the *Spring and Autumn* which will make men know me, and it is the *Spring and Autumn* which will make men condemn me.[270]

Because of its condensed style, a number of commentaries have been written to explain and expand the meanings of *Spring and Autumn*. The most noticeable ones are the *Commentary of Gongyang* [*Gongyang Zhuan*], the *Commentary of Guliang* [*Guliang Zhuan*], and the *Commentary of Zuo* [*Zuo Zhuan*], which form the so-called "*Three Commentaries on Spring and Autumn Annals*" [*Chunqiu San Zhuan*].[271]

The volumes of *Spring and Autumn* are considered to be the practical applications of the Confucian doctrine of rectification of names.[272] In application of the rectification of names, *Spring and Autumn* together with the *Commentaries*, according to Hsu's generalization, provide four important functions: giving names and definitions to phenomena; defining the fundamental principles of organization of the state and outlining the limits of individual spheres of action in political and social organizations; passing critical judgment ("praise-and-censure") upon the actions of men; and illustrating the possible tendencies of various phenomena.[273] In fact, these functions were not separately classified in the classic. The functions are implied in the fact that Confucius used correct names to record the historical events. As mentioned above, names, according to Confucius, are more than words to identify people and things; they indicate the relationships, the roles of people and inherent values. Therefore, by using accurate terminology, Confucius implicitly gave definitions to political actions, defined basic principles of organization and operations of the government, adjudicated political actions, and showed causes and effects that demonstrate political tendencies.

A number of remarks have been given for the governmental importance of the *Spring and Autumn*. An interpreter cited in the Kung-yang Commentary states that "for restoring order in chaotic times and effecting a return to what is correct, nothing comes closer than the *Spring and Autumn*."[274] Describing the political applications of the text of a Confucian disciple and a pre-Han interpreter, namely Tzu-hsia, in *Chunqiu Fanlu* [*Luxuriant Dew of the Spring and Autumn Annals*], Dong Zhongshu writes:

> The ruler of state must not fail to study the *Spring and Autumn*. If he does not study the *Spring and Autumn* he will not have means to observe the dangers around him, and will not understand the state's great handle of authority or the chief responsibilities of the ruler.[275]

Dong Zhongshu himself realizes that: "*The Spring and Autumn* rectifies right and wrong, consequently it strengthens human governance."[276]

Remarkably, in late nineteenth-century China, such proponents of modern constitutionalism as Kang Youwei and Liang Qichao drew on commentaries of *Spring and Autumn* to justify their constitutional proposals.[277] Kang Youwei owed much to Kung-yang's interpretation of the *Chunqiu*, which he began to study in earnest in the late 1880s.[278] As noted by Liang Qichao, Kang Youwei was

> the first man to interpret the ideas of reform as found in the *Chunqiu*. From this text, he explained the Three Ages. He considered the *Chunqiu* a work designed to curb the authority of the emperor and enlarge the right of people to remove domestic struggle and bring unification.[279]

More recently, Jiang Qing also draws from *Commentary of Gongyang of the Spring and Autumn Annals* [*Gongyang Zhuan*] to develop his distinctive proposal of Confucian constitutionalism for future China.[280] The fact that Chinese modern constitutionalists have invoked *Spring and Autumn* to justify their proposals indicates that this chronicle has social intellectual power.

It is my contention that the aforementioned functions of *Spring and Autumn* are relatively similar to the modern functions of constitutional judges in exercising their judicial review power. Hsu states that "*Spring and Autumn* assumes the position of the chief justice of a supreme court deciding upon the actions and laws of sovereigns, princes, and ministers."[281] *Spring and Autumn*'s function of accuracy of terminology is analogous to the constitutional judges' function of constitutional interpretation. In addition, the role of *Spring and Autumn* in judging political actions is seemingly equal to the function of the constitutional judges in adjudicating the constitutionality of the political institutions' actions. Hsu compares:

> *Spring and Autumn* performs the function of rational judgment. To point out the good as good and the bad as bad means, in modern terminology, the final judgment as to whether or not the law is constitutional, whether or not the action is legal, or whether or not the man is criminal. It eulogizes those who obey the law and condemns those who violate it. This is rectification.[282]

Hence, it can be said that Confucius, by composing *Spring and Autumn* as a free scholar functioned as a de facto constitutional judge. As Mencius says, "Confucius completed the *Spring and Autumn*, and rebellious ministers and villainous sons are struck with terror."[283] So, Confucius, by composing *Spring and Autumn*, inserted limits on the public power by social intellectual authority.

By the case of *Spring and Autumn* and the role of Confucius as a de facto constitutional judge, it can be concluded that Confucianism widely opens the door for scholastic constitutionalism. The practice of constitutionalism cannot be totally dependent on institutional structural limits. Confucianism suggests that scholars' public discourse can play the role of limiting the governmental power by their social intellectual authority. By scholarship of government, public intellectuals can limit the public power by defining political terms, clarifying the foundational principles of political institutions, praising and censuring the actions of power holders on the grounds of legality and morality, and anticipating the political tendencies that can help align the practice of public power and rectify the governors' malfeasances. The scholars' social intellectual authority is constitutionally meaningful in part because it serves as the guide for formal practices. When official people practice their power with a scholastic orientation, their arbitrariness can be limited. Moreover, scholastic constitutionalism is meaningful in the sense that the scholarship may usefully raise the popular awareness of constitutionalist values which in turn help to popularize the constitutionalist community.

To conclude this section, consider these words in the memorial of Li Si, the prime minister of the first unified empire in China, requesting Qin Shi Huang to burn the Confucian books and to execute the Confucian scholars:

> At the present Your Majesty possesses a unified empire … and has firmly established for yourself a position of sole supremacy. And yet these independent schools, joining with each other, criticize the codes of laws and instructions. Hearing of the promulgation of a decree, they criticize it, each from the standpoint of his own school. At home they disapprove of it in their hearts; going out they criticize it in the thoroughfare. They seek a reputation by discrediting their sovereign; they appear superior by expressing contrary views, and they lead the lowly multitude in the spreading of slander. If such license is not prohibited, the sovereign power will decline above and partisan factions will form below. It would be well to prohibit

> it.... All persons in the empire, except from members of the Academy of Learned Scholars, in possession of the *Book of Odes*, *The Book of History*, and discourses of the hundred philosophers should take them to the local governors and have them indiscriminately burned. Those who dare to talk to each other about the *Book of Odes* and the *Book of History* should be executed and their bodies exposed in the market place. Anyone referring to the past to criticize the present should, together with all members of his family, be put to death.[284]

Li Si inadvertently provided the real testimony for the practice of scholastic constitutionalism. Social intellectual authority of political discourse by the Confucian scholars was so influential that Qin Shi Huang had to burn the Confucian books and to execute the Confucians. Yet, Qui polity was not a Confucian constitutionalist polity as it practiced draconian legal enforcement, the practice recommended by legalists like Li Si. Therefore, social intellectual authority had to pave the way for rampant power.

Conclusion

The present chapter has challenged the perception that the philosophy of constitutionalism is distinctively western. It suggests that there are constitutionalist provenances in the Confucian intellectual repository. Classical Confucianism is the antithesis of arbitrary rule; it is opposite to despotic government. In reflection on the antidote for despotism, classical Confucianism on the philosophical foundation of humaneness (*ren*) proposes a rectified government (*zheng ming*) responsible for the people (*minben*) functioning in concordance with the parameter of prior traditional norms and institutions (*li*) protected by internal moral cultivation and external scholastic restraints ("scholastic constitutionalism").

I conclude this chapter by using the findings to engage in conversations with some comments on Confucian philosophy of government. Some scholars do recognize that classical Confucianism endorses limited government, but refuse to conceive such Confucian construction of limited government as a model of constitutionalism. Edward Shils, for example, agrees that Confucianism supports limitations on government but asserts that: "Confucius makes no provision for a constitution."[285] This is correct to the extent that the constitution is viewed through the positivistic lens as the monistic written basic law ordained by "we the people." But if the constitution is understood from a Diceyan perspective as "all rules which directly or indirectly affect the distribution or the exercise of the sovereign power in the state,"[286] it is far from true that Confucius and other classical Confucians are silent about it. In the Confucian governmental theory, the *li* that includes traditional moral norms and governmental institutions, which establish normative standards for rectification of government, can be recognized as a variant of unwritten constitution – a Confucian constitution. This does not mean that a Confucian constitution (or *li*) was not written down. As mentioned above, many traditional norms and institutions were written in the Confucian Classics.

The "unwrittenness" of the Confucian constitution (*li*) means that it, like the English Constitution, was not codified in a monistic charter.

Like Edward Shils, Joseph Chan concurs that classical Confucianism strongly supports limited government in the sense that it requires political authority to be responsible for the well-being of the people and subjected to Dao or *li* as objective principles and rituals regarding the well-being of the people.[287] However, Chan refuses to conceive Confucian construction of limited government as a vision of constitutionalism because Confucian limited government is not backed by "higher institutional authority to effectively bind rulers who choose not to follow them."[288] In Chan's understanding, constitutionalism is "a European concept and practice,"[289] essentially defined by the separation of legislative, executive, and judicial powers, and institutional checks and balances.[290]

Chan's argument is untenable. First, while focusing exclusively on institutional authority, Chan fails to appreciate that constitutionalism can be alternatively implemented by social intellectual authority. Confucian construction of constitutionalism gives more attention to social intellectual authority than to institutional authority. Second, Chan tends to understand constitutionalism in a modern, liberal sense and fails to realize that such institutional limits of the public power as the separation of legislative, executive, and judicial powers and checks and balances are developed in modern constitutionalism, not the essential features of constitutionalism in general. Even in modern constitutionalism, these institutional limits are common but not essential. The fusion of powers is a distinguished feature of parliamentary government. Even in presidential government, which is normally characterized by strict separation of powers, there is also considerable degree of fusion of powers.[291] In addition, judicial review is a common tool of institutional limits but not the *sin qua non* of modern constitutionalism. Ginsburg, who is well known for his scholarship on judicial review, affirms that:

> Judicial enforcement of constitutional norms is the exception rather than a sine qua non.... Neither judicial review nor judicialized constraint is an essential feature of constitutionalism, though they certainly reflect the fullest development of the phenomenon as conventionally understood.[292]

Stéphanie Balme and Michael W. Dowdle also state that: "Even in the most effective constitutional system, significant aspects of constitutional structure are invariably non-justiciable."[293]

Pre-modern constitutionalism developed functional and institutional restraints other than the separation of powers and judicial review. In the case of Confucian constitutionalism, the ministries are institutional limits of the royal power, backed by the power of tradition and the power of wisdom and morality. In the next chapter, I shall examine in detail the institutionalized fora allowing the ministries, the Confucian scholar-officials, to rectify the ruler in concordance with Confucian constitutional norms.

Notes

1 Scott Gordon, *Controlling the State: Constitutionalism from Ancient Athens to Today* (Cambridge, MA: Harvard University Press, 1999), 5. The term "constitutionalism" was first used in 1832, according to the *Oxford English Dictionary.*
2 Ibid., 107–115; Raymond Polin, *Plato and Aristotle on Constitutionalism: An Exposition and Reference Source* (Aldershot: Ashgate Publishing Ltd, 1998); Charles Howard McIlwain, *Constitutionalism: Ancient and Modern* (Clark, NJ: The Lawbook Exchange, Ltd., 2005).
3 Xinzhong Yao, *An Introduction to Confucianism* (Cambridge: Cambridge University Press, 2000), 271.
4 Shaohua Hu, *Explaining Chinese Democratization* (Westport, CT and London: Praeger, 2000), 24.
5 Peter Zarrow, *China in War and Revolution 1895–1949* (New York: Routledge, 2005), 134.
6 Sor-Hoon Tan, *Confucian Democracy: A Deweyan Reconstruction* (Albany, NY: State University of New York Press, 2003), 7.
7 Chaihark Hahm, "Confucian Constitutionalism" (SJD dissertation, Harvard Law School, 2000); Chaihark Hahm, "Conceptualizing Korean Constitutionalism: Foreign Transplant or Indigenous Tradition?" *Journal of Korean Law* 1(2) (2001): 151; Chaihark Hahm, "Ritual and Constitutionalism: Disputing the Ruler's Legitimacy in a Confucian Polity," *The American Journal of Comparative Law* 57 (2009): 135; Sungmoon Kim, "Confucian Constitutionalism: Mencius and Xunzi on Virtual, Ritual, and Royal Transmission," *The Review of Politics* 73(3) (2001): 347.
8 Louis Henkin, "A New Birth of Constitutionalism: Generic Influences and Generic Defects," *Cardozo Law Review* 14 (1992–1993): 534.
9 Thomas C. Grey, "Constitutionalism: Analytic Framework," in *Constitutionalism, Nomos XX*, ed. J. Roland Pennnock and John W. Chapman (New York: New York University Press, 1979), 190 (italic in original).
10 Stanford Encyclopedic Philosophy, "Constitutionalism," http://plato.stanford.edu/entries/constitutionalism.
11 McIlwain, *Constitutionalism*, 24.
12 Carl J. Friedrich, *Man and His Government* (New York: Mc-Graw Hill, 1963), 271.
13 Grey, "Constitutionalism," 190–207.
14 C.H. McIlwain, *Constitutionalism and the Changing World* (Cambridge: Cambridge University Press, 1969), 244.
15 Carl J. Friedrich, *Constitutional Government and Democracy* (New York: Ginn and Company, 1950), 123.
16 Ibid.
17 Craham Walker, "The Idea of Nonliberal Constitutionalism," in *Nomos XXXIX: Ethnicity and Group Rights*, ed. Ian Shapiro and Will Kymlicka (New York and London: New York University Press, 1997), 165.
18 For a comprehensive treatment on sham constitutions, see David S. Law and Mila Versteeg, "Sham Constitutions," *California Law Review* 101 (2013): 863.
19 Chaihark Hahm, "Constitutionalism, Confucian Civic Culture, and Ritual Propriety," in *Confucianism for the Modern World*, ed. Daniel A. Bell and Hahm Chaibong (Cambridge and New York: Cambridge University Press, 2003), 33.
20 Grey, "Constitutionalism," 190 (italic in original).
21 Alec Stone Sweet, "Constitutionalism, Legal Pluralism, and International Regimes," *Indiana Journal of Global Legal Studies* 16(2) (2009): 626.
22 David Landau, "Abusive Constitutionalism," *U.C. David Law Review* 47 (2013): 189.
23 Nicholas Tsagourias, "Introduction: Constitutionalism," in *Transnational Constitutionalism: International and European Models*, ed. Nicholas Tsagourias (Cambridge: Cambridge University Press, 2007), 3.

24 Leslie Lipson, *The Great Issues of Politics: An Introduction to Political Science* (New Jersey: Prentice- Hall, 1960), 236.
25 Jon Elster, *Ulysses and the Sirens: Studies in Rationality and Irrationality* (Cambridge: Cambridge University Press, 1979); Jon Elster, *Ulysses Unbound: Studies in Rationality, Precommitment, and Constraints* (Cambridge: Cambridge University Press, 2000); Stephen Holmes, *Passions and Constraint: On the Theory of Liberal Democracy* (Chicago, IL: University of Chicago Press, 1995).
26 Holmes, *Passions and Constraint*, 163. ("Constitutional rules are enabling, not disabling.")
27 John Ferejohn and Lawrence Sager, "Commitment and Constitutionalism," *Texas Law Review* 81 (2003): 1930.
28 Holmes, *Passions and Constraint*, 163.
29 Tom Ginsburg, "Constitutionalism: East Asian Antecedents," *Chicago-Kent Law Review* 88 (2012): 15. ("The basic idea is that an individual's long-term choices may not align with their short-term choices for each period.") See also Steven R. Ratner, "Precommitment Theory and International Law: Starting a Conversation," *Texas Law Review* 81 (2003): 2055. ("To restrain oneself from doing something that one would otherwise do because such restraint will itself directly improve one's future welfare.")
30 Ginsburg, "Constitutionalism," 15.
31 Walker, "Nonliberal Constitutionalism," 164.
32 Ibid.
33 Ibid., 160.
34 Ibid., 162
35 Ibid., 163.
36 Ibid., 163–164.
37 Kay, "American Constitutionalism," 21.
38 See generally, Carl J. Friedrich, *Transcendent Justice: the Religious Dimension of Constitutionalism* (Durham, NC: Duke University Press, 1964).
39 Walker, "Nonliberal Constitutionalism," 165.
40 Ibid.
41 Richard S. Kay, "American Constitutionalism" in *Constitutionalism: Philosophical Foundations*, ed. Larry Alexander (New York: Cambridge University Press, 1998), 27.
42 Ibid.
43 A.V. Dicey, *Introduction to the Study of Law of the Constitution* (London: Macmillan, 1920), 23–24.
44 Giovanni Sartori, "Constitutionalism: A Preliminary Discussion," *The American Political Science Review* 56(4) (1962): 853.
45 Vernon Bogdanor, "Britain: The Political Constitution," in *Constitutions in Democratic Politics*, ed. Vernon Bogdanor (Aldershot: Gover Publishing Company Limited, 1988), 56.
46 Tiedeman, *The Unwritten Constitution of the United States*; Thomas C. Grey, "Do We have an Unwritten Constitution?" *Stanford Law Review* 27 (1975); Michael S. Moore, "Do We have an Unwritten Constitution?" *Southern California Law Review* 63 (1989).
47 Moore, "Do We have an Unwritten Constitution," 137.
48 Grey, "Unwritten Constitution," 16.
49 Akhil Reed Amar, *America's Unwritten Constitution* (New York: Basic Books, 2012).
50 Robert Lowry Clinton, *God and Man in Law: The Foundations of Anglo-American Constitutionalism* (Lawrence, KS: University Press of Kansas, 1997), 58.
51 Ibid., 61
52 Ibid., 60.

53 Ibid.

54 Michael W. Dowdle, "Popular Constitutionalism and the Constitutional Meaning of Charter 08," in *Liu Xiaobo, Charter 08 and the Challenges of Political Reform in China*, ed. Jean-Philippe Béjia *et al.* (Hong Kong: Hong Kong University Press, 2012), 206.

55 Ibid., 208 (italic in original).

56 Ibid., 209.

57 In this study, *ren* and humaneness are interchangeably used.

58 Kung-chuan Hsiao, *A History of Chinese Political Thought, Volume One: From the Beginnings to the Sixth Century A.D*, trans. F.W. Mote (Princeton, NJ: Princeton University Press, 1979), 102.

59 Liang Qichao, *History of Chinese Political Thought*, trans. L.T. Chen (London: Routledge, 2000), 38.

60 Xuezhi Guo notes that *ren* is discussed a total of 105 times in the *Analects*. Xuezhi Guo, *The Ideal Chinese Political Leader: A Historical and Cultural Perspective* (Westport, CT and London: Praeger, 2002), 6.

61 Herbert Fingarette, *Confucius: The Secular as Sacred* (New York, Evanston, San Francisco and London: Harper & Row, 1972), 37–56; Tu Wei-ming, *Humanity and Self-Cultivation: Essays in Confucian Thought* (Berkeley, CA: Asian Humanity Press, 1979); 5–17; Kwong-loi Shun, "Jen [ren] and Li in the Analects," *Philosophy East & West* 43(3) (1993): 457.

62 Donald J. Munro, *The Concept of Man in Early China* (Stanford, CA: Stanford University Press, 1969), 71.

63 James Legge, *The Chinese Classics with Translations, Critical and Exegetical Notes, Prolegomena, and Copious Indexes, Volume I, Confucian Analects, The Great Learning, The Doctrine of the Mean* (Hong Kong: Hong Kong University Press, 1960), 405.

64 Legge, *Volume II, The Works of Mencius*, 485 (slightly modified).

65 See Herbert Fingarette, "The Music of Humanity in the *Conversations* of Confucius," *Journal of Chinese Philosophy* 10(4) (1983): 339.

66 Legge, *Analects*, 334.

67 In a different vein, Tu Wei-ming refutes the notion that *ren* is primarily a concept of human relations, for he suggests that *ren* is "basically linked with the self-reviving, self-perfecting, and self-fulfilling process of an individual. Tu Wei-ming, "The Creative Tension between Jen and Li," *Philosophy East & West* 18 (1968): 34.

68 Legge, *Analects*, 260.

69 Fung Yu-lan, *A History of Chinese Philosophy Vol. 1*, trans. Derk Bodde (Princeton, NJ: Princeton University Press, 1952), 70.

70 Hsiao, *Chinese Political Thought*, 102.

71 Yongping Liu, *Origins of Chinese Law: Penal and Administrative Law in Its Early Development* (Hong Kong: Oxford University Press, 1998), 92.

72 Fung, *Chinese Philosophy*, 71.

73 Legge, *Analects*, 251.

74 Ibid., 194 (slightly modified).

75 Fung Yu-lan, *A Short History of Chinese Philosophy* (New York: The Free Press, 1948), 43.

76 Ibid.

77 Legge, *Analects*, 194 (modified).

78 Fung states: "to say that the all pervading principle of Confucius is *chung* and *shu* is the same as saying that it is *ren*." Fung, *Chinese Philosophy*, 71.

79 Legge, *The Doctrine of the Mean*, 394 (modified).

80 Mohism is the rival of Confucianism, established by Mo Tzu. The fundamental principle of this school of thought is the indiscriminate mutual concern of each other. For more details, see Hsiao, *Chinese Political Thought*, 214–272

81 Liu, *Origins of Chinese Law*, 94.
82 Ibid.
83 McIlwain, *Constitutionalism*, 24.
84 "Arbitrary rule," "despotism" and "tyranny" are terms closed in meaning. "Despot (Greek *despotes*) related to someone who resorts to arbitrary rule." Eric Carlton, *Faces of Despotism* (Aldershot: SCOLAR Press, 1995), 10. "Despotism and tyranny are virtually synonymous terms for governments uncontrolled by law or custom. Power in such government is typically concentrated in the hands of a single authoritarian ruler." Frank N. Magill, ed., *International Encyclopedia of Government and Politics, Volume One* (London and Chicago, IL: Salem Press, 1996), 365.
85 Legge, *Volume III., The Shoo King* [*Shu Jing*], 175.
86 Kuo-Cheng Wu, *Ancient Chinese Political Theories* (Shanghai: Commercial Press, 1974), 19.
87 Legge, *The Shoo King* [*Shu Jing*], 196.
88 James Legge, *Li Ki: Sacred Books of the East, Vol. XXVIII* (Oxford: Clarendon Press, 1885), 190–191.
89 Legge, *Analects*, 353–354.
90 Leonard Shihlien Hsu, *The Political Philosophy of Confucianism* (London: Curzon Press, 1975), 110.
91 Legge, *Analects*, 269.
92 Legge, *The Works of Mencius*, 164–165.
93 Hsiao, *Chinese Political Thought*, 157. ("His examples refer to the military campaigns that led to the downfall of the Hsia and Shang dynasties, and their displacement by the Shang and Chou dynasties; in these cases the tyrant last rulers were deposed, banished, or killed.")
94 Legge, *The Works of Mencius*, 167.
95 John Knoblock, *Xunzi: A Translation and Study of the Complete Works, Volume III* (Stanford, CA: Stanford University Press, 1994), 35.
96 Ibid.
97 McIlwain, *Constitutionalism and the Changing World*, 271.
98 Chung-ying Cheng, *New Dimensions of Confucian and Neo-Confucian Philosophy* (Albany, NY: State University of New York Press, 1991), 221.
99 Chenyang Li, *The Tao Encounters the West: Explorations in Comparative Philosophy* (Albany, NY: State University of New York Press, 1999), 63.
100 Legge, *Analects*, 263.
101 Historically, the Prince of Wei was Lord Zhe of Wei who fought with his father Kuai Kui for the rulership of the state. Kuai Kui, the eldest son of Duke Ling of Wei (493 BC), offended his father and was forced into exile. When Duke Ling died, the people chose his grandson Zhe to be their ruler but Kuai Kui sought the help of the state of Jin to gain the throne. Zhang Dainian, *Key Concepts in Chinese Philosophy*, trans. Edmund Ryden (New Haven, CT and London: Yale University Press; Beijing, Foreign Languages Press: 2002), 462.
102 For more elaborations on Sima Qian's perspective, see John Makeham, *Name and Actuality in Early Chinese Thought* (Albany, NY: State University of New York Press, 1994), 36; see also John Makeham, *Transmitters and Creators: Chinese Commentators and Commentaries on the Analects* (Cambridge, MA and London: Harvard University Asia Center, 2003), 334. Vietnamese scholar Nguyễn Hiến Lê equally explains Confucius' doctrine of rectification of names basing on the historical events related to the Lord of Wei. Nguyễn Hiến Lê, *Khổng tử* [*Confucius*] (Hanoi: Cultural Publishing House, 1996), 131.
103 Dainian, *Key Concepts in Chinese Philosophy*, 463.
104 Xunzi develops a separate chapter in his work to discuss the theme. Knoblock, *Xunzi, Volume III*, 113–138. Giản Chi and Nguyễn Hiến Lê, two Vietnamese exponents of Chinese classical works, believe that Confucius and Mencius comprehend

rectification of names in moral meaning while Xunzi's disposition of rectification of name is of both moral and logical meanings. Giản Chi and Nguyễn Hiến Lê, *Tuân tử* [*Xunzi*] (Hanoi: Cultural Publishing House, 1994), 162–163. I believe that the rectification of names in Xunzi philosophy is both governmental and nominal in that Xunzi writes the chapter for both defining governmental responsibilities and differentiating different things. Han commentators' expansive deconstruction of Confucius' doctrine of rectification may be attributable to Xunzi's chapter. Consequently, in the modern time, the doctrine has been studied beyond the political sphere. Apart from having been the topic of political philosophy, the doctrine has been the concern of linguistic and nominalistic studies. Zhang Dainian categorizes the doctrine to the section of "philosophy of language." Dainian, *Key Concepts in Chinese Philosophy*, 461. Makeham equally studies the doctrine under the light of nominalism. Makeham, *Name and Actuality*.

105 Li, *The Tao Encounters the West*, 64.
106 Fung, *Chinese Philosophy*, 59.
107 Since, as mentioned above, by rectification of names, what Confucius really means is to rectify the names of persons, especially the ones in authority, we should focus on the people's names.
108 Henry Rosemont Jr., "Two Loci of Authority: Autonomous Individuals and Related Persons," in *Confucian Cultures of Authority*, ed. Peter D. Hershock and Roger T. Ames (Albany, NY: State University of New York Press, 2006), 10.
109 Cheng, *New Dimensions*, 222.
110 Ibid.
111 Rosemont, in explaining Confucius' self, writes: "I am a son, husband, father, grandfather, teacher, student, friend, colleague, neighbor, and more. I live, rather than 'play' these roles." Rosemont, "Two Loci of Authority," 10.
112 Li, *Tao Encounters the West*, 67.
113 Fung, *Chinese Philosophy*, 59–60.
114 Legge, *Analects*, 256.
115 Likewise for "minister," "father," and "son."
116 Legge, *Analects*, 213.
117 Cheng, *New Dimensions*, 222.
118 Legge, *Analects*, 258.
119 Beau Breslin, *The Communitarian Constitution* (Baltimore, MD and London: Johns Hopkins University Press, 2004), 115.
120 Thomas Hobbes, *Leviathan*, ed. Richard E. Flathman and David Johnston (New York and London: W.W. Norton & Company, 1997), 55.
121 Montesquieu, *The Spirit of the Laws*, trans. Thomas Nugent (New York: Hafner Publishing Company, 1962), 150.
122 Thomas Jefferson, *The Papers of Thomas Jefferson, Volume 30*, ed. Barbarra B. Oberg (Princeton, NJ: Princeton University Press, 2003), 541.
123 Hahm, "Conceptualizing Korean Constitutionalism," 163; Kim, "Confucian Constitutionalism," 376.
124 Legge, *Analects*, 182.
125 Ibid., 1.
126 Yao, *An Introduction to Confucianism*, 162.
127 Knoblock, *Xunzi, Volume III*, 150.
128 Fung, *A History of Chinese Philosophy*, 287.
129 Knoblock, *Xunzi, Volume III*, 159.
130 Legge, *The Shoo King* [*Shu Jing*], 158–159.
131 Ibid., 254–255.
132 Ibid., 262–263.
133 For detailed discussions on the concept of *tianming*, see Tan, *Confucian Democracy*, 136–144.

134 Legge, *Analects*, 194.
135 Ibid., 269.
136 Ibid., 266–267.
137 Legge, *Analects*, 352. For more detailed explanation of these principles, see Hsu, *Political Philosophy*, 106–111.
138 Hsiao, *Chinese Political Thought*, 148.
139 To go further in Mencius' doctrine on the goodness of human nature is beyond the present study. Suffice to say that Mencius believed that the four virtues – humaneness, righteousness, propriety, and wisdom – all came into being as extensions and developments of every human being's innate sense of commiseration, of shame, of respect, and of right and wrong. See ibid. Mencius introduces the doctrine in his reply to the disciple Kung-tu's inquiry on the nature of the human. Legge, *The Works of Mencius*, 401–403.
140 The three dynasties are the Hsia, Shang, and Zhou.
141 Legge, *The Works of Mencius*, 293 (slightly modified).
142 Ibid., 288 (slightly modified).
143 Ibid., 138.
144 Ibid., 483.
145 Hsiao, *Chinese Political Thought*, 152. For a similar assertion, see Viren Murthy, "The Democratic Potential of Confucian *Minben* Thought," *Asian Philosophy* 10(1) (2000): 35.
146 Legge, *The Works of Mencius*, 147–148 (slightly modified).
147 Ibid., 148.
148 Hsiao, *Chinese Political Thought*, 152.
149 Legge, *The Works of Mencius*, 251.
150 These institutions are named. Ibid., 242.
151 Knoblock, *Xunzi, Volume III*, 150–151.
152 Ibid., 151.
153 Ibid., 151–152.
154 Tan, *Confucian Democracy*, 136.
155 Knoblock, *Xunzi, Volume III*, 224.
156 Knoblock, *Xunzi, Volume II*, 97.
157 Ibid., 181.
158 Ibid., 101.
159 Tan, *Confucian Democracy*, 141–142.
160 Cited in Polin, *Plato and Aristotle*, 12.
161 Legge, *Analects*, 152.
162 Ibid., 340.
163 Ibid., 265.
164 Ibid., 140.
165 Andrew J. Nathan, *Chinese Democracy* (New York: Alfred A. Knopf, 1985), 127.
166 Lucian W. Pye, *Asian Power and Politics: The Cultural Dimensions of Authority* (Cambridge, MA: Belknap Press of Harvard University Press, 1985), 81.
167 *Kant's Political Writings*, trans. H.B Nisbet (London: Cambridge University Press, 1970), 74.
168 Ibid. (italic in original).
169 Legge, *Great Learning*, 370 ("in the Announcement to K'ang (of the Book of Historic Documents), it is said, 'Act as if you were watching over an infant.' "); 374 ("in the Book of Poetry, it is said, 'How much to be rejoiced in are these princes, the parents of the people!' When a prince loves what the people love, and hates what the people hate, then is he what is called the parent of the people"); Knoblock, *Xunzi, Volume III*, 35 ("Tang and Vu were considered as the father and mother of the people.")
170 Hsu, *Political Philosophy*, 93.

171 Homer Dubs, *The Works of Hsun Tze* (London: Arthur Probsthain & Co., 1928), 113.
172 Masayuki Sato, *The Confucian Quest for Order: The Origin and Formation of the Political Thought of Xunzi* (Leiden: Koninklijke Brill NV, 2003), 166.
173 The pictogram *li* 禮 indicates a sacrificial vessel with two pieces of jade above it. Liu, *Origins of Chinese Law*, 63.
174 Hahm, "Ritual and Constitutionalism," 144.
175 For a comprehensive treatment on the development of the concept of *li*, see: Masayuki Sato, *Confucian Quest*, 173–236.
176 Knoblock, *Xunzi, Volume II*, 51.
177 Benjamin I. Schwartz, *The World of Thought in Ancient China* (Cambridge, MA: Harvard University Press, 1985), 67.
178 Hsu, *Political Philosophy*, 95.
179 Qu Tongzu [T'ung-Tus Ch'u], *Law and Society in Traditional China* (Paris: Mouton, 1961), 231.
180 Kuo-Cheng Wu, *Ancient Chinese Political Theories* (Shanghai: Commercial Press, 1928), 37.
181 Song, "The *Zhou Li* and Constitutionalism," 13.
182 Hahm, "Confucian Constitutionalism," 141.
183 Legge, *Analects*, 146.
184 De Bary is an exceptional case. Wm. Theodore de Bary, "The 'Constitutional Tradition' in China," *Journal of China Law* 9(7) (1995): 8.
185 Legge, *Analects*, 169.
186 Ibid., 161.
187 Ibid., 265.
188 Legge, *Mencius*, 288–289.
189 Cheng, *New Dimensions*, 314.
190 Ibid., 314–315.
191 Ibid., 315.
192 De Bary, "Constitutional Tradition," 10.
193 Sato, *Confucian Quest*, 406.
194 Knoblock, *Xunzi, Volume II*, 229.
195 Hahm, "Ritual and Constitutionalism," 144–145.
196 Hsu, *Political Philosophy*, 96–99.
197 Ginsburg, "Confucian Constitutionalism," 794.
198 See John Knoblock, *Xunzi: A Translation and Study of the Complete Works, Volume III* (Stanford, CA: Stanford University Press, 1994), 151–152. ("In antiquity the sage kings took man's nature to be evil, to be inclined to prejudice and prone to error, to be perverse and rebellious, and not to be upright or orderly. For this reason they invented ritual principles and precepts of moral duty.")
199 Carl J. Friedrich, *Tradition and Authority* (London: Pall Mall Press, 1972), 14.
200 Legge, *Analects*, 195.
201 Ibid., 160.
202 For more elaboration, see Fung, *Chinese Philosophy*, 108–111.
203 Ibid., 282.
204 Herbert Fingarette, *Confucius*, 6 (italic in original).
205 William P. Alford, *To Steal a Book is an Elegant Offense: Intellectual Property Law in Chinese Civilization* (Stanford, CA: Stanford University Press, 1995), 9–29.
206 Ibid., 211.
207 Hahm, *Confucian Constitutionalism*, 88–106.
208 Fingarette, "The Music of Humanity," 335 (italic in original).
209 Ibid., 335.
210 According to Masayuki Sato, in Xunzi's works *li* is juxtaposed to *yi* 104 times to form the two Chinese characters *liyi*. Sato also points out that when *li* and *yi* are used

separately, the meaning of *li* overlaps that of *yi* to some extent. Sato, *The Confucian Quest*, 345–347. The subtext is that *li* is normally related to what is right.

211 Wejen Chang, "Confucian Theory of Norms and Human Rights," in *Confucianism and Human Rights*, ed. de Bary and Tu Weiming (New York: Colombia University Press, 1998), 126.

212 Knoblock, *Xunzi, Volume III*, 211.

213 Gilbert Keith Chesterton, *Orthodoxy* (London, Sydney and Auckland: Hodder & Stoughton, 1996), 62–63

214 Dante Germino, "Carl J. Friedrich on Constitutionalism and the 'Great Tradition' of Political Theory," in *Nomos XX: Constitutionalism*, ed. Roland Pennock and John W. Chapman (New York: New York University Press, 1979), 19.

215 Ibid., 20–25.

216 Ibid., 23.

217 Robert Lowry Clinton, *God and Man in the Law: The Foundations of Anglo-American Constitutionalism* (Lawrence, KS: University Press of Kansas, 1997).

218 Ibid., 55.

219 Walker, "Nonliberal Constitutionalism," 165; Beau Breslin, *The Communitarian Constitution* (Baltimore, MD and London: Johns Hopkins University Press, 2004), 112–133.

220 Schwartz, *The World of Thought*, 67 (italic added).

221 Cheng, *New Dimensions*, 323 (italic added).

222 Breslin, *Communitarian Constitution*, 126 (italic in original).

223 Ibid.

224 Ibid., 129.

225 Ibid., 130.

226 Alasdair MacIntyre, *Whose Justice? Which Rationality?* (Notre Dame, IN: University of Notre Dame Press, 1988), 383

227 Hsu, *Political Philosophy*, 96–99.

228 Legge, *Li Ki* [*Li Ji*], 90.

229 Herrlee Glessner Creel, "Legal Institutions and Procedures during the Chou Dynasty," in *Essays on China's Legal Tradition*, ed. Jerome Alan Cohen, R. Randle Edwards, and Fu-mei Chang Chen (Princeton, NJ: Princeton University Press, 1980), 39.

230 Legge, *Analects*, 305.

231 Hahm, "Confucian Constitutionalism," 153.

232 Ibid., 79.

233 Wm. Theodore de Bary, *The Liberal Tradition in China* (Hong Kong: The Chinese University Press, 1983), 28.

234 Legge, *Analects*, 250.

235 Legge, *Great Learning*, 359.

236 Ibid.

237 Daniel A. Bell, *Beyond Liberal Democracy: Political Thinking for an East Asian Context* (Princeton, NJ: Princeton University Press, 2006), 153–154.

238 Legge, *The Work of Mencius*, 210–211.

239 Ibid., 213–214

240 Ibid., 387.

241 Ibid., 214.

242 Ibid., 445.

243 Legge, *Doctrine of Means*, 409.

244 Confucius himself wishes to participate in the government. After he resigned from his position as a Minister of Crime in his native state (Lu), he traveled to other states in the hope of being employed. Additionally, Confucius initiated the private school to educate the prospective officials. In fact, some of his students became officials.

245 Legge, *Analects*, 297 ("the determined scholar and the man of virtue will not seek to live at the expense of injuring their virtue. They will even sacrifice their lives to preserve their virtue complete."); Legge, *Mencius*, 458. ("They [great ministers] rectify themselves and others are rectified.")
246 Tu Wei-ming regards *li* as the process of humanization. See Tu Wei-ming, "Li as Process of Humanization," *Philosophy East & West* 22(2) (1972): 187–201.
247 Rosemont, "Two Loci of Authority," 11.
248 Chang, "Confucian Theory," 171.
249 Legge, *Analects*, 256.
250 Ibid., 161.
251 Li Fu Chen, *The Confucian Way*, trans. Shih Shun Liu (London: KPI limited, 1986), 489.
252 Legge, *Mencius*, 318.
253 Hawkling L. Yen, "A Survey of Constitutional Development in China" (PhD dissertation, Columbia University, 1911), 85.
254 Legge, *Analects*, 245–246. Confucius himself practiced the principle of the "great minister." At the age of 50, he was the Minister of Crime of Lu state. When the Duke of Lu was enamored of a gift of female musicians sent by the Duke of Chi'i and did not send him a portion of flesh from the solstitial sacrifice (the indicator that he was neglected), he resigned from his position and went to other states. Hsiao, *Chinese Political Thought*, 82.
255 Legge, *Analects*, 285.
256 Legge, *Mencius*, 161.
257 Ibid., 392.
258 Ibid., 392
259 Ibid., 393
260 Ibid., 467. (Î Yin is the regent of Shang dynasty after the death of King Tang. T'â-chiâ is the paternal grandchild of Tang and the contemporary king.)
261 Knoblock, *Xunzi, Volume II*, 199.
262 Ibid., 200.
263 Ibid., 199.
264 Legge, *Mencius*, 310.
265 Legge, *The Doctrine of the Means*, 406.
266 Legge, *Analects*, 342.
267 Ibid., 172.
268 Others are the *Book of Records*, the *Book of Poetry*, the *Book of Rites*, and the *Book of Change*. In fact, Confucian classics also include the *Book of Music* but it was destroyed by Qin's fires and its remnant was incorporated into the *Book of Rites*.
269 Legge, *Volume V*, *Ch'un Ch'in* [*Chunqiu*], 1.
270 Legge, *Mencius*, 281–282.
271 Legge, *Ch'un Ch'in* [*Chunqiu*], 22–38.
272 Hsu, *Political Philosophy*, 54.
273 Hsu, *Political Philosophy*, 54–58.
274 Quoted in Sarah A. Queen, *From Chronicle to Canon: The Hermeneutics of the Spring and Autumn, according to Tung Chung-shu* (New York: Cambridge University Press, 1996), 122.
275 Ibid.
276 Ibid., 123.
277 Winberg Chai, "The Political Thought of Kang Youwei: A Study of Its Origin and Its Influence" (PhD dissertation, New York University, 1968), xi.
278 Ibid., 28–29.
279 Quoted in ibid., 29.
280 Jiang Qing, *A Confucian Constitutional Order: How China's Ancient Past Can Shape Its Political Future*, ed. Daniel A. Bell and Ruiping Fan, trans. Edmund Ryden (Princeton, NJ: Princeton University Press, 2012).

281 Hsu, *Political Philosophy*, 56.
282 Ibid., 56–57.
283 Legge, *Mencius*, 283.
284 Wm. Theodore de Bary, Wing-tsit Chan, and Burton Watson, ed., *Sources of Chinese Tradition* (New York: Columbia University Press, 1060), 154–155.
285 Edward Shils, "Reflections on Civil Society and Civility in the Chinese Intellectual Tradition," in *Confucian Traditions in East Asian Modernity: Moral Education and Economic Culture in Japan and the Four Mini-Dragons*, edited by Tu Wei-ming (Cambridge, MA: Harvard University Press, 1996), 53.
286 A.V. Dicey, *Introduction to the Study of Law of the Constitution* (London: Macmillan, 1920), 22.
287 Joseph Chan, *Confucian Perfectionism: A Political Philosophy for Modern Times* (Princeton, NJ: Princeton University Press, 2013), 50.
288 Ibid., 51.
289 Ibid., 47.
290 Ibid., 60.
291 Richard Albert. "The Fusion of Presidentialism and Parliamentarism," *American Journal of Comparative Law* 57 (2009): 531.
292 Ginsburg, "Constitutionalism," 17.
293 Stéphanie Balme and Michael W. Dowdle, "Introduction: Exploring for Constitutionalism in 21st Century China," in *Building Constitutionalism in China*, ed. Stéphanie Balme and Michael W. Dowdle (New York: Palgrave Macmillan, 2009), 2.

2 Imperial Confucian constitutionalism

Introduction

The preceding chapter has examined Confucian constitutionalism at the conceptual level. The present chapter turns to consider it at the practical level. The chapter will demonstrate how the constitutionalist ideas in classical Confucianism were put into practice by imperial governments in East Asia.

Up until the middle of the twentieth century, imperial government in the history of East Asia was conventionally understood under the lens of "Oriental despotism," according to which the supreme power was conceived to be concentrated in the hands of a single, unlimited monarch.[1] In a comprehensive survey of "Oriental despotism," Karl A. Wittfogel tries to argue about the "absence of effective constitutional checks" of the imperial ruler. Although there were systematic law codes, Wittfogel writes,

> The ruler who exercises complete administrative, managerial, judicial, military, and fiscal authority may use his power to make whatever laws he and his aides deem fit. Expediency and inertia favour the perpetuation of most of these laws, but the absolutist regime is free to alter its norms at any time.[2]

However, recent scholarship has considerably challenged the traditional understanding of the East Asian imperial regime. Scholars in different disciplines, such as philosophy, history, political science, and particularly constitutional law and theory, have engaged in discussions on the practice of the form of Confucian constitutionalism in imperial East Asia. Chaihark Hahm, for example, has explored the practice of Confucian ritualist constitutionalism in Choson Korea.[3] Pierre-Étienne Will has examined Confucian virtual Constitutionalism in Ming China.[4]

Generally speaking, there is a tendency to rethink East Asian Confucian polity. The phantasm of Oriental despotism dominating our conventional thinking of East Asian imperial government has been significantly challenged. Notwithstanding that, the manifestations of Confucian constitutionalism have not yet been fully examined as scholars tend to focus on particular aspects of Confucian tradition, like *li* or virtue. This chapter alternatively introduces a fuller and more systematic investigation of the practice of Confucian constitutionalism.

To a certain extent, more specific investigations of the Confucian constitutional norms and institutions in this chapter are conceptually based on Hahm's study of ritual constitutionalism in the Choson dynasty and Will's study of virtual constitutionalism in the late Ming dynasty. Particularly, I accept Hahm's idea that *li* could function as constitutional norms in Confucian polities as it encompasses a set of political and moral rules, percepts, principles, and conventions that regulated and limited the royal power.

However, I do not focus on the "disciplinary" dimension of *li* as Hahm did. I admit that *li* could be used to discipline the ruler as Hahm suggests, but I contend that the idea of "discipline" does not well denote the constitutionalist purpose of application of *li*. I would suggest the alternative lexicon, namely "rectification" understood in the very Confucian sense, which, I believe, is more appropriate. My previous consideration of classical foundations of Confucian constitutionalism suggests that *li* is derivatively linked to the Confucian doctrine of rectification of names (*zheng ming*). A *zheng ming* government is a limited government in which the physical power holders are required to function in accordance with their "names" or the metaphysical normative and institutional standards defining their authorities, duties, and expected virtues. *Li* is the embodiment of such standards. *Li* is articulated and enforced to rectify (*zheng ming*) the ruler to ensure their responsibility to the people (*minben*). The rectification of the use of public power in accordance with the *li* in a Confucian polity might be achieved by positive means, including internal cultivation, and institutionalized external advice, education, criticism, remonstrance, and praise-and-censure.

It is also necessary to reveal the manifestations of Confucian constitutionalism in different eras in imperial East Asia. As the cases of imperial Korea and China have been explored by other scholars, I focus here on the case of imperial Vietnam. Confucianism was introduced from China into Vietnam during the millennial period of Chinese dependency ("*Bắc thuộc*," 111 BC–AD 905). In an era of national independence, Confucianism was promoted by the Lý (1009–1225) and Trần (1225–1400) dynasties. Confucianism reached its heyday in imperial Vietnam in the Lê dynasty in the fifteenth century. After the golden age, Confucianism suffered a decline in the period of North–South partition. Defeating the Tây Sơn force, Nguyễn Ánh (1762–1820) founded the Nguyễn dynasty in 1802. The Nguyễn dynasty completely put an end to the national partition and consolidated the traditional monarchic government in a united territory. The new peaceful context provided an advantageous environment for the reinvigoration of Confucianism.[5]

I illustrate the practice of Confucian constitutionalism in imperial East Asia by the case of the Nguyễn dynasty, one of the major Confucian monarchies and the last dynasty in imperial Vietnam, with a focus on its early development. The Nguyễn dynasty existed for 143 years in total, from 1802, when Nguyễn Ánh (Gia Long) acceded to the throne, to 1945, when emperor Bảo Đại (1913–1997) abdicated the throne after the August Revolution led by the Indochina Communist Party (presently the Communist Party of Vietnam). The Nguyễn dynasty independently ruled the country in the early period of its existence from 1802 to 1884, with the successive emperors Gia Long, Minh Mệnh or Minh Mạng (1791–1841), Thiệu Trị (1807–1847), and Tự Đức (1829–1883), who were all ardent proponents of Confucianism. In the latter period from 1884 to 1945, the French colonized Vietnam and the position of the Nguyễn court was titular. The independent Nguyễn dynasty governed the country with great *éclat* under the reign of Emperor Minh Mệnh from 1820 to 1841.[6] This chapter focuses on the independent period of the dynasty.

The chapter reveals numerous constitutional norms as the embodiment of the Confucian *li* used to restrain the royal authority, namely the models of ancient kings, the political norms in the Confucian Classics, the ancestral precedents, and the institutions of the precedent dynasties. In addition, the chapter explores structuralized forums enabling the scholar-officials to use the norms to limit the royal power, including the royal examination system, the deliberative institutions, the educative institution, the remonstrative institution, and the historical institution. The practice of imperial Confucianism was limited due to the lack of institutional independence and popular mobilization, but could be achieved to a certain degree due to the power of tradition.

This chapter is structured as follows. The first section examines the Confucian constitutional norms as the articulation of the *li*. The second section considers the structuralized forums enabling the scholar-officials to use the norms to limit the royal power. The third section provides discussions on the practice of Confucian constitutionalism. The final part concludes the chapter.

Confucian constitution

In the preceding chapter, I have argued that in classical Confucianism, *li* that includes traditional norms and institutions which directly or indirectly control the distribution and the operation of the public power can be recognized as a Confucian constitution. In this section, I shall examine the manifestation of this idea.

However, some conceptual issues should be clarified first. Grey distinguishes written and unwritten constitutional norms. The written constitutional norms are those that derive their status from the fact of their "enactment of some authorized body" and their content is derived by "interpretation" of the enacted constitutional text.[7] In contrast, the unwritten constitutional norms have sources of authority other than enactment, and correspondingly their content must be identified by means other than interpretation.[8] Grey further divides the unwritten constitutional norms into two categories. First are norms whose authority is based on their "general acceptance" and their content is elucidated by "investigation, impressionistic or scientific, of the usages generally accepted as binding the community in question."[9] Second are those norms whose authority rests on their status as "moral and political truths" and the content of these norms is determined by some method of "arriving at true moral and political value judgments."[10]

With the above conceptual framework, we can proceed to study constitutional norms in Confucian polity. Certainly, there is no enacted single charter like a modern written constitution in a Confucian regime. However, there actually existed unwritten norms that regulated and limited the actions of the ruler and hence can be regarded as "unwritten constitutional norms." They are derived from two sources, to borrow Grey's category, namely "universal and immutable moral or political truth" and "the shared and strongly felt values and beliefs of the community" (usage and acceptance).[11] They were traditional norms expressing political and moral truths and generally accepted values and beliefs, gathered under the Confucian terminological umbrella, namely *li* (ritual).

Hahm has illuminatingly elaborated on constitutional norms in Confucian polity. He reveals that law in Confucian polities in the imperial history of China and Korea included three types of norms or codes, namely ritual (*li*), penal, and administrative. Within the tripartite legal framework of the Confucian governments, *li* can be understood as a set of constitutional norms as they were used to regulate and restrain the ruler.[12] Hahm compares: "Indeed, the ruler's observance of ritual regulations was of paramount importance in Confucian political theory, much like the duty of a modern-day president to uphold the constitution.... Ritual was norm that even the king was expected to obey."[13] He then goes on to elaborate three constitutional principles or norms of the Confucian government as the embodiment of *li*, namely "the way of former kings," political norms in the Confucian Classics, and the ancestral precedents.

By the case of the Ming dynasty, Will also discovers three elements of the "dynastic constitution," namely the values and precedents embodied in the Confucian Classics; the ancestral institutions of the dynasty; and the administrative constitution as embodied in certain official treatises, and in a body of penal and administrative law which controlled the activities of the bureaucracy.[14]

It can be seen that Hahm and Will share the commonalities that the political principles in the Confucian Classics, and the ancestral norms could function as constitutional norms but hold different views on the constitutional status of the penal and administrative laws. I agree with Hahm that, for constitutionalist purposes, the penal and administrative laws were less meaningful as they were only applied to the commoners and the officials, respectively, rather than the ruler.[15] The norms, to be constitutionally meaningful, must be the ones that affect (regulate and limit) the power of the sovereign.

Let us consider in more detail the discursive constitutional norms. The first is "the way of former kings." The former kings referred to the mythical sage kings, including Yao and Shun in the ancient history of China, whom the classical Confucians eulogized as the paradigm of governance. The constitutional importance of the way of the ancient kings is that the scholar-officials were able to use the way of the ancient kings to restrain their ruler. In the case of the Choson dynasty, Hahm writes:

> They constantly urged the monarch to discipline himself by taking the ancient kings as his model. They capitalized on the ancient past as the criterion by which to judge and criticize the present. If there were disruption of peace and order in the realm, it was attributed to the current king's deviation from the way of the former kings.[16]

The second are political norms in the Confucian Classics. In the Choson dynasty, according to Hahm, "the Confucian classics such as the *Five Classics* and the *Four Books* did function as sources for political norms."[17] Similarly, in the Ming dynasty, as Will demonstrates,

> They [the Classics] had important political implications, because they constituted a sort of superior orthodoxy and because the ones who considered themselves to be in charge of interpreting *The Classics* and protecting the orthodoxy were the literati. The intellectual power of the literati derived from their social position made them, in a way, the functional equivalents of guardians of the "constitution" – except that in this case it was not a legal document that they guarded, but the scriptures with which dynastic policies were supposed to be in conformity.[18]

The third are the ancestral precedents. The contents of ancestral institutions were the complex mixture of proclamations, laws, legislations, and structural institutions created by the dynastic founder or sometimes by the first few emperors of a dynasty.[19] What characterizes these institutions as ancestral is the fact that it was considered highly difficult for the contemporary ruler to alter them without risking an accusation of lack of *xiao* (filial piety).[20] However, this does not mean that changes to ancestral laws were impossible. Hahm notes: "Even in the tradition-bound constitutional culture, changes in laws were inevitable and indeed necessary."[21]

Like the Choson dynasty of Korea and the Ming dynasty of China, the Nguyễn dynasty of Vietnam also had the three types of constitutional norms mentioned above. However, I would add a fourth set of norms that controlled the early Nguyễn rulers, namely the institutions of the precedent dynasties. The four types of unwritten constitutional norms are the embodiment of *li* as a set of normative rules used to rectify the ruler.

The way of former kings

As adherents of Confucianism, the early Nguyễn rulers acknowledged the principle of following the ancient kings.[22] To illustrate, Minh Mệnh's ambitious aspiration was to be comparable to "the precedent sages and enlightened kings."[23] Thiệu Trị also committed to this percept, as described by a Confucian mandarin:

> The present-day Emperor clearly understands the wills of the precedent emperors, follows the sage and enlightened kings, and accords with the way of the mean of King Yao. His morality is unadulterated, such as the respect to King Wen [of Zhou].[24]

The model of the Chinese ancient kings – their governments, institutions, laws, and conduct which were mainly recorded in the *Shu Jing* (*Book of Historical*

Documents) – provided normative precepts for the Nguyễn rulers in their legislation, policy decisions, and daily behaviors. It is in this sense that the model of the ancient kings could superimpose limitative effects upon the royal authority. The scholar-officials of the Nguyễn dynasty often invoked the models of the ancient kings to rectify their ruler.

Political norms in the Confucian Classics

Early Nguyễn rulers publicly articulated particular political norms emanating from the Confucian Classics. To illustrate, drawing from the Confucian Classics, Minh Mệnh declared four indispensable norms of rule, namely: *kính thiên* (*respecting the Heaven*), *pháp tổ* (*following the ancestors*), *cần chính* (*being diligent in political affairs*), and *ái dân* (*loving people*).[25] How these norms practically controlled his legislations and his policies was meticulously described in the "*Minh Mệnh Chính yếu*" (*Minh Mệnh's Principal Policies*)[26] composed by the Quốc sử quán (National Historian Office) of the Nguyễn dynasty, which recorded principal policies implemented by Minh Mệnh. Following his father, Thiệu Trị publicly proclaimed his loyalty to these four norms. He composed an anthology in which he collected statements from the Confucian Classics which directly expressed the meaning of the norms, and disseminated the work among the community of Confucian scholars and officials.[27] The subsequent emperor Tự Đức was also amenable to the four norms and supplemented four others, namely, *thân hiền* (*cherishing the talents*), *đồ trị* (*arranging the order*), *chí thiện* (*having great virtues*), and *đôn thân* (*supporting the relatives*). He even composed a poem to popularize the eight norms.[28]

The political norms stemming from the Confucian Classics could function as "constitutional norms" in the sense that they were paramount standards for rectifying the practice of the royal power. Scholar-officials of the Nguyễn dynasty often used the political norms in the Confucian Classics as normative standards to judge and criticize the ruler. The ruler was supposed to legislate, formulate national policies, lead the administrative system, and cautiously control his quotidian behaviors in such a way as to be in concordance with the political norms in the Classics. To illustrate, let us consider how the two important norms called *kính thiên* (*respecting the Heaven*) and *ái dân* (*loving people*) could control the political discourse and practice of the emperors.

The norm *kính thiên* (*respecting the Heaven*) originated from the Confucian concept of "Mandate of Heaven" (Vietnamese: *thiên mệnh*; Chinese: *tianming*), which suggests that the king is "the Son of Heaven" receiving the Mandate from the Heaven to govern the kingdom to benefit the people.[29] Tạ Văn Tài pointed out that as a kind of fundamental constitution, or as an equivalence to a constitution, the founders of the major dynasties in Vietnam (Lý, Trần, Lê, and Nguyễn) repeatedly used the Confucian notion of the Mandate of Heaven to claim legitimacy of rule.[30] However, he failed to discover the other aspect of the constitutional significance of the practice of the concept of the Mandate of Heaven, which is more practical. That is, the commitment to the concept could control the ruler's concrete policies and his daily behaviors. In the case of the early Nguyễn dynasty, the doctrine of the Mandate of Heaven was not merely invoked to justify the legitimacy of the enthronement. Beyond that, the doctrine induced the principal norm *kính thiên* (*respecting the Heaven*), which practically controlled the royal authority in concrete matters and the conduct of the ruler.

In theory, the legitimate rule in concordance with the Mandate of Heaven demands the ruler to respect the Heaven in the concrete sense that he must meticulously observe natural phenomena which are supposedly the indicators of the heavenly feeling.[31] The abnormal phenomena, for example, might be the manifestation of divine anger. Furthermore, the ruler is required to keep watch over the living conditions of the people. As popular will is the embodiment of heavenly will, the annoyance of the people, which normally stemmed from high taxes, harsh punishments, and officials' corruption, might be evidence of heaven's dissent of the governance of the contemporary ruler. In these cases, the ruler has to rectify his policies to satisfy the desires of the public and to further cultivate his personal morality. It is in this sense that the commitment to respecting the Heaven potentially induced the limitations of the practice of imperial power.

Importantly, the norm "*kính thiên*" is consequential in its relations to other norms of the Nguyễn dynasty. To respect the heaven, the ruler should limit the annoyance of the people by *ái dân* (*loving the people*), *cần chính* (*being diligent in political affairs*), *thân hiền* (*cherishing the talents*), and *chí thiện* (*having great virtues*). Let us consider in more detail the norm "*ái dân*" ("*loving people*") as the consequence of the norm "*kính thiên.*"

Minh Mệnh, Thiệu Trị, and Tự Đức simultaneously regarded "*ái dân*" as the essential norm for national governance. Particularly, during the regime of Minh Mệnh, "to love people" was the overriding principle.[32] In this regard, the two books entitled "*ái dân*" ("*loving people*") in *Minh Mệnh's Principal Policies*, which addressed Minh Mệnh's commitment to the Confucian *minben* together with his practical policies to implement this principle, should be examined.

For classical Confucianism, to love the people means to work for their happiness. On the occasion of his fiftieth birthday, Minh Mệnh delivered nationwide a royal proclamation in which, drawing from the Confucian Classics, he professed adherence to that concept: "The kingly way is to consider peace the criterion and to accumulate five happinesses for the people."[33] "Five happinesses" refers to the ninth division of "the Great Plan" in the *Shu Jing*, which consists of long life, riches, soundness of body and serenity of mind, the love of virtue, and an end crowning the life.[34] Generally, following the classical teachings of Confucianism, Minh Mệnh believed that good government should be responsible for public standards of decent life for the people.

To work for the people means that the ruler should not be selfish and should be sympathetic to the will of the people. In the aforementioned declaration, Minh Mệnh stated: "Consider people's wishes our wishes. Therefore, consider the people's joys our joys."[35] These sentences are based on the teaching in the *Great Learning* that: "when a prince loves what the people love, and hates what the people hate, then is he what is called the parent of the people."[36] In *Minh Mệnh's*

Principal Policies there are a number of statements further illustrating his unselfish spirit and the sense of responsibility for the people. For example, Minh Mệnh said: "Since I have ascended the throne, I neglect eating and clothing all day long, just taking care of rescuing the people.... On the business of loving the people and nurturing the people, I am never parsimonious."[37] In a similar vein, he said on another occasion:

> When the people are miserable or faced with catastrophe, I further cultivate myself, and only consider how to lavish favor and nurture the people, all day long I mediate, and do not dare to relax. How can I enjoy luxury and ignore loving the people![38]

He explained that:

> Being an affluent king, I do not worry about how to satisfy my wishes but I think about my people who are suffering destitution, widowhood, orphanhood, and uneasy livelihood. To satisfy the wishes of one person not only implicates his own body but also inculcates the people with that bad habit.[39]

Apart from *Minh Mệnh's Principal Policies*, Minh Mệnh's deep solicitude for the people was reflected in his thousands of poems. With 5,000 pages of woodblock, Minh Mệnh's poems expressed his concern for the living conditions of the people, especially the misery that the people had to suffer due to catastrophes and the corruption of the mandarins.[40]

Interestingly, as the highest examiner of the royal examination, Minh Mệnh tended to formulate the questions in close relation to the mechanisms of practicing the Confucian requirement of responsible government for the people. To illustrate, it is useful to cite one of his examination questions:

> I think that for the Son of Heaven, the Heaven is the Father, the Earth is the Mother, and he is the Son. The mass of people are compatriots and are consanguineous. Therefore, it is said that the king is the firstborn child. The firstborn child inherits the throne from his parent to become the king of the people with great responsibilities. Certainly, he has to have the way to nurture and educate the people so that the people in the whole of the country can all be peaceful. Only when he can do that, he completes his tasks.... Now, I receive the Mandate of Heaven to maintain the great achievements of the ancestors and all day long concentrate on how to complete the responsibilities of the firstborn child to compare with the precedent sages and enlightened kings. On the sequence to practice this, what are the priorities? You, students who have fully studied classics and historical works and now are waiting to be questioned, are supposedly knowledgeable. Please compose a careful essay and I will myself examine it.[41]

The ancestral precedents

As previously mentioned, the early monarchs of the Nguyễn dynasty considered *pháp tổ* (following the ancestors) the ruling norm. Emperor Thiệu Trị helpfully depicted the norm:

> The ancestors established the dynasty and arduous careers. The echo of their virtues has been smooth.... They must be comprehended, followed, studied, and looked at. To the inferiors, it must be humble. To the people, it must be generous.... The talented and virtuous must be all appointed as mandarins.... Follow the ancestors to stabilize the dynasty.[42]

Who were the ancestors of the Nguyễn dynasty? The ancestry of the dynasty referred to both Gia Long – the dynastic founder – and the Lords of Nguyễn family who ruled the Southern part of Vietnam during the time of the Trịnh Lords–Nguyễn Lords rivalry.

To practice the principle of following the ancestors, the Nguyễn rulers particularly paid attention to recording the ancestral institutions and works, which led to the advent of the voluminous work entitled *Đại Nam Thực Lục* (*Veritable Records of Đại Nam*).[43] The work recorded the institutions and works of the rulers of the Nguyễn family, consisting of two components, namely, *Đại Nam Thực Lục Tiền Biên* (*Previous Compilation of Veritable Records of Đại Nam*), which covered nine Lords of the Nguyễn family during the time of the Trịnh Lords–Nguyễn Lords rivalry, and *Đại Nam Thực Lục Chính biên* (*Primary Compilation of Veritable Records of Đại Nam*), which covered seven emperors of the Nguyễn dynasty from Gia Long to Khải Định. *The Previous Compilations and the Primary Compilation's First Era* (*Đệ nhất kỷ*), which concerns Emperor Gia Long, can be considered as the textualized embodiments of the ancestral precedents which were supposed to be followed by the later Nguyễn emperors.

In addition, the *Hoàng Việt Luật Lệ* (*Laws of Imperial Viet*) or *Luật Gia Long* (*Gia Long Code*)[44] promulgated by Emperor Gia Long can also be considered the ancestral precedents which were applicable to later rulers of the dynasty. The "constitutional" implication of the binding force of the laws of the founding emperor was that they constituted limitations on the practice of the legislative power of the later rulers. The contemporary ruler might introduce some new laws but it was not easy for him to change the laws established by his ancestors. Therefore, the arbitrariness in law-making was restricted. Practically, the Gia Long Code remained in effect throughout the time of the Nguyễn dynasty,[45] despite the fact that subsequent emperors – Minh Mệnh, Thiệu Trị, and Tự Đức – also supplemented new laws which were codified in the other *Hoàng Triệu Luật Lệ* (*Laws of the Dynasty*).[46]

Finally, the structural institutions of the central government created by the founder of the dynasty can also be recognized as the ancestral precedents. Particularly, these structural institutions were characterized by the principle of "*tứ bất*" ("*four negations*"), which negated four titles, namely royals, prime minister, queen, and first doctorate laureate. The "*tứ bất*" principle was putatively established by Gia Long and became the normative percept of the dynasty.[47]

Institutions of precedent dynasties

Early emperors of the Nguyễn dynasty particularly realized the need to inherit the institutions of the precedent dynasties, which, in their belief, were the expression of lasting political principles. This can be verified by their particular concern for recording them. To illustrate, Gia Long delivered a royal proclamation requesting the collection of materials concerning the institutions of the precedent dynasties, saying that:

> On the way to govern a country, there must be permanent principles; on the way to order, it should be sought from old institutions. In our Viet nation, there were successive dynasties of Đinh, Lý, Trần, and Lê. In their politics, there were some things changeable and some things stable. During that period, should there be institutions and laws worthy of recording?[48]

Gia Long then demanded that among the public those who stored materials concerning the institutions, laws, and general history of the precedent dynasties should donate them to the court.[49] Gia Long's campaign induced a nationwide movement of book donation. A number of valuable materials regarding the precedent dynasties – including the *Completed Annuals of Đại Việt* and the *Hông Đức Code* – were gathered in the imperial depository.[50]

A similar campaign was initiated under the early rule of Minh Mệnh. In a royal proclamation requesting the continuous collection of materials relating to the precursors' institutions, the emperor stated:

> I think that when the precedent emperors emerged, there must be books of each dynasty recording their words, actions, and political affairs to bequeath to the later generations. Every house which stores the documents of the precedent dynasties, regardless of thoroughness or brevity, must submit the original versions to the government or let the government transcribe them.[51]

As a consequence of that, a number of books of the precedent dynasties stored in private families or works later composed by individual authors were discovered and delivered to the court.[52] Most notable was the lucubration entitled "*Lịch triều Hiến chương Loại chí*" (*Categorical Records of Institutions of the Precedent Dynasties*), authorized by Phan Huy Chú.

Phan Huy Chú was an erudite Confucian scholar widely celebrated in Vietnam. A son of a *tiến sĩ* (*doctoral laureate*) and Confucian scholar-official, Phan Huy Ích, he only obtained *tú tài* (*the degree of baccalaureate*) after several attempts in the royal examinations. Failing to pursue an advanced degree to gain access to the imperial government, Phan Huy Chú concentrated his time on studying the history of dynastic institutions, which led to his compilation of the

Categorical Records of Institutions of the Precedent Dynasties. In 1821, Emperor Minh Mệnh knew of him and exceptionally appointed him as a *biên tu* (editorial official) of the *Hàn Lâm Viện* (Hanlin Academy). Phan Huy Chú took this opportunity to submit the *Records* to the emperor. The emperor rated the work highly and rewarded him lavishly with valuables.[53]

At the time, *The Records of Institutions of the Precedent Dynasties* was the most thorough disquisition on the theme. This encyclopedic work consists of 49 books recording the institutions of the successive dynasties to the end of the Lê period, which were classified in ten categories: geography, historical figures, mandarin system, rituals, examination system, public finance system, criminal laws, military system, literatures, and diplomatic relations.[54] Phan Huy Chú's *Records* can be regarded as the comprehensive textualized embodiment of the precedent dynastic institutions that were supposed to be inherited by the Nguyễn dynasty.

Among various institutions of different precedent dynasties, early Nguyễn emperors particularly endorsed the ones established during the golden age of the early Lê dynasty under the reign of Lê Thánh Tông.[55] In particular, Minh Mệnh's ambition was to be a second "Lê Thánh Tông."[56] He said: "Among precedent kings in our country, Lê Thánh Tông can be considered the virtuous king who I constantly adore."[57] He even believed that Lê Thánh Tông established the laws and institutions, which could be forever bequeathed to the later generations.[58]

The institutions of the predecessors were the embodiments of stable principles of government whose effectiveness was testified by the lasting endurance in the tradition. Therefore, practically, the early Nguyễn dynasty largely followed the established institutions of their precursors. Traditional rules of monarchial hereditary succession were followed. Governance based on the Confucian ideology was continuingly practiced. As far as the legal system is concerned, Gia Long, when ordering his officials to draft the code of the dynasty, stated that laws of the precedent dynasties should be considered the foundations.[59] In addtion, the Nguyễn dynasty was largely amenable to the precedent model of the central government characterized by the recruitment of officials by the method of royal examinations, the six ministries system, and specialized institutions such as the imperial lecture, the censorial institution, and the historian office.

To be sure, the Nguyễn dynasty introduced unprecedented institutional reforms, as evident under the rule of Minh Mệnh.[60] However, such administrative institutional changes were technical rather than substantial. The invocation of the precedent institutions remained the distinctive character of institutional arrangements. The principles of royal transmission through consanguineous heredity in normal situations and the fundamental characteristics of the organization of the central government were substantially retained.

In short, the constitutional norms of the Nguyễn dynasty included four kinds, namely: models of ancient kings; the political and moral principles in the Confucian Classics; the ancestral precedents; and the institutions of the precedent dynasties. They all derived from the tradition. They were unwritten in nature, which means that they were not enacted in a single charter. In the subsequent section, I will consider institutional settings designed to rectify the ruler in concordance with those Confucian unwritten constitutional norms.

Institutionalized scholastic constitutionalism

Grey asserts, "There are a number of mechanisms of constitutional enforcement."[61] Modern constitutionalism largely relies on judicial review and the political mechanisms of the separation of powers and checks and balances to enforce constitutional norms.[62] However, these mechanisms are only established in mature constitutionalist states in the modern time and hence should not be used as fixed standards of constitutional enforcement in general. With that in mind, we can proceed to consider the constitutional enforcement mechanisms of premodern constitutionalism of Confucian societies.

In Confucian regimes there were some mechanisms of constitutional enforcement which were neither judicial nor political, but "scholastic." It should be recalled that classical Confucianism considers the wise and virtuous scholars as the external forces to limit the actions of the ruler in concordance with the *li* or the constitutional norms. I have labeled this idea as "scholastic constitutionalism." In practice, the scholar-officials of imperial governments in East Asia, by their scholarship and through discursive structuralized forums, were responsible for ensuring the conformity of the ruler's actions to the constitutional norms. These mechanisms were not political as the scholar-officials were just the members of the administrative system. Neither were they judicial as the scholar-officials were not the independent judges vested with judicial review power. Instead, the Confucian mechanisms of constitutional enforcement were "scholastic" in the sense that they depended on special structural institutions which allowed the scholar-officials to use their scholarship to restrain the ruler.

Hahm's study helpfully demonstrates various such institutions, namely the prime minister, the imperial lecture, the censorate, and the historian office.[63] In the case of the Nguyễn dynasty, the three latter institutions did exist, but the prime minister was abolished in accordance with the principle of "four negations" due to the fear that the prime minister might usurp the emperor's power. Alternatively, the dynasty established some deliberative institutions which can be regarded as potential checks of the emperor's power.

Apart from that, to examine the scholastic enforcement of constitutional norms in Confucian polities in East Asia, I suggest that we should take the royal examination system into account. First, this is because the system was the beginning of the scholastic enforcement of constitutional norms. It was largely dependent on this system that the wise and virtuous scholars could gain access to the government to restrain the power of the ruler. Second, the royal examination system itself was the restraint of the ruler on the matter of personnel. In theory, the ruler could not arbitrarily appoint persons without passing the exams to hold governmental positions. Therefore, in the subsequent section, the royal examination system will be examined before proceeding to other institutions.

Royal examination system

As elaborated in the preceding chapter, Confucian elitism holds that government should be administrated by intellectuals who are previously educated about the *li*, which consisted of traditional principles of government discovered in ancient times by enlightened thinkers and traditional norms and institutions practiced by the sage kings. To put this idea into practice, since the Han dynasty or perhaps earlier, imperial China developed the famous royal examination system as a strict gateway for Confucian scholars to gain access to governmental positions. As Franklin W. Houn remarks,

> Facilitating social mobility and ensuring the government a continuing supply of the learned and, on the whole, capable personnel, this system soon became one of the most cherished Chinese political institutions. Consequently, to the old store of beliefs was added the new notion that holding unrestricted, competitive examinations regularly was an essential mark of good government and that discontinuing them would lead to social injustice and political disorder.[64]

The system of royal examination was introduced in Vietnam in the Lý dynasty and remained a principal institution for recruiting officials in the subsequent dynasties of Trần, Lê, and Nguyễn.[65] Particularly, in concordance with the political norm *thân hiền* (*cherishing the talents*), the early Nguyễn dynasty considerably developed Confucian education and the royal examination system to train competent personnel for the imperial government.[66]

To begin with, the early Nguyễn dynasty initiated various policies to reinforce Confucian education to prepare students for royal examinations. In addition to the *Quốc tự giám* (*national university*), which was moved from Hà Nội to the new capital at Huế, a number of local schools were established at provincial and district levels. Furthermore, to promote Confucian studies, the dynasty constructed the *văn miếu* (*temples of Confucius*) and the stone steles to inscribe the names of graduates in every province. The court even ordered the establishment of the societies of the *hội tư văn* (*Confucian scholars*) in every village.[67]

Along with the promotion of Confucian education and studies, the Nguyễn dynasty intensified the royal examination system with reference to the Chinese experience and especially the previous achievements of the Lê dynasty. The titles of the winners, the system of multi-stage examination consisting of *thi hương* (*provincial examination*), *thi hội* (*metropolitan examination*), and *thi đình* (*palace examination*), and rules of the exam area were meticulously regulated.[68] Notably, the dynasty established stringent disciplines for the examination. Corruption and cheating at the exams would be seriously sanctioned as crimes. The regulations of the exam even excluded from the exam students who violated the Confucian moral norms like lack of *xiao* (filial piety) or *li* (ritual) in their familial behaviors.[69]

Throughout its existence, the Nguyễn dynasty held 47 *thi hương* (provincial examinations) with 6,165 graduates titled as cử nhân (bachelor) and *tú tài* (baccalaureate) and 39 *thi hội* (metropolitan examinations) with 558 *tiến sĩ* (doctoral laureates).[70] The holders of the titles of doctoral laureates would be invited to the palace for the *thi đình* (palace examination) in which the king would ask questions and read candidates' responses and then rank them.[71] In the course of the policy of "four negations" (*tư bất*), the Nguyễn dynasty eliminated the title *Trạng nguyên* (first doctoral laureate) and only conferred two *Bảng nhãn* (second doctoral laureate) and nine *Thám hoa* (third doctoral laureate).[72]

During the beginning of the dynasty under Emperor Gia Long, the royal examination system had not been developed, and the officials were selected among the meritorious men and the graduates in the exams organized by the precedent Lê dynasty. However, since the time of Minh Mệnh, as the royal examination system was significantly enhanced, the practice of recruitment of officials through the royal exams was mandatory,[73] except in some special cases, such as recommendation by incumbent officials at the request of the emperor.[74]

The constitutional significance of the royal examination system should be recognized. The system enabled the Confucian scholars from ordinary families to gain access to governmental positions. Appointment through royal exams might sometimes not be in the imperial interest, but because the practice was deeply rooted in the tradition as an embodiment of cultural politics and was underpinned by the great endorsements of the public, especially the community of Confucian intelligentsia, the emperor was not free to repudiate it.[75] The recruitment of officials through the mechanism of royal examination therefore constricted the imperial authority in the matter of personnel. Furthermore, the practice of this institution ensured that the emperor would be surrounded by Confucian scholars who would rectify the ruler in concordance with the constitutional norms.

Deliberative institutions

As discussed in Chapter 1, classical Confucian theory of government holds that the ruler should govern his kingdom with the advice of the wise and virtuous scholars. Institutionalizing this idea, the Nguyễn dynasty established important deliberative institutions which allowed the Confucian scholar-officials to participate in the policy-making process.

During the period of the partially de facto control of the country in the Gia Định territory with a military government, Nguyễn Ánh (later emperor Gia Long) introduced the institution called "*Nhà Công Đồng*" (literally *the* House of Public Agreement) in 1787. It was the assembly of key ministers where they deliberated and decided on military affairs and sometimes economic and social issues. The resolutions of the House were verified by the seal with the inscription 添言允協 (*thiêm ngôn doãn hiệp* – well-matched additional words).[76] After his formal enthronement, Gia Long retained this institution in his early reign at the capital, Huế.[77] In 1803, however, Gia Long replaced the *Nhà Công Đồng* with a more systematized institution, namely *Hội đồng Đình thần* (Council of Courtiers). The members of the Council consisted of senior ministers who resided in the capital. Four times a month, it assembled to resolve four categories of affairs: trans-ministerial affairs; legal cases appealed to the court; petitions against local bullies; and denouncements of corrupted mandarins.[78]

From the reign of Minh Mệnh onwards, the Council of Courtiers experienced some reforms. According to a regulation in 1822, its members were more extensive, including not only the officials residing in the capital but also some selected provincial officials. In terms of its functions, the Council was the forum for the scholar-officials to debate and to propose national policies. Practically, important national decisions, such as the abolition of the intermediate administrative unit Bắc Thành or the establishment of the *Đô sát Viện* (*Censorate*), were proposed and carefully deliberated by the Council and accepted afterward by the emperor. In addition, the Council was responsible for recommending candidates for important positions in the educational and supervisory institutions of the central government and the governors in the provincial and district levels. Finally, it was authorized to hear legal cases concerning felonies committed by senior ministers and other cases with capital punishment.[79]

Concerning its operation, the Council of Courtiers assembled monthly on the second, eighth, sixteenth, and twentieth days. The agendas of the session consisted of two categories of matters: the ones regularly put forward by the Council and the ones occasionally raised by the emperor. To prepare for a session, the relevant institutions (ministries, departments, and boards) would draft and distribute the proposals two days in advance to the members of the Council. After each session, if the Council reached an agreement, it would prepare a suggestion with the signatures of the members and submit it to the emperor. Opposing opinions were recorded for later references. In some crucial sessions, the Censorate would attend and supervise the operation of the Council.[80]

The Council of Courtiers was seemingly a "dynastic parliament." It can be considered the external scholastic check of the imperial authority. In fact, the decisions of the Council were advisory rather than definitive.[81] However, even though the emperor could in theory determine all national affairs, he was not free to practice this arbitrarily as the Council of Courtiers was the platform for the Confucian scholar-officials to restrain his discretion. A priori, practically, the emperor often accepted the decisions of the Council or just made some minor modifications.[82] Minh Mệnh even believed that to override the decisions of the Council would be autocratic. To illustrate, in 1827, he requested the Council to recommend some candidates for some districts, and when the suggestion was submitted, he said: "The Council of Courtiers is my arms and legs and my eyes. Once I authorize it to select the candidates, but still I retain the determination, is it autocratic?" He then followed the suggestion.[83]

The practice of the Council of Courtiers indicates that the Nguyễn rulers could not decide national policies on their own. The process of national policy-making required deliberation among the Confucian scholar-officials in the Council before definitive decisions could be made. In short, the Council can be considered the structural limit of the imperial power.

Another deliberative institution which allowed the Confucian scholar-officials to participate in the national policy-making process was the *Viện Cơ mật* (*Privy*

Council). Emulating the Office of Military Plans of the Qing dynasty in China, in 1834 Minh Mệnh contrived the Privy Council "which will concern itself with secret strategies of a military country and confidential business."[84] The members of the body were selected from advanced Confucian scholar-officials. They consisted of four "*đại thần*" (great ministers) who served in other positions[85] concurrently and eight subordinate "*hành tẩu*" (apprentices) who were chosen by the Council of Courtiers among the personnel of the offices like the Six Ministries.[86]

In the early Nguyễn dynasty, the Privy Council was a rather powerful organ. It was the most prestigious organ for the senior Confucian scholar-officials to discuss and advise the ruler on a range of crucial issues concerning military, internal security, diplomatic relations, economic development and people's livelihoods. In addition, it was responsible for supervising the activities of the court. Finally, the Privy Council was the place where confidential documents and precious objects of the court were reserved.[87]

The Privy Council seemed to be a "dynastic cabinet." Consequential national affairs, rather than being individually decided by the ruler, required careful consideration by the senior Confucian scholar-officials through the medium of the Privy Council. It is in this sense that the Privy Council together with the Council of Courtiers could constitute structural limits of the royal authority.

Educative institution: imperial lecture

Lecturing political leaders may be an audacious idea today but it was actually a classical idea in Confucianism. As elaborated in Chapter 1, it was the view of classical Confucians that for a peaceful and orderly polity, the ruler should not only fully internalize moral principles but also be externally indoctrinated by wise and virtuous scholars.

Practically, the history of imperial East Asia witnessed the phenomenon of "imperial lecture" which refers to "the doctrination session in which Confucian scholars taught the emperor moral principles of government while explicating Confucian classics and history."[88] Its provenance was traceable back to the Han dynasty in China. During this period, there were often informal sessions in which the emperor summoned Confucian scholars for expositions of the Confucian Classics. But it was not until the Sung dynasty in tenth-century China that the imperial lecture was institutionalized under a concrete form rendered in Chinese as *jingyan* (literally "the classics mat"). In the subsequent dynasties of China (Yuan, Ming, Qing) the institution continued to be an integral part of the imperial government.[89] The institution of imperial lecture from the Sung dynasty was adopted in Korea, referred to in Korean as *kyong-yon*, at the beginning of the twelfth century during the reign of King Yejong of Koryo dynasty, but remained rather nominal in the next two centuries before becoming effective under the Choson dynasty.[90]

The institution of imperial lecture, in Vietnamese *kinh diên*, was introduced in Vietnam in 1128 under the reign of King Lý Thần Tông (1128–1138) of the

Lý dynasty[91] and remained a permanent institution in the government of the subsequent dynasties of Trần and Lê. In the Nguyễn dynasty, the institution was re-established under the rule of Emperor Thiệu Trị.[92] Thiệu Trị explained that the reason he constituted the imperial lecture stemmed from the proposal submitted by two censors of circuits Trần Văn Ý and Võ Tự. The proposal suggested that on days of leisure, the emperor should together with "great ministers" construe the meanings of the classics and discuss the principles of governance in order to comprehend the good things as well as the bad things of the past and to realize the annoyance of the people.[93] After reading the proposal, Thiệu Trị stated:

> These mandarins said reasonable words. I think that the formerly sage and enlightened kings who created great achievements which have been consistently exalted were all hard learners.... Now I, a junior who accedes to the throne to order the nation and rule the people, need assistance and establish the *kinh diên*.[94]

Kinh diên, then, became the forum for the Confucian scholar-officials to lecture the classics to the emperor and to discuss with him theoretical and practical issues concerning national governance.[95]

With the Nguyễn government, there was a special organ named *Viện Tập Hiền* (literally the institute where the talented and virtuous assemble) responsible for various affairs concerning the *kinh diên* (imperial lecture). Its directors were two advanced *kinh diên giảng quan* (mandarin-lecturers) selected among the great ministers. It had six *nhật giảng quan* (daily mandarin-lecturers) responsible for delivering the lectures. Additionally, there were various other scholars (with different titles, such as *Thị độc học sĩ*, *Thị độc*, *Thừa chỉ*, *Trước tác*, *Tu Soạn*) whose functions were to prepare and reserve the materials of the lectures and to record the words and actions of the emperor during the sessions.[96]

The site for imperial lectures was located at the *Điện Khâm Văn* (Hall of Imperial Literature) during the rule of Thiệu Trị and later moved to *Điện Văn Minh* (Hall of Civilization) under the rule of Tự Đức.[97] This implied that the location of the imperial lectures was the place for enlightenment.

Annually, the imperial lecture was inaugurated in February and ended on 28 November with a royal ceremony. Monthly, six sessions were held on the second, eighth, twelfth, eighteenth, twenty-second, and twenty-eighth days.[98] Attendants of the imperial lectures consisted of the emperor, royals (*hoàng thân*), and all great ministers (*quan đại thần*).[99] In the sessions, the mandarin-lecturers were seated instead of standing,[100] implying that they were not acting as the servants of the emperor. The curriculum of the imperial lectures included the *Four Books* and the *Five Classics*. Some neo-Confucian texts were also studied, such as the *Extended Meaning of the Great Learning* (Chinese: *Daxue Yanji*, Vietnamese: *Đại học Diễn nghĩa*).[101] In addition, the Nguyễn *kinh diên* appropriated a number of books made use of in the *jingyan* of the Qing dynasty. Finally, some particular textbooks prepared by the *Viện Tập Hiền* were also included in the curriculum of the imperial lectures.[102]

Scholars have pointed out the constitutional significance of the imperial lectures. In the case of traditional China, Yon-Ung Kwon believes that the imperial lectures played the role of moralizing the imperial government.[103] Hahm contends that the imperial lecture was "a forum in which the ruler could be educated and disciplined by Confucians in the 'kingly way'" and "did not cease to function as constitutional check, or regularized restraint, on the ruler."[104]

It can be anticipated that Confucian scholar-officials' exposition of the principles of government, political norms, traditional institutions, and ruling models of the ancient kings recorded in the classics and other Confucian works could influence the understanding and action of the monarch. Through the medium of the imperial lectures, the Confucian scholar-officials became the interpreters and the guardians of the classics as a source of the dynasty's "constitutional norms." They hence could constrict the ruler's monopolization of the interpretation of the Confucian Classics for his egoistic interests. It is in this sense that the imperial lectures could play the role of constitutional protection. Another implication of the imperial lecture was its potential contribution to the discernibility of the "dynastic constitution." The imperial lectures were a fairly open forum for the Confucian scholar-officials to make clear to various members of the court the political principles, percepts, norms, and institutions which were controlling the operation of the polity, and this induced the latent limitation of the individual calculations of the ruler. In short, the imperial lectures can be recognized as an institutionalized forum for the scholar-officials to rectify the use of royal power.

Remonstrative institution: censorate

In Chapter 1 I demonstrated that remonstrance against the ruler is a constitutional principle in classical Confucian theory of government. Candid admonishment to the ruler to guarantee his practice of imperial power in accordance with the *li*-civilized norms and institutions is both the legitimate right and the humanizing duty of the Confucian scholar-officials. Imperial government in the history of East Asia institutionalized this Confucian principle.

In Chinese imperial government, all the officials of the mandarin system were expected to fulfill the task of criticizing the ruler. According to Franklin W. Houn, every regular bureaucrat of the administrative system, apart from particularly assigned administration, might sporadically admonish the ruler either on his own initiative or in the course of response to a royal consultation.[105] In imperial China, there was, however, a specialized institution named censorate (*yushitai*, latter *duchayuan*), particularly designed for the group of scholar-officials called "talking officials" to impeach the corrupt or incompetent mandarins and to remonstrate against the emperor.[106] The specialized censorship in imperial China, according to Charles O. Hucker, was

> highly organized, highly systemized, and highly institutionalized, concentrated in particular governmental agencies and officials whose prescribed function was to impeach or remonstrate or both, vested with high prestige

> and special sanctions, providing a routine surveillance over all governmental activities.[107]

The Chinese censorial system was traced back to the Qin dynasty, and, in the Ming dynasty, it achieved a high degree of complexity in terms of both its structure and its function.[108] In the subsequent dynasties in China, the censorate, in spite of its changes in name, personnel, and institutional relation to other agencies, remained a permanent component of the Chinese imperial governments.[109]

Imperial Korea also institutionalized the Confucian principle of remonstrance. In the Choson dynasty, an institution named Office of Remonstrance (*Saganwon*) was a forum for the Confucian scholar-officials to criticize the ruler on all national affairs. In addition, there was another institution called Office of Inspection (*Sahonbu*) responsible for investigating and impeaching misconduct by officials. The two institutions normally operated in tandem, and hence were commonly rendered as an entity under the name *taegan* (censorate).[110]

In imperial Vietnam, generally speaking, occupants of the throne were adherent to the Confucian teaching of frank criticism to the ruler. The early Nguyễn rulers were also loyal to this tradition. To illustrate, when Emperor Gia Long initially ascended the throne, he delivered a royal proclamation requesting *chiếu cần lời nói thẳng* (straightforward words).[111] Interestingly, Minh Mệnh composed a poem to mock the fact that Tang-dynasty Emperor Xuanzong neglected the royal business because of his being amorous with concubine Yang Guifei, and Minh Mệnh then talked to his ministers:

> Since I have ascended the throne, I have wholeheartedly taken care of the affairs ... I do not dare to be leisured. But I do not know whether I can keep being like this in the future. The virtue of the king is not to be leisured. In case afterwards I am tired or not as diligent as before, you should read this poem to mock me. This will certainly make me repent.[112]

Practically, there is much historical evidence indicating that the Nguyễn rulers were often criticized by the scholar-officials, and even the common people.[113]

Apart from social criticism and the regular officials' criticism, there existed an institution within the Nguyễn government for the Confucian scholar-officials to censure the ruler. The institution of censorate was introduced from China into Vietnam in the Lý dynasty, named as *Ngự sử đài* (equivalent to the Chinese *yushitai*). The successive Trần and Lê dynasties followed this practice.[114] In the Nguyễn dynasty, the censorial institution was established under the reign of Minh Mệnh in 1832, renamed as *Đô sát viện* (equivalent to the Chinese *duchayuan*). For convenience, in this study it is referred to as "the Censorate."

Minh Mệnh realized that the censorial institution was highly relevant to the *phong hóa kỷ cương* (morality and order) of the polity and requested the Council of Courtiers to discuss the founding of the institution. In the view of the Council,

> The establishment of the institution of talking officials (*ngôn quan*) was ancient. [In China], dynasties from Han, Tang, Sung to Ming and Qing all found it. Its name was different [in different dynasties] but its permanent functions were supervision and impeachment. With the advent of the *Collected Institutions* (*Hội Điển*) of the Qing dynasty, the regulations on the Censorate were sufficient. Our dynasty has institutions which are different from those of the Qing. Hence, it should be based on this to adjust what should be used.[115]

On this ground, it can be said that the establishment of the Censorate in the Nguyễn dynasty was critically drawn from the Chinese experience, especially the Qing's censorial system.[116]

The structure of the Nguyễn Censorate was rather complex. Its leaders consisted of four senior officials entitled *Tả đô Ngự sử* (Censor-in-chief of the Left), *Hữu đô Ngự sử* (Censor-in-chief of the Right), *Tả phó đô Ngự sử* (Vice Censor-in-chief of the Left), and *Hữu phó đô Ngự sử* (Vice Censor-in-chief of the Right). The institution was traditionally headed by the Censor-in-chief of the Left.[117] The Nguyễn Censorate sheltered six *lục khoa* (Offices of Scrutiny) led by six *chưởng ấn cấp sự trung* (senior supervising secretaries).[118] Each Office of Scrutiny supervised several specific central institutions. In addition, there were 16 *giám sát ngự sử* (investigating censors) assigned in 16 *đạo* (circuits), which included all Vietnam, which supervised the officials of the capital city of Huế and one or several provinces.[119]

The Censorate had important functions vis-à-vis the emperor. It could remonstrate with the emperor on misconduct of the court and submit recommendations with respect to the livelihood of the people and consequential and confidential affairs of the court.[120] By this power, the Censorate could put some limitations on the practice of the imperial power. The Censorate was the institutionalized forum for the Confucian scholar-officials to rectify the ruler in accordance with the Confucian principles of good governance. Through frank criticism, the Confucian scholar-officials could help restrain the usurpation of authority for personal benefit and hence ensure that the emperor's policies were for the benefit of the people as required by the *minben* principle. The Censorate could also help guarantee the operation of the imperial royal power in accordance with traditional civilized norms and institution or the *li*. Finally, by rebuking the misconduct of the emperor through the medium of the censorial system, the Confucian scholar-officials could help ensure the conformity of the emperor's personal conduct with Confucian morality. In short, such structuralized disposition had the potential of restraining the ruler from acting in accordance with his personal propensity.

Apart from the remonstrant function, the Nguyễn Censorate had the historiographical function, which was highly relevant to both formal and informal activities of the emperor. It was allocated the task of recording every word and action of the ruler both in formal imperial audiences and in his outside trips. The original reference of this practice can be found in the *Liji* (*Book of Rites*), one of the Five Classics: "His [the emperor's] actions were written down by the recorder of the Left, and his utterances by the recorder of the Right."[121] There existed special officials of the so-called *qijuzhu* (*Diaries of Activities and Repose*) which were maintained erratically throughout the imperial history of China, apparently from the beginning of the Han dynasty.[122] The officials of *qijuzhu* were responsible for recording in detail all governmental actions of the emperor and all matters dealt with in official imperial audiences.[123] This institution was practiced in the Nguyễn dynasty. According to the *Veritable Records of Đại Nam*, in the official imperial audiences there were two censors appointed as officials of *khởi cư chú* (Vietnamese equivalent of the Chinese term *qijuzhu*), responsible for recording all words and actions of the emperor. Even in outside trips, the emperor was also accompanied by these two historiographers. At the end of each month, they compiled and handed the records to the National Historian Office (*Quốc Sử Quán*).[124] The emperor was not allowed to read these records to guarantee the objectivity and truthfulness.[125] The records of the officials of *Diaries of Activities and Repose* served as the raw materials for the National Historian Office to compose the verifiable records of the dynasty.

Remarking on the above quotation in the *Liji*, Wolfgang Franke helpfully identified the constitutional function of the historiographer: "This statement shows clearly the traditional Chinese conception of the task of the historiographer: to restrain the ruler from irresponsible or criminal actions by recording minutely and imperturbably all affairs coming to his knowledge."[126] In the case of the Nguyễn dynasty, it is intriguing that the task of recording the imperial diary was allocated to the Censorate and hence the censors become the historiographers. This can be explained by the fact that historiography implied censorial effect. By accompanying the ruler both in his imperial audience and in outside trips, and meticulously recording his verbal transactions and physical motions, the censorial historiographers functioned as constant surveillance of the ruler.

Historical institution: National Historian Office

It has been mentioned that the historiographers of the Censorate were the routine watchdogs of the ruler. There was, however, a special institution called the National Historian Office (*Quốc sử Quán*) within the Nguyễn government which provided the concentrating forum for the Confucian scholar-officials to fetter the imperial power by the special means of history.

It should first be noted that history occupies an important position in Confucian political philosophy. As illustrated previously, in Confucianism, the rule of *li* actually means the rule of tradition. Traditionalist discourse in Confucian theory on government naturally leads to the emphasis on the role of history. Confucius particularly emphasizes the role of history in good governance. He repeatedly invoked the historic paragons of governance recorded in the *Shu Jing* to extrapolate principles of government. Most notably, he composed the famous historical work *Spring and Autumn Annals* or *Chunqiu*, whose goals were not merely to record the history of the Lu state but more substantially to provide governing standards and prophecy for the contemporary and future generations of governors. Tu Wei-ming helpfully generalizes that, in Confucian vision, history is

> not a chronological record of what happen.... Rather, history's function is that of wise counsel about the future as well as the present, which is offered as a communal verdict written by an informed observer and not as private opinion. The historian so conceived is the conscience of the collective memory we all share. His responsibility is not only to show what has already been done but also to suggest, whenever appropriate, what other possibilities may have existed and why the failure to realize them has led to disastrous consequences. To write history is therefore a political act committed in the name of the human community as a whole.[127]

Following the Confucian teachings, imperial governments in Confucian nations such as China and Korea took history seriously, which is mostly evident by the fact that in each dynasty in the two countries there were regular historian offices in the imperial government.[128]

On the grounds of Confucian tradition and Chinese experience, imperial rulers of Vietnam also recognized the significance of history and institutionalized the historiography. Specialized historian institutions variously named as Historian Office (*Sử quán*) or National Historian Institute (*Quốc sử Viện*) were a permanent agency in the imperial government from the Trần dynasty to the Lê dynasty.[129] Following this practice, the early emperors of the Nguyễn dynasty were highly conscious of the important role of history, and established a specialized agency responsible for historical work. Gia Long established the Historical Bureau (*Sử cục*) in 1811. However, it was a small-scale agency and deficient in terms of its personnel.[130] It was not until the reign of Minh Mệnh that an extensive and well-structured historian institution, namely the National Historian Office (*Quốc sử Quán*), was established, in 1820; it existed until 1945, with great achievements. The institution is the author of voluminous annuals and a number of other works regarding Vietnamese culture, literature, geology, government, and law. Most notable are: *Veritable Records of Đai Nam* (*Đại Nam Thực Lục*) – a 588-volume annual of the reign of the Nguyễn family; *Collected Institutions of Đai Nam* (*Đại Nam Hội điển Sử lệ*) – a 262-volume work describing the governmental structure of the Nguyễn dynasty; *Minh Mệnh's Principal Policies* (*Minh Mệnh Chính yếu*) – the records of essential policies implemented by Minh Mệnh; and *Imperial Annals of Việt* (*Việt sử Thông giám Cương mục*) – a 53-volume chronicle of Vietnamese history from antiquity to the Lê dynasty.

The historians of the Nguyễn dynasty in particular, and of the Vietnamese imperial government in general, as students of the Confucian school, normally regarded Confucius' *Chunqiu* as the model for their works. Like the *Chunqiu*, major historical works of imperial Vietnam like the *Completed Annals of Đại Việt* by Ngô Sĩ Liên and other historians of the Lê dynasty, the *Veritable Records of Đại Nam* and *Imperial Annals of Viet*, by the National Historian Office of the

Nguyễn dynasty, recorded historical events in chronological order. More importantly, the writing style of the *Chunqiu*, based on the spirit of *zheng ming* (*rectification of names*), significantly influenced the Vietnamese court historians. Consequently, by authorizing imperial chronicles, the Vietnamese court historians could position the constitutional *zheng ming* roles similar to those of Confucius in his *Chunqiu*. Let us illustrate by the case of the historians of the Nguyễn court, mainly with the *Veritable Records of Đại Nam* – the most important annual of the dynasty – and the other relevant historical work, the *Collected Institutions of Đại Nam*.

First, in the *Veritable Records of Đai Nam*, the historians of the Nguyễn court, like Confucius in the *Chunqiu*, gave names and definitions to political phenomena. The *Records* clearly defined governmental terms and clarified governmental events. However, different from the *Chunqiu*'s concise style, the *Veritable Records of Đại Nam* interpreted the terms and events in quite a verbose manner. The "constitutional" meaning of the interpretation is that it made clear to the court and the general public governmental terms and phenomena, which is the base for the operation of public power in a transparent and objective manner.

Second, the historians defined fundamental principles of governmental organization and particular spheres of actions of the government's members. This can be found in the *Veritable Records of Đại Nam*, but more evidently in the *Collected Institutions of Đại Nam*, which defined in detail the principles of organization and operation, the authorities and the duties of various governmental institutions of the Nguyễn dynasty. By this, the historians objectified the standards of the polity and established a transparent foundation for the practice of the public authority.

Third, through recording historical events, the historians passed critical judgments ("*praise-and-censure*" – Chinese: *pao-pien*; Vietnamese: *bao biếm*) on the action of the ruler and other members of the imperial government. However, different from Confucius' judgment by the strategy of meticulous terminology, the Nguyễn court historians practiced this in a more explicit and verbose style. In theory, the constitutional meaning of the historians' praise-and-censure is that it affected the practice of imperial power by encouraging good deeds and limiting bad deeds by the ruler. Practically, a comparison of the *Completed Annals of Đại Việt* with the *Veritable Records of Đai Nam* suggests that the court historians of the Lê dynasty were more active and willing in censuring the emperor than those of the Nguyễn dynasty. The *Veritable Records of Đại Nam* recorded historical events in either a neutral or praising manner.

That is why Vietnamese historical scholars tend to conclude that the Nguyễn dynasty appropriated the National Historian Office and historical means in general to legitimize its rule and elevate the position of the Nguyễn family in Vietnamese history.[131] The monarch could take advantage of the means of history to legitimize and honor his rule. However, he might be well aware of the fact that to be recorded in history was to be subject to the critical judgment of not merely the historians, but ultimately entire future generations.[132] This consciousness could constantly remind him to be considerate and responsible in his actions and hence be instrumental in preventing him from bad deeds. It is in this way that the historians could curb the arbitrariness of the imperial power.

Moreover, as the court historians were normally selected from the Confucian scholars who possessed a high level of probity, the ruler was not free to force them to distort the historical events according to his personal interests. The *Veritable Records of Đại Nam*, as its name indicates, recorded the true events. Consequently, to be legitimized and honored by history, the ruler had to act in a way that was consistent with the Confucian requirements of an ideal and legitimate king (such as receiving the Mandate from Heaven, being virtuous and talented, working for the happiness of the people, following the rule of *li*, employing wise and virtuous men and respecting their advice and criticisms), about which the court historians were educated prior to their appointment to the National Historian Office. Therefore, to be praised by history, the ruler was expected to limit his wrongdoings and govern the kingdom in a way that could provide meaningful standards and lessons for later governors. History and the historians could hence become the special means to rectify the use of imperial power.

Discussion

It is no longer proper to view government in imperial East Asia as pure despotism. First, this is because the ruler was subject to numerous constitutional norms: the models of ancient kings, the political norms in the Classics, the ancestral precedents, and the institutions of the precedent dynasties. One may reject that argument by stating that any polity has a set of constitutive norms as fundamental principles by which it is organized, and the Confucian polity is not an exceptional case. To be sure, constitutionalism is not merely about the norms by which the state is organized but is about the norms by which the state *ought* to be organized. Louis Henkin states that the practice of constitutionalism involves not a constitution merely describing "the kind of government and the institutions of government that have already been established" but a constitution "establishing a blueprint for how government is to be organized and what the governors must do if government and governors are to have constitutional legitimacy."[133]

One may question whether the Confucian norms mentioned above are qualified to be called "constitutional." They are "constitutional" because they are normative limits of the royal power. The Confucian norms do not merely describe the existing polity. Instead, they establish prescriptive standards that a ruler must follow if he and his court are to have legitimacy. As the embodiments of the tradition, the Confucian norms subjected the ruler to the universal moral and political truths and the shared values and beliefs of the community, generally accepted from generation to generation and hence presenting the social consensus. They constitute the prescriptive Confucian constitution and are hence meaningful to the practice of constitutionalism.

In addition, there were multiple structural institutions designed for the wise and virtuous scholars to participate in the imperial government to deliberate national affairs and to restrain the ruler's power in accordance with the traditional norms by various means, namely remonstrance, teaching, and praise-and-censure. With such complex institutional arrangements, the arbitrary power could be controlled and the constitutional norms could be put into practice to a certain degree. Particularly, the willingness and the audacity of the scholar-officials and even of the commoners to criticize the emperor were useful for enforcing the constitutional norms.

Those who deny the practice of Confucian constitutionalism in imperial East Asia may argue that the imperial polity lacks effective institutional mechanisms to enforce the Confucian norms in the case that the ruler chose to infringe them. It is true that governments in the imperial history of East Asia did not have effective institutions of constitutional enforcements like modern constitutional governments. The following are among many stories drawing from the experiences of the Nguyễn dynasty showing the failure of the norms and the institutions in controlling the arbitrary practice of imperial power.

First is the case of the construction of Tự Đức's Imperial Mausoleum. Tự Đức constructed the Mausoleum when he was alive. In the statement about the Mausoleum, Tự Đức himself revealed the rejection of "heaven" and the people of that highly costly project:

> Since the Mausoleum has been built, lightning struck the *Hòa khiêm* palace, people rebelled, and deceived people invaded the doors of the palace. As the heaven has blamed and the people has resented, how can I do not dare to respect?[134]

Notwithstanding that, the construction of the Mausoleum was finished at the cost of the people's lives. These Vietnamese folk verses remain today: "*Vạn Niên*[135] *là Vạn Niên nào! Thành xây xương lính, hào đào máu dân*" ("Alas the *Vạn Niên*! Alas the *Vạn Niên*! It walls are built by the soldier's bones, and its trenches are dug by people's bloods"). Tự Đức's construction of his own mausoleum infringed the norms of *kính thiên* (*respecting the Heaven*) and *ái dân* (*loving the people*).

Another case is related to the fate of a scholar-official serving in *the institution of imperial lecture* (*Viện Tập hiền*) named Phạm Phú Thứ, who is popularly known in Vietnam today. He was a doctorate and appointed as a member of the *Viện Tập hiền* in the second year of Tự Đưc's reign (1849) to give lectures to the emperor. It is said that, as a junior emperor, Tự Đưc indulged in pleasures and neglected national affairs. One year after his appointment (1850), Phạm Phú Thứ submitted a remonstrant statement against the emperor. In response, the emperor dismissed and imprisoned him. Fortunately, thanks to the advice of the queen mother, Từ Dũ, the emperor recalled him to the palace and appointed him to hold a new position. Although Phạm Phú Thứ was reappointed, the story indicates that the scholar-officials in some cases failed to practice their remonstrant power.

Let us consider another case involving Minh Mệnh. Although he is more positively evaluated by the Vietnamese historical scholars among the early emperors of the Nguyễn dynasty, the following case shows his disregard of outright remonstrances. In 1831, Minh Mệnh took a journey to Ngũ Hành Sơn – a famous tourist site of Quảng Nam province. The emperor had visited this place in 1825 and 1827, but in 1831, while the province was suffering from serious drought which caused lean harvest for four suburban districts, he decided to take a trip to the place again. Many ministers admonished his tourist plan but the emperor ignored them. Phan Thanh Giản, a mandarin of Quảng Nam province, was in charge of receiving the emperor, but he also remonstrated against the tour and unfortunately was demoted for that action. The tour eventually did happen.[136]

When the emperor was on the road to return, a poor student stopped the emperor's palanquin and proposed a long impeachment of the emperor's trip. Invoking the models of the ancient kings and the Confucian Classics, the student stated:

> Whenever your Majesty takes long-day trip, this costs greatly, not to account for the burdensome and the annoyance of the people. Today, your Majesty has again visited Quang Nam, and the great ministers and other mandarins have remonstrated against this. Although I am an alone and mediocre inferior, I candidly submit to your Majesty some words. If your Majesty happens to be vexed and upset because of this, your Majesty forgets the Yu dynasty's mirror of listening to criticism of king's mistakes. In contrast, if your Majesty happens to be considerate and to treat the people as the most important element,[137] this will be the base of the dynasty. In this case, the lord is nothing more than a boat and the people are nothing more than water. It is only said that water sustains the boat; never is it said that the boat sustains water.[138] I dare to demand your Majesty not to disdain my stupid ideas in this suggestion and aspire you to practice them. In case you disdain and ignore my ideas and incriminate me because of the offense against the sovereign, I am ready to suffer the penalty without any regret.[139]

It is said that the audacious student was immediately arrested and punished with the death penalty, but some officials suggested the emperor let him live under surveillance by the court. The actual fate of the student is unclear.[140]

As Joseph Chan demonstrates, the perennial challenge of Confucianism is the gap between its political ideal and its political reality.[141] The above stories illustrate the gap between the ideal of Confucian constitutionalism promoted by classical Confucian thinkers and the reality of Confucian government in imperial East Asia. However, this is not specific to Confucian constitutionalism but is a common challenge to constitutionalism in general. Constitutionalism is always faced with the gap between the constitutional ideal and political reality. Even in the modern world, the constitutions and the courts are used in many places not for the ideal of constitutionalism but for the practical interests of authoritarianism.[142] Particularly, the phenomenon called "abusive constitutionalism" suggests that the mechanisms of constitution-making have been misappropriated by would-be autocrats to undermine constitutionalism.[143]

There are several factors that limited the practice of Confucian constitutionalism in imperial East Asia. To begin with, the Confucian institutions which had the potential to restrain the ruler's actions in accordance with the constitutional norms lacked the necessary independence. They were merely the institutions of the imperial government whose members were appointed by the ruler. In addition, Confucian constitutionalism is scholarly, not popular. The constitutional discourse of Confucian scholar-officials was not sustained by "we the people" due to imperial restrictions of political freedoms, such as freedoms of expression, assembly, and demonstration. This limits the impact of social intellectual authority. Consequently, when the siren song of despotic power was strong, the ruler would ignore Confucian institutional and normative restraints.

However, that does not mean that Confucian norms and institutions are merely a sham. In fact, Confucian constitutionalism in imperial East Asia can be achieved to a certain degree. To illustrate, consider how the norms *kính thiên* (*respecting the Heaven*) and *ái dân* (*loving the people*) could meaningfully control the actions of Emperor Minh Mênh of the Nguyễn dynasty. The chapter entitled *kính thiên* in *Minh Mệnh's Principal Policies* records such abnormal phenomena as droughts, inundations, epidemics, and earthquakes, and the emperor's attitude and corresponding policies. It indicates that the emperor often acknowledged that these were because of his imperfect governance and conduct, and this actually led to the further self-cultivation of his personal morality and his amelioration of the public policies, especially criminal policies.[144] In addition, *Minh Mệnh's Principal Policies* records numerous policies which Minh Mệnh introduced to practice the Confucian requirements of *minben* governance. For the livelihood of the people, Minh Mệnh reduced taxes, punished criminal slightly, distributed rice to the poor, provided rice, medicines, and financial aid to the victims of catastrophes, and the likes.[145] With regard to the officialdom, he employed the talented and virtuous and punished corrupt mandarins.[146] Concerning his own works, he was highly diligent in his businesses.[147]

Apart from that, there were cases suggesting that the emperor really respected the remonstrance of the scholar-officials. Tự Đức can be considered again. Nguyên Đắc Xuân, the most well-known specialist of the Nguyễn dynasty and past Huế in Vietnam, stated that although the construction and expenditure under the rule of Tự Đức were highly costly, he was not a despotic ruler.[148] During his reign, many scholar-officials remonstrated against him, and in many cases the emperor actually showed consideration for their words. The following are some examples.

Mandarins Trương Đăng Quế, Nguyễn Tri Phương, Lâm Gia Thiệp, Nguyễn Đăng Giai, and Phan Thanh Giản concurrently submitted a report to Tự Đức to criticize themselves but implicitly criticized the emperor. They said in the report:

> We hold key political positions. The one who is responsible for the employment affair is not selective enough to create a transparent mandarinate and hence the talented and the incompetent cannot be distinguished. The one who is responsible for finance and tax do not often clarify the profits and

> hence the corrupted has not all been penalized. While the deities demand candour, the one who is responsible for the state's rites is not respectful enough. While no one among the people do not want leisure, the one who is responsible for the military affairs do not know how to love the arduous people. The one who is responsible for criminal affairs is not upright and hence there are many unjust cases.... We do not know what to do. We request you to interrogate our unfulfillment of the responsibilities.

It is recorded that Tự Đức examined the report and also self-realized his mistakes.[149]

More direct criticism of the emperor and the court is shown in the case of Trương Quốc Dụng, a doctorate who is famous for his upright personality and his erudition. He passed through many positions in the imperial government, including serving as the head of the National Historian Office.[150] In 1848, when Tự Đức had just acceded to the throne, Trương Quốc Dụng submitted a letter to the emperor to criticize the affairs of the court, stating that the court's expenditures were lavish, trials of crimes were arbitrary and lacked respect for the laws, the appointments of mandarins were not selective, administrative procedures were complicated, and taxes were high. He then suggested corresponding remedies. After reading the letter, Tự Đức requested the Council of Courtiers to examine the problems and implement the suggested remedies.[151]

Another case concerning Thân Văn Nhiếp should be recalled. He was a doctorate, who also passed through many positions in the imperial government, and is famous for his probity talks.[152] In 1866 he submitted a petition to Tự Đức to criticize his luxurious life, saying that:

> Reigning in the precious nine-storey palace, think about the destroyed houses of the Southern people. Viewing the beautiful storey of the mausoleum, think about the graves on fields' mounds of the Southern people. Seizing sapphires, think about the empty productions in the South.

The emperor responded that the statements were "plain but pressing" and requested the Council of Courtiers and the Privy Council to consider the possible implementation of the proper suggestions.[153] As the situation was not considerably ameliorated, in 1868 Thân Văn Nhiếp sent the second petition to Tự Đức, particularly rebuking his construction of the imperial Mausoleum. In the conclusion, he stated:

> As your Majesty possesses the nation but does not regret it, I do not regret my head. I have made petitions for many times, but the problems have not been handled. Now I offend the taboos again I am ready for death.

The emperor replied that: "the things you rebuke are my faults."[154]

Thus, Confucian constitutionalism was actually implemented in imperial East Asia to a certain degree. Although Confucian institutions lacked necessary independence and Confucian constitutional discourse was not sustained by the people, Confucian constitutionalism can be achieved to a certain degree thanks to a special power, namely the power of tradition. The Confucian norms were the embodiments of reasonable principles authenticated in the tradition, which presented the social consensus and conditioned the activities of the ruling class. The continuation of the traditional norms could stabilize the dynasty while the discontinuation of them might result in social chaos. As the Confucian norms and the institutions were firmly established in the past with social acceptance, the ruler was not free to go against them without risking the ruin of his reign. Although there were no independent institutions to protect the scholar-officials from the ruler's chastisement, it was the power of tradition that could regularly compel the ruler to follow the established norms and advice, teachings, and frank remonstrance of the scholar-officials as a constitutional culture. This is more justifiable if we take into account the fact that even the practice of modern constitutionalism also relies on the power of tradition or constitutional culture.[155]

In short, Confucian governments in imperial East Asia are neither purely despotic nor purely constitutional. It is fairer to view them as governments of a complex nexus of both despotic practices and constitutional practices.

Conclusion

The present chapter has examined the practice of imperial Confucian constitutionalism in pre-modern East Asia. The investigation has revealed numerous norms as the embodiment of *li* used to rectify the royal authority, namely the models of ancient kings, the political norms in the Classics, the ancestral precedents, and the institutions of the precedent dynasties. In addition, the chapter has also discovered structuralized fora enabling the scholar-officials to use the norms to rectify the royal power, including the royal examination system, the deliberative institutions, the educative institution, the remonstrative institution, and the historical institution. The chapter concludes that the practice of imperial Confucianism was limited due to the lack of institutional independence and popular mobilization, but could be achieved to a certain degree thanks to the power of tradition.

This exploration is important not only for our improved understanding of imperial government and the law in pre-modern East Asia, but also for the development of constitutional government in modern East Asia. In a less positive scenario, the cultural traditions cannot be imputed as impediments of the development of modern constitutional government in modern East Asia. In a more positive scenario, traditional Confucian norms and institutions may be used and integrated in the modern projects of promoting constitutionalism in modern East Asia. In the next chapter I will consider how modern Confucianists integrated Confucian tradition with Western values of modern constitutionalism to formulate their vision of modern Confucian constitutionalism.

Notes

1 This view can be traced back to C.S. Montesquieu's description of imperial China as a despotic state. C.S. Montesquieu, *The Spirit of the Laws*, trans. Thomas Nugent (New York: Hafner Publishing Company, 1962), 125.
2 Karl A. Wittfogel, *Oriental Despotism: A Comparative Study of Total Power* (New Haven, CT and London: Yale University Press, 1963) 101–102.
3 Chaihark Hahm, "Confucian Constitutionalism" (SJD dissertation, Harvard Law School, 2000); Hahm Chaihark, "Constitutionalism, Confucian Civic Virtue, and Ritual Propriety," in *Confucianism for the Modern World*, ed. Daniel A. Bell and Hahm Chaibong (Cambridge: Cambridge University Press, 2003), 31–53; Chaihark Hahm, "Conceptualizing Korean Constitutionalism: Foreign Transplant or Indigenous Tradition?" *Journal of Korean Law* 1(2) (2001): 15; Chaihark Hahm, "Ritual and Constitutionalism: Disputing the Ruler's Legitimacy in a Confucian Polity," *American Journal of Comparative Law* 57 (2009): 135.
4 Pierre-Étienne Will, "Virtual Constitutionalism in the Late Ming Dynasty," in *Building Constitutionalism in China*, ed. Stéphanie Balme and Michael W. Dowdle (New York: Palgrave Macmillan, 2009), 261–274.
5 See, generally, Trần Trọng Kim, *Nho Giáo* [*Confucianism*] (Hanoi: Culture and Infomation Publishing House, 2001).
6 Nguyễn Minh Tường, *Cải cách Hành chính dưới Triều Minh Mệnh (1820–1840)* [*Administrative Reform under the Reign of Minh Mệnh (1820–1840)*] (Hanoi: Social Science Publishing House, 1996).
7 Thomas C. Grey, "Constitutionalism: Analytic Framework" in *Constitutionalism, Nomos XX*, ed. J. Roland Pennnock and John W. Chapman (New York: New York University Press, 1979), 202.
8 Ibid.
9 Ibid.
10 Ibid.
11 Ibid., 204.
12 Hahm, "Korean Constitutionalism," 169–179.
13 Ibid., 174.
14 Will, "Virtual Constitutionalism," 262.
15 Hahm, "Korean Constitutionalism," 174–175.
16 Ibid., 182.
17 Ibid., 182–183.
18 Will, "Virtual Constitutionalism," 262 (original italic).
19 Ibid., 263.
20 Ibid.; Hahm, "Korean Constitutionalism," 184.
21 Hahm, "Korean Constitutionalism," 182.
22 Trần Văn Giàu, *Sự Phát Triển của Tư tưởng ở Việt Nam, Tập I* [*The Development of Thoughts in Vietnam, Volume I*] (Hanoi: Social Science Publishing House, 1973), 306. The Confucian concept of the way of the mean is principally expressed in the work *Doctrine of the Mean*, one of the Four Books, reportedly authorized by Zisi, a grandson of Confucius.
23 Nguyễn Dynasty's National Historian Office, *Khâm định Đại Nam Hội điển Sự Lệ, Tập VII* [*Collected Institutions of Đại Nam, Volume VII*], translated into modern Vietnamese by Trần Huy Hân and Nguyễn Thế Đạt (Huế: Thuận Hóa Publishing House, 1993), 477–478.
24 Cited in Trần Văn Giàu [*The Development of Thoughts in Vietnam, Volume I*], 307.
25 Nguyễn Dynasty's National Historian Office, *Đại Nam Thực Lục Chính Biên, tập XXIII* [*Veritable Records of Đại Nam, Volume XXIII*], translated into modern Vietnamese by the Translation Group of the Institute of Historical Studies (*Viện Sử học*) (Hanoi: Social Science Publishing House, 1970), 145.

26 Nguyễn Dynasty's National Historian Office, *Minh Mệnh Chính yếu, Tập I* [*Minh Mệnh's Principal Policies, Volume I*], translated into modern Vietnamese by the Translation Committee [*Ủy ban Dịch Thuật*] (Huế: Thuận Hóa Publishing House, 1994). (*Quyển 1, Thiên thứ nhất- Kính thiên* [*Book 1, First Chapter – Respecting the Heaven*], 23–50; *Quyển 1 – Thiên thứ hai- Pháp tổ* [*Book 1, Second Chapter – Following the Acenstors*], 51–62; *Quyển 5 – Cần Chính* [*Book 5 – Being Diligent in Political Affairs*], 205–230; *Quyển 6, 7 – Ái dân* [*Books 6 and 7 – Loving People*], 231–347.)

27 Trần Văn Giàu, [*The Development of Thoughts in Vietnam, Volume I*], 289–291.

28 Ibid., 292.

29 Sor-Hoon Tan, *Confucian Democracy: A Deweyan Reconstruction (*Albany, NY: State University of New York Press, 2003), 136–144.

30 Tạ Văn Tài, "Confucian Influences in the Traditional Legal System of Vietnam, with Some Comparisons with China: Rule by Law and Rule of Law," *Vietnamese Social Science Review* 1 (2009): 22–26.

31 Inside the Nguyễn government, there was a specialized institution helping the emperor in this task, named as *Khâm Thiên Giám* (Astronomical Office). Nguyễn Dynasty's National Historian Office, *Đại Nam Hội điển, Tập XV* [*Collected Institutions of Đại Nam, Volume XV*], 444.

32 Nguyễn Minh Tường, [*Administrative Reform*], 64.

33 Nguyễn Dynasty's National Historian Office, [*Minh Mệnh's Principal Policies, Volume I*], 341–342.

34 Legge, *Volume I, The Great Learning*, 374.

35 Nguyễn Dynasty's National Historian Office, [*Minh Mệnh's Principal Policies, Volume I*], 233.

36 Legge, *Volume I, The Great Learning*, 374.

37 Nguyễn Dynasty's National Historian Office, [*Minh Mệnh's Principal Policies, Volume I*], 233.

38 Ibid., 241.

39 Ibid., 283.

40 Nguyễn Minh Tường, "Vua Minh Mệnh với hai Tư tưởng Chính trị lớn của Ông: Củng cố Nền Thống nhất Quốc gia và Yêu Dân" ["King Minh Mệnh and His Great Political Thoughts: Reinforcing the National Unity and Loving the People"] in *Những Vấn đề Lịch sử và Văn Chương Triều Nguyễn* [*Historial and Literacy Issues of the Nguyễn Dynasty*], ed. Nguyễn Phong Nam (Hanoi: Educational Publishing House, 1997), 31.

41 Nguyễn Dynasty's National Historian Office, [*Collected Institutions of Đại Nam, Volume VII*], 477–478.

42 Cited in Trần Văn Giàu, [*The Development of Thoughts in Vietnam, Volume I*], 290–291.

43 Nguyễn Dynasty's National Historian Office, *Đại Nam Thực Lục* [*Veritable Records of Đại Nam*].

44 Nguyễn Q. Thắng *et al.*, translated into modern Vietnamese, *Hoàng Việt Luật Lệ (Luật Gia Long)* [*Laws of Imperial Viet or Gia Long Code*] (Hanoi: Culture and Information Publishing House, 1994).

45 Lương Ninh, *Lịch sử Việt Nam Giản yếu* [*Introduction of Vietnamese History*] (Hanoi: National Politics Publishing House, 2000), 318.

46 Trần Văn Giáp, *Tìm hiểu Kho sách Hán Nôm, Tập I* [*A Study of the Sino-Vietnamese Depository, Volume I*] (Hanoi: National Library, 1970), 97.

47 Đỗ Bang, ed., *Tổ chức Bộ Máy Nhà nước Triều Nguyễn (1802–1884)* [*Organization of State Apparatus of the Nguyễn Dynasty (1802–1884)*] (Huế: Thuận Hóa Publishing House, 1997), 14–16.

48 Nguyễn Dynasty's National Historian Office, [*Veritable Records of Đại Nam, Volume I*], 816.

49 Ibid.

50 Nguyễn Hữu Tâm, "Quá trình Hình thành Quốc sử Quán Triều Nguyễn" ["The Birth of the National Historian Office of the Nguyễn Dynasty"], *Journal of Historical Studies* 3 (2008): 42.

51 Nguyễn Dynasty's National Historian Office, [*Veritable Records of Đại Nam, Volume II*], 63.

52 Nguyễn Hữu Tâm, ["The National Historian Office"], 43.

53 Nguyễn Dynasty's National Historian Office, [*Veritable Records of Đại Nam, Volume II*], 128. For more detail on the biographies of Phan Huy Chú and his father Phan Huy Ích, see Nguyễn Q. Thắng and Nguyễn Bá Thế, *Từ điển Nhân vật Lịch sử Việt Nam* [*Dictionary of Vietnamese Historical Figures*] (Hanoi: Social Sciences Publishing House, 1991), 762–764.

54 The work was originally in Chinese. In 1957, the Saigon University Law School published in South Vietnam the modern Vietnamese translation of three parts of the Records concerning the mandarin system, public finance system, and criminal laws. Phan Huy Chú, *Lịch triều Hiến chương Loại Chí* [*Categorical Records of Institutions of the Precedent Dynasties*], trans. Cao Nãi Quang (Saigon: Saigon University Law School, 1957). The Records was completely translated into modern Vietnamese by Nguyễn Thọ Dực and published in South Vietnam in 1972. Phan Huy Chú, *Lịch triều Hiến chương Loại Chí, 10 Tập* [*Categorical Records of Institutions of the Precedent Dynasties, Ten Volumes*], trans. Nguyễn Thọ Dực (Saigon: Translation Committee, 1972). Under unified Vietnam, another Vietnamese version of the work was introduced by the Institute of Historical Studies. Phan Huy Chú, *Lịch triều Hiến chương Loại Chí, 4 Tập* [*Categorical Records of Institutions of the Precedent Dynasties, Four Volumes*], trans. Translation Group of the Institute of Historial Studies (Hanoi: Social Sciences Publishing House, 1992).

55 Đỗ Bang, [*The Nguyễn Dynasty*], 44.

56 Nguyễn Minh Tường, [*Administrative Reform*], 44.

57 Nguyễn Dynasty's National Historian Office, [*Veritable Records of Đại Nam, Volume X*], 16.

58 Ibid., 17.

59 Nguyễn Q. Thắng and Nguyễn Văn Tài, trans., *Hoàng Việt Luật Lệ (Luật Gia Long)* [*Laws of Imperial Viet or Gia Long Code*], 2.

60 Nguyễn Minh Tường, [*Administrative Reform*].

61 Grey, "Constitutionalism," 196.

62 Constitutional law scholars have recently tended to distinguish legal and political constitutionalism according to which the former depends on the court for the judicial review power to enforce the constitutional norms, while the latter relies on the mechanism of separation of powers and various forms of checks and balances for constitutional enforcement. See Marco Goldoni, "Two Internal Critiques of Political Constitutionalism," *International Journal of Constitutional Law* 10(4) (2012): 926–949.

63 Hahm, "Confucian Constitutionalism." For more details, see the subsequent sections.

64 Franklin W. Houn, *Chinese Political Traditions* (Washington, DC: Public Affairs Press, 1965), 70–71.

65 For the royal examination system in imperial Vietnam in general, see: Nguyễn Q. Thắng, *Khoa cử và Giáo dục Việt Nam* [*Vietnamese Examination and Education*] (Hanoi: Culture and Information Publishing House, 1993); Nguyễn Thế Long, *Nho học ở Việt Nam: Giáo dục và Thi Cử* [*Confucian Studies in Vietnam: Education and Examination*] (Hanoi: Education Publishing House, 1995); Bùi Xuân Đính, *Giáo dục và Khoa cử Nho học Thăng Long-Hà nội* [*Thăng Long-Hà nội's Education and Confucian Examination*] (Hanoi: Hanoi Publishing House, 2010); Phan Ngọc Liên, *Giáo dục và Thi cử Việt Nam Trước Cách mạng Tháng Tám 1945* [*Education and Examination in Vietnam Prior to the August 1945 Revolution* (Hanoi: Encyclopedia Publishing House, 2006).

66 See, generally, Lê Thị Thanh Hòa, *Việc Đào tạo và Sử dụng Quan lại của Triều Nguyễn từ Năm 1802 đến Năm 1884* [*Education and Use of Mandarins in the Nguyễn Dynasty from 1802 to 1884*] (Hanoi: Social Sciences Publishing House, 1998).

67 Nguyễn Thế Long, [*Confucian Studies in Vietnam*], 37.

68 Nguyễn Khắc Thuần, *Tiến trình Văn hoá Việt Nam từ Khởi thuỷ đến Thế kỷ thứ XIX* [*The Process of Vietnamese Culture from Antiquity to the 19th Century*] (Hanoi: Education Publishing House, 2007), 875.

69 Nguyễn Dynasty's National Historian Office, [*Veritable Records of Đại Nam, Volume X*], 340.

70 Phan Ngọc Liên, [*Education and Examination*],104.

71 Hữu Ngọc and Lady Borton, *Thi Cử Nho Giao – Royal Exams* (Hanoi: The World Publishing House, 2004), 19 (bilingual book).

72 Nguyễn Khắc Thuần, [*The Process of Vietnamese Culture*], 878–879.

73 Lê Thị Thanh Hòa, [*Education and Use of Mandarins*], 169.

74 Nguyễn Dynasty's National Historian Office, [*Minh Mệnh's Principal Policies, Volume I*], 161.

75 Even the princes and relatives of senior mandarins were also required to take royal exams to be appointed as officials. Lê Thị Thanh Hòa, [*Education and Use of Mandarins*], 182.

76 Lê Nguyễn Lưu, "Từ Ấn Công đồng và Đình thần đến Tiếng trống Đăng văn" ["From the Seals of the Court to the Drumbeat of Claiming Innocence"], *Journal of Research and Development* 84 (2011): 19.

77 Đỗ Bang, [*Nguyễn Dynasty*], 43.

78 Ibid.

79 Ibid., 45–46.

80 Ibid., 46–47.

81 Vũ Minh Giang, ed., *Những Đặc trưng Cơ bản của Bộ máy Quản lý Đất nước và Hệ thống Chính trị Nước ta Trước Thời kỳ Đổi mới* [*The Basic Characteristics of the Mechanism of National Governance and the Political System in Our Country Prior to the Renovation Period*] (Hanoi: National Political Publishing House, 2008), 100.

82 Lê Nguyễn Lưu, ["The Seals of the Court"], 22.

83 Nguyễn Dynasty's National Historian Office, [*Veritable Records of Đại Nam, Volume II*], 637.

84 Nguyễn Dynasty's National Historian Office, [*Veritable Records of Đại Nam, Volume XV*], 335; Nguyễn Dynasty's National Historian Office, *Đại Nam Hội điển, Tập I* [*Collected Institutions of Đại Nam, Volume I*], 199; Alexander Woodside, *Vietnam and the Chinese Model: A Comparative Study of Nguyen and Ch'ing Civil Government in the First Half of the Nineteenth Century* (Cambridge, MA: Council on East Asian Studies, Harvard University, 1988), 96–97.

85 Practially, they were often the ministers of the Six Ministries. Đỗ Bang, [*Nguyễn Dynasty*], 60.

86 Woodside, *Vietnam and the Chinese Model*, 99.

87 Đỗ Bang, [*Nguyễn Dynasty*], 59.

88 Yon-Ung Kwon, "The Imperial Lecture of Sung China," *Journal of Social Sciences and Humanities* 48 (1978): 103.

89 Ibid.; see also, Wm. Theodore de Bary, *Neo-Confucian Orthodoxy and the Learning of the Mind-and-Heart* (New York: Columbia University Press, 1981), 29–38.

90 Yon-Ung Kwon, "The Royal Lecture of Early Yi Korea," *Journal of Social Sciences and Humanities* 50 (1979): 56; Hahm, "Confucian Constitutionalism," 179.

91 Nguyễn Q. Thắng, [*Vietnamese Examination and Education*], 28.

92 Nguyễn Sĩ Giác, trans., *Đại Nam Điển Lệ Toát Yếu* [*Sumary of Institutions of Đại Nam*] (Ho Chi Minh City: Ho Chi Minh City Publishing House, 1993), 7.

93 Nguyễn Dynasty's National Historian Office, [*Collected Institutions of Đại Nam Volume I*], 218.

94 Ibid., 219.
95 Nguyễn Sĩ Giác, trans., [*Sumary of Institutions of Đại Nam*], 7.
96 Ibid.
97 Nguyễn Dynasty's National Historian Office, [*Collected Institutions, Volume I*], 217–219.
98 Ibid., 219.
99 Đỗ Bang, [*Nguyễn Dynasty*], 86.
100 Nguyễn Dynasty's National Historian Office, [*Collected Institutions of Đại Nam Volume I*], 222.
101 Ibid., 220.
102 Đỗ Bang, [*Nguyễn Dynasty*], 87.
103 Yon-Ung Kwon, "The Imperial Lecture of Sung China," 113.
104 Hahm, "Confucian Constitutionalism," 180–185.
105 Houn, *Chinese Political Traditions*, 61
106 Ibid., 62.
107 Charles O. Hucker, "Confucianism and the Chinese Censorial System," in *Confucianism in Action*, ed. David S. Nivison and Arthur F. Wright (Stanford, CA: Stanford University Press, 1959), 187.
108 Ibid.
109 Charles O. Hucker, *China's Imperial Past* (Stanford, CA: Stanford University Press, 1975), 162–163, 308–314.
110 Hahm, "Confucian Constitutionalism," 187. For more illustrations, see Yongryn Mo, "The Challenge of Accountability: Implications of the Censorate," in *Confucianism for the Modern World*, ed. Daniel A. Bell and Hahm Chaibong (Cambridge: Cambridge University Press, 2003), 54–68.
111 Đỗ Bang, [*Nguyễn Dynasty*], 19.
112 Nguyễn Dynasty's National Historian Office, [*Veritable Records of Đại Nam, Volume X*], 29.
113 Văn Tạo, "Tổ chức và Thực hiện Nhiện vụ 'Giám sát và Phản biện Xã hội' của Nhà nước Việt Nam trong Lịch sử" ["Organization and Implementation of the Duty of 'Social Supervision and Critic' in the Vietnamese State in History,"] *Journal of Historical Studies* 4 (2009): 14–25.
114 Đỗ Văn Ninh, *Từ Điển Quan Chức Việt Nam* [*Dictionary of Madarinate in Vietnam*] (Hanoi: Youth Publishing House, 2002), 449–450.
115 Nguyễn Dynasty's National Historian Office, [*Veritable Records of Đại Nam, Volume XI*], 151–152.
116 Đỗ Văn Ninh, [*Dictionary*], 227–228. See also, Woodside, *Vietnam and the Chinese Model*, 71.
117 Nguyễn Dynasty's National Historian Office, [*Collected Institutions of Đại Nam Volume II*], 66.
118 In the Lê dynasty, the six "*Offices of Scrutiny*" (*lục khoa*) were independent agents responsible for correspondingly supervising THE *six ministries* (*lục bộ*). In the Nguyễn dynasty, they were incorporated in the Censorate.
119 Nguyễn Dynasty's National Historian Office, [*Veritable Records of Đại Nam, Volume XI*], 153–154; Woodside, *Vietnam and The Chinese Model*, 72–73.
120 Nguyễn Dynasty's National Historian Office, [*Veritable Records of Đại Nam, Volume XI*], 153. Apart from the functions concerning the emperor, the Nguyễn Censorate was empowered to supervise, investigate, and impeach the misconduct by the princes and all officials of the administrative system. Ibid.
121 James Legge, *Li Ki* [*Liji*] – *Sacred Books of the East, Vol. XXVIII* (Oxford: Clarendon Press, 1885), 2.
122 Charles O. Hucker, *A Dictionary of Official Titles in Imperial China* (Stanford, CA: Stanford University Press, 1985), 135.
123 Wolfgang Franke, "The Veritable Records of the Ming Dynasty (1368–1644)," in

Historians of China and Japan, ed. W.G Beasley and E.G Pulleyblank (London: Oxford University Press, 1961), 61.

124 Nguyễn Dynasty's National Historian Office, [*Veritable Records of Đại Nam, Volume XI*], 155.

125 Vũ Minh Giang, ed., [*The Basic Characteristics*], 99.

126 Franke, "The Veritable Records of the Ming Dynasty," 61.

127 Tu Wei-ming, *Way, Learning, and Politics: Essays on the Confucian Intellectual* (Albany, NY: State University of New York Press, 1993), 7–8.

128 Hahm, "Confucian Constitutionalism," 194.

129 Đỗ Văn Ninh, [*Dictionary*], 447–448.

130 Nguyễn Hữu Tâm, ["The Historian Office"], 42.

131 Ibid., 39.

132 Hahm, "Confucian Constitutionalism," 194.

133 Louis Henkin, "Elements of Constitutionalism," *Review of the International Commission of Jurists* 60 (1998): 11.

134 Cited in Trần Văn Giàu, [*The Development of Thoughts*], 282–283.

135 *Vạn Niên* is the first name of the Mausoleum. The name is later changed to *Khiêm Cung* and finally to *Khiêm Lăng*.

136 "Cuộc Tuần du Ngũ Hành Sơn của Vua Minh Mạng năm 1831 và Bản Điều trần của Người Học trò Huyện Duy Xuyên" ["Minh Mang's Journey to Ngũ Hành Sơn in 1831 and the Petition of a Student at Suburban District Duy Xuyên"], accessed March 4, 2012, www.danang.gov.vn/TabID/65/CID/1483/ItemID/27594/default.aspx.

137 This is a reminding of Mencius' famous statement: "the people are the most important element in a nation; the spirits of the land and grain are the next; the sovereign is the lightest." See Legge, *Volume 2: The Works of Mencius*, 483.

138 This famous simile can be found in the *Works of Xunzi*. It is on record in the *Works of Xunzi 9.4* that: "A tradition says: the lord is the boat; his subject the water. It is the water that sustains the boat, and it is the water that capsizes the boat." See John Knoblock, *Xunzi: A Translation and Study of the Complete Works, Volume II* (Stanford, CA: Stanford University Press, 1994), 97. In another book of the *Works of Xunzi, 31.4*, Confucius is reported to respond to Duke Ai by recalling the king to the metaphor with the beginning "I have heard that…" John Knoblock, *Xunzi: A Translation and Study of the Complete Works, Volume III* (Stanford, CA: Stanford University Press, 1994), 262. The classical locus of the simile belies that the saying belongs to Xunzi. In fact, the words "*a tradition says*" in the 9.4 and Confucius' words "*I have heard that*" in 31.4 indicate that the statement is the traditional expression of the ancient Chinese people's conventional credence in the significant role of the people vis-à-vis the government.

139 The story is recalled according to a letter by the bishop Taberd of South Vietnam from 1830 to 1940, cited in ["Minh Mạng's Journey to Ngũ Hành Sơn"].

140 Ibid.

141 Joseph Chan, *Confucian Perfectionism: A Political Philosophy for Modern Times* (Princeton, NJ: Princeton University Press, 2013), 2–24.

142 See, generally, Tom Ginsburg and Alberto Simpser, *Constitutions in Authoritarian Regimes* (New York: Cambridge University Press, 2014); Tom Ginsburg and Tamir Moustafa, *Rule by Law: The Politics of Courts in Authoritarian Regimes* (Cambridge and New York: Cambridge University Press, 2008).

143 David Landau, "Abusive Constitutionalism," *UC Davis Law Review* 47 (2013): 186.

144 Nguyễn Dynasty's National Historian Office, [*Minh Mệnh's Principal Policies, Volume I, Book 1, First Chapter – Respecting the Heaven*], 23–50.

145 Ibid., [*Books 6 and 7 – Loving People*], 231–347.

146 Ibid., [*Book 4 – Seeking the Talent*], 147–164.

147 Ibid., [*Book 5 – Being Diligent in Political Affairs*], 205–231.

148 Nguyễn Đắc Xuân, *Nghiên cứu Triều Nguyễn và Huế xưa, Tập II* [*Studies of Nguyễn Dynasty and Past Huế, Volume II*] (Huế: Thuận Hóa Publishing House, 2012), 221.

149 Nguyễn Dynasty's National Historian Office, [*Veritable Records of Đại Nam, Volume XXVII*], 113–114.
150 Nguyễn Đắc Xuân, *Nghiên cứu Triều Nguyễn và Huế xưa, Tập I* [*Studies of Nguyễn Dynasty and Past Huế, Volume I*] (Huế: Thuận Hóa Publishing House, 2011), 303.
151 Ibid., 59–63.
152 Nguyễn Đắc Xuân, [*Nguyễn Dynasty and Past Huế, Volume II*], 218.
153 Nguyễn Dynasty's National Historian Office, [*Veritable Records of Đại Nam, Volume XXXI*], 83–84.
154 Ibid., 244–246.
155 John Ferejohn, Jack N. Rakove, and Jonathan Riley, eds., *Constitutional Culture and Democratic Rule* (Cambridge: Cambridge University Press, 2001) (conceiving of constitutionalism as an ongoing process in which most members of a given community rely on certain cultural norms and practices to identify and interpret constitutional rules that limit government power).

3 Modern Confucian constitutionalism

Introduction

Modern constitutionalism, whose common ingredients include written constitution, popular sovereignty, separation of powers, and the protection of fundamental human rights, conceptually backed by liberal ideas of Enlightenment thinkers like Locke, Rousseau, and Montesquieu, emerged in the West in the last quarter of the eighteenth century from the two revolutions in North America and France.[1] In the late nineteenth and early twentieth centuries, western modern constitutionalism spread all over Europe, some parts of Asia, and other parts of the world.

Japan was the first East Asian nation to adopt a written constitution under the influence of western modern constitutionalism during the Meiji Restoration (1868–1898).[2] Meiji constitutionalism was somewhat influenced by the German-continental constitutionalism. Although Meiji constitution was enacted not by "we the people" but by the emperor, it established structural limits on the emperor's power by creating the parliament (the Diet). It also adopted the German idea of *Rechtssaat*, but mixed it with the indigenous principle of *Kotutai*, which underlines the importance of national identity.[3] Meiji constitutionalism is an integrating project for national modernization and national identity.

Together with Japan, other East Asian societies, such as China and Vietnam, were also influenced by western modern constitutionalism. At the same time, Confucianism, which informed law and government in these societies for a long history, continued to have its role in shaping constitutional vision in modern East Asia. Substantial western ideas of modern constitutionalism were first introduced in East Asian counties like China and Vietnam, ironically not by western intellectuals, but by Confucian intellectuals, such as Kang Youwei, Liang Qichao, and Sun Yat-sen in China, and Phan Bội Châu, Phan Chu Trinh, and Huỳnh Thúc Kháng in Vietnam.

In this chapter I examine their constitutional thoughts from an integrating perspective. I argue that East Asian Confucian intellectuals have combined values of western modern constitutionalism with values of Confucianism to develop their distinctive vision of modern Confucian constitutionalism, which can be explained by the logic of constitutional learning, the expression of national identity, and the limits of western liberal constitutionalism.

In Japan, Itagaki "devised the terms 'patriot' and 'public' to revise the Confucian ideal of a disinterested public service so as to combat individualist attempts to advance personal ambitions or sectional interests."[4] Similarly, in Korea, modern intellectuals at the end of the nineteenth century, according to Chaihark Halm, discussed the western idea of human rights "by using translations derived from Confucian vocabulary," and their rights discourse features "emphasizing people's rights and making state more responsive to the demands of the people."[5] In other words, they tend to blend the western idea of rights with the Confucian idea of *minben*, which highlights responsive government.

In China, Confucianism still occupied an important role in the intellectual climate in the late nineteenth century, although there were some exceptional criticisms of Confucianism from the western liberal point of view.[6] While attacking the old imperial regime, "reformers in general stopped short of criticizing the religio-ideological foundation of the old order – namely, Confucianism."[7] One of the reasons for this was that: "For most of these reformers this moral-ideological conservatism underlay and tempered the radicalness of their political reformism."[8] Consequently, reformers' approach to western values tends to be instrumentalist, while their position regarding Confucian tradition is more foundationalist. Hao Chang demonstrates that: "Western learning was given a value – but only an instrumental and secondary one, whereas traditional Confucian learning was still regarded as the lofty locus of intrinsic values."[9] This observation is effective in regard to constitutionalism. Chinese constitutionalists supported some values of western modern constitutionalism as an instrument to modernize the political system as a response to the rising power of the west and other industrial nations. However, Confucianism continued to influence their thinking as foundational values. This makes Confucian tradition retain its role in Chinese modern constitutional vision. For example, Kang Youwei (1858–1927) and his student Liang Qichao (1873–1929) attempted to blend western ideas (such as rights, democracy, and constitution) with Confucian ideas (such as *minben* or people as basis and *datong* or great harmony), and other intellectual sources.[10] Sun Yat Sen's doctrine of five-power constitution (*wuquan xianfa*), which includes legislature, judiciary, executive, civil service examinations, and censorship, was also an integration of the Montesquieuian theory of separation of power with the Confucian tradition of elitism and remonstration.[11]

This chapter focuses on the Vietnamese modern Confucianists.[12] I limit the study to the figures whose projects are more systematic and most influential. For this reason, I choose the two cases of Phan Bội Châu and Phan Châu Trinh. During the Vietnamese anti-colonial history in the first quarter of the last century, Phan Bội Châu and Phan Châu Trinh emerged as the most influential figures. Their revolutionary thoughts, together with the anti-colonial movements under their leadership, were the early concerns of some western historians.[13] Additionally, the commendable efforts toward the translation of some Vietnamese and western scholars have helpfully introduced their major political writings to English readers.[14] Notwithstanding that, a paucity of attention has been paid to the constitutionalist dimensions of their revolutionary odysseys. In the present chapter, I hope to fill this gap by investigating their constitutionalist visions.

The chapter pursues dual purposes. First, it aims to draw academic attention to the foundational contribution of the modern Confucian intellectuals in the introduction of modern constitutionalism. Second, it raises a more general argument on the possibility of integration of Confucianism with western modern constitutionalism. I will demonstrate how Phan Bội Châu and Phan Châu Trinh supported and introduced western modern constitutionalism into Vietnam and how they at the same time adhered to classical Confucianism and integrated some constitutionalist ideas of classical Confucianism with western modern constitutionalism to formulate their particular constitutionalist projects.

The chapter is organized as follows. The first section considers the historical context. The second section examines the case of Phan Bội Châu, while the third section considers the case of Phan Châu Trinh. The fourth section considers the legitimacy of their project, and concludes with further discussions.

Historical context

France first fired at Vũng Thùng (presently Đà Nẵng) in 1858, initiating its invasion of Vietnam. After 25 years of belligerent colonization, the French held complete dominion over Vietnam by 1883, followed by 15 years (1883–1896) of so-called "pacification" (*bình định*).[15] Under French domination, Vietnam was part of a larger colonial system known as the Indochinese Union, established in 1887 and consisting of the colony of Cochinchina (Nam Bộ or Southern Vietnam) and the protectorates of Annam (Trung Bộ or Central Vietnam), Tonkin (Bắc Bộ or Northern Vietnam) and Cambodia, together with the protectorate of Laos after its annexation in 1893.[16] In 1897 the arrival of Paul Doumer as governor-general of Indochina led the French colonialism in the territory to the new phase characterized by the consolidation of the colonial governmental institutions which were maintained until the August Revolution in 1945 and the exploitation of the local resources on a large scale.[17]

Institutionally, at the peak of the colonial governing pyramid sits a French governor-general, residing in Hanoi, appointed by the French Councils of Ministers with the approbation of the French Parliament, and authorized to issue decrees and laws that regulated the conduct and behavior of all people living in Indochina.[18] Cochinchina, as a full colony, was governed under French law by a French governor named as the lieutenant governor at Saigon, while Annam and Tonkin, as the protectorates, were under the rule of the Hanoi governor-general and two French "resident superiors," one in Hanoi and one in Huế.[19] The lieutenant governor and the resident superiors were appointed by the governor-general and held all powers in their own hands, except the legislative power. These heads of the state ruled their bureaucracies with the advice of the appointive and elective bodies.[20] The elective body in Cochinchina was the Colonial Council established in 1867. In Tonkin and

Annam, the protectorates had separate institutions for French citizens and indigenous people. The Council of French Economic and Financial Interests consisted of 20 French members elected by French and naturalized French citizens, responsible for giving opinions on the annual budget. For the local people, there were the indigenous consultative councils, namely Chambers of the People's Representatives of Tonkin and Annam, constituted in 1908 and 1925, respectively.[21]

At the same time, the monarchy of Nguyễn dynasty at Huế still remained, together with its bureaucratic apparatus and its Confucian education and examination system, juxtaposed to the colonial schools.[22] However, the traditional institutions only had titular or subservient status.[23] Nguyễn Khắc Viện notes that all important services – security, finances, public works, posts, agriculture, health, trade, and so forth were in the hands of the French, while the Vietnamese administrations were preserved *proforma* or were only assigned minor tasks.[24]

At the very beginning of the French invasion of Vietnam, national resistance was rife, with the refusal of collaboration with the French on the part of local officials and members of the scholar-gentry.[25] Most conspicuous during the early years of the modern Vietnamese anti-colonialism was the *Cần Vương* (Loyalist) movement edict by monarch Hàm Nghi and Tôn Thất Thuyết since 1885, which ended in failure with the Hương Sơn uprising led by Phan Đình Phùng in 1897.[26] Frustrated by the precursors, the twentieth-century Vietnamese anti-colonialists sought other remedies.

This new stage dramatically resonated with the overseas historical milieu. The impact of the Meiji Restoration should be mentioned first. The Meiji Restoration had triumphed during the period 1868–1898, which radically initiated Japan's economic, social, and political metamorphosis from a decentralized feudal kingdom into a powerful modern capitalist state with a constitutionalist government.[27] At that time, the Vietnamese anti-colonialists had only an inkling of the Japanese restoration as they were grappling with the abortive uprisings. It was not until Japan's victory in the Russo-Japanese War (1904–1905) that the twentieth-century Vietnamese nationalists were transfixed by the power of the Japanese restoration in maintaining national autonomy and modernizing the nation.[28]

In conjunction with the Meiji Restoration, Chinese revolutionary movements equally served as external catalysts for the Vietnamese nationalists to move forward to modern revolutionary alternatives. They were particularly inspired by the institutional reform movement known as the Wuxu Reform or the Hundred Days' Reform led by Kang Youwei (Vietnamese: Khang Hữu Vi), the 1911 Republican Revolution led by Sun Zhongshan (Vietnamese: Tôn Trung Sơn), and the constitutional reform movement under the radical influence of Liang Qichao (Vietnamese: Lương Khải Siêu).[29]

It is because of these revolutionary movements that the Vietnamese nationalists gravitated with great alacrity toward Chinese reformists' writings known as "New Books." The term "New Books" (Japanese: *shin sho*; Chinese: *hsin shu*; Vietnamese: *tân thư*) refers to the literature encompassing western modern knowledge, deviating from traditional teachings – including the Confucian teachings – which were introduced into Japan, China, and Vietnam during the late nineteenth and early twentieth centuries. The wave of "New Books" hit Vietnam via winding paths.[30] The wave was initiated in Japan during the Meiji Restoration, period when radical figures like Fukuzawa translated western books to introduce the western modern knowledge of natural science, technology, philosophy, politics, law, and social sciences to Japan, which contributed significantly to the success of the restoration programs. The Japanese versions were in turn disseminated in China via the writings of such reformists as Kang Youwei and Liang Qichao. For the early modern Vietnamese nationalists, due to the fact that the exclusive foreign language in which they were competent was Chinese, the sole way they could have access to the "New Books" was indirectly via the Chinese medium. The Chinese "New Books" were initially introduced great volume in Vietnam in the 1920s through the harbors of Hải Phòng, Sài Gòn, and Đà Nẵng, which were teeming with Chinese inhabitants and where some Chinese revolutionary cliques were in exile.[31]

The Chinese "New Books," in particular the writings of Liang Qichao, served as the stimulus for the early modern Vietnamese nationalists to search for novel paradigms of revolution. The 8 January 1929 edition of the Vietnamese newspaper called *Morning Bell* (*Thần Chung*), published in Saigon, verified that Liang Qichao's writings "have nearly directly aroused our Confucian scholars because they discuss the Chinese story but there are many contents coincident with our pathologies."[32] After the death of Liang Qichao, the newspaper compared the effect of his *Collected Works of Yinbingshi* on the Vietnamese Confucian scholars as "the proper antidote for a person with a chronic disease."[33]

Notably, in the early twentieth century, reformist thought and western democracy were propagandized in the country, which agitated the popular anticolonial movements, not through the direct conveyance of the western-style scholars and the French books, but the indirect medium of Confucian scholars and Chinese books.[34] The western-style intellectuals educated in the French schools were inclined to a functionary career in the colonial bureaucracy, which thwarted them from becoming the introducers of western reformist thoughts. As far as the students of the Confucian schools were concerned, they were bifurcated into two groups: the Confucian mandarins and the free Confucianists. The Confucian mandarins stayed in the same line with the western-style intellectuals in that they tended to be careerists within the existing system rather than transmitters of novel western knowledge concerning political renovation. In contrast, the free Confucianists were the scholars who refused to participate in the traditional bureaucracy and chose the arduous odyssey to fight for national independence and socio-political modernization; this explains why they were the active propagandists of western reformist theories.

The early constitutional movements in Vietnam were initiated in the above-discussed general context. It was the Confucianists rather than the western literati who were the first evangelists and activists for modern constitutionalism in Vietnam. Meiji constitutionalism coupled with the Chinese constitutional movements served as the practical sources for them to formulate new concepts of republic and parliament. In addition, the "New Books" familiarized them with the philosophical foundations of western liberal constitutionalism detailed in the works of the Enlightenment thinkers, particularly *The Social Contract* of Jean-Jacques Rousseau and *The Spirit of Laws* of Charles-Louis de Secondat Montesquieu, which galvanized them with novel notions of fundamental law, popular sovereignty, human rights, and the separation of powers. Furthermore, through the hortative "New Books," the Confucianists have been aware of the modern practices of constitutional governments in the western world, especially American and French constitutionalism. Consequently, constitutionalism became an inextricable part of their revolutionary campaigns since they believed that constitutionalist institutions and values were instrumental to modernization of the nation and could ultimately restore sovereignty from the invaders.

Phan Bội Châu (1867–1940)

Outside Vietnam, the name of Phan Bội Châu may not be well recognized, but within the country he has gained a status comparable to that of Sun Yat-sen in China.[35] Phan Bội Châu was the most influential protagonist of the national liberation movement in the first quarter of twentieth-century Vietnam. Nguyễn Ái Quốc (Hồ Chí Minh) regards him as "the hero, the apostle, and the martyr of independence venerated by twenty million enslaved compatriots."[36] He was the historic figure for the leadership of the anti-colonial organizations and movement, namely Restoration Association (*Duy Tân Hội*) (1904), Eastern Exodus Movement (*Phong trào Đông Du*) (1905), and Vietnam Restoration League (*Việt Nam Quang phục Hội*) (1912).

Phan Bội Châu was the son of a Confucian family in Nghệ An, the central province of Vietnam. He was instilled with Confucian values through familial education from an early stage. When Phan was five years old, his mother, Nguyễn Thị Nhàn, recited to him passages from *Classic of Poetry* (Chinese: *Shijing*; Vietnamese: *Thơ Kinh*). It is reported in his autobiography that at this age it took Phan merely three days to memorize verbatim the *Three-Character Classic* (Chinese: *San-tzu-ching*; Vietnamese: *Tam tự Kinh*). He was then taught by his father, a village teacher, other Confucian texts, especially the *Analects*. Phan subsequently spent 15 years preparing for the Confucian traditional examination and eventually graduated as a valedictorian in the regional exam by 1900. After graduation, he spent five itinerant years inside the country to establish a friendship with the patriotic Confucian community/society. During this time Phan Bội Châu and other Confucianists founded the Restoration Association in 1904. One of their main strategies was to seek foreign help to restore sovereignty to Vietnam. In concordance with the program of the Association, Phan went to Japan in 1905, initiating the Eastern Exodus Movement which allowed approximately 200 Vietnamese people to surreptitiously travel to Japan to study for revolutionary missions. After the movement was disrupted by the Franco-Japan treaty in 1909,[37] Phan moved to Hong Kong and then to Guangdong, where he and his comrades dispersed the Modernization Association and established the

Vietnam Restoration League in 1912. In 1925, Phan was arrested by French authorities, and tried and condemned to capital punishment. However, due to public demonstration, the punishment was converted to house imprisonment in Huế. Phan spent his final 15 years taking trips on the Hương River to receive his friends and to talk to young admirers. Due to this period, he is remembered as the "Old Man of Imperial Quay" (*Ông già Bến Ngự*).[38]

As a nationalist, Phan Bội Châu's ardent preoccupation was the independence of Vietnam. However, it is unlikely that "his program consisted of one point: getting rid of the French."[39] The fallacy stems from ignoring the constitutional dimension of his revolutionary journey. In fact, Phan's goals were twofold: regaining national autonomy and establishing a constitutional government. With regard to the latter, Phan Bội Châu can be considered the first constitutionalist in the modern history of the Vietnamese constitutional development. Phan's constitutionalism was formulated on the grounds of his traditional Confucian knowledge and modern understanding of western constitutionalism, which resulted from the influences of Meiji constitutionalism, Chinese revolutionary movements, the "New Books," and the Chinese reformists like Liang Qichao and Sun Yat-sen, with whom he had directly held audience and exchanged modernizing projects.

Despotic monarchy vs. constitutional democracy

In a similar vein to the percept that constitutionalist ideas are generated from the apprehension of despotic power, Phan Bội Châu developed his constitutionalist vision by criticizing the despotic monarchy and calling for a constitutional democracy. It should be noted that when Phan Bội Châu was in Vietnam and when the Modernization Association was founded in 1904, his sole mission was to regain national independence. It was not until Phan and the other members of the Association were in exile that the plan for a constitutional government for a future Vietnam was formulated, which accrued from the influences of the western works of constitutionalist theory and the experience of foreign governments and politicians. Phan explained in his autobiography:

> Ever since my arrival in Japan, I had been studying the origins of revolutions in other countries and the advantages and disadvantages of various political systems. I was fascinated by the theories of Rousseau, Montesquieu, and others. Rousseau's *Social Contract* and Montesquieu's *De l'Espirit des Lois* [*The Spirit of Laws*] I had read for the first time only after I went overseas. Moreover, as a result of my many contacts with Chinese comrades, monarchism had been relegated to the back of my mind.[40]

Consequently, after Phan Bội Châu and his comrades travelled overseas, the political program of the Modernization Association was supplemented with constitutional content. The new program was declared in 1905 as follows: "to subjugate the French, to restore Vietnam, and to establish a constitutional monarchism."[41] Phan publicly enunciated in detail the new platform for the Modernization Association in his *New Vietnam* (*Tân Việt Nam*), written in 1907.[42] The document is actually a revolutionary manifesto with the central objective of a constitutional monarchism for a future independent Vietnam. It was inchoate, with implacable castigations of the colonial tyrannical power and absolutist monarchism:

> Ever since the French came to protect us, Frenchmen hold every level of power; they hold the power of life and death over everyone. The life of thousands of Vietnamese people is not worth that of a French dog; the moral prestige of hundreds of our officials does not prevail over that of a French woman.... The poison of absolutism coming from those people who have oppressed others for thousands of years spread from China into our country so thoroughly that a single individual surrounded by a few thousand mediocre men were able to treat our people like fish and meat. And yet our people are so naïve and stupid that they do not know how to wrest back their democratic rights, how to preserve their country's destiny. Day and night, they simply think of how best to provide the ruler and his cohorts with their own blood for beverage and their own flesh for food.[43]

The *New Vietnam* envisages that in the brilliant prospect of an independent Vietnam the protectorate power shall be abrogated and the dogma of monarchial sovereignty shall be replaced by the modern principle of popular sovereignty. Accordingly, the people shall be girded with the supreme power to decide the destiny of the country and the structure of the government, and shall pass definitive adjudications upon the actions of the power holders through their representatives.

Later, when the Republican Revolution of 1911, led by Sun Yat-sen, subjugated the Manchu monarchy in China, Phan Bội Châu and his comrades adjusted their political organization and program. In 1912, the Restoration Association was replaced by the Vietnam Restoration League, with the goals of restoring autonomy to Vietnam and establishing a democratic republic like the new China.[44] Phan explains that previously he was committed to the (limited) monarchy because he wished to "keep faith with the people at home" who still strongly advocated for the monarchy, but with the establishment of the Chinese republican government, he believed that the circumstance had changed and was quickly absolved from the monarchic plan.[45] Therefore, Phan Bội Châu and his Vietnam Restoration League introduced a new plan for the democratic republic of an independent Vietnam. The *Military Strategies for Vietnam Restoration* (*Việt Nam Quang phục Quân phương Lược*) (1912) declares:

> We must eliminate the (traditional) monarchism because it is an egregious polity.... Democratic republic is an excellent polity.... The power in the nation shall belong to the plenary people and shall be decided by the people. The noisome vestiges of despotism will be absent.[46]

Written constitution

The new government in Phan's vision would be articulated by a written constitution. This is first due to the influence of Meiji constitutionalism. In the *Ballad to Awaken Countrymen* (*Đề Tỉnh Quốc dân Ca*),[47] written in 1906, Phan inflammatorily reminded his people that "the Constitution was created at the beginning of the Meiji regime. Within thirty years, the morale of the people was powerfully invigorated."[48] Phan then suggested that his compatriots should follow in Japan's footsteps to pursue a written constitution.[49]

In addition, the *New Vietnam* implicitly suggests that a constitution will be promulgated in the future of an independent Vietnam. That is why the prosecutor general, the chief of the Judicial Service in Indochina, reported to the governor-general of Indochina on 28 April 1909 that:

> It [the *New Vietnam*] deals with laws and regulations to be enacted by the future government of independent Vietnam.... Nothing has been left out of that draft for a new constitution and the chapter which spells out the promises for the future is one of the most elaborate in this document.[50]

After his dismal failure, Phan Bội Châu never abandoned his pursuit of a constitution for Vietnam, even when he was under house arrest in Huế. In 1926, Phan produced a constitutional draft and sent it to his friend Lê Văn Miến. Lê replied:

> In my opinion, it is not necessary to add anything but it should be reduced. It requires an entire abscission. Do not let any words and sentences remain. As the country is lost and the people are the slaves, how can we create a constitution!

Phan subsequently personally destroyed the constitutional draft.[51] However, Phan's desire for a constitution in Vietnam was unquenchable. In 1932, in answering the interview of the *East and West Magazine* (*Đông Tây*), he again stated that "creating a constitution is not only worthy but also necessary. There shall be a constitution. This is a truism."[52] Phan then sketched his constitution:

> I myself have a constitution in mind. My constitution will be the balance of the monarchic constitutions of England and Japan and model the constitutions of America, Germany, and Russia.... It is also necessary to depend on our people's background to select the appropriate things for perfection."[53]

Liberal rights

Phan Bội Châu's constitutionalism demands the responsibility of the government for human rights defined by him as "the rights of human and the rights to be human."[54] The *New Vietnam* anticipates that in the new polity "the sense of rights" of the people will be developed. As an echo of western liberalism, the document particularly emphasizes the normative values regarding political liberal rights, including equal and free right to vote, freedom of thought, freedom of press, the rights of petitions and law-suits. Furthermore, the new constitutional government is envisaged to be responsible for social rights, especially, educational right, women's rights, and gender equality.[55] As an enticing addendum, in a poem entitled "The Rights" (*Quyền lợi*), Phan delivered a panegyric for constitutional rights, ranging from the rights to freedom of speech, freedom of thought, freedom of movement, freedom of press, to the rights to freedom of associations and freedom of doing business.[56]

The separation of powers

In order to safeguard the liberal rights, Phan suggests structural limitations of state power. The *New Vietnam* proposes a limited government in which the monarch and his mandarins are constrained by an independent congressional system. The Congress shall be created by popular vote and be responsible for all political matters. Remarkably, Phan suggests a tricameral system in which the congressional body is divided into three chambers, namely the Higher Assembly, the Middle Congress, and the Lower Congress, operating with internal counterbalances.[57] The Congress is also conceived as the public forum for checking and balancing the monarchic and administrative authorities:

> Whether to preserve or to do away with the monarchy, whether to promote or demote the mandarins: our people will have the ultimate right to make these decisions. The mismanagement done by the ruler or the abuses perpetrated by the mandarins, all behaviour that is not conformity with the public good, can be reprimanded or punished by our people in their deliberations in the Congress.[58]

Unquestionably, Phan Bội Châu is a modern constitutionalist. Although Phan received Confucian traditional education, he was genuinely amicable to western modern constitutionalist notions and institutions. Consequently, in his vision, the new government in Vietnam would follow key elements of western modern constitutionalism: popular sovereignty, a written constitution, liberal rights, and the separation of powers.

Confucianism

Phan Bội Châu, while gravitating to modern constitutionalist values, remained a bona fide Confucianist. After embarking upon a number of revolutionary activities struggling for national independence and constitutionalist polity, the Old Man of the Imperial Quay spent the late stage of his life in quiescence to mediate traditional values. During this time that he was still fixated on Confucianism, which led him to publish two renowned lucubrations, namely *Khổng học Đăng* (*The Light of Confucianism*) and *Chu Dịch* (*The Book of Change or I Ching*).[59] A perusal of the works will reveal that the Old Man is genuinely a sagacious Confucianist. Importantly, in these two magna opera, Phan Bội Châu affirms Confucianism as the foundational and immortal axiology. Interestingly, in the parallel sentences he composed to mourn himself, Phan stated that he would carry with him the Way of Confucius and Mencius to cross the Styx.[60]

What was Confucianism in Phan Bội Châu's mind? Phan was a free Confucian scholar who had departed from the mandarin bureaucracy. Moreover, he had criticized the Confucian educational system designed for the selection of candidates for the officials of the court. Consequently, the Confucianism that he expounded is the tradition of philosophy rather than the politicized ideology of the imperial dynasties.

This can be well illustrated by his work *The Light of Confucianism*. Characterizing Confucianism as the "old studies," Phan writes in the prelude: "By 'old studies' I mean the Asian genuine philosophy in the ancient time.... The nomenclature 'old studies' is not the instrument to steal the trappings at all."[61] The allusion is that Confucianism is considered as a tradition of philosophy, not as the imperial ideology that was traditionally appropriated for the mandarin positions. Hence, Phan sarcastically writes that it is inadvisable for careerists to read this book.[62] Conceiving Confucianism as a tradition of philosophy, Phan goes further to categorize various schools of Confucianism throughout its history. Accordingly, the teachings of Confucius in the *Analects* are the essence of Confucianism; the teachings of the *Great Leaning* and the *Doctrine of Mean* constitute the genuine Confucian school (*đích phái*); Mencian and Xunzian studies are considered the adjacent Confucian school (*phái rất gần*); meanwhile, the Confucianism from Han dynasty to Qing dynasty is considered as the distant Confucian school (*viễn phái*).

Phan Bội Châu's two Confucian works indicate his belief in the revivification of Confucian values. More importantly, the works show that Phan gives credence to the possible coexistence of Confucianism with modern values. In the foreword of *The Light of Confucianism*, Phan offers a metaphor:

> Substantial learning can be compared with constructing a building: old studies are the foundation while new studies are the material; the two can help each other to constitute a gorgeous building. There is never a building without materials but the essential thing is that there is never a building without foundations. I write this book to temper the old studies with the new studies; the two form each other; definitely, they are not contradictory.[63]

The outlook is really effective in his constitutionalism. Phan's constitutionalist project is virtually the mélange of Confucianism as "the old studies" and the western liberal constitutionalism as "the new studies." This is evident in Phan's wish to combine the Confucian principle of *minben* (*people as base*) with the western liberal principle of rights. He states:

> At the present age, if (the doctrine of) Mencius is absent, the meaning of "*dân quý*" (*people as the most important element*) cannot be illuminated; if (the doctrine of) Montesquieu is absent, who can raise the flag of "*dân quyền*" (popular rights)?[64]

Phan's aspiration in this statement is to marry "*dân quý*" and "*dân quyền*," which is actually to integrate Confucian *minben* with western liberalism.

Western liberalism, as developed by enlightened thinkers like Montesquieu and Rousseau, focuses on liberal rights of individuals. Inspired by this tradition, western constitutional theorists tend to define the goal of constitutionalism as to safeguard individual liberal rights. From the Confucian perspective in East Asian tradition, the objectives for government to pursue, rather than individual rights, are the material and spiritual needs of people, as indicated in the concept of *minben*.

It seems that Phan Bội Châu is unsatisfied with western liberal constitutionalism's emphasis on liberal rights and neglect of public good. Therefore, Phan incorporated the Confucian *minben* in his distinctive constitutionalist vision.

As a reflection of the *minben* tradition, even though Phan Bội Châu placed significant emphasis on individual rights, he never considered individual rights the sole and ultimate end of the new government; rather, in his project, the constitutionalist government is responsible for the public good of the people. His literature is rife with sentiment for "*nhân dân*" (people) instead of "*cá nhân*" (individual). For example: "Take our hearts to think about the people"; "The people are the people of the country and the country is the country for the people"; "Without the people, nothing is valuable"; "The cleaned face of the country is thanked to the people."[65] In fact, as an echo of the Confucian *minben* concept, Phan's constitutionalism was designed to promote the accountability of the government to the public good of the people rather than solely to individual rights.

The distinguishing feature of Confucian *minben* is the responsibility of the government in educating the people, especially on spiritual values concerning culture and morality. Under the influence of this tradition, the normative values of the new constitutionalist government in Phan Boi Châu's plan are not only fundamental rights, but also fundamental virtues: the people should not only be entitled to the rights, but also be educated with moral and cultural values. To instill these values in the people, Phan Bội Châu outlines the educational function of the government. Phan believes that once the government fulfills its edificatory function, and the people are imbued with patriotism, attend to public business, conform to legislations, and pursue the civilized values, criminal law will be trivial.[66] Structurally, in the *New Vietnam* Phan Bội Châu suggests establishing a Reeducation Center (*Viện Cảm hóa*) at the capital of the independent Vietnam. This institution would be presided over by a judge appointed by the Supreme National University and be specifically responsible for the edificatory task.[67] This is a genuine reflection of the Confucianism emphasis on the importance of morality and the government's duty to educate.

In addition to moral education, Phan also emphasizes the significance of education on the constitution for the success of constitutionalism. Phan demands that the people should be educated by constitutional knowledge. He believes that "people's rights are respected due to the high level of people's intelligence. The republics of France and America are stemmed from people's intelligence. The constitutionalism in Japan, England, and Germany also established as a result of their intelligence."[68] This explains the fact that Phan wrote prolifically to criticize despotism and disseminate constitutional knowledge. Phan Bội Châu utilized his literary talent developed in the Confucian educational system to propagandize the constitutionalist values to the people.

Denouement

Phan Bội Châu himself underestimated his influence when he began his autobiography with these words: "My history is entirely a history of failure."[69] In fact, his revolutionary thought and activities in general and his constitutionalism in particular had considerable influences on the modernization process and constitutional development in the history of early twentieth-century Vietnam.

The significance of the Eastern Exodus Movement should first be noted. Vinh Sinh and Nicholas Wickenden argue that the movement, albeit short-lived, "was the first step toward giving Vietnam full access to modern ideas."[70] In particular, Phan's constitutionalism described in the *New Vietnam* was the first attempt to bring into Vietnam comprehensive ideas and institutions of modern constitutionalism, such as popular sovereignty, representative democracy, fundamental rights, and separation of powers. Additionally, his strong commitment to democracy during the time of the Vietnam Restoration League "appears as the first effective step toward the abandonment of the traditional form of polity in Vietnam."[71] To a certain extent, Phan effectively directed the development of Vietnamese modern politics to the constitutional democracy. Finally, the impact of Phan's literature should be emphasized. As Vinh Sinh and Nicholas Wickenden write:

> Phan's voluminous writings, in particular his passionate poetry, were perfectly attuned to appeal to the feelings and desires of his countrymen then and since, arousing their patriotic sentiments and national pride in times of crisis. Many participants in the Vietnamese resistance movement of the later years cite a few lines of Phan's poetry that had awakened their enthusiasm in their youth. Phan was far from unconscious of his literary gifts, but their effect was greater than he could know.[72]

Constitutional matters are important issues in his voluminous writings. Phan's writings helpfully diffused constitutional knowledge to the people. His writings familiarized the people to modern terms and notions like "democracy" (*dân chủ*), "popular rights" (*dân quyền*), and "constitution" (*hiến pháp*) and inspired them to fight for these values. In conclusion, Phan's works considerably aroused the constitutional consciousness of the public and motivated the people to strive for a modern constitutional government in Vietnam.

Phan Chu Trinh (1872–1926)

Phan Chu Trinh (also spelled as Phan Châu Trinh), the coeval of Phan Bội Châu, was another renowned Confucian patriot, recognized as the stalwart activist for democracy in the early twentieth century in Vietnam. He is nationally celebrated as the key figure of the Restoration Movement (*Phong trào Duy Tân*) and the Tonkin Free School (*Đông kinh Nghĩa thục*).

Phan Chu Trinh was born in Quang Nam, a central province of Vietnam. As a military official's son, Phan was enamored with martial arts, spending his childhood on "swords" instead of "words." It was not until after his father's death in 1887 that Phan became a fledgling of the Confucian school, with particular interests in the *Analects* and *Mencius*. After passing the first level examination (*cử nhân*) in 1900 and the next level (*phó bảng*) the following year, Phan was assigned as a secretary (*thừa biên*) in the Ministry of Rites in 1903. Disappointed with the corruption of the mandarin bureaucracy and partially due to his gaining access (in 1904) to the *New Books* of Liang Qichao, Phan resigned from his position in 1905 to travel together with his two intimate friends Trần Qúy Cáp and Huynh Thúc Kháng to listen to the *vox populi* as preparation for later revolutionary activities. In 1906, Phan Chu Trinh arrived in Hong Kong to establish a liaison with Phan Bội Châu, and from there the two Phans went to Japan where they exchanged their contentious political ideas.

After returning to Vietnam from Japan, Phan Chu Trinh composed the *Letter to Governor-General Paul Beau* (1907) in which he attributed the abysmal condition in Vietnam to the corrupt mandarin bureaucracy together with the vicarious onus of the French colonial government and appealed for reforms with emphasis on promoting popular rights through the selection of proficient officials, expanding press freedom, reforming the legal codes, abolishing the civil service examinations, expanding the school system, and encouraging industrial and commercial education.[73]

When the demands were disregarded, Phan and his two friends – Huỳnh Thúc Kháng and Trần Quý Cáp – initiated the Restoration Movement to struggle for modernization and liberal rights. The outcome of the movement was beyond that anticipated by the leaders. The movement reached its apogee by the farmers' insurrection in Central Vietnam, appealing for the reduction of taxes initially and later on liberal rights in general. The colonial authorities aggressively quelled the movement. Many members (including Trần Quý Cáp) were executed, while Phan Chu Trinh and Huỳnh Thúc Kháng were exiled to Poulo Condore Island.[74]

Fortunately, thanks to the French League for Human Rights, Phan Chu Trinh was released in 1910. However, the colonists tried to hold him under house punishment in Mỹ Tho city but later acquiesced to his demand for expatriation to France in 1911. During his 14-year stay in France, he incessantly wrote to demand the reform of colonial policies in Indochina. He wrote *On Indochinese*

Politics (*Đông Dương Chính trị luận*) and *History of the Insurrection of Central Vietnam* (*Trung Kỳ Dân biến Thỉ Mạt Ký*) to disclose the affliction of the colonized regions, which led to some changes of French colonial policies in Indochina.[75] Additionally, a remarkable event during this time which drew special attention from French politicians and popular opinion was the dissemination of Phan Chu Trinh's *Letter of Seven Clauses* (*Thất Điều Thư*) on 14 July 1922, in which he listed seven crimes of the Emperor Khải Định when the emperor had visited the Marseille Exposition at the invitation of the French government.[76]

Repatriating to Saigon in 1925, Phan continued advocating for democracy in Vietnam. Most notable are his two public lectures entitled "Morality and Ethics in the Orient and the Occident" (*Đạo đức và Luân lý Đông Tây*)[77] (hereinafter Morality and Ethics) and "Monarchy and Democracy" (*Quân trị Chủ nghĩa và Dân trị Chủ nghĩa*).[78] Phan Chu Trinh died in Saigon on 24 March 1926 and his funeral was an occasion for the eruption of a national movement of democracy.

Although Phan Chu Trinh and Phan Bội Châu pursued the same purpose of national independence and constitutional government for Vietnam, they were differentiated by the priorities of political campaigns and revolutionary means. Phan Bội Châu writes on the commonality and the disjunction between him and Phan Chu Trinh:

> He and I were pursing one and the same goal, but our means were considerably different. He wished to start by relying on the French to abolish the monarchy, but I wished to start by driving out the French to restore Vietnam.[79]

While Phan Bội Châu regarded the retrieval of national autonomy from French colonist by violent insurrection as the foremost mission and the establishment of the constitutionalist government as the sequel, Phan Chu Trinh suggested expediting liberal rights and formulating the constitutional democracy within a self-rule (*tự trị*) system under French patronage as the non-violent means for incrementally restoring unadulterated sovereignty.

Interestingly enough, there is a poem entitled "The Ballad for Wakening up the National Spirit 2" (*Tỉnh Quốc hồn Ca 2*) (hereinafter, *The Ballad*) written in the late phase of his life (1922), whose last stanzas helpfully encapsulate Phan Chu Trinh's political program, which is in accordance with his other political writings and activities.[80]

Phan's cachet is his instrumentalist approach to France for modernizing the nation as the prerequisite for the nation's move to independence.[81] With the belief that "to resort to violence is self-deconstructive" (*bạo động tắc tử*) Phan raises the slogan "relying on French to look for progress" (*Ỷ Pháp cầu tiến bộ*).[82]

This leads Phan to suggest that "the primal agreement is to set up the self-rule system." What Phan Chu Trinh really means by "self-rule" is that Vietnamese people must be allowed to govern themselves albeit without obviating the French's aegis.[83] His contemplation on the prospect of a rapprochement (the amicable relationship, the "coexistence of interests," Asian and European in "the same family") indicates that he was thinking of Vietnam as a dominion like Canada.

Within the dominion, Phan calls for a constitutionalist regime. His constitutionalist vision is formulated by his traditional education, his access to western political theories (especially, the theories of Montesquieu and Rousseau[84]) through the "New Books," and his experiences in Japan and France.

Despotic monarchy vs. constitutional democracy

Like Phan Bội Châu, Phan Chu Trinh had an animus to despotic monarchy. Phan Bội Châu wrote about Phan Chu Trinh when they exchanged revolutionary ideas in Kwangtung:

> Every day when we talk about the affairs of our country, he singled out for bitter reproach the wicked conduct of the monarchs, the enemies of the people. He ground his teeth when talking about the ruler of the day, who was bringing calamity to the country and disaster to the people; as much as to say that if the system of the monarchial autocracy were not abolished, simply restoring the country's independence would bring no happiness.[85]

Phan Chu Trinh's animosity toward monarchy is well illuminated by his *Letter of Seven*. Beginning with the declaration "I love democracy, abhor the tyranny of autocratic monarchy,"[86] the letter is in fact an indictment of the contemporary monarch. The letter was written with an adamant conviction that

> unless people in our country make a united and strenuous effort to fight against the despotic monarch and corrupt mandarins, unless we extirpate the evil influence of the several-thousand years autocracy once and for all, it will be impossible for people in our country to see the daylight again.[87]

Phan then alleged that Emperor Khải Định had committed seven offences (reckless promotion of autocratic monarchy, unfair rewards and punishments, reckless demand for kowtow, improper dressing, excessive pleasure outings, and shady deals behind the present visit to France) and called for his dethronement.[88]

Why did Phan Chu Trinh abhor the despotic monarchy? His explanation was that the loss of Vietnam's independence was principally attributed to the despotic monarchy and the suppression of public rights as its consequence. In 1906, Phan Chu Trinh commented to Phan Bội Châu during their farewell in Hong Kong that: "since the nineteenth century when countries vehemently competed with each other, the destiny of a country is in the hands of the majority and never is there a country without public rights which can avoid losing the country."[89]

In the public lecture "Morality and Ethics" Phan Chu Trinh further persuades his people that the monarchy was the cause of the loss of the country. Drawing from historical evidence, Phan ascribed to the monarchy the invasion of Korea by Manchus, Mongols, and Japan, respectively, and in the case of China, the replacement of the Song dynasty by the Yuan dynasty and subsequently the replacement of the Ming dynasty by the Qing dynasty.[90] He then concludes:

> Is it not silly to entrust a monarch with the governing power over a country of millions of people. Even in the case of an intelligent monarch, it would be difficult for him to accomplish every responsibility, and things would be even worse under the ignorant monarch who committed cruelties and prohibited the learned people from participating in national affairs. Who would then dare to shoulder the burden? If a family has no one to take care of it, or if a country is not tended, how can that family and that country not collapse and disappear?[91]

Attributing the loss of the country to the monarchy and the suppression of liberal rights, Phan Chu Trinh calls for the abolishment of the monarchy and the establishment of a democratic republic as the gradual path to regain sovereignty.[92] That is why he writes in *The Ballad*: "the monarch's power should be exchanged with the people's power." Phan's rationale is that in a democratic republic, popular rights are developed, the people participate more actively in and are responsible for the national affairs, the patriotism is hence intensified, and ultimately sovereignty can be entirely retrieved.

Written constitution

Conceiving the miasma of the traditional monarchy together with the Augean stable of the mandarin bureaucracy as the juggernauts for modernization and independence, Phan proceeded to propose a new government in which the public power is distributed and constrained by law, especially a written constitution. In the *Letter of Seven Clauses*, Phan laments that the absence of a constitution in Vietnam was the cause of the monarch's arbitrary rule and therefore the suppression of liberal rights: "It is only in our country that popular rights are still being suppressed, a constitution has not been adopted, the monarch is still allowed to make arbitrary decisions, and the people do not have the freedom of public expression."[93] In *The Ballad* Phan suggests: "Political platform should be somewhat transparent." The implication is that the governmental power should be divided and operates under a stable and clear legal framework like a written constitution. In concordance with his suggestion in *The Ballad* that "the law shall be based on the French law," in the "Monarchy and Democracy," Phan particularly extols the French constitutional system and implicitly calls for a written constitution like that of the French as the basic law for the political platform.

In the "Monarchy and Democracy," Phan equates democracy with rule of law:

> Democracy is a government of laws [Vietnamese: *pháp trị*]. The right and the duty of everyone in the country are well described by the laws.... Before the law, everyone is equal, regardless of whether they are officials or common people.[94]

In particular, Phan underlines the distribution and constraint of public power by a written constitution: "Everyone in the country must observe the constitution. The power of the government is also stipulated in the constitution, and therefore there is little room for negligence and autocracy."[95] Conceiving monarchy as the rule of man and democracy as the rule of law, and after making some comparisons, Phan concludes: "democracy is better than monarchy."[96] He then, in the peroration of the speech, orients his compatriots to a democratic government with a written constitution:

> To govern a country solely on the basis of the personal opinions of one individual or an imperial court is to treat the people of that country as if they were a herd of goats – their prosperity and joy, or their poverty and misery, are entirely in the hands of the herder. In contrast, in a democracy, people create their own constitution and select officials, who will act according to the will of the people to look after their nation's business.[97]

Phan in fact suggests a democratic government with a written constitution ordained by the people mirroring the French paradigm.

Liberal rights

Phan Chu Trinh's constitutionalism is largely influenced by western modern liberalism. One of the principal goals of his constitutionalist government is to protect and promote liberal rights. Phan is an admirer of western enlightenment liberals. In particular, he is a prurient adherent of Rousseau and Montesquieu, whose political philosophies he read through the Chinese reformist literature as a young official in Huế. Additionally, his 14 years "living in the land of democracy and breathing the air of liberty"[98] constitutes important practical sources formulating his liberalist discourse. In fact, Phan Chu Trinh is characterized as the most ardent democrat who held aloft the banner of liberal rights in early twentieth-century Vietnam. Huynh Thúc Kháng, in his funeral eulogy for Phan Chu Trinh, virtually espied the essential spirit of his defunct friend "The philosophy of the Nestor (*Tiên sinh*) is to capsize despotism and to liberalize popular rights."[99] Nguyễn Sinh Sắc, father of Hồ Chí Minh, condoled him by the inscription: "the first organizer of popular rights in the Southern Nation."[100]

Indeed, Phan's revolutionary path aims at mobilizing the practice of liberal rights. To begin with, his *Letter to Governor-General Paul Beau* (1907) after his return to Vietnam from Japan appealed for reforms with an emphasis on promoting popular rights. Later, the Restoration Movement, together with the Tonkin Free School, under his leadership mainly aimed at promoting liberal rights. In spite of the punishment for his liberal campaigns, during his years in France, Phan had never stopped urging the French government to practice liberal rights in Indochina, as evident in his *On Indochinese Politics* and the *History of the Insurrection of Central Vietnam*. Particularly, he spent a great deal of his time in France (around 1912–1914) to retranslate into the Vietnamese language Liang

Qichao's Chinese version of the Japanese novel *Kajin no kigu*[101] to inspire the Vietnamese people with liberal values expressed via the literary form. Moreover, the *Letter of Seven Clauses* in which he castigated the monarch also manifests his profound concern for the liberal rights of the Vietnamese people. Last but not least, his crucial public speeches, especially "Monarchy and Democracy," delivered after his return to Vietnam from France, were heavily intended to arouse the Vietnamese people about the prospect of their liberal rights. It is clear that Phan, in *The Ballad*, called for enfranchising people with political participation, freedom of assembly, freedom of thought, and freedom of speech, the prerequisites for other public rights.

However, it should be noted that Phan Chu Trinh's approach to public rights is instrumentalist. When the two Phans exchanged reformist ideas in Japan, Phan Chu Trinh advised Phan Bội Châu:

> Please stay on in Tokyo to take a quiet rest and devote yourself to writing, and not to make appeals for combat against the French. You should only call for "popular rights and popular enlightenment." Once popular rights have been achieved, then we can think about other things.[102]

The implication is that Phan Chu Trinh considered the practice of liberal rights as instrumental to incrementally regaining the national independence.

The separation of powers

In order to implement liberal rights, Phan Chu Trinh envisaged a political system in which the governmental functions were divided. At an early stage, he called for the separation of powers in his petition of "laws and the establishment of supplementary courts" on 4 June 1911. He laments that: "In Indochina, the worst thing is that the judiciary power and the administrative power are concentrated in one hand; hence, if the mandarins injure the people, the people do not dare to do anything."[103] He then suggests "renovating the laws, constituting supplementary courts, separating the powers: administrative officials will be responsible for governing affairs and the judicial officials will be responsible for legal affairs."[104] It was clear that Phan had already developed the concept of judicial independence.

Additionally, his time in France helped Phan intensify his understanding of the doctrine and the practice of the separation of powers. Therefore, after his return to Saigon from Paris, in his "Monarchy and Democracy," Phan demonstrated his more profound comprehension of the government's Montesquieuian scheme. In the speech, Phan describes with admiration the French constitutional system in which, he observed, "the judicial power, the administrative power of the government, and the legislative power of the parliament are separate, not controlled by a single person."[105] This explains his vision of the new Vietnam where "there shall be the Parliament to represent the people" and "there shall be a responsible prime minister to serve the public." In fact, the structural limitation of the government that Phan envisaged follows the parliamentary model of separation of power with a representative legislature, a responsible executive, and an independent judiciary.

To recapitulate briefly, similar to Phan Bội Châu, Phan Chu Trinh was a modern constitutionalist in early twentieth-century Vietnam. Phan Chu Trinh, albeit formally trained with Confucian knowledge, was an admirer of western modern constitutionalism, particularly the practice of French constitutionalism, which led him to advocate constitutional democracy, written constitution, liberal rights, and the separation of powers.

Confucianism

In spite of supporting modern constitutionalism, Phan Chu Trinh himself declared that "I am a Confucianist"[106] when he was taking in the liberal atmosphere in France. Additionally, in "Morality and Ethics," Phan Chu Trinh extolled western moral values but explicitly attested his loyalty to Confucianism:

> I have thus far criticized our ethics and praised western ethics; probably the audience is astonished, thinking that I am betraying the teachings of Confucius and Mencius. I would like to tell you that ever since I came to understand Confucian morality to a certain extent, I have adored it.[107]

What was Confucianism in Phan Chu Trinh's understanding? Phan became a free Confucian scholar after serving for the imperial administration for a short period of time. He called for the abolishment of the traditional Confucian examination system and criticized the corruption of the Confucian mandarins. Therefore, like Phan Bội Châu, Phan Chu Trinh claimed Confucianism views as a tradition of philosophy rather than an ideology of the imperial government. However, what was remarkable about Phan Chu Trinh's perspective, which was clearly demonstrated in his "Monarchy and Democracy" and "Morality and Ethics," was that he only regarded the classical principles practiced by the Chinese ancient kings like Yao, Shun, Yu, Tang, Wen, and Vu, and philosophized by Confucius and Mencius as Confucianism.[108] He contended that the monarchs of the later generations in East Asia had actually abandoned Confucianism while claiming that they were following it:

> When one looks into the history of monarchy in East Asia, one finds that, since Qin dynasty [221–206 BC], though the East Asian countries would consider they were practicing Confucianism, in actuality there was nothing Confucian in the policy practiced, only one or two things remained in the family traditions, and, apart from that, the absolute monarchs relied on Confucianism only to exert pressure upon their peoples.[109]

He then laments that the teachings of Confucius and Mencius have been misunderstood and misappropriated, and therefore countries like China, Vietnam, and Korea have just practiced the "heretical form of Confucianism" (*tà Nho*).[110]

What is the authentic form of Confucianism, according to Phan Chu Trinh? Interestingly, while it is customary to think about Confucianism as the foundation of despotic monarchy in East Asia, Phan states in "Monarchy and Democracy" that: "Monarchy in East Asia did not originate in Confucianism."[111] In "Morality and Ethics," he also claims: "Confucianism is not an ideology that serves the autocratic monarchs."[112] Instead, Phan Chu Trinh conceptualized that Confucianism is antagonistic to autocracy.

On this point, it is worth a return to his castigation of the Emperor Khải Định in the *Letter of Seven Clauses*. Phan Chu Trinh has invoked Confucianism to justify the illegitimacy of the monarch. Phan argued that while "from the olden days our country held Confucianism in reverence," in practice the emperor's reckless promotion of autocracy had been the opposite of Confucianism.[113] To show that the emperor had lost the Confucian legitimacy, Phan summoned the Confucian criticism of despotism and the Confucian concept of *minben*. After reminding the emperor about Confucius' saying that an unopposed ruler may lead the nation to ruin, and Mencius' famous statement on the people as the most important element, Phan states that:

> If your Majesty opened the *Five Classics* and the *Four Books*, could you find an indication that autocracy should be promoted? If your position is above everyone, you should place your heart below everyone – that is the essence of Confucianism.[114]

Acerbically, Phan related Khải Định to Jie and Zhou, the notorious tyrants in Chinese ancient history. Phan reminded the emperor about the favorable attitude of Confucius toward the castigations of the two tyrants and Mencius' stigmatization of Jie as "a robber," "a ruffian," and "a mere fellow." Phan then concluded:

> Is it not genuine Confucianism? The Classics and the Books are still available, all were compiled from the sayings of Confucius and Mencius – I did not fabricate them to deceive myself and then go on to deceive others. By issuing edicts for promotion of autocracy, are you yourself not acting against Confucianism? Is there any king who, acting against the national religion (*quốc giáo*) can remain on the throne for long?[115]

It can be seen that, in adherence to classical Confucianism, in particular Mencian studies, Phan Chu Trinh conceives the core values of Confucianism as the antagonism of despotism and responsible government for the people.

On that ground, Phan suggests that the classical Confucian paradigm of government is comparable to constitutional government in that the people and the government are equal in their values and responsibilities: "Confucianism is very fair, teaching that the monarch and the people are both equally important. The monarch and the people both need to be equipped with morality and ethics."[116] Interestingly, Phan believes that modern constitutional government is just the practice of the Confucian classical governmental model:

> In the *Great Learning*, Master Zeng quoted Confucius, saying: "From the emperor down to the mass of the people, all must consider the cultivation of the person the root of everything." Self-cultivation is such a crucial aspect, one which Confucius insisted the people and the monarch must practice. Was he not fair? This form of government has been practiced in Europe for a long time, i.e., the form of government in which power is divided between the monarch and the people, which has been translated into Chinese as *junzhu lixian* [Vietnamese: *quân chủ lập hiến*]. At present, Britain, Belgium, and Japan practice this form of government.[117]

As both classical Confucian governmental inquiry and modern constitutional democracy practiced in Europe accentuate the important role of the people and equality between the government and the people, Phan concludes: "There is nothing in the present civilization of Europe that goes against the teachings of Confucius and Mencius."[118] Hence, Phan's "Monarchy and Democracy" and "Morality and Ethics" are the encomiums of both modern western constitutionalism and Confucianism. Phan concurrently eulogized both western liberal thinkers (Rousseau, La Fontaine, Montesquieu, Pascal, and Voltaire) and the practice of French constitutionalism and the Confucian classical thinkers (Confucius and Mencius).[119]

Since Confucianism has been misunderstood and misused under autocratic influence, Phan Chu Trinh, in the belief in the shared values of Confucianism and European modern civilization, proposes that the reasonable way to revitalize authentic Confucianism is by introducing European democracy:

> Democracy is a wonderfully efficacious remedy against the autocratic disease of our country. To bring in European civilization is to bring back the teachings of Confucius and Mencius.... The introduction of European civilization would not cause any harm, but it will help to enhance the teachings of Confucius and Mencius.[120]

Finally, Phan emphasizes that this introduction is the harmonization of the authentic civilization (*chân văn minh*) in the west with the authentic Confucianism (*chân Nho giáo*) in East Asia.[121] Consequently, Phan's constitutionalism is in fact the amalgamation of western liberal constitutionalist values and Confucian classical values. Like in Phan Bội Chau's case, this is well elaborated on by Phan Chu Trinh's integration of the Confucian *minben* concept into his constitutionalist project.

Despite being an ardent activist for liberal rights, Phan is far from a pure liberalist. As the echo of Confucian *minben*, like Phan Bội Chau, the *telos* of Phan's constitutionalism concerns the public goods of the people rather than merely liberal rights. On this point, attention should return to his program for the Restoration Movement encapsulated in the motto: "*chấn dân khí, khai dân trí, hậu dân sinh*" ("invigorate the people's spirit, broaden the people's mind, and enrich the people's well-being").

Within the movement, "*chấn dân khí*" means by education and public speech, revitalizing the national catharsis that had been at a low ebb due to the miasma of despotism and colonialism; "*khai dân trí*" means educating the people on new values by establishing free schools to teach a new curriculum; and "*hậu dân sinh*" means improving the living conditions by developing domestic products and industry.[122] Obviously, Phan Chu Trinh's concerns encompass widely moral, intellectual, and material dimensions of people's lives. It should be noted that these are also Phan's enduring considerations rather than only the ephemeral slogan for the movement. That explains why Phan has written in *The Ballad* that "there shall be a responsible prime minister to serve the public." Understanding the verse within his philosophy, "the public" can be construed as the general standards comprehensively concerning people's moral, intellectual, and material dimensions.

In particular, following the teachings of Confucius and Mencius on educating the people as the practice of the *minben* principle, "Phan Chau Trinh strongly believed education was the most important element in modernization."[123] In Phan's project, the people must not only be entitled to liberal rights but also be educated with moral values. Importantly, he especially underlines the foundational value of classical Confucian morality. This is most evident in his "Morality and Ethics." After returning to Saigon from Paris, he chose to deliver a speech on the traditional theme of morality and ethics instead of more topical or modern issues. His explanation for the choice actually reflects his attachment to the Confucian moral foundationalism: "I have chosen this subject because I believe that, from ancient times to the present day, regardless of the people, regardless of the country, regardless of the race, and regardless of the national power, once a nation is standing in the world to compete against other nations, it cannot count only on its material strength but must also rely on morality as its foundation."[124] His understanding of morality is in fact shaped by Confucian morality. He states: "To be a human being, one is expected to have *nhân* (humaneness), *nghĩa* (righteousness), *lễ* (propriety), *trí* (wisdom), *tín* (trustworthiness), *cần* (diligence), and *kiệm* (frugality)."[125] These are fundamental moral values fostered in classical Confucianism, but Phan considers them the universal moral values which can serve as the foundation for every society "regardless of time and place."[126]

Apart from the moral values, Phan Chu Trinh believes that people should be educated with contemporary western knowledge for modernization in general, and constitutional knowledge for the success of modern constitutionalism in particular. In this regard, it should be recalled that Phan Chu Trinh, together with Huỳnh Thúc Kháng and Trần Quý Cáp, created the Tonkin Free School (*Đông kinh Nghĩa thục*) in Hanoi in March 1907.[127] The school was established with the mission of expanding the people's knowledge (*khai dân trí*) of the Restoration Movement. By the establishment of this school, Phan Chu Trinh and other modern Confucianists in Vietnam continued the teachings of Confucius and Mencius in educating the people, but with novel content. Although the school had a short life of only nine months,[128] it played an important role in the change of Vietnamese modern culture and in the movement toward modern constitutionalist values in particular.[129] Through the materials[130] and the activities[131] of the school, among other things, the new terms and ideas of "*chính thể lập hiến*" (constitutionalist polity), "*cộng hòa*" (republic), "*nghị viện*" (parliament), and "*dân chủ*" (democracy) were disseminated to the public. In short, Phan Chu Trinh seems to agree with Phan Bội Châu that the success of constitutionalism requires the education of constitutional knowledge to the people.

Phan Chu Trinh, in a similar manner to Phan Bội Châu, was highly active in writing to criticize the despotic monarchy and to distribute constitutional knowledge to the people. It is worth remembering Phan Bội Châu's inscription for Phan Chu Trinh: "by words instead of swords and guns, you disquieted the dynasty of the autocrat; by nibs instead of drums or gongs, you illuminated the atrium of democracy."[132] Like an old bottle used for storing new liquid, Phan Chu Trinh utilized his literary capacity nurtured in the Confucian educational system to diffuse constitutionalist values. Particularly, he composed the poem (which has been appropriated in the present study) to propagandize his constitutionalist project.

Denouement

The history of Vietnam has taken a path different from that anticipated by Phan Chu Trinh. Instead of becoming a French dominion, the country has gained autonomy through the revolution in August 1945 and a written constitution was subsequently enacted. However, this does not mean that Phan's constitutionalist project was fruitless. On this point, Phan Chu Trinh's unique funeral in 1926 should be noted. This unprecedented funeral, in which the entire country mourned a Confucian patriot, has served as the occasion for the breaking out of Vietnamese modern nationalism. Reportedly, it was attended by 16,000–100,000 people in Saigon, where the main funeral took place, while the total population there was around 300,000. Apart from the main event in Saigon, around 40 provinces throughout the country also held funerals to mourn Phan Chu Trinh.[133] The nationwide funerals demonstrated the significant influence of Phan Chu Trinh's revolutionary thoughts and activities, including his constitutionalism. Phan Bội Châu helpfully represented the national impact of Phan Chu Trinh's works:

> Our Phan Hy Mã [Phan Chu Trinh's other name] studied Montesquieu's philosophy and illuminates Mencius' sayings, took the two words "popular rights" (*dân quyền*) to cry throughout the country like the resounding thunders wakening up a myriad of dreams and thanks to that our nation henceforth gradually realizes that we have rights.... Now he has passed away but his philosophy has become more and more luminous. The whole of our compatriots, even children, has genuflected and worshipped him. Hence, the meaning of "popular rights" has imbued in their minds.[134]

Phan Chu Trinh never witnessed the realization of his constitutionalist ideas. However, his evangelism was very influential in introducing to the Vietnamese people the fundamental principles of modern constitutionalism during that period. Like Phan Bội Châu, Phan Chu Trinh considerably enlightened and galvanized the people with modern constitutionalist values, especially the modern discourse of liberal rights.

Conclusion

Utilizing the cases of Phan Bội Châu and Phan Chu Trinh, the present chapter has demonstrated the efforts of modern intellectuals in promoting modern constitutionalism in early twentieth-century East Asia. As far as Vietnam is concerned, even though the two Phans never witnessed the realization of their constitutionalist projects, the meaningfulness of their work is considerable. The establishment of the Democratic Republic of Vietnam in 1945 and the subsequent enactment of the first written constitution in 1946 are the denouement of various constitutional movements and the contribution of the Confucian movements should be recognized. The Confucianists were the first generation of the modern constitutionalists in Vietnam, who have familiarized and inspired the Vietnamese people with novel vocabularies and notions of western constitutionalist theories, such as popular sovereignty, written constitution, liberal rights, and the separation of powers. They have actually established the foundational steps in helping Vietnam to have full access to the ideas and institutions of western modern constitutionalism. Therefore, scholarly inquiry into modern constitutional history in Vietnam should be started with not the 1946 constitution, but the constitutionalist discourse of the Confucianists in the early twentieth century. I conclude this chapter with more general observations.

First, Confucianism is not the impediment of the development of modern constitutionalism in East Asia. The Confucianists like Phan Bội Châu, Phan Chu Trinh, Kang Yuwei, and Liang Qichao, albeit educated in the traditional system of education, were sympathetic to notions and institutions of western modern constitutionalism. They were concurrently the students of Confucius, Mencius, Montesquieu, and Rousseau. This indicates that identification with Confucianism, putatively the political ideology of authoritarian governments in pre-modern East Asia, needs not constrain attraction to Western modern constitutionalism. This is a meaningful observation when we consider the real predicates for the development of modern constitutionalism in the East Asian Confucian societies.

However, Chengyang Li argues that the fact that Chinese Confucian intellectuals such as Yan Fu (1853–1921), Kang Yuwei, Liang Qichao, Zhang Binglin (1868–1936), and Liu Shipei (1884–1927) first welcomed the western idea of democracy in China does not necessarily suggest that Confucianism has an intrinsic affinity for democracy. Li explains:

> In a country like nineteenth-century China, only intellectuals had the opportunity and political sensitivity to be exposed to the Western idea of democracy. In a Buddhist or Islamic country it is likely for Buddhist or Islamic intellectuals to be among the first to be exposed to and perhaps welcome democracy.[135]

Li's argument is debatable. As previously mentioned, the intelligentsia of early twentieth-century Vietnam consisted of not only the Confucian intellectuals but also the western-style intellectuals. Unfortunately, the western-style intellectuals trained in the French schools were inclined to functionary careers in the colonial bureaucracy.[136] The students of the Confucian schools criticized this. Phan Chu Trinh regarded "those who have followed western studies and worked as clerks or interpreters" as the "licensed robbers"[137] in the sense that they appropriated the colonial governmental offices for their egoistic benefits. This limited their role in introducing western modern thought into Vietnam. Commenting on the western-style intellectuals, Huỳnh Thúc Kháng lamented: "who are concerned with the philosophy and the essence of Western studies so as to develop ourselves and introduce them to our people?"[138] Instead, it was the students of Confucianism who were the first advocates of western modern constitutionalism in early twentieth-century Vietnam. To explain this, consider this reminiscence of Nguyễn Khắc Viện, a typical western-style intellectual of the time:

> We [I use the word "we" because the author of these lines is one of those intellectuals graduated from the University of Hanoi or returned home from France after the colonial period] learned what the Confucian scholars lacked: physics, algebra, biology, electoral politics, and republic constitutions. But when we compared ourselves with the traditional scholars, whom we still saw on a regular basis, we definitely felt they had something we lacked.
>
> Their knowledge was relatively limited, but they were "men," they were the "bamboo trees" which remained tall, "pines" that withstood the adversities of winter.... With their deeply-rooted moral convictions, the scholars had principles to which they adhered. The validity of these convictions could be debated, but their existence was certain, since these men never acted against these convictions. Ethics was the very base of their education.
>
> Our training was different. In high school and in the university, we paid special attention to chemistry, trigonometry, and geography courses. When it was time for ethics, we secretly read novels or played naval battles. The scholars never knew what a scientist was, whereas we never knew what a worthy man was. And most of us, although not all, were like clay when it came to stand up with opposing forces that played with us at will.[139]

These words suggest that the genuine students of Confucianism possess distinctive moral qualifications enabling them to actively struggle for social reformation in general, and western modern constitutionalism in particular. Mencius famously declares the moral convictions of "the great man" as follows:

> to dwell in the wide house of the world, to stand in the correct seat of the world, and to walk in the great path of the world; when he obtains his desire for office, to practice his principles for the good of the people; and when that desire is disappointed, to practice them alone; to be above the power of

> riches and honours to make dissipated, of poverty and mean condition to make swerve from the principle, and of power and force to make bend.[140]

The western-style intellectuals lacked these Confucian qualifications, and the Confucian mandarins betrayed them. Differently, the bona fide Confucianists, the ones who adhered to the standards of classic Confucianism and moved away from imperial Confucianism, have persistently retained the Confucian qualifications of "the great man,"[141] which necessarily led them to engage in the arduous odyssey, struggling for socio-political modernization in general and modern constitutionalism in particular. As the loyal adherents of these moral characteristics, the Confucianists have sacrificed their own interests for the betterment of the public and this led them to fighting for modernization of the Vietnamese society, including the practice of western modern constitutionalism, despite the circumstances, such as incarceration, they suffered. Particularly, "the stuff of transcending the bending to power and force" is the impetuous characteristic invigorating the Confucianists to valorously censure despotic power in favor of constitutionalism. In short, the genuine Confucianists have intrinsic affinity for modern constitutionalists: the magnanimous spirit of struggling against despotic government in favor of government responsible for general public standards.

Indeed, the fact that the Confucianists actively fought for western modern constitutionalism suggests that Confucianism has elements hospitable to western modern constitutionalism. In the Confucianists' perspective, the essence of Confucianism – to be accurate, classical Confucianism – is the antagonism of despotism and the governmental responsibility; I have explained these as constitutionalist ideas in Confucian philosophy in Chapter 1. The antagonism of despotism in favor of responsible government is truly the junction of classical Confucianism and western modern constitutionalism. However, western modern constitutionalism is distinguished from Confucian constitutionalism by its means, namely written constitution and the institutionalized separation of powers. The Confucianists were euphoric to welcome these western constitutionalist contrivances as instruments to realize their Confucian dream of the welfare of the people.

The second observation concerns the logic of the Confucianist's learning from outside. Comparative constitutional law scholars have pointed out "learning" as an important mechanism of constitutional diffusion. Its logic is that: "Success breeds imitation, and constitutionalism is no exception. Countries copy legal and constitutional innovations from their most successful rivals in the hope of achieving similar success."[142] This logic can explain the transnational sources of constitutional projects of the two Phan revolutionaries. They adopted some elements of western constitutionalism to modernize the Vietnamese society because they learned from the triumph of Meiji Japan and the successful Chinese creation of the republic, which stemmed from their adoption of values of western constitutionalism; the two contexts shared the Confucian culture with Vietnam. Particularly, Japan has modernized its political system by adopting western constitutional values, from which it became a strong nation capable of defeating

Russian power. The two Phans were aware of that successful story and adopted western constitutional institutions in the hope that Vietnam could gain similar success: defeating the French. The stories of the two Phans demonstrate a common thing: in the late nineteenth and early twentieth centuries, when East Asia was confronted the western power of imperialism, Confucian intellectuals learned from each other and from the West in adopting values of western constitutionalism in the hope that their nations could be modernized and become strong enough to compete with and combat the external power. So, the Confucian intellectuals' approach to Western constitutionalism is instrumentalist rather foundationalist. Western constitutionalism is welcomed as an instrument for modernization.

The third observation relates the logic of the role of Confucianism in modern constitutionalism in East Asia. While modern East Asian constitutionalists like Phan Bội Châu and Phan Chu Trinh supported common institutions of western modern constitutionalism, they do not abandon Confucianism. One possible argument is that as Confucianism was still the prevailing model of thought among intellectuals at the time, they strategically rather than substantially employed Confucianism to enhance the legitimacy of their constitutional projects and political activities. This argument is, however, rebuttable. In fact, they employed Confucianism for substantial expressivist reasons. Confucianism constitutes the national identity of East Asian nations like China, Vietnam, and Korea. It is logical that modern constitutionalism in these nations must express Confucian culture. This explains the fact that the East Asian modern intellectuals adhered to Confucianism and integrated its elements in their distinctive constitutional vision. Another reason explaining why the East Asian modern intellectuals adhered to Confucianism may stem from the limits of western liberal constitutionalism. They seemed unhappy with Western constitutional government's chief goal of protecting liberal rights. Therefore, they drew from Confucian moral principles to redefine the goal of constitutionalism. Consequently, in their visions, their projects of modern Confucian constitutionalism incorporated basic elements of Western modern constitutionalism, such as written constitution, popular sovereignty and democratic government, fundamental political rights constitutive to the democratic government, and the separation of powers, but redefined them by disconnecting them from their underpinning of liberalism and replacing liberalism with Confucianism. In the new formulation of modern Confucian constitutionalism, western constitutional ingredients are merely for the sake of protecting liberal rights, but are redefined by Confucianism, especially the concept of *minben*, to ultimately serve the moral and material well-being of the people.

One possible critical response may be that the Confucian intellectuals misunderstood western modern constitutionalism when they disconnected it from liberalism, for which they instrumentally employed its institutions for communitarian purposes. Recall Robert Cover's theory on *nomos* and narrative, which suggests that legal concepts, principles, and institutions would be reasonably differently understood in different narratives.[143] Since the particular narratives of East

Asia in the early twentieth century are less concerned with individuals' liberty and more with public goals, especially state-building, the Confucian constitutionalists reasonably understood the institutions of western modern constitutionalism in different ways and for different purposes. They, however, did not abandon the essence of constitutionalism as the legal limitations on the public power. They just understood constitutional limitations in a positive way.

The Confucianists actually integrated some classical Confucian political principles into their particular constitutionalist visions. Despite supporting western liberal constitutionalism, they might think that it is not perfect and could be improved by Confucian political wisdom in the Confucian context. Particularly, to them, liberal rights are important but might not be the ultimate goal of a constitutionalist state. Consequently, the constitutionalist state in their understanding is not the neutral state merely providing legal protection for rights. Rather, in their Confucian constitutionalist projects, persons should be not only girded with fundamental rights, but also be instilled with fundamental moral virtues, and there should be the requirement of educating the people with constitutional knowledge provided by both the state and the community. In this sense, the state necessarily engages in the promotion of civic virtue rather than being neutral regarding the individual's choice of a good life.

In the next chapter I will consider the possibility of further mixing Confucianism with western liberal constitutionalism in contemporary East Asia.

Notes

1 Dieter Grimm, "The Achievement of Constitutionalism and its Prospects in a Changed World," in *The Twilight of Constitutionalism?* ed. Petra Dobner and Martin Loughlin (Oxford: Oxford University Press, 2010); Alan S. Rosenbaum, ed., *Constitutionalism: The Philosophical Dimension* (New York: Greenwood Press, 1988).

2 For a comprehensive study of the Meiji Restoration, see W.G. Beasley, *The Meiji Restoration* (Stanford, CA: Stanford University Press, 1972). For particular accounts on Meiji constitutionalism, see Takii Kazuhiro, *The Meiji Constitution: The Japanese Experience of the West and the Shaping of the Modern State*, translated by David Noble (Tokyo: International House of Japan, 2007); G. Akita, *Foundations of Constitutional Government in Modern Japan: 1868–1900* (Cambridge, MA: Harvard University Press, 1967).

3 Christopher A. Ford, "The Indigenization of Constitutionalism in Japanese Experience," *Case Western Reserve Journal of International Law* 28 (1996): 3.

4 BaoGang He, "Four Models of the Relationship Between Confucianism and Democracy," *Journal of Chinese Philosophy* 37(1) (2010): 25; Richard Henry Mason, *Japan's First General Election* (Cambridge: Cambridge University Press, 1969), 74.

5 Chaihark Halm, "Human Rights in Korea," in *Human Rights in Asia: A Comparative Legal Study of Twelve Asian Jurisdictions, France, and the United States*, ed. Randall Peerenboom *et al.* (New York: Routledge, 2005), 267.

6 Hao Chang, "Intellectual Change and the Reform Movement, 1890–8" in *The Cambridge History of China, Vol. 11*, ed. John F. Fairbank and Kwang-Ching Liu (Cambridge and New York: Cambridge University Press, 1978), 281–282.

7 Ibid., 282.

8 Ibid.

9 Ibid., 283.

10 See, generally, Alison Adcock Kaufman, "One Nation Among Many: Foreign Models in the Constitutional Thought of Liang Qichao" (PhD dissertation, University of California, Berkeley, 2007).

11 Sun Yat-sen, *San Min Chu I: The Three Principles of the People*, trans. Frank W. Price (Taiwan: China Publishing Co., 1927), 145.

12 For studies on constitutional thoughts of Chinese Confucianists, see: Kaufman, "One Nation Among Many"; Eric Chiyeung Ip, "Building Constitutional Democracy on Oriental Foundations: An Anatomy of Sun Yat-sen's Constitutionalism," *Historia Constitucional* 9 (2008): 328.

13 William J. Duiker, "Hanoi Scrutinizes the Past: The Marxist Evaluation of Phan Boi Chau and Phan Chu Trinh," *Southeast Asia: An International Quarterly* 1(3) (1971): 242–254; William J. Duiker, *The Rise of Nationalism in Vietnam, 1900–1941* (Ithaca, NY and London: Cornell University Press, 1976); William J. Duiker, "Phan Boi Chau: Asian Revolutionary in a Changing World," *The Journal of Asian Studies* 31(1) (1971): 77–88; David G. Marr, *Vietnamese Anticolonialism, 1885–1925* (Berkeley, Los Angeles, London: University of California, 1971); Buttinger, *Vietnam: A Dragon Embattled, Volume 1: From Colonialism to the Vietminh* (New York, Washington, London: Frederick A. Praeger, Publishers, 1976), 111–158; Alexander B. Woodside, *Community and Revolution in Modern Vietnam* (Boston, MA: Houghton Mifflin Company, 1976), 36–42.

14 David G. Marr, ed., *Reflections from Captivity* (Athens, OH: Ohio University Press, 1978) (Christopher Jenkins, Trần Khánh Tuyết, and Huỳnh Sanh Thông's translation of Phan Bội Châu's *Ngục Trung Thư* [*The Book Written in Prison*] is included); Vinh Sinh and Nicholas Wickenden, trans., *Overturned Chariot: The Autobiography of Phan Bội Châu* (Honolulu: University of Hawaii Press, 1999); Trương Bửu Lâm, trans., *Colonialism Experienced* (translations of Phan Bội Châu's *The New Vietnam* and Phan Chu Trinh's *Letter to Governor-General Paul Beau* are included); Vinh Sinh, trans., *Phan Chau Trinh* (providing an excellent introduction of Phan Châu Trinh's life and political thought, and translation of his four critical political writings).

15 Trần Văn Giàu, *Sự Phát Ttriển của Tư tưởng ở Việt Nam, Tập II* [*The Development of Thoughts in Vietnam, Volume II*] (Hanoi: Social Science Publishing House, 1973), 14.

16 Thomas Hodgkin, *Vietnam: The Revolutionary Path* (London and Basingstoke: Macmillan, 1981), 173. For more details on the making of Indochina, see Pierre Brocheux and Daniel Hémery, *Indochina: An Ambiguous Colonization, 1858–1954*, trans. Ly Lan Dill-Klein *et al.* (Berkeley, Los Angeles, London: University of California Press, 2009); Donald Lancaster, *The Emancipation of French Indochina* (London, New York, Toronto: Oxford University Press, 1961), in particular Part II, 59–71; Joseph Buttinger, *Vietnam: A Dragon Embattled*, 3–43.

17 Trần Văn Giàu, [*The Development of Thoughts*], 16–17.

18 Trương Bửu Lâm, trans., *Colonialism Experienced: Vietnamese Writings on Colonialism, 1900–1931* (Anna Arbor, MI: University of Michigan Press, 2000), 9.

19 Alexander B. Woodside, *Community and Revolution in Modern Vietnam* (Boston, MA: Houghton Mifflin Company, 1976), 3.

20 Trương Bửu Lâm, *Colonialism Experienced*, 12.

21 Ibid., 13.

22 For French colonial schools in Vietnam, see Trần Thị Phương Hoa, "Franco-Vietnamese Schools and the Transition from Confucian to a New Kind of Intellectuals in the Colonial Context of Tonkin" (Working Paper Series, Harvard-Yenching Institute, 2009).

23 Trần Văn Giàu, [*The Development of Thoughts*], 20; Woodside, *Community and Revolution*, 3.

24 Nguyễn Khắc Việ*n, Vietnam: A Long Hist*ory (Hanoi: Foreign Languages Publishing House, 1987), 168.

25 Vinh Sinh, trans., *Phan Chau Trinh and His Political Writings* (Ithaca, NY: Cornell Southeast Asia Program Publications, 2009), 6.
26 For more elaborations of the *Can Vuong Movement*, see Marr, *Vietnamese Anticolonialism*, 44–76.
27 For a comprehensive study of theMeiji Restoration, see Beasley, *The Meiji Restoration*. For particular accounts on Meiji constitutionalism, see Takii Kazuhiro, *The Meiji Constitution: The Japanese Experience of the West and the Shaping of the Modern State*, trans. David Noble (Tokyo: International House of Japan, 2007).
28 Trần Văn Giàu, [*The Development of Thoughts*], 25.
29 Ibid., 27. For Chinese reformists and revolutionary movements, see Wang Juntao, "Confucian Democrats in Chinese History," in *Confucianism for the Modern World*, ed. Daniel A. Bell and Hahm Chaibong (Cambridge: Cambridge University Press, 2003), 72–81; Tseng Yu-hao, *Modern Chinese Legal and Political Philosophy* (Shanghai: The Commercial Press, 1930), 39–133.
30 For a collection of essays indicating Hanoi's views on the influences of the "new books" in Vietnam, see, Đinh Xuân Lâm, ed., *Tân thư và Xã hội Việt Nam cuối Thế kỷ XIX đầu Thế kỷ XX* [*New Books and Vietnamese Society in the Period of the Late 19th Century to the Early 20th Century*] (Hanoi: National Political Publishing House, 1997).
31 Trần Văn Giàu, [*The Development of Thoughts*], 26.
32 Ibid., 27–28. After the fiasco of the Wuxu Reform due to the coup d'etat led by the Empress Dowager, Liang Qichao escaped to Japan. Liang established here the *Qing Yi Bao* in around 14 November to 12 December 1898. After the fire in the printing plant in Yokohama put an end to this journal in 1900, Liang initiated the *Xinmin Congbao* in early spring of 1902. Based on the journalist form, Liang commented on current affairs, attacked the Empress Dowager's regime in Beijing, and disseminated new western democratic ideas. For Liang's journalist activities during exile in Japan, see Joseph R. Levenson, *Liang Qichao and the Mind of Modern China* (Berkeley, CA: University of California Press, 1970), 55–83. *The Collected Works of Yinbingshi* is an anthology of Liang Qichao's writings, first published in 1902. The phrase "*yinbingshi*" literally meaning "ice-drinker's room" is putatively stemmed from this sentence in Zhuang Tzu's work: "This every morning I was given my commission and this evening I am drinking iced water." Martin Palmer and Elizabeth Breuilly, trans., *The Book of Chuang Tzu* (London: Penguin Books, 1996), 30.
33 Trần Văn Giàu, [*The Development of Thoughts*], 27.
34 Ibid., 26.
35 Vinh Sinh and Wickenden, "Introduction" in *The Autobiography of Phan Bội Châu*, 1.
36 Nguyễn Ái Quốc, "Những Trò Lố hay là Varenne và Phan Bội Châu" ["The Jazz or Varenne and Phan Bội Châu"] in *Phan Bội Châu trong Dòng Thời đại* [*Phan Bội Châu in the Stream of Time*], ed. Chương Thâu (Nghệ An: Nghệ An Publishing House, 2007), 15.
37 The treaty reaches for the modus vivendi by which the two countries respect each other's spheres of interests in East Asia. Vinh Sinh and Wickenden, "Introduction," 12.
38 For a comprehensive picture of Phan's life, see Vinh Sinh and Wickenden, "Introduction." For particular accounts on the Eastern Exodus Movement, see: Marr, *Vietnamese Anticolonialism*, 120–155; Vinh Sinh, ed., *Phan Bội Châu and the Dong-Du Movement* (New Haven, CT: Yale Southeast Asia Studies, 1988). For more illustrations of the last course of his life in Huế, see Trần Huy Liệu, "Nhớ lại 'Ông già Bến Ngự' " ["Recalling the 'Old Man of Imperial Quay' "] In *Ông già Bến Ngự: Hồi ký* [*Old Man of Imperial Quay: Memoir*], ed. Tôn Quang Phiệt *et al.* (Huế: Thuận Hóa Publishing House, 1982), 40–54.
39 Buttinger, *Vietnam*, 158.

40 Vinh Sinh and Wickenden, *The Autobiography of Phan Ḅôi Châu*, 190. Among his "many contacts with Chinese comrades," most notable are the audiences with Liang Qichao and Sun Yat-sen, which considerably impact on his modernizing projects. Phan was able to write but not speak and listen in Chinese. Therefore, Phan's conversations with Liang Qichao and Sun Yat-sen were conducted mainly through brush-conversation. Ibid., 85–90 (with Liang Qichao); 101–102 (with Sun Yat-sen).
41 Phan Bội Châu, *Toàn tập, Tập 2* [*Complete Works, Volume 2*] (Huế: Thuận Hóa Publishing House, 1990), 112.
42 The document was written in Chinese characters when Phan went to Hong Kong from Japan. The original version is restored in the National Archives in Hanoi. The modern Vietnamese language version can be found at ibid. 250–277. The English translation can be found at Trương Bửu Lâm, *Colonialism Experienced*, 105–124. I will follow Lâm's translation.
43 Ibid., 107–108.
44 Vinh Sinh and Wickenden, *The Autobiography of Phan Ḅôi Châu*, 191.
45 Ibid., 190.
46 Phan Bội Châu, *Toàn tập, Tập 3* [*Complete Works, Volume 3*], 135.
47 The authorship of *The Ballad* is somewhat confused. Different materials note the author as Phan Bội Châu, Nguyễn Thiện Thuật, Tăng Bạt Hổ, and Dương Bá Trạc. However, some coevals of Phan Bội Châu such as Hồ Chí Minh verify Phan's authorship. Phan himself did not mention *The Ballad* in his autobiography. However, Chương Thâu noted that *The Ballad* appeared in the collections of posthumous manuscripts of Phan Bội Châu that Chương received from Phan's daughter-in law (Nguyễn Thị Phúc) in 1961. Originally, *The Ballad* was written in both literary Chinese character (*chữ Hán*) and Vietnamese demotic character (*chữ Nôm*). The modern Vietnamese romanized script (*quốc ngữ*) version appears in Chương Thâu, *Đông Kinh Nghĩa Thục* [*Tonkin Free School*] (Hanoi: Hanoi Publishing House, 1982), 159–168.
48 Ibid., 162.
49 Ibid., 167.
50 Trương Bửu Lâm, *Colonialism Experienced*, 123–124.
51 Phan Bội Châu, *Toàn tập, Tập 4* [*Complete Works, Volume 4*], 71.
52 Ibid., 244.
53 Ibid.
54 Ibid., 261.
55 Trương Bửu Lâm, trans., *Colonialism Experienced*, 108–114.
56 Phan Bội Châu, *Toàn tập, Tập 5* [*Complete Works, Volume 5*], 256.
57 Trương Bửu Lâm, trans., *Colonialism Experienced*, 108.
58 Ibid.
59 Phan Bội Châu, *Chu Dich* [*The Book of Change*] (Hanoi: Cultural Publishing House, 1996); Phan Bội Châu, *Khổng học Đăng* [*The Light of Confucianism*] (Hanoi: Cultural and Information Publishing House, 1998).
60 Lê Sỹ Thắng, "Phan Bội Châu và Nho giáo" ["Phan Bội Châu and Confucianism"] in *Nho giáo: Xưa và Nay* [*Confucianism: Ancient and Modern*], ed. Vũ Khiêu (Hanoi: Social Sciences Publishing House, 1991), 225.
61 Phan Bội Châu, [*The Light of Confucianism*], 13–14
62 Ibid., 14.
63 Ibid., 13.
64 Phan Bội Châu, [*Complete Works, Volume 4*], 32.
65 Cited in Trần Văn Giầu, [*The Development of Thoughts*], 119.
66 Trương Bửu Lâm, *Colonialism Experienced*, 112.
67 Ibid.
68 Phan Bội Châu, [*Complete Works, Volume 4*], 60.
69 Vinh Sinh and Wickenden, *The Autobiography of Phan Ḅôi Châu*, 45.

70 Vinh Sinh and Wickenden, "Introduction," 32.
71 Ibid.
72 Ibid., 33.
73 The English translation of the letter can be found at Trương Bửu Lâm, *Colonialism Experienced*, 125–140.
74 For more details on the Restoration Movement, see Đỗ Thị Minh Thúy and Nguyễn Hồng Sơn, ed., *Phong trào Duy dân với Sự Chuyển biến của Văn hóa Việt Nam đầu Thế kỷ XX* [*Restoration Movement and the Transition of Vietnamese Culture in the Early Twentieth Century*] (Hanoi: Encyclopedic Publishing House and Cultural Institute, 2010).
75 Nguyễn Q. Thắng, *Phan Châu Trinh- Cuộc đời & Tác phẩm* [*Phan Châu Trinh: The Life and the Works*] (Hanoi: Literacy Publishing House, 2006), 113.
76 Formally known as *Việt Nam Quốc dân Phan Châu Trinh Ký thư ư Việt Nam Đương kim Hoàng đế* [*A Letter by Phan Châu Trinh, a Vietnamese Citizen, Addressed to the Contemporary Emperor of Vietnam*], the letter is originally in Chinese and translated into French to publish in French magazines. The Vietnamese modern-language version of the letter translated by Phan Chu Trinh and Lê Ấm is included in ibid., 421–446. The English translation of the letter can be found in Vinh Sinh, *Phan Chau Trinh*, 87–102. In this study, I follow Vinh Sinh's translation.
77 For the Vietnamese version, see Nguyễn Q. Thắng, *Phan Châu Trinh*, 475–508. For the English version, see Vinh Sinh, trans., *Phan Chau Trinh*, 103–123. In this study, I follow Vinh Sinh's translation.
78 The Vietnamese version can be found at Nguyễn Q. Thắng, *Phan Châu Trinh*, 447–473. The English translation is included in Vinh Sinh, *Phan Chau Trinh*, 125–139. In this study, I follow Vinh Sinh's translation.
79 Vinh Sinh and Wickenden, *The Autobiography of Phan Bội Châu*, 109.
80 The Vietnamese version of *The Ballad* can be found at Lê Thị Kinh (Phan Thị Minh), ed., *Phan Châu Trinh qua Những Tài liệu Mới Phát hiện, Tập 1* [*Phan Châu Trinh through Newly Discovered Materials, Volume 1*] (Đà Nẵng: Đà Nẵng Publishing House, 2001), 242. The English translation is my own.
81 Duiker, *Nationalism in Vietnam*, 51.
82 Vinh Sinh, "Introduction" in *Phan Châu Trinh*, 43.
83 Phan Chu Trinh clearly expressed his ideas on self-rule in *Pháp-Việt Liên hiệp Hậu chi Tân Việt Nam* [*A New Vietnam Following the Franco-Vietnamese Alliance*] (1910–1911). For English translation of the writing, see Vinh Sinh, *Phan Chau Trinh*, 57–86.
84 It is recalled that after Phan Chu Trinh returned to Saigon from Paris, there were many young admirers visiting him and at the beginning of every conversation, Phan asked every visitor the same question: "Have you read *The Social Contract* of Rousseau or *The Spirit of Law* of Montesquieu?" Trần Văn Giầu, [*The Development of Thoughts*], 451.
85 Vinh Sinh and Wickenden, *The Autobiography of Phan Bội Châu*, 105.
86 Vinh Sinh, *Phan Chau Trinh*, 87.
87 Ibid., 88.
88 Ibid.
89 Cited in Nguyễn Đình An, "Phan Châu Trinh: Nhà Cách mạng Chính trị, Nhà Dân chủ Đầu tiên của Nước ta" ["Phan Châu Trinh: A Political Revolutionary and The First Democrat of Our Country"] in [*Restoration Movement*], 358.
90 Vinh Sinh, *Phan Chau Trinh*, 119.
91 Ibid.
92 After his death, the *Eastern French Magazine* (*Đông Pháp Thời Báo*) published a picture of Phan Chu Trinh standing on the podium, with a caption reading: *Uphold Republicanism* (*Thủ Xướng Cộng hòa*). Vinh Sinh, "Introduction," 37.
93 Vinh Sinh, *Phan Chau Trinh*, 88.

94 Ibid., 139.
95 Ibid.
96 Ibid.
97 Ibid.
98 Ibid., 88.
99 Trần Văn Giầu, [*The Development of Thoughts*], 437.
100 Nguyễn Q. Thắng, *Phan Châu Trinh*, 77.
101 *Kajin no kigu* is a political serialized novel that explores popular rights and revolution, first published in Japan from 1885 to 1897 by the Japanese ex-samuri Tokai Sanshi. Liang Qichao translated the novel into Chinese when he was in Japan in 1899. Because Phan was unable to read Japanese, he retranslated via Liang's version. Phan's Vietnamese poetic version is known as "*Giai nhân Kỳ ngộ Diễn ca*." For more details, see Vinh Sinh, "Elegant Females Re-encountered: From Tokai Sanshi's *Kajin no kigu* to Phan Chau Trinh's *Giai nhân Kỳ ngộ Diễn ca*" in *Essays into Vietnamese Pasts*, ed. K.W. Taylor and John K. Whitmore (Ithaca, NY: Cornell University Southeast Asia Program, 1995), 195–206.
102 Vinh Sinh and Wickenden, *The Autobiography of Phan Ḅôi Châu*, 108.
103 Lê Thị Kinh, [*Newly Discovered Materials*], 37.
104 Ibid., 38.
105 Vinh Sinh, *Phan Chau Trinh*, 139.
106 Vinh Sinh, *Phan Chau Trinh*, 45.
107 Ibid., 117.
108 Ibid., 129.
109 Ibid., 130.
110 Ibid., 118–119.
111 Ibid., 127.
112 Ibid., 117.
113 Ibid., 88.
114 Ibid., 89.
115 Ibid., 89.
116 Ibid., 117.
117 Ibid., 117–118.
118 Ibid., 118.
119 Ibid., 116.
120 Ibid., 118.
121 Ibid.
122 Vinh Sinh, "Introduction," 20–21.
123 Ibid., 22.
124 Vinh Sinh, *Phan Chau Trinh*, 103.
125 Ibid., 104 (slightly retranslated).
126 Ibid.
127 According to Vinh Sinh and Wickenden, the Tonkin Free School (*Đông Kinh Nghĩa Thục*) was modeled after the *Keiō Gijuku*, the school found in Tokyo in 1868 by Fukuzawa (1835–1901), a famous educator. "*Đông Kinh*" is both the old name of Hanoi and the Vietnamese equivalent of Tokyo. "*Nghĩa Thục*" is the Vietnamese equivalent of *Gijuku*, a private "community school." Vinh Sinh and Wickenden, "Introduction," 12. I believe the name of the school implies Confucian meaning. "*Thục*" means school and "*Nghĩa*" is a Vietnamese word for the Confucian term *yi* (righteousness). The implication is that the school is aimed at generating a new Vietnamese generation who will embark upon righteous actions. For more on the school, see Chương Thâu, [*Tonkin Free School*]. For English writings about the school, see Vu Duc Bang, "The Dong Kinh Free School Movement," in *Aspects of Vietnamese History*, ed. Walter F. Vella (Honolulu: University of Hawaii Press, 1973), 30–95; Marr, *Vietnamese Anticolonialism*, 156–184.

128 The colonial authority closed the school in February 1908 as a result of the tax-protest riots.
129 For a collection of essays indicating Hanoi's current reapprasial of the meaning of the school, see Hoàng Như Mai, ed., *Một Trăm Năm Đông Kinh Nghĩa Thục* [*Centenary of the Tonkin Free School*] (Hanoi: Intellectual Publishing House, 2008).
130 For a corpus of materials produced and used by the school, see Chương Thâu, ed., *Đông Kinh Nghĩa Thục và Văn thơ Đông Kinh Nghĩa Thục* [*Tonkin Free School and the Literatures of Tonkin Free School*] (two volumes) (Hanoi: Hanoi Publishing House, 2010).
131 Phan Chu Trinh's public speeches as the activity of the school were extremely popular and attracted a number of audiences, as verified by this poem: "Those who went to hear the speeches were crowded as if at the festival, then came the time of composition expositions, guests come like rains." Vinh Sinh, "Introduction," 23.
132 Cited in Trần Văn Giầu, [*The Development of Thoughts*], 437.
133 For information about Phan Chu Trinh's funeral, see Nguyên Ngọc, "Phan Châu Trinh Hiện đại Một cách Lạ lùng" ["Phan Chu Trinh is Unusually Modern"], accessed 19 April 2013, http://phapluattp.vn/20110322113816778p0c1021/phan-chau-trinh-hien-dai-mot-cach-la-lung.htm.
134 Phan Bội Châu, [*Complete Works, Volume 4*], 32–33.
135 Chengyang Li, *The Tao Encounters the West* (Albany, NY: State University of New York Press, 1999), 171.
136 It should be noted that during the early twentieth century in Vietnam, there were a few western-style intellectuals, the Francophiles, who suggested the practice of some ideas and institutions of western modern constitutionalism within colonial Vietnam. Bùi Quang Chiêu, for example, created the Constitutionalist Party in 1919 in South Vietnam. R.B. Smith, "Bui Quang Chieu and the Constitutionalist Party in French Cochinchina, 1917–1930," *Modern Asian Studies* 3(2) (1969): 131; Hue-Tam Ho Tai, "The Politics of Compromise: The Constitutional Party and the Electoral Reforms of 1922 in French Cochinchina," *Modern Asian Studies* 18(3) (1984): 371. Phạm Quỳnh, another colonial collaborator, also proposed the constitutional monarchy within colonial Vietnam in 1930. Gerard Sasges, "'Indigenous Representation is Hostile to All Monopolies': Phạm Quỳnh and the End of the Alcohol Monopoly in Colonial Vietnam," *Journal of Vietnamese Studies* 5(1) (2010): 1. It was not until after World War II that Vietnam witnessed the presence of nationalist western-style intellectuals, like Phan Anh and the Thanh Nghị group, who continued to call for the practice of modern constitutionalism in an independent Vietnam. Phan Đăng Thanh, *Tư tưởng Lập hiến Việt Nam nửa đầu Thế kỷ 20* [*Vietnamese Constitutional Thoughts in the First Half of the Twentieth Century*] (Hanoi: Judicial Publishing House, 2006).
137 Vinh Sinh, *Phan Chau Trinh*, 115.
138 Nguyễn Q. Thắng, *Huỳnh Thúc Kháng: Con người & Thơ Văn* [*Huỳnh Thúc Kháng: Person and Literature*] (Ho Chi Minh City: Literature Publishing House, 2001), 615.
139 Nguyễn Khắc Viện, *Tradition and Revolution in Vietnam*, ed. David Marr and Jayne Werner (Berkeley, CA: Indochina Resource Center, 1974), 43–44.
140 James Legge, *The Chinese Classics with Translations, Critical and Exegetical Notes, Prolegomena, and Copious Indexes, Volume II, The Works of Mencius* (Hong Kong: Hong Kong University Press, 1960), 265.
141 Nguyễn Hiến Lê notes that these moral convictions helped to spawn the revolutionary spirit of the Confucians during the French colonial period. Nguyễn Hiến Lê, *Mạnh Tử* [*Mencius*] (Hanoi: Cultural Publishing House, 1996), 186.
142 David S. Law and Mila Versteeg, "The Evolution and Ideology of Global Constitutionalism," *California Law Review* 99 (2011): 1173
143 Robert Cover, "Nomos and Narrative," in *Narrative, Violence, and the Law: The Essays of Robert Cover*, ed. Artha Minow, Michael Ryan, and Austin Sarat (Ann Arbor, MI: University of Michigan Press, 1992), 95–96.

4 Toward an East Asian model of constitutionalism

Introduction

The recent emergence of scholarship on Confucian constitutionalism in traditional East Asia has considerably challenged the conventional thinking of the *origins* of constitutionalism as the sole purview of the west.[1] However, it is indubitable that *modern* constitutionalism – a new form of limited government defined by written constitution as supreme law, popular sovereignty, the separation of powers, judicial review, and protection of human rights – is a distinctively western innovation.[2] Importantly, the achievement of modern constitutionalism has reached beyond its native land.[3] In the last three decades, western ideas and institutions of modern constitutionalism have spread to all corners of the globe, including the Confucian East Asian region.[4]

Japan was the first nation in Asia to adopt values of western liberal constitutionalism in the herculean effort of the Meiji regime to modernize the nation and to cope with the rising western power of the late nineteenth century. The Meiji Constitution of 1889 incorporated some western modern constitutionalist values, albeit enacted by a monarchical rather than popular constituent power. Following the Prussian Constitution in Germany, the Constitution provided for a parliament (the Diet), separated the public power to some extent, and protected some individuals' rights.[5] In the 1930s, however, Meiji nascent constitutionalism was wrecked by the belligerent military government, which eventually initiated the Pacific War (1941–1945).[6]

Japan was defeated in the Pacific War, and a post-war Constitution was enacted in November 1946 under the influence of Douglas MacArthur, Supreme Commander of the Allied Powers.[7] Apart from the distinctive principle of pacifism, the Constitution adopted fundamental principles of western modern constitutionalism, including popular sovereignty and democratic government, the separation of power, individualism and protection of fundamental human rights, rule of law, and Marshallian judicial review, which are aimed at transforming Japan into a full constitutional democracy.[8] The Constitution remains in effect in Japan today, without any amendments despite occasional calls for revision.[9]

Under the Constitution, Japan dramatically reconstructed the nation after the war, developed its economy into one of the largest economies in the world, and firmly established itself as a western-style modern constitutionalist state. Despite its enactment under international pressure, the Constitution widely receives popular domestic endorsement[10] and continuously underpins peaceful transfers of power, dynamic democracy with periodical free and equal parliamentary elections, protection of human rights, and capable and independent (albeit conservative) judicial review.[11]

South Korea is another typical example of a western-style constitutionalist state in East Asia.[12] Although South Korea's post-war Constitution adopted in June 1948 "provided for a Western-style liberal constitutional democracy,"[13] informed by the US Constitution, German Weimar Constitution, and the Constitution of the Republic of China (ROC),[14] the Constitution was subsequently subject to many amendments and substantial rewritings under authoritarian and military rule.[15] It was not until 1987 that South Korea successfully established a true liberal constitutional democracy, with an extensively revised Constitution and a new Constitutional Court.[16]

Under the new constitutional framework, public power has been peacefully transferred. Notably, the Korean Constitutional Court typically represents the successful story of judicial review in new democracies in Asia.[17] The Court has actively protected constitutional rights, declared statutes and government actions unconstitutional in hundreds of cases, and decided on critical political issues involving the trial of two former presidents and the parliamentary impeachment of President Roh Moo-hyun.[18] Albert Chen concludes that: "South Korea today, one of Asia's major economic powers, has thus become one of the strongholds of liberal constitutional democracy in Asia."[19]

Like South Korea, Taiwan has successfully transitioned from authoritarian rule to a western-style constitutional regime since the late twentieth century. The 1946 Constitution of the ROC, which has been implemented in Taiwan since 1949 after the Chinese Nationalist Party – or Kuomintang (KMT) – retreated here following its defeat by the Chinese Communist Party (CCP) in mainland China, was "based on the Western model of the liberal democratic state,"[20] although it also reflected some Confucian values, such as the idea of public welfare and the institutions of examination called Yuan and Supervisory Yuan as the result of Sun Yat-sen's influence.[21] However, the *jieyan* or martial law decree enacted in Taiwan by the KMT government in May 1947 disabled the constitutionalist aspirations of the 1946 ROC Constitution.[22]

It was not until July 1987 that the martial law decree was lifted, which opened a new era for Taiwan's incremental transition from authoritarianism to western-style modern constitutionalism.[23] A series of constitutional amendments to the 1946 ROC Constitution known as Additional Articles was promulgated in 1992, 1994, 1997, 1999, 2000, and 2005.[24] These amendments – which stipulate, among other things, popular elections of the national legislature, directly elected presidency, and constitutional referendum[25] – are constructive for Taiwan's gradual transformation into a true modern constitutionalist regime. The new constitutional framework has facilitated peaceful transfer of power between the two parties (the KMT and the Democratic Progressive Party) through free parliamentary and presidential elections undertaken periodically.[26] In addition, after decades of dormancy, since the second half of the 1980s, the Council of Grand Justice of the Judicial Yuan, Taiwan's specialist constitutional court following the Kelsenian style like South Korea, has become active and progressive in its practice of judicial review power, facilitative to Taiwan's transition to western-style constitutionalism and democracy.[27]

Different from the three aforementioned stories, China and Vietnam have rejected the "third wave of democratization" and consistently maintained the socialist polity under the single rule of the communist party. In fact, before the domination of communist power, constitutional thinking and practices in China and Vietnam in the early twentieth century were considerably shaped by western modern constitutionalism.[28] Recently, these two nations have witnessed the re-emergence of western-style constitutionalist discourse.

After triumphing over the KMT, the CCP founded the People's Republic of China (PRC) in October 1949, with four constitutions enacted in 1954, 1975, 1978, and 1982.[29] The current 1982 Constitution embodies Deng Xiaoping's reform and opening policy, amended several times in 1988, 1993, 1999, and 2004. The constitutional amendments feature commitments to socialism with Chinese characteristics, socialist market economy, rule of law state, and the protection of human rights and private property rights.[30] These amendments reflect the influences of some ideas of western modern constitutionalism. In addition, the Chinese discourse of "judicialization of the constitution" (*xianfa sifahua*) may have some connections with the global spread of judicial review.[31] Further, more radical proposals, such as the "Charter 08" signed in December 2009 by over 350 Chinese intellectuals and human rights activists including 2010 Nobel Peace Prize laureate Liu Xiaobo, have been calling for China's transformation into a western-style constitutionalist regime.[32]

More recently, China's constitutionalism (*xianzhing*) debate in early 2013 indicates that pro-constitutionalist arguments are implicitly informed by substantial ideas of western liberal constitutionalism, such as human rights protection, judicial independence, and constitutional review.[33] Therefore, anti-constitutionalists accused the pro-constitutionalists of mobilizing for westernization of the Chinese government.[34]

Like China, Vietnam has recently witnessed the re-attraction to western liberal constitutionalism. Under the leadership of the Communist Party, Vietnam has experienced five constitutions. The first Constitution in 1946, despite its enactment under the communist power, had some features of a western-style constitution. The two subsequent constitutions enacted in 1969 and 1980 strictly followed the Soviet constitutional tradition. The 1992 Constitution, which was promulgated as the expression of the Party's policy of "renovation" (*Doi moi*), initiated in 1986, an equivalence to Deng Xiaoping's reform and opening policy, continued the soviet-style constitutional system but stipulated the practice of socialist market economy and protection of private property rights. The 2001 amendments to the 1992 Constitution provided for, among other things, the creation of a socialist rule of law state and clear distribution of the public power, which indicates the influence of some ideas of western modern constitutionalism.

After nearly three decades of Renovation, the State of Vietnam decided to replace the 1992 Constitution with a new constitution adopted in November 2013. Constitutional debate during the 2010s constitution-making process was informed by core ideas of western liberal constitutionalism, including popular constituent power, popular sovereignty, universal human rights, the separation of power, and judicial review. Notably, a group of 72 Vietnamese intellectuals submitted a radical petition to the constitution-makers, which is now known as Petition 72, an equivalent of China's Charter 08, calling for the transformation of Vietnam into a western-style constitutional democracy.[35] The 2013 Constitution of Vietnam explicitly rejects substantial contents of Petition 72 and other radical proposals, but includes some constitutional rhetoric, such as constitution-making by the people, constitutional referendum, and mutual control among the state branches, which reflects certain ideas of western liberal constitutionalism.[36]

It can be seen that western modern constitutionalism has spread to East Asia. Liberal constitutionalist regimes have been successfully established in Japan, South Korea, and Taiwan, following western standards, while constitutional discourse and some constitutional practices in socialist regimes in China and Vietnam have also been informed by western liberal constitutionalism to a certain degree.

Is Western liberal constitutionalism the final end of constitutional history in East Asia? Is it possible for East Asia to develop a distinctive model of constitutionalism or just converge with western liberal constitutionalism? This is an important question for the development of constitutionalism in both established constitutionalist polities in Japan, South Korea, and Taiwan, and developing constitutional systems in China and Vietnam. In this chapter, I argue that it is possible and desirable for East Asia to develop a distinctive model of constitutionalism by integrating ethico-political ideas and values of Confucianism. This chapter develops a normative theory of mixed constitutionalism in the East Asian context. East Asian constitutionalism is defined by the axiological, ideational mixtures of ingredients from Confucianism and western liberal constitutionalism.

The structure of this chapter is as follows. The first section considers whether empirically there is an East Asian model of constitutionalism. The second and third sections clarify the theoretical frameworks of the study, namely moral constitutional theory and mixed constitutional theory, respectively. Sections four and five develop a normative theory of mixed constitutionalism in the East Asian context. The fourth section deals with general issues of mixed constitutionalism as an East Asian model, while the fifth articulates its distinctive features. The final section concludes the chapter.

Is there an East Asian constitutionalism?

There are two main arguments regarding this question, which can be called regionalism and universalism.

Regionalism

Regionalists argue that a distinctive model of constitutionalism exists in East Asia. Professors Jiunn-Rong Yeh and Wen-chen Chang represent this model of thinking.[37] According to them, "Japan, South Korea and Taiwan are now lively and stable constitutional democracies."[38] They demonstrate "similar political and social contexts" shared among these democracies, including: stable economy after rapid growth, open political environment with a vibrant civil society, fast-changing family relationships and social structure, and ethnic homogeneity despite local divisions.[39] Yeh and Chang then identify four distinctive features of constitutional developments in these East Asian democracies: (1) constitution-making undertaken as an ancillary component instrumental to a larger project of modernization; (2) textual and institutional continuity despite incremental constitutional progress and change; (3) reactive and cautious judicial review; and (4) a wide range of rights responsive to social and political progress.[40] These features, Yeh and Chang argue, suggest the existence of a distinctive model of "East Asian constitutionalism," which is different from the standard western constitutionalism, transitional constitutionalism in post-communist Europe, and the discourse of "Asian values."[41] They conclude:

> Owing to these unique features, constitutional developments in East Asia can no longer be simplistically regarded as a lagging version of standard (Western) constitutionalism nor as a twin of transitional constitutionalism experienced by new European democracies nor a reflection of predetermined Asian values. Instead, East Asian constitution's features – while consistent with some aspects of those models or theories – are distinctive in their own right. They are unique responses to the widely shared historical, cultural, social and political contexts in the region.[42]

Universalism

Universalists, in contrast, believe that constitutionalism in East Asia in fact has common features of generic constitutionalism, and therefore there is no distinctive model of East Asian constitutionalism. Professor Albert Chen, for example, argues that:

> Constitutionalism, albeit originating in the Western world, seems to have a universal appeal and to address the fundamental problems of governance, government, and political power in many modern societies in Asia.... No distinctly Asian mode of constitutionalism or political-constitutional practices can be identified.[43]

Recently, Professor Chen further engaged in a scholarly dialogue with Professor Yeh and Professor Chang on the question of whether there is a distinctive model of constitutionalism in East Asia.[44]

Chen demonstrates that constitutionalism in Japan, South Korea and Taiwan have common features of liberal constitutionalism, which presents the maturity of constitutional practice in the region. These common features include free elections operating as the platforms for fair political competition for political power; the existence of healthy legal systems capable of protecting human rights and civil liberties; the effectiveness of the rule of law which guarantees the capacity of legal enforcement and largely frees administrative authorities from corruption; the clear establishment of separation of powers and judicial independence; judicial review of the constitutionality and legality of legislative and executive actions; and the flourishing of freedom of the press and civil society.[45] On these grounds, Chen doubts whether any of the four features of constitutionalism in East Asia identified by Yeh and Chang, or their combination together, is really distinctive to the three East Asian democracies and hence is constitutive of a distinctive model of constitutionalism in East Asia.

As to the first instrumentalist feature, Chen refuses to consider it as distinctive to East Asia by stating that:

> a broader view of the emergence of constitutions in the non-Western world would suggest that the phenomenon identified by Yeh and Chang is in fact common among non-Western states in the late nineteenth and early twentieth centuries whose survival were threatened by the expansion of the West, and states that emerged towards the end of the age of colonialism and imperialism which used their newly promulgated constitutions to assert their newfound national identity and to legitimize their newly established political systems.[46]

Regarding the second feature of constitutional continuity, Chen suggests that:

> constitutional histories of different countries display varying degrees of constitutional continuity or discontinuity, and it is by no means clear or obvious that the East Asian states exhibit a high degree of continuity in this regard that distinguishes them from other countries in the world.[47]

To illustrate, Chen points out that "the degree of constitutional continuity in East Asia cannot be said to be high" compared to older democracies in the West, such as Britain, the United States, Canada, and Australia, or some other Asian states, such as India, Malaysia, and Singapore.[48]

Chen also refuses to consider reactive and cautious judicial review as distinctive to East Asia. He argues that: "being reactive and cautious (and politically prudent) are probably the traits of successful constitutional or supreme courts engaged in constitutional adjudication all over the world."[49]

Finally, concerning the willingness to recognize a wide range of rights, including civil and political rights as well as social and economic rights, Chen believes that this can hardly be said to be distinctive to constitutional adjudication in East Asia.[50] He indicates that "progressive constitutional and supreme courts all over the world share such willingness; hence the trends of the globalization of constitutional law and the increasing judicialization of constitutional rights and of governance as a global phenomenon."[51]

Assessment

Successful constitutionalism must be deeply embedded in the institutional, doctrinal, social, and cultural contexts of a polity or a broader region.[52] So, from this contextualist perspective, Yeh and Chang's attempt to search for a distinctive model of constitutionalism appropriate to the East Asian context is legitimate. However, in my point of view, their arguments are less tenable. I agree with Chen that some features of constitutionalism arguably specific to East Asia are in fact ubiquitous. For example, reactivity and cautiousness are actually the traits of any successful constitutional adjudication. As Tom Ginsburg points out

> All successful constitutional courts must be sensitive to their political environments, and the experience of other courts in Asia makes this all too evident. All constitutional courts must frame their adverse decisions in a way that is most palatable to those in the best position to hurt them. And all constitutional courts are engaged in dialogues with the legislature.[53]

Also, the globalization of constitutional law which leads to the judicial recognition of human rights is actually the global phenomenon.[54] I would like to add more arguments justifying that constitutional instrumentality and constitutional continuity are not distinctive to constitutionalism in East Asia.

Consider first the instrumentality of constitution-making. Instrumentality is a general feature of global constitutionalism and global constitution-making. Constitutionalism is not a panacea for every socio-economic and political problem emerging in a modern society. It is mainly an antidote to the pathology of arbitrary power. To ensure the proper use of the public power and to prevent capricious power is not an end but a means for national goals. Therefore, constitutionalism and constitution-making are instrumental to broader national projects, whether liberation, state building, socio-economic and political construction and reconstruction, modernization, or more recently global economic and political integration.[55] Even constitution-making in the standard western constitutionalism, like American constitutionalism, is also instrumental to broader national goals. The making of the 1787 Philadelphia Constitution was a component of a larger project for forming "a more perfect Union," establishing "Justice," ensuring "domestic Tranquillity," providing for "the common defence," promoting "the general Welfare," and securing "Liberty"[56] as explicitly declared in its preamble. Thus, the US Constitution was enacted not as an end, but as an instrument to construct a powerful and wealthy federal nation and a just and liberal society.

Let us consider next the quality of constitutional continuity. As constitutions are often written in turbulent times, say, after a revolution or the collapse of an authoritarian or dictatorship regime, they are normally regarded as the rupture from the past and envisagement of a new future.[57] Constitutional discontinuity, then, seems to be necessary for the operation of a new constitutional government. With this prevailing consideration, it seems that constitutional continuity is the distinctive feature of constitutionalism in East Asia. However, constitutional discontinuity has been overstated. In fact, constitutional continuity is pervasive in any viable constitutionalism.

Drawing from Hannah Arendt's *Beyond Past and Future*[58] and *On Revolution*,[59] Kim Lane Scheppele has helpfully dispelled the conventional image of constitutional rupture.[60] She demonstrates that at the moment of constitutional drafting, "too much is uncertain for constitutional drafters to feel decisive and confident" about the future.[61] Constitutional drafters "*know* about the past experiences of their country and its people," but they "do not know and in fact *cannot know*" the future.[62] Therefore, "Constitutions in their moments of creation cannot be inspired solely by imagined futures," but "more crucially, they encode imagined pasts."[63] Scheppele concludes that: "Constitutional drafters ultimately understand and react most of all to what they take to be the crucial histories of their own countries."[64] Given that, constitution-making is by no means a rupture from the past. The constitution embodies the continuous constitutional legacies of a country. Scheppele put this as follows:

> After all, at any given moment, any country with an existing constitution might have a constitution that will fail in the future, and yet the country may well have a sense of a constitutional inheritance successfully passed on. If such a government hands off power through a successor constitution that maintains elements of the same legacy, then it is not clear that anything of an enduring sort has been lost.[65]

To illustrate, Scheppele points out that France has changed its written constitutions repeatedly, but "preserved a certain common baseline of principles and traditions. On this model, a daisy chain of constitutions can be just as 'successful' as one single constitution that appears to last forever."[66] Similarly, in Germany, although the drafters of the Boon Constitution rejected any continuation of the Nazi past, they "nonetheless found elements of German constitutional history to draw from in creating a new government."[67] So, despite constitutional changes, constitutional continuity is guaranteed in France and Germany.

In a quite similar vein, Jed Rubenfeld argues that a constitutionalist polity is comprehensible only when the constitutional being – the people – is conceived as a cross-generation entity: "A people consists of not a set of persons here and now, but of the temporally extended sets of persons – past, present, and future – who will have lived under the rule of a particular political and legal order."[68] Constitutionalism is therefore the process of ongoing experiences which involve different generations. Consequently, a written constitution adopted in a given time cannot provide the panoply of consequential aspects of the polity in proviso that it is not an authoritarian constitution, the opprobrium to a true constitutionalism. For viable constitutionalism, a written constitution is always supplemented by continuing constitutional writings and practices. In short, any truly viable constitutionalism must involve the continuing constitutional evolvement across generations.

Constitutional continuity is also evident in standard western constitutionalism such as American constitutionalism. Ruti Teitel provides useful guidance in this regard. She demonstrates the continuing constitutional developments in the United States since the 1776 Revolution, stating that:

> The Revolution did not immediately culminate with a foundational constitution, but rather produced a number of constitutive documents. In the first postrevolutionary five-year period, the Articles of Confederation constituted a transformative, critical response to a regime distinguished by minimal state power. A more expansive scheme of state power was created only upon the adoption of the Constitution of 1787. The addition of the Bill of Rights and the post-Civil War amendments to the American Constitution represented yet additional constitutive stages.[69]

Thus, constitutional continuity is the common characteristic of viable constitutionalism, not distinctive to constitutionalism in East Asia.

However, I do not mean to say that constitutionalism in East Asia is a simple copy of western liberal constitutionalism. Yeh and Chang are correct in stating that the East Asian region has distinctive historical, cultural, social and political contexts, and constitutional practice in the region has responded to these contexts.[70] Therefore, some common features of liberal constitutionalism have been practiced differently in East Asia. But this is a common constitutional phenomenon rather than distinctive to East Asia. It is common that similar constitutional tasks are performed differently in different contexts. Therefore, functional differences are not substantial enough to suggest the existence of an East Asian "model" of constitutionalism.

What makes a model of constitutionalism distinctive? Constitutionalism is substantially defined by axiological or ideational attributes and structural or institutional attributes.[71] The former shapes the latter. A distinctive model of constitutionalism must have distinctive ideational and/or institutional attributes. The axiological or ideational underpinning of western liberal constitutionalism is the enlightenment liberalism that conceptually emphasizes liberal rights of individuals and the protection by a limited government created through a social contract and with separate powers. Western liberal constitutionalism transformed these abstract liberal principles into material institutions – the written constitution, democratic government, structural separation of the three state branches, and the bill of rights, and its protection by judicial review. A distinctive model of constitutionalism must possess substantial distinctions respecting axiological foundation and/or institutional arrangement. Meanwhile, constitutionalism in

East Asia substantially adheres to western liberalism and its institutional consequences. Constitutionalist polities in East Asia adopt the western principles of justice associated with liberalism and its institutional consequences, namely written constitution, pluralist and multi-party democracy, Montesquieuian government, the Bill of Rights, and the Marshallian or Kelsenian judicial review.

It should be noted that constitutional experience in Taiwan has some institutional distinctions, namely the Examination Yuan and the Supervisory Yuan deriving from Chinese institutional traditions. However, these institutions are not the central drivers of Taiwan constitutionalism. These marginal institutions make Taiwan constitutionalism piquant rather than substantially different from western constitutionalism.

One may also argue that constitutional experiences in socialist polity of China and Vietnam possess more substantial ideational and institutional differences, and hence "socialist constitutionalism" may be a distinctive model. It is true that these socialist constitutional systems are established in substantially different ideational backgrounds compared with western constitutional systems, namely Marxism–Leninism, and ideologies of local leaders (Ho Chi Minh thought in Vietnam; Mao Zedong thought, Deng Xiaoping theory, and Jiang Zemin thought of the "Three Represents" in China).[72] On these ideological bases, the socialist constitutional institutions are articulated substantially differently from western constitutional institutions, defined by the single leadership of the Communist Party entrenched constitutionally,[73] the unity of power lacking institutional checks and balances, and the statist rights judicially unenforceable.

Yet, it is proper to state that constitutional experiences in China and Vietnam present a distinctive model of *constitutional* rather than *constitutionalist* system. Although there have been nascent constitutionalist discourses and practices in China and Vietnam recently,[74] the two nations are still far from a mature constitutionalist polity. Some practical and intellectual manifestations of constitutionalism in China and Vietnam, such as the protection of private property rights and the discourse of controlling the state power, human rights, judicial review, and judicial independence, are informed by ideas of western liberal constitutionalism rather than socialist ideology.

In short, empirically, no distinctive model of constitutionalism can be found in East Asia. Constitutionalism in East Asia is the transplant of western constitutionalism into the East Asian soil. Its practices have some functional distinctions as a response to the particular contexts.[75] But these distinctions are not substantial enough to suggest the existence of an "East Asian constitutionalism."

However, it is possible and desirable to develop an East Asian model of constitutionalism by considering the relevance of Confucianism. The integration of Confucian moral principles will redefine the axiological or ideational foundation of constitutionalism in East Asia, making it a distinctive model. Yet, for many constitutionalists, moral normative inquiry into constitutional questions is problematic. Therefore, it is important to justify moral normativity in constitutional inquiry.

Moral normative constitutional theory

Existing literature indicates that studies of comparative constitutional law are predominantly conceptual and empirical. Constitutional comparativists are occupied by conceptual themes (such as the conceptions of constitution, constitutionalism, rule of law, and rights), and empirical themes (such as constitution-making, structural arrangement, judicial review, constitutional interpretation, and constitutional convergence.)[76] Scholarship of comparative constitutionalism in Asia is also predominantly empirical.[77]

To be sure, there are normative *institutional* studies in contemporary constitutional law. Prominent examples include the normative discussions on the legitimacy of constitutional review and how to reconcile constitutionalism with democracy.[78] However, contemporary constitutional comparativists tend to evade normative *moral* inquiry. This may have connections with liberal constitutional theories, such as constitutional neutralism,[79] and democratic proceduralism,[80] which accentuate jurisdictions, functions, and processes and remain skeptical of normative considerations of moral fundamental values. Constitutional skepticism of normative morality mainly derives from the Rawlian premise that in a pluralist society, as citizens as rational self-choice individuals possess different opinions of moral values, a constitutional government must provide a neutral framework for individual citizens to pursue their own moral goals.[81] Given the global spread of liberal constitutionalism, the "normative evasions"[82] in contemporary comparative constitutional law are comprehensible. But, is the refraining from normative moral constitutional inquiry desirable? May not the normative moral evasions in comparative theories of constitutionalism defeat the essential purpose of constitutionalism?

Constitutionalism itself is a normative endeavor and enterprise. Constitutionalism requires a normative constitution, not every constitution. Descriptive constitutions, which merely describe the existing government's structure and policy programs, are largely irrelevant to constitutionalism. Constitutionalism necessitates a normative constitution which commands authoritatively what the government should do, by which the public power is properly effectuated for general public ends. Constitutionalist normativity is not merely institutional but fundamentally moral. Constitutional institutions and rules are erected on fundamental moral principles respecting humans' decent and just political lives. Consequently, every influential theory of constitutionalism explicitly and implicitly presupposes some premises of normative morality,[83] including the theories about American liberal constitutionalism.[84] Let me further justify this argument by rereading and expanding of Ronald Dworkin's moral reading of the US Constitution.

Constitutionalism is the government under law, and constitutional law, like other laws, as Ronald Dworkin authoritatively argues, includes not only rules but more substantially moral principles.[85] To illustrate, Dworkin argues that the bill of rights, which is expressed in an abstract language in the US Constitution as well as in most contemporary constitutions, refers to abstract moral principles.[86] According to him, the US bill of rights refers to the following moral principles:

> Government must treat all these subject to its domination as having equal moral and political status; it must attempt, in good faith, to treat them all with equal concern; and it must respect whatever individual freedoms are indispensable to these ends, including but not limited to the freedom more specifically designated in the document, such as the freedom of speech and religion.[87]

Human rights provisions in constitutions are actually the expression of moral principles. Constitutionalism requires government to protect and respect these rights. This normative requirement is not merely institutional but substantially moral. Beneath the institutionalized rights lie fundamental moral principles. But this does not mean that moral principles must be expressed under the form of the Bill of Rights. Constitutional rights are among variant forms embodying moral principles. Moral principles can be expressed elsewhere in the constitutions and may concern values beyond rights.

Constitutional preambles, for example, normally express fundamental moral principles of the polity. To illustrate, according to the preamble of the US Constitution, moral principles underlying the whole US constitutionalist polity are associated with not only an individual's liberty but also "general welfare."[88] So, Dworkin's list of US constitutional moral principles can be supplemented with the principle that the US government must pursue the welfare for all the people, which is not less important than the protection of the rights of individuals, if not the supreme moral constitutional duty of the US government.[89] Another example is the preamble of France's 1958 Constitution. It declares three fundamental moral ideals deriving from the revolutionary era, namely liberty, equality and fraternity, which are also conceived as the objectives of the French democratic government.[90] Particularly, the principle of fraternity is concerned with constitutional duties rather than rights.

Constitutional provisions regarding the separation of the three legislative, executive, and judicial powers can also be understood as referring to moral principles. Constitutional separations are not merely the functional enterprises but express fundamental moral premises. Montesquieu's theory of separation of power rests on the ontological moral premise of the nature of the human being that: "Every man invested with power is apt to abuse it."[91] Yet, constitutional separations can also be explained as associated with the teleological moral premise that it is morally wrong to vest all powers into a single hand because this enables the power holders to convert public power into private possession and use it for their egoistic benefits at the cost of the public general purposes. Understood this way, constitutional separations may be the tool to protect human rights from the infringement of the power's holders, but they may have more general moral purpose of effecting the proper use of the public power for the common good.

Even rules of the constitution-making process are not merely procedural or technical. The global rule of participation in the constitution-making process, for example, expresses the fundamental principle respecting what Nobel laureate

James M. Buchanan called "ethics of constitutional citizenship."[92] Buchanan argues that we, as individual citizens, make choices from not merely "particularized policy alternatives" but more fundamentally "grand organizational alternatives."[93] To choose among grand organizational alternatives, citizens must actively participate in the discussion of constitutional change, whether amendment or replacement.[94] Importantly, Buchanan suggests that citizens' discussions of constitutional change "must reflect the presence of some ethical precept that transcends rational interest for the individual."[95] Citizens' behavior according to such a precept "embodies an ethical responsibility for the choices among regimes."[96] If the citizens fail to engage in discussion on constitutional change and fail to choose the grand alternatives, "the constitutional regime that we inherit must be vulnerable both to nonprincipled exploitation and the natural erosion of historical change."[97] Buchanan suggests that ideal vision of constitutional order must embody the constitutional principle and recognition that "the individual, as citizen, must accept the ethical responsibility of full and informed participation in a continuing constitutional convention."[98] Therefore, public participation in the constitution-making process, as globally practiced, is not merely a practical political necessity or a human right, but more substantially the moral responsibility of citizens in choosing a constitutional regime; otherwise, they will live under an exploited or naturally eroded regime. Public participation in the constitution-making process, therefore, embodies the fundamental moral principle of constitutional citizenship constructive to political decency and justice.

In short, a serious theory of constitutionalism is inevitably a normative moral inquiry. This can be justified by a re-reading and expansion of Dworkin's moral reading of the US Constitution. In term of jurisdictional scope, the moral reading is valid to any normative constitutions, not only the US Constitution. Any constitutionalist constitutions must include fundamental moral principles which direct the power holders toward achieving general public standards. In term of substantial contents, the moral constitutional principles may concern things beyond rights, such as citizen's duties, public welfare, and other common goods.

Opponents of normative moral constitutional theory may invoke the rule of law argument. It can be argued that normative moral constitutional theory may foster the rule of man rather than the rule of law. Constitutionalism as the rule of moral principles may lead to the rule of constitutional judges and lawyers as moral philosophers. Moreover, morality seems to be ambiguous and indeterminate, and this may contradict one of the virtues of the rule of law, namely predictability.[99] Dworkin's theory of constitutional *integrity* is instructive to dispel the fear that normative moral constitutional inquiry is detrimental to the rule of law. Dworkin states:

> Judges may not read their own convictions into the Constitution. They may not read the abstract moral clauses as expressing particular moral judgment, no matter how much that judgment appeals to them, unless they find it consistent in principle with the structural design of the Constitution as a whole,

> and also with the dominant lines of the past constitutional interpretation by other judges. They must regard themselves as partners with other officials, past and future, who together elaborate a coherent constitutional morality, and they must care to see that what they contribute fits with the rest.[100]

So, normative moral constitutional inquiry remains the concern for the rule of law, with law understood as including moral principles foundational to rules. Moral principles are interpretative, especially by judges. Judges' interpretation of constitutional principles is not personal and arbitrary, but is constrained by "history, practice, and integrity."[101] This first dispels the worry about moral ambiguity and indeterminacy. Second, this dispels the fear that judges will become philosophical kings, as their jurisprudence is anchored in "history, practice, and integrity." Third, the virtue of constitutional integrity guarantees the predictability of law and legal system. People can anticipate the motion of the law and the legal system by looking at the whole constitutional polity, constitutional history, and constitutional antecedents.

Yet, Dworkin's constitutional integrity can be reread and expanded. Articulation of constitutional principles is not the exclusive business of judges.[102] Juridical reasoning by professional jurists is just one way to articulate constitutional principles. Articulation of constitutional principles may involve all actors of the entire constitutional community in consistence with the requirement of constitutional integrity. Judges and lawyers, the people and their representatives, all participate in the collaborative grand enterprise of articulating the moral foundations of their constitutional community in concordance with the requirement of constitutional integrity. The requirement of constitutional integrity suggests that they will look at the whole constitutionalist polity, consider past generations' arguments, and regard themselves as fellows with others in order to elaborate coherent moral constitutional principles. Depending on their positions, they may employ different means to articulate constitutional principles, such as legal reasoning in courtrooms, scholarly discourse in law schools, political discourse in presidential and congressional fora, moral and religious discourse, popular discourse, demonstration, and even new channels of social media.

Having justified the legitimacy of normative moral inquiry into constitutionalism, it is now safe to inquire into the normative moral foundation of the potential model of East Asian constitutionalism. The potential model of East Asian constitutionalism is defined by mixing Confucian moral principles with western constitutional principles. In this regard, mixed constitutional theory is instructive.

Mixed constitutional theory

Constitutional mixture is a common practice in modern constitutionalism. A typical example is the wide practice of semi-presidentialism which combines elements of presidentialism and parlimentarism.[103] Other structural or institutional mixtures include bicameralism, federalism, and different forms of checks and balances. However, a more underlying dimension of constitutional mixture, which is "axiological or ideational,"[104] receives less scholarly attention.

In this regard, Graham Walker is instructive.[105] He argues that structural or institutional mixtures are the embodiment of "axiological, ideational mixtures, i.e., the (usually deliberate) juxtaposition of rival principles of justice or legitimacy – popular versus aristocratic, democratic versus oligarchic, moral versus consensual – so as to offset their respective defects."[106] The idea of axiological, ideational mixtures is antique, evident in Aristotle and Polybius' theories of the mixed constitution.[107] However, Walker's mixed constitutional theory is novel in that he deliberately applies "the concept of principled constitutional mixtures" to "today's rival legitimacy principles, those of liberalism and its opposites."[108]

Walker opines that constitutionalism and liberalism can be conceptually disentangled. He argues that it is possible to anticipate a constitutionalism which is disconnected from liberal legitimacy principles of autonomous individuals and neutral government, or a form of non-liberal constitutionalism, but still "retains constitutionalism's appeal as a superior objectivity that limits power-holders and impedes despotism."[109] The normative model of principled mixed constitutionalism belongs to this pedigree of constitutionalism.[110]

To justify the legitimacy of the new model of principled mixed constitutionalism, Walker first offers two political arguments drawing from the constitutional experiences of post-communist Eastern Europe in the late twentieth century. The first argument is that the enactment of a mixed constitution is greater likely because "diverse and fragmented peoples are unlikely to agree on the constitutional enthronement of any single justice principle."[111] Yet, it can be argued that in divided societies, liberal government is more likely because it treat different individuals and groups fairly and remains neutral toward all of them.[112] However, Walker argues,

> many people now see a tendency in liberalism to privatize and relativize the substantive differences it claims to respect. Many peoples around the world realize this and are hostile to liberal "westernization." Such peoples are hardly likely to enact a predominantly liberal constitution.[113]

The second political justification of the new mixed constitution is that it can provide an answer to the question at the moment of constitutional founding, "the question of what shall form sufficiently enduring bonds of political community to give people enough cohesion to live together at a viable level of voluntary cooperation."[114] Liberal constitution, which would encourage "individuals to calculate their private material advantage," "is a notoriously weak incentive to social harmony."[115]

Apart from political justifications, Walker provides moral justifications of the new model of mixed constitutionalism. Principled mixed constitutionalism is morally desirable because it avoids the lamentable outcome generated by liberal constitutionalism, namely "a trivially diverse society dominated by morally indifferent consumer-individualists."[116] Walker further elaborates the moral limits of liberal constitutionalism as follows:

> The social power of advanced liberalism is alchemy without fanfare, for a scrupulous liberalism does not respect the plurality it organizes. Instead, it trivializes pluralism by transforming substantive differences, in such matters as religion, morality, and ethnic culture, into differences of private choice and personal taste. In other words, untempered liberal norms, especially when reinforced by a commercial marketplace organized around choice and contract, have a diffuse but unmistakable social consequence. Liberal neutrality, or privatism, effectively operates as the substantive commitment that displaces rather than tolerates its predecessors.[117]

Having justified the political and moral legitimacy of mixed constitutionalism, Walker offers a general principle that governs its concrete features, namely that "explicit constitutional preference for a non-liberal, communal value should be constructed so as to deter the legal or political abolition of dissenting alternatives, except in the case of dissenters whose value systems exalt murder, genocide, torture, theft, and slavery."[118] In a principled mixed constitutional scheme, a government can promote "one side of a value polarity without always having to require it," and "without having to go so far as to outlaw the other."[119]

In terms of practice, Walker points out examples of institutional arrangements embodying a mixed constitutionalism, drawing from Canada's Charter of Rights and Freedom, Israel's 1948 Declaration of Independence, and US constitutional norm of property during the New Deal.[120] Yet, these empirical workings of constitutional mixtures are inadvertent or compromised, as the liberal tendency of the regime remains dominant. Instead, the mixed constitutionalism Walker is proposing is deliberately principled.[121]

To guarantee the nature of the mixed constitutionalism and to avoid the degeneration of the polity into either its liberal or non-liberal poles, Walker proposes the principle of "partial establishment of moral, religious, ethnic, or other cultural affirmations of meaning."[122] He argues that a mixed constitution of "partial establishment" better appreciates the plural values of a divided society than a liberal constitution:

> Unlike a liberal establishment, it does not colonize dissenters. Unlike an illiberal establishment, it does not extirpate dissenters. The most potent basis of difference or dissent is an alternative truth claim; a mixed constitution of partial establishments respects dissent because it values public truth-seeking. Unlike liberalism, it sanctions truth-seeking as potentially significant beyond idiosyncratic private preference. It does not insist in advance that truth-seekers can never find any truth deserving public validation because, in fact, it partially validates some claims to truth (in "partial establishments"). Unlike illiberalism, it systemically deflects truth-seeking from hubris, that is, from prematurely calling a halt to the search in the name of a comprehensive possession of the truth. Its constitutional structure implies and promotes the belief that truth-seeking never secures more than a partial grasp of its object, and the belief that

> that partial grasp validates whatever deserves public validation, including the search itself.[123]

If the essence of constitutionalism is the limit of any form of absolutism, whether personal, institutional, or ideational, then "only the mixed constitution authentically deserves to be called constitutionalism" as it excludes any absolutized principle.[124] If this is the case, "the term 'liberal constitutionalism' may itself turn out to be an oxymoron."[125]

Walker has provided a powerful theoretical device to understand new directions of modern constitutionalism. First, his theory suggests diversifying normative inquiry of modern constitutionalism, which does not necessarily pivot at liberal constitutionalism. In a similar vein, Mark Tushnet has recently proposed "pluralizing the object of study in comparative constitutional law" to include "forms of constitutionalism other than liberal constitutionalism."[126] His normative theory of "authoritarian constitutionalism" is developed in this attempt.[127] Another importance in Walker's theory is that it suggests the possibility of principled mixtures rather than merely institutional mixtures.[128] Modern constitutionalism needs not be exclusively defined by liberal principles, but can be jointly defined by both liberal and non-liberal principles.

However, Walker tends to ignore the principle of unity which is necessary to the viability of a mixed constitutionalism. There must be a minimum united framework under which the constitutionalist polity which mixes rival legitimacy principles can operate; otherwise, the polity may degenerate into chaos. William A. Galston's theory of "pluralist constitutionalism" can support and supplement Walker's theory.[129]

Galston's theory is based on the ground of value pluralism adumbrated by Isaiah Berlin.[130] Galston summarizes five arguments of value pluralism as follows.[131] First, the human being operates within "a shared horizon of moral meaning and justification."[132] Second, "objective goods cannot be fully rank-ordered."[133] Third, there are some goods which "provide a ground of unity on which diverse individual and collective lives may be built."[134] Fourth, beyond these basic goods, "there is a wide range of legitimate diversity – diversity of individual conceptions of good lives, and also of public cultures and public purposes."[135] Fifth, value pluralism rejects monism, a theory of value "either (a) reduces goods to a common measure or (b) creates a comprehensive hierarchy or ordering among goods."[136]

Galston suggests that "social peace and stability," albeit not dominant in all circumstances, can be recognized as basic goods which "typically help create the framework within which the attainment of other goods becomes possible."[137] To ensure social peace and stability, the public order needs what he calls "minimum conditions," which include clear and stable property relations, the rule of law,[138] a public authority capable of enforcing the law, an economy that does not divide the rich and poor, and a sense of membership in the political community "strong enough to override ethnic and religious differences."[139] To secure these "minimum conditions," there must be "the conditions of the conditions" – a suitably regulated market economy, a basic level of social provision, and a system of education sufficient to promote economic competence, law-abidingness, and civic attachment.[140]

These minimum conditions and "the conditions of conditions" provide ground of unity under which the pluralist constitutionalism can operate. A constitution in a pluralist society

> represents an authoritative *partial ordering* of public values. It selects a subset of worthy values, brings them to the foreground, and subordinates others to them. These preferred values then become the benchmarks for assessing legislation, public policy, and even the condition of public culture.[141]

Constitutional ordering of value is only *partial* in three senses. First, a community's distinctive constitutional values will not always be consistent with the minimum requirements of public order. Second, constitutional values will not always dominate an individual's ensemble of personal values. Third, constitutionally established pluralist values will unavoidably come into conflict with one another.[142]

Galston's theory of pluralist constitutionalism bears some affinities to Walker's theory of mixed constitutionalism. First, methodologically, they both advocate pluralizing the concept of modern constitutionalism. Liberal constitutionalism is not conceived as the exclusive object of normative constitutional inquiry. Second, substantially, they both agree on the coexistence of different constitutional values in a constitutionalist polity. Constitutional values can be different but must not be radically diverse to coexist with the same polity. Galston, therefore, suggests that even a pluralist constitution must be coherent.[143] Similarly, Walker's mixed constitutionalism is not about combining various illiberal principles hostile to one another.[144] Third, Galston and Walker both have the teleological concern of the state's partially promotion of certain constitutional values. Galston's idea of a constitution of "partial ordering" relatively resembles Walker's idea of a constitution of "partial establishment." "Comprehensive" ordering or establishment of value would induce constitutionalism to transform into authoritarianism. In short, arguments of pluralist constitutionalism help enhance the legitimacy of mixed constitutionalism.

Yet, Galston is different from Walker in that he pays more attention to the necessity of a ground of unity conditional to a workable constitutionalism. Drawing from Galston's theory, a theory of mixed constitutionalism needs to be supplemented with the concern of constitutional unity or the basic public goods of "social peace and stability" ensured by the "minimum conditions," and "the conditions of the conditions."

Mixed constitutionalism in the East Asian context

Let us now move on to apply the general theory of mixed constitutionalism to articulate a specific normative theory of mixed constitutionalism in the particular context of East Asia. The normative inquiry into the potential model of East Asian constitutionalism distinctive from western liberal constitutionalism is congruent with the new scholarly propensity towards pluralizing the categories of constitutionalism. An East Asian model of constitutionalism defined by mixing western liberal principles and Confucian principles represents the version of principled mixed constitutionalism.

This normative theory of the potential model of East Asian constitutionalism is more concerned with underlying axiological or ideational mixtures. The integration of Confucian moral principles will substantially redefine the nature of the axiological foundation and institutional arrangement of constitutionalism in East Asia, making it a distinctive model appropriate to the region.

In the mixed constitutional scheme, Confucianism would experience a process which Stephen C. Angle calls "creative transformation."[145] For Confucianism to have continued relevance to today's constitutionalism, it must be put into the broad-ranging dialogue with other values, through which process Confucianism will be creatively transformed. In other words, Confucianism will be reconstructed. In fact, Confucianism does not have fixed meanings but has always experienced reconstructions to meet the new circumstances. Within classical Confucianism, several ideas were reconstructed in different times. To illustrate, from the original meaning of religious ceremony, the meanings of *li* have gradually expanded over time to include traditional institutions, moral norms, and cosmological principles. In a similar vein, Han Confucianism and Sung Confucianism reconstructed classical Confucian concepts. In contemporary time, the reconstruction of Confucianism for constitutional purposes is connected with similar reconstructions of Confucianism to respond to the challenges of human rights and democracy advanced by political scientists and philosophers.[146]

This theory is primarily concerned with normative theoretical articulations of the legitimacy, principles, conditions, and features of mixed constitutionalism in East Asia, although some empirical observations are included. This part considers the legitimacy, principles, and conditions, while the next part articulates the normative features.

The legitimacy

The legitimacy of mixed constitutionalism in East Asia is justified by six arguments: pluralist, critical, expressivist, learning, coherent, and empiricist.

First, mixed constitutionalism in East Asia can be justified by the argument that the nations of the East Asia region are increasingly *pluralist*. The East Asia region is a place of different systems of value associated with Confucianism, Taoism, Buddhism, Christianity, Islamism, and other religions and traditions of belief. Diverse and fragmented East Asian peoples are unlikely to be open to constitutional entrenchment of a single principle of justice. Mixed constitutionalism is more likely to accommodate the plurality of values in East Asia. Yet, it may be argued that a liberal state may treat different people and groups magnanimously by remaining neutral to all of them. However, as Walker argues, the neutral liberal state tends to privatize and relativize the substantive differences. It also highlights individual concerns, which is hostile to the cohesion of the political community. Liberal aspirations of free-choice individuals and neutral government eventually trivialize diverse society, dominated by morally indifferent consumer-individualists. I cite the commercialist and individualist spirit of cosmopolitan cities of East Asia.

Second, the theory of mixed constitutionalism in East Asia holds a *critical* view towards liberal constitutionalism. The critical argument is twofold. First, although western liberal constitutionalism has received a global paean, it is by no means impeccable. Scholars have identified certain defects internal to liberal constitutionalism.[147] As epitomized by Li-ann Thio, "liberal constitutionalism has been criticized for its conceptions of the self, polity, and secularity as organizing ideals, and the constraint-oriented liberal state's inability positively to address multiculturalism and development issues."[148] Second, while liberal constitutionalism may be more or less rational and progressive and may function well in its western homeland, it may malfunction in external contexts which do not have a tradition of individualism and Christianity – like East Asian societies. So, although liberal constitutionalism has dominated new East Asian democracies, this does not mean that it functions perfectly here. Legislative violence in South Korea and in Taiwan provides an illustration.[149]

Third, the *expressivist* argument justifies the legitimacy of the Confucian component in the mixed constitutional scheme. A successful constitutionalism must express the national identity and the political tradition of a given community.[150] Meanwhile, Confucianism constitutes an important ingredient of national identity and political culture of East Asian nations. This suggests that a distinctive model of East Asian constitutionalism must seek to express Confucian values. One may ask: given the diversity of values in East Asia, why Confucianism matters to the mixed constitutionalism. Three answers can be offered. First, a constitution does not seek to express every value; rather, it seeks to express values that it considers most important to the *political* architecture. Compared with other systems of value, Confucianism is more concerned with the grand political architecture. It is preoccupied by the aspiration on how to organize a decent and just political life. Therefore, Confucianism is more relevant to the expressive nature of constitutionalism. Second, Confucian influence is evident in not only the pedestrian life of the lay people, but also in the political and constitutional sphere in contemporary East Asia.[151] Third, Confucianism encompasses constitutionalist values and principles capable of tempering or supplementing the deficiencies of liberal constitutionalism.

Fourthly, the argument of *learning* concerns the western ingredients of the mixed constitutional scheme. From a global perspective, constitutional learning is in fact a common mechanism for different countries to develop their constitutional systems.[152] Although western liberal constitutionalism has its own deficiencies, it comprises some rationalist notions and institutions which can be learned from and can be successfully transplanted outside the west if they experience a process of indigenization by their interaction and incorporation with the local values. In addition, the learning argument can be justified from a Confucian perspective. First, learning from the others is the spirit that the authentic Confucians always welcome. Confucius says: "When I walk along with two others, they may serve me as my teachers. I will select their good qualities and follow them, their bad qualities and avoid them."[153] So to select good qualities of western liberal constitutionalism and follow them and to recognize its bad qualities and to avoid them is consistent with this Confucian learning logic.

Moreover, learning from western liberal constitutionalism can bridge the gap between Confucian constitutionalist ideals and Confucian political reality. The perennial problem with Confucianism is the gap between its ideals and its reality.[154] As discussed in Chapter 3, Phan Chu Trinh laments that the teachings of Confucius and Mencius have been misunderstood and misappropriated, and therefore imperial government in China, Vietnam, and Korea have only practiced the "heretical form of Confucianism" (*tà Nho*).[155] Phan then suggests that the best way to bring back the genuine teachings of Confucius and Mencius is to bring in western democracy.[156] In a similar vein, Tu Weiming contends that: "Confucian personality ideals – the authentic person, the worthy, or the sage – can be realized more fully in the liberal–democratic society than either in the traditional imperial dictatorship or modern authoritarian regime."[157]

I partially concur with Phan and Tu's positions. Western liberal constitutionalism and democracy are not the exclusive way to fully realize Confucian ideals. Neither should modern constitutionalist institutions be employed as instruments to fully realize Confucian moral ideals of personality. Yet, when we particularly focus on Confucian constitutional ideals, not on Confucian moral ideals of personality, I believe that the incorporation of ideas and institutions of western liberal constitutionalism would help better realize Confucian constitutionalist ideals. As I discussed in Chapter 1, Confucian constitutional ideals are a rectified (*zheng ming*) government as an antidote for despotism, responsible for the people (*minben*), functioning in concordance with the parameter of traditional norms and institutions (*li*), and protected by internal moral cultivation and external scholastic restraints.[158] These classical Confucian constitutionalist ideals were not fully practiced in imperial East Asia, although some level of their realization could be achieved due to the power of tradition.[159] The powerful monarchs and the lack of good institutional designs restricted the realization of Confucian constitutionalist ideals. Modern authoritarian polity is also incompatible with these ideals. Alternatively, the integration of western liberal ideas and institutions so as to create a modern mixed constitutionalist polity would provide an expedient environment to realize Confucian constitutionalist ideals.

Fifth, the *coherent* argument suggests that Confucian values can coexist with western values of liberal constitutionalism within a mixed constitutional scheme. Confucianism and western liberal constitutionalism are competing visions, but they are not hostile to each other. Several scholars have argued that Confucianism is compatible with western liberal constitutional democracy.[160] Although the compatibilist argument is normatively problematic in the sense that it implies that Confucian societies eventually converge with western liberal constitutionalism, it is empirically instructive in that Confucianism and western constitutionalism have something in common, which makes them possibly coexist in a single polity. Most importantly, Confucianism and western liberal constitutionalism share the same concern that public power must be limited for general public standards, although they develop different mechanisms of constitutional limits and pursue different public values. The coexistence of competing Confucian and western constitutional values in a single polity is not prejudicial to the unity of the polity, but moreover is fruitful to the evolution of the constitutional identity of the polity. The dialogical interactions of Confucian and western constitutional values would create the condition of "constitutional disharmony"[161] which helps animate the dynamics of constitutional development.

The last, but not least, argument suggests that mixed constitutionalism in the context of East Asia has some *empirical* grounds. This empiricist argument is twofold. First, the integration of western constitutionalism with Confucianism has some empirical grounds in modern East Asia. As demonstrated in Chapter 3, public intellectuals in early twentieth-century East Asia anticipated the possible combination of elements of western modern constitutionalism with traditional elements of Confucianism. But their projects have not yet been fully theoretically developed for the practical reason that they were revolutionaries rather than pure constitutional theorists. However, their projects provide empirical grounds for further theorizing the mixed constitutionalism in the future of East Asia.

The second dimension of the empiricist argument is that constitutional experiences in contemporary East Asia present some evidence of constitutional mixtures. Taiwanese constitutionalism has materialized, to a certain degree, Sun Yat-sen's constitutional theory of five powers. In Taiwan's constitutional system, apart the three branches of legislature, executive, and judiciary, there are two additional institutions of Control Yuan and Examination Yuan, drawing from Confucian tradition.[162] In South Korea, the Constitutional Court, in deciding a case in 1998,[163] indicated an integrating jurisprudence when it upheld both liberal values and Confucian family rituals.[164]

In China and Vietnam, the constitutions also comprise some mixtures between socialist values and Confucian values. The Preamble of the Constitution of Vietnam underlines the importance of both the achievement of the Communist Party and the traditional value of "humaneness-righteousness" derived from Confucianism.[165] Article 8 of this Constitution can be considered the reflection of the Confucian principle of *minben* (people as base), which demands the power holders' responsibility for the people: "All state bodies and state officials and employees shall respect the people, serve the people with utmost dedication, maintain close ties with the people, listen to the opinions of the people and accept their supervision."[166] In the same *minben* spirit, Article 3 of the Constitution of China requires the National People's Congress and the local people's congresses at different levels to be "responsible to the people and subject to their supervision."[167] In addition, the echo of the Confucian moral principle of filial piety (*xiao*) can be found in Article 49 of the Constitution of China, which requires that: "Parents have the duty to rear and educate their minor children, and children who have come of age have the duty to support and assist their parents."[168]

However, some aforementioned empirical constitutional mixtures are sporadic and inadvertent. Constitutionalism in Taiwan and South Korea remain predominantly liberal in nature, while the constitutional systems in China and Vietnam remain predominantly socialist in nature. A distinctive model of constitutionalism in East Asia seeks to deliberately mix western liberal constitutional principles with Confucian ethico-political principles. So, East Asian constitutionalism is a principled mixed constitutionalism.

The governing principle: "partial establishment"

To modify Walker,[169] a general principle that governs the concrete features of the mixed constitutionalism in East Asia can be stated as follows: explicit constitutional preference for Confucian values should be partially established so as to deter the legal or political abolition of dissenting alternatives, except in the case that the dissenters exalt murder, genocide, torture, theft, and slavery. The government in East Asian jurisdictions where the remnants of Confucian legacies are evident can promote some Confucian values without always having to require them, and without having to go so far as to outlaw other systems of value, religions, and belief.

In that sense, mixed constitutionalism in the context of East Asia is neither wholly liberal nor wholly Confucian. Neither liberalism nor Confucianism dominates the polity. They jointly operate to maintain the balance of the polity and to prevent the polity from collapsing into the domination of a single political principle or, one may say, the "principled despotism." Liberal aspirations are tempered by Confucian aspirations to make them not go so far to generate apolitical hyper-individualists and amoral and machine-like government. The partial incorporation of Confucian values can increase the humanity of the polity by promoting the responsibility of both citizens and the government for their polity, which helps to generate a more active civic citizenship and a moral government more concerned with general humanity values. Yet, Confucian aspirations are tempered by liberal values to make them not go so far as to always dominate individuals' ensemble of personal values and to turn the polity into authoritarianism. This way of partial constitutional establishment of Confucian values guarantees the freedom of thought, belief, and religion of individuals following the values of Buddhism, Christianity, Islamism, and others. To modify Galston,[170] in the inevitable cases when the enforcement of Confucian and other public norms significantly interferes with individual or group practices, constitutionally authorized persons or institutions should consider the ways of diminishing human costs without eviscerating the norms. The reasonable consideration and determination depend on the facts of particular cases and need not be transformed into "universal-decision rules."[171]

The theory of mixed constitutionalism in East Asia would reject Jiang Qing's comprehensive appropriation of Confucianism as a state religion and doctrine for a "Confucian constitutional order."[172] Qing's approach to Confucianism presents a sort of "monism." From the perspective of value pluralism, partial establishment or ordering of Confucianism is more sensible than its monist comprehensive enthronement, for two reasons. First, "monistic accounts of value lead to Procrustean distortions of moral argument."[173] In a similar vein, it can be said that the comprehensive establishment of Confucianism will lead to Procrustean distortions of moral argument and belief in the East Asian nations where diverse systems of value exist. Consider, for example, how the Christian community in China would respond if Confucianism were comprehensively established as a state religion and as a doctrine to organize and operate the state. Second, "our moral experience suggests that the tension among broad structures or theories of value ... is rooted in a genuine heterogeneity of value."[174] Arguing from this line, the comprehensive ordering of Confucianism would enthrone its heterogeneity, which would exacerbate value conflicts and tensions.

In addition, from a constitutionalist perspective, the partial establishment of Confucianism is more reasonable than the comprehensive one. To create a constitutionalism comprehensively based on Confucianism would go against the essential spirit of constitutionalism itself. The essence of constitutionalism is to restrain any forms of tyranny or absolutism, regardless of personal, institutional, or ideological absolutism. So, a polity comprehensively permeated and controlled by Confucianism as a state religion is less qualified as constitutionalist. In addition, comprehensive establishment of Confucianism would remove the condition of constitutional dynamics, namely the dialogical interaction of competing constitutional visions.

Moreover, from a Confucian perspective, its partial establishment is more tenable than the comprehensive one. To begin with, Confucian philosophy itself rejects intellectual monism in favor of intellectual pluralism. Confucianism, particularly with its emphasis on benevolence or humaneness (*ren*), is essentially an inclusive tradition. One of the important Confucian characters is the spirit of learning from others. Even though Confucianism contains profound wisdom of good life and good government, it was created more than two millennia ago and could not envisage ideas of modern constitutional government, such as a written constitution, democratically elected government, constitutional rights, and constitutional review. Confucians would be happy to learn these values from others. Apart from the spirit of learning there is the Confucian "Doctrine of the Mean"[175] (中庸; *chung yung*), which denies any form of extremism in favor of a balanced and harmonious manner of reflection, behavior, and action. So, the domination of a particular just principle would go against the spirit of *chung yung*.

Furthermore, empirically, Confucianism was created and developed in an intellectually pluralist context. It was the blossom of the "Hundred Schools of Thought" (*zhuzibaijia* 诸子百家) during the Spring and Autumn (770–476 BC) and Warring States (475–221 BC) Periods in the history of China that provided fertile soil for the flowering of Confucianism. It was through the dialogical interactions with Maoists, Daoists, legalists, logicians, and Ying-Yang scholars that the Confucians developed their distinctive arguments.[176] After the Warring States

Period, Qin apotheosized legalism as the dominant ideology, and consequently Confucianism became the hapless victim of the ideological monopoly. Following the suggestion of the legalist Li Si, the First Emperor of Qin burned Confucian books and executed Confucian scholars.[177] In the subsequent dynasties in China, Confucianism replaced the dominant position of legalism and this adversely affected its development, because this limited its interaction with other schools of thought. But when there was a chance to engage in dialogical conversations with other schools of thought, Confucianism could be revitalized, as the case of neo-Confucianism in the Sung dynasty indicates, although it was impossible to return to its heyday. New Confucianism or contemporary Confucianism is equally developed by creatively combining Confucian tradition with western civilization.[178] In short, the comprehensive appropriation of Confucianism to design a new constitutional order will restrict its competitive, incorporative, and argumentative dialogues with other schools of thought, and this in turn will be prejudicial to the dynamics of the constitutional discourse and the health of Confucianism itself.

Constitutional unity

Mixed constitutionalism in the context of East Asia would operate under the ground of unity. Galston's theory is relevant in this regard.[179] "Social peace and stability" can be recognized as the common basic goods for the "paired dance" of both liberal constitutional values and Confucian values. These basic goods are ensured by the "minimum conditions" – clear and stable property relations, the rule of law procedurally understood, public authority capable of enforcing the law, an economy without a gap between the rich and poor, and a sense of membership – and the "conditions of the conditions" – a suitably regulated market economy, a basic level of social provision, and a system of education sufficient to promote economic competence, law-abidingness and civic attachment.

Let us proceed to articulate in more detail normative features of mixed constitutionalism as an East Asian model.

Normative features of mixed constitutionalism in East Asia

Negative and positive constitutionalism

The first feature of East Asian constitutionalism concerns a revised ontological understanding of constitutionalism in the East Asian context informed by the Confucian doctrine of rectification of names. The normative theory of East Asian constitutionalism seeks to combine the western idea of negative constitutional limitations with the Confucian idea of constitutional rectification, which is more positive. The addition of the concept of constitutional rectification redefines the nature of constitutionalism in East Asia as the balance between negative and positive constitutionalism, distinctive from western liberal constitutionalism, which is predominantly negative.

Western liberal constitutionalism is predominantly a form of negative constitutionalism. The principles of autonomous individuals and neutral government naturally lead to the negative conception of constitutional "limits" or "restraints." The idea is that to guarantee the independent space for individuals, which is considered by liberals as the condition for individuals to live meaningful lives, government must be limited from interfering with individual space. The negative conception of constitutional limits is also connected with the negative conception of the corruptible and imperfect nature of humans, especially the natural tendency to abuse power, adumbrated by enlightenment thinkers like Thomas Hobbes[180] and Jean-Jacques Rousseau,[181] and supported by American framers like George Washington,[182] James Madison,[183] and Thomas Jefferson.[184]

To be sure, constitutionalism cannot abandon constitutional limits. However, constitutional limits are not necessarily understood in the negative sense. In fact, several western constitutionalists and political scientists have challenged the negative understanding of constitutional limits. To illustrate, Leslie Lipson laments that:

> Some are so fearful of its abuses that their picture of constitutionalism is a series of prohibitions. Their rule of law develops into a roll of negatives. To devise checks, controls, restraints, and limitations become the essence of constitutionalism and the prime guarantee of human freedom. But is it really necessary to lean so far backwards? May not this overattention to abuses defeat its own purpose?[185]

Stephen Holmes is equally skeptical about the fact that: "The common metaphors of checking, blocking, limiting and restraining all suggest that constitutions are, in the main, negative devices used to prevent abuses of power."[186] Holmes, then, goes further to develop a positive constitutionalist vision. He distinguishes negative constitutionalism from positive constitutionalism. Defining negative constitutionalism as "the doctrine that constitutions are primarily preventive or inhibitory devices, meant to check or repress tyranny and other abuses of power,"[187] Holmes criticizes it as "the most formidable obstacle to a fruitful theoretical exploration of the relation between constitutionalism and democracy."[188] He points out that: "What this negative constitutionalism neglects is that a constitution also creates institutions, assigns responsibilities, inculcates aims, and makes a country governable."[189] Drawing theoretical inspirations from Jean Bodin and John Stuart Mill, Holmes advocates the positive constitutionalism. Holmes proposes rethinking the conventional concept of limits: "Limits do not necessarily weaken; they can also strengthen.... Constitutions, moreover, can be binding in a way that engenders unprecedented possibilities."[190]

Properly understood, constitutionalism is essentially about not weak or strong, but proper, power. The central nature of constitutionalism is the political-legal order assuring the existence of a structural and normative matrix in which the government can effectively hold proper communion with its people. The proper communion means that the power holders are responsible to the public rather than being free to pursue their own interests. To guarantee the power holders' constant responsibility for the public, the proper performance of the public power needs both negative limitations of arbitrary power and positive arrangement, distribution, and use of power. Lipson provides a useful metaphor:

> Just as it is one thing to harness a horse and another to hobble it, so it is one thing to control a government and another to cripple it.... Since government is indispensable and no one can govern without power, it is evident that constitutionalism should first be concerned with how power must be used, then with the prevention of its abuse. The state should be envisaged as a canal through which political power may flow, releasing its energy for the benefits of humankind, rather than as a dam to hold it back.[191]

So, constitutionalism has both negative and positive dimensions under which the purpose is the same: to hold the government responsible to the public. The negative limitations are necessary to preclude the power holders' lamentable objectives of pursuing their selfish benefits to hold their accountability for the public, but are not aimed at paralyzing the government by eviscerating its governing devices. The positive dimension of constitutionalism includes positive arrangement, distribution, and use of the public power. This is not intended to lavishly augment the government. In contrast, the structural and normative constitutional framework facilitates the government to progress in the proper direction and destination to ensure its responsibility to the public. To use Leslie Lipson's words, the constitutions can be regarded as the dykes, not the dams. They are not the dams to block the power, but the dykes to keep the power smoothly flowing in the proper direction and toward the proper destination to lease its energy for the public standards.

Within the East Asian context, the Confucian doctrine of "rectification of names" or *zheng ming* can correct the deficiency of negative constitutionalism. As discussed in Chapter 1, for the classical Confucians, "names" (*ming*) are not simply words to call persons but denote personal relationships – a person's functions, duties, and expected virtues. So, in the governmental context, to rectify the names is not merely to correct the misuse of words or to use the correct words, but to maintain the concordance between the real actions of governors like kings and ministers with the standards defining their duties, functions, and expected values.[192] Rectification of names, in fact, connotes the negative limitations of arbitrary power. Negative rectification of names is to avert the situation in which those who carry the social titles do not act correspondingly to the roles and the values that the titles stand for. Elitist remonstrance against the encroachments of imperial power is an example of the negative rectification. But the classical Confucians are more concerned with positive rectification, which involves various constitutive activities to promote the correspondence between the physical political institutions and the metaphysical political-moral standards. In more detail, the rectification of the government first requires the articulation of standards for proper organization, distribution, and use of public power and then to implement these standards in actual politics by positive activities, such as, lecture, recommendation, "praise and censure," and "pure discussion."

In modern government in East Asia, the public power is no longer concentrated in the hands of a single ruler, but instead distributed to different political institutions through the modern mechanism of separation of powers. The authorities and duties of the state's branches are defined by a written constitution. Yet, the modern East Asian people have persistently expected their political leaders to be rectified, in the sense that they should both correct their misconduct and do right things for the people by morally self-cultivating on the one hand, and learning from the elite's advice and criticisms on the other.

The promotion of constitutionalism, to be successful, must be based on the language and understanding the local people are familiar with. Therefore, the normative theory of the East Asian model of constitutionalism seeks to combine the western idea of negative constitutional limits with the Confucian idea of constitutional rectification. The introduction of the concept of constitutional rectification would redefine the nature of constitutionalism in East Asia. Unlike western liberal constitutionalism, East Asian constitutionalism would not be predominantly negative constitutionalism. East Asian constitutionalism pursues the balance between negative and positive dimensions of constitutionalism. East Asian constitutionalism marries constitutional limitations with constitutional rectifications, and both seek to ensure the concordance of the actions of the physical constitutional institutions (the legislature, executive, and the judiciary) and persons (legislators, president, primer, and judges) with constitutional metaphysical standards publicly articulated, conducted by both positive and negative means and for both positive and negative ends.

Constitutional rights and virtues

The second feature of East Asian constitutionalism relates a teleological reconsideration of constitutionalism in the East Asian context. The normative theory of East Asian constitutionalism attempts to mix the negative issue of constitutional protection of human rights with the positive issue of constitutional promotion of civic virtues informed by the Confucian concept of *ren* (humaneness or benevolence).

Western liberal constitutionalism is predominated by the negative concern of protecting human rights. To liberal constitutionalists,

> government should be neutral toward the moral and religious views its citizens espouse. Since people disagree on the best way to live, government should not affirm in law any particular vision of good life. Instead, it should provide a framework of rights and respects persons as free and independent selves, capable of choosing their own values and ends.[193]

Western liberal constitutionalism tends to refrain from a teleological concern of the uses of public power. However, western liberal constitutionalism's evasion of teleological concern has met with challenges. Whittington argues that:

> Constitutionalism is equally concerned with setting limits on government and defining the ends of government. Constitutionalism grew out of an effort to redefine the appropriate uses of the public power, and its history has been marked by a progressive effort to refine the instruments for appropriately channelling that power and recurrent efforts to rethink the foundations of government authority. A constitutionalism modelled simply as a system of rules implies an interest only in the boundaries of political power, eschewing a teleological concern with the uses of that power.[194]

Any normative constitutions, which are essential to constitutionalism, must include explicitly or implicitly teleological concerns and moral principles; liberal constitutions are not exceptions. Proponents of state neutrality may argue that a constitutionalism with teleological concerns will fail to respect individuals as rational selves capable of pursuing their own moral ends. The thesis of constitutional neutrality is, however, empirically and normatively problematic. Empirically, Michael J. Sandel illuminatingly indicates that, even in the United States, which is the typical liberal polity, the government is not able to act neutrally regarding moral issues. Recalling the cases of abortion, stem cell, and same-sex marriage, Sandel demonstrates the failure of the aspiration to neutrality. He asserts that it is impossible for the state to decide questions of justice and rights without resolving substantive moral questions.[195]

Yet, one needs not summon communitarians like Sandel to argue against state neutrality. Some liberal constitutionalists and liberals are also skeptical about constitutional neutrality. Whittington, for example, argues that: "Constitutions cannot be neutral to how public power is used. Constitutional law is only one tool amongst many for directing political power toward achieving genuinely public ends."[196] In a similar vein, Galston argues:

> No political community is, or can be, wholly neutral regarding all ends that individuals and associations may seek to pursue; each community encourages some while discouraging others (or prohibiting them outright). While some regimes are more capacious than others, none can accommodate on equal terms the full range of human possibilities. It is often said that to govern is to choose; so too is to create a government.[197]

Normatively, when constitutional neutrality is possible, it is undesirable. Sandel argues that neutral government fails to foster active citizenship. He then calls for "a strong sense of community," cultivating "in citizens a concern for the whole, a dedication to the common good," and "a politics of moral engagement."[198] In fact, the Rawlsian liberal principle of neutrality has been considerably challenged by western communitarian philosophers, such as Alasdair MacIntyre,[199] Charles Taylor,[200] Michael Walzer,[201] and especially Sandel.[202] Western communitarianism rejects the autonomous selves, priority of individual rights, and neutral state in favor of the encumbered selves, civic virtue, and a politics of moral engagement. Whether communitarian arguments are valid is debatable, but they at least suggest that it is unclear that state neutrality can lead to desirable political life.

A constitutionalist polity with neutral government, if possible, will merely be concerned with institutional setting of limits on the government and neglects substantial moral values of a human's decent and just political life. Such an amoral neutral government will resemble a machine. Is such government desirable for human? Constitutional government is a man-made societal artifice. It is created by humans, and is just one specific tool for humans to achieve general goals, including moral goals. It is undesirable that a man-made societal constitutional government can work like a physical machine independent from humans' moral ends.

The above considerations suggest that East Asian constitutionalism need not evade the teleological concerns. In the East Asian context, the Confucian concept of *ren* can be introduced to justify the teleological concerns of constitutionalism. East Asian constitutionalism would concern not only human rights, but also human virtues.

To Confucians, there is something more important than human rights for a human to pursue: that is humaneness or *ren*. The ultimate goal of humans (人, *ren*) is to become fully humane (仁, *ren*) human. As elaborated in Chapter 1, *ren* means the love or concern for others. *Chung* (conscientiousness) and *shu* (altruism) are the duplex realization of the *ren*, which means refraining from doing harmful things to others, and doing beneficial things to others, respectively. To Confucians, *ren* is the highest moral quality. *Ren* is the overall virtue, and in particular social relationships there are particular virtues guiding personal behaviors stemming from the overall virtue of *ren*. To realize *ren* is the endless process of human beings. A man who fully achieves *ren* would become a sage.[203]

Mixed constitutionalism in East Asia with the principle of "partial establishment" would adopt a minimalist approach to the Confucian *ren*. Its telos is not to maximize *ren* or to transform all citizens into Confucian superior persons (*junzi*) or even sages, because maximization of the Confucian ideals would not respect the plurality of values and would transform the polity into totalitarianism. Therefore, mixed constitutionalism in East Asia seeks to incorporate the minimal spirit of Confucian *ren*, namely the spirit of caring for others. In this manner, the virtue of caring for the others is married with the liberal concern for human rights.

However, can Confucian virtue and human rights coexist? Epistemologies of Confucianism and human rights[204] helpfully dispel the worry that Confucianism is an obstacle to human rights.[205] Confucianism did not advance a theory of human rights[206] but embraces human values which are compatible with human rights and hence can be reconstructed for constitutionalist purposes. Theodore de Bary states:

> It is obvious enough that Confucianism itself did not generate human rights concept and practices equivalent to those now embodied in the Universal Declaration; it is not obvious that Confucianism was headed in another

> altogether different authoritarian or "communitarian" direction, incompatible with the rights affirmed in the Declaration. Thus our aim is not to find twentieth century human rights in Confucianism, but to recognize certain human values – historically embedded in, but at the same time at odds with, repressive institutions in China – that in the emerging modern world could be supportive of those rights."[207]

Joseph Chan proposes that Confucianism can adopt an instrumentalist approach to human rights, which means to take "human rights as an important device for protecting people's fundamental interests."[208] He argues that Confucianism is compatible with human rights, and hence human rights can be employed as a fallback mechanism in case Confucian virtues fail. According to Chan, "in the ideal Confucian society, people are more or less virtuous and act in the spirit of benevolence."[209] In a non-ideal situation, however, human rights "can serve as an important fallback apparatus to protect one's basic interests and needs."[210] Fan Ruiping adopts a similar view, suggesting that: "even if rights are not necessary when the virtues prevail in society ... they are necessary when the virtues do not prevail."[211] Chinese new Confucian Mou Zongsan adopts a deeper instrumentalist view. He believes that: "Constitution, laws, and rights are not merely *compatible* with Confucianism; these objective political structures are *required* by Confucianism if it is to realize its own goals."[212] In other words, human rights are employed as an instrument to realize Confucian goals.

The instrumentalist approach can only work in a strong Confucian society. Consider first Chan's fallback approach. Only in a society where Confucian virtues are deeply instilled can human rights be conceived as the fallback mechanism when virtues fail. In addition, the fallback position implicitly views human rights as inferior Confucian virtues. This view is insensible in the societies where different systems of values exist. It is insensible to require non-Confucian communities to adopt human rights as subordinate to Confucian virtues.

More importantly, the fallback mechanism is unworkable at a constitutional level. In other words, it cannot be applied to constitutional rights. Rights become constitutional because they are conceived as fundamentally significant to the polity and because they are higher than ordinary legal rights.[213] Constitutional rights establish the relationship between citizens and government. Constitutional rights set up the legal limitations on the practice of public power, particular legislative power. The fallback is hopeless at this constitutional level. If human rights are employed as merely the fallback mechanism when virtues fail, they turn out to be subordinate to virtue, less fundamental. In this case, there is little incentive to positively transform human rights into constitutional rights. Yet, one may argue, even human rights as a fallback mechanism should be constitutionalized. This, however, makes the fallback argument contradictory given its preoccupation of virtues. The entrenchment of rights at constitutional level would raise people's awareness of their fundamental rights and encourage them to use their rights. As Justin Tiward argues: "The mere existence of [a] right, even when unclaimed, has a remarkable effect on group dynamics."[214] A priori, the existence of rights at a constitutional level triggers more remarkable effects on people's awareness and practice of rights. So, the fallback approach lack reasons to constitutionalize human rights.

Different from Chan's fallback approach, Mou Zongsan's thick instrumentalism is more concerned with constitutionalizing human rights. However, like the case of Chan, Mou's approach can only work in a strong Confucian society. Only in a society which comprehensively subscribes to Confucianism can human rights be employed as a means to realize Confucian goals. From an empirical point of view, it is unlikely that human rights can be a means to serve Confucian ends in value-pluralist societies in contemporary East Asia. An empirical observation of East Asia suggests that different systems of values (Confucianism, Buddhism, Islam, Catholicism, Protestantism, and others) exist here, and they develop different moral positions on the nature of human dignity and pursue different moral ends. In this context, employing human rights as an instrument to realize Confucian moral ideals may engender value conflicts and resistance to human rights protection.

Alternatively, the normative theory of mixed constitutionalism in East Asia would adopt a supplementary approach to Confucian virtues. As Angle argues, "in order to place their role in protecting vital interests against powerful entities like modern states and global corporations, human rights must be publicly known, readily enforceable, and maximally unambiguous."[215] For this purpose, mixed constitutionalism in East Asia seeks to subjectively constitutionalize human rights. However, unlike western liberal constitutionalism, mixed constitutionalism in East Asia seeks to combine constitutional rights with Confucian virtues. East Asian constitutionalism would employ Confucian virtues as a supplement, not as an instrument or replacement to constitutional rights.

The legitimacy of the addition of the concern of virtues lies in the need to temper excessive legal litigation, hyper-individualism, and egocentric pursuit of interests. One needs not subscribe to communitarianism to promote civic virtues. "Many liberals nowadays acknowledge the need to promote civic virtue and to educate people with the habits, belief, and attitudes necessary for citizenship. These writers argue that even a liberal government is dependent on the habits and dispositions of its citizens and that the liberal states need not – indeed should not – be neutral as to the process of character formulation."[216] These liberal writers include Stephen Macedo, William Galston, and Joseph Raz.[217] Liberals' concern for civic virtues "is closely associated with the excessive-rights-bearing individualism in contemporary liberalism, the corresponding erosion of community in liberal-democratic life, and the disappearance of common good in liberal political discourse."[218]

It is problematic for a society in which social conflicts are always resolved by claiming a right against another. This is even graver at the constitutional level. Excessive and aggressive claim of constitutional rights against the government would erode the civic foundations of the constitutionalist regime. It is certainly true that powerful governments are the most vulnerable to human rights. But, a government in itself is not an evil. It is an essential necessity for human civilization. A government is a cooperator of people, not their enemy. Once they create the government through democratic procedures, people should trust their government rather than look at it with dubious eyes by frequently and aggressively claiming their constitutional rights against their government. Excessive constitutional claims and litigations may also increase hyper-individualism and egocentrism.

To live together in a peaceful and stable constitutionalist polity, citizens and government should resolve constitutional conflicts in a proper manner, which adds the importance of virtues to the claim of constitutional rights.[219] In the East Asian context, the employment of constitutional rights can be supplemented by the consideration of Confucian virtues.[220] To follow Michael J. Meyer,[221] normative mixed constitutional theory in East Asia would agree with the Confucian virtuous use of constitutional rights. Yet, this constitutional mixture of rights and Confucian virtues does not equate to giving priority to Confucian virtues over rights. Neither does it suggest that the legitimacy of constitutional rights lies in the Confucian moral principles. The argument here is that the employment of constitutional rights in East Asian contexts can be supplemented with the consideration of Confucian virtues so that constitutional rights would not be abused for destructive and selfish purposes and would not be conducted in an antagonist manner.

As Meyer argues, the dictates of virtue in proper use of rights will be complex, and this depends on particular situations.[222] So, there is no simplistic formula for the virtuous use of constitutional rights. Depending on particular situations and particular constitutional rights, citizens may consider particular virtues suitable for claiming a constitutional right. However, *ren* or humanity can serve as the overreaching spirit guiding the proper employment of constitutional rights. The minimal employment of the Confucian overreaching virtue of *ren* suggests that citizens, when deciding to claim or not to claim a constitutional right and how far the claim can go, should have concern for the others: their government, their fellows, and their community as a whole. This means that they should consider the balance between their pursuit of their fundamental and legitimate interests and the potential threats to the peace and stability of the polity, the normal functioning of the government, and the fundamental and legitimate interests of other citizens. The employment of constitutional rights in this benevolent manner may help prevent constitutional conflicts between the citizens and their government at the beginning, or limit the escalation of the conflicts which have the potential to damage the peace and stability of the polity.

In Confucianism, there are particular virtues deriving from *ren*, including: respectfulness, lenience, truthfulness, industry, and beneficence (*Analects*, 13.19; 17.6). If these human virtues are disconnected from the Confucian perfectionist aspiration of gentlemen or sages, they will be useful for proper employment of constitutional rights.[223] Citizens need the virtues of respectfulness, lenience, truthfulness, industry, and beneficence, not as personal virtues to become superior men or sages according to Confucian ideal personality, but as civic virtues to practice their constitutional rights in a proper manner and to properly interact with the government, other fellows, and the community when practicing their rights. When Confucian virtues are employed as civic virtues for constitutional purposes, not as personal virtues for perfectionist purposes, members of non-Confucian communities, as *citizens* of the constitutionalist community who share the Confucian culture as a constitutional culture, can practice constitutional rights with the consideration of Confucian virtues as civic virtues without forfeiting the pursuit of their own systems of moral values which they believe are meaningful to their personal moral life.

While the consideration of virtues depends on the uses of particular constitutional rights in particular situations, the marriage of constitutional rights and Confucian virtues in general is not ad hoc but principled. Whether in the preamble or in an individual provision of the constitution, an explicit aspirational preference for Confucian virtues in using constitutional rights is necessary. In addition, civic education by the government and the civil society is necessary for proper employment of constitutional rights. Recall that modern Confucian constitutionalists have already proposed that citizens should be not only vested with fundamental rights, but also educated with fundamental virtues.[224] Virtuous use of constitutional rights can be promoted by the government and the society as a constitutional culture.

Yet, one may doubt that the political promotion of virtues is more likely to lead to paternalistic authoritarianism rather than to constitutionalism. Walker's theory of nonliberal constitutionalism is instructive in this regard. He states:

> Any system claiming the title of nonliberal constitutionalism must frame public life in a way that implements self-limitation across multiple dimensions simultaneously. In other words, nonliberal constitutions must make their positive moral purposes systematically nontotalist, and they must frame structures for the exercise of governmental power that are systematically nontyrannial.[225]

In the same vein as the nonliberal constitutionalist argument, it can be said that citizens in mixed constitutionalist regimes of East Asia "feel rather sure that some ways of life are better than others" but at the same time "feel sure that there are some good reasons to put some limits on the political promotion of even the best way of life."[226] Recall the principle of partial establishment. Constitutional preference is a partial establishment of Confucian virtues. This preference means to promote virtues in practicing constitutional rights without having them be required. Partial constitutional establishment of Confucian virtues would not lead to any legislation that allows the government to go so far so as to outlaw or criminalize unvirtuous (but legal) practice of constitutional rights. Moreover, the government is not the single educator of virtues. The public will also engage in vibrant discourses on the meaning of virtues, and civil society will also engage in civic education. Finally, the citizens, not the government, are the main actors defining the virtuous ways of practicing their constitutional rights in particular circumstances.

Popular sovereignty and people as basis

The third distinctive feature of the proposed East Asian constitutionalism concerns democracy. The normative theory of mixed constitutionalism in East Asia seeks to marry the western liberal principle of popular sovereignty with the Confucian principle of people as base (*minben*). Accordingly, democratic elections operate principally as a mechanism to select representatives who can better serve the people, and peripherally as a mechanism to sanction them.

Popular sovereignty is the core principle of western liberal constitutionalism. This principle recognizes the people as the author of the public power, and the government's officials are created and removed by the people through free and equal elections. Elections practiced with the "one person, one vote" policy as the expression of popular sovereignty and political equality of individual citizens are essential to the operation of democracy in the contemporary world. In East Asian liberal constitutional democracies, free and equal elections have been widely practiced.

It is obvious that liberal elections are a distinguished mechanism of western liberal constitutionalism to create a legitimate government and to peacefully transfer power. However, liberal elections are far from perfect. Confucian democrats, such as Daniel A. Bell, Joseph Chan, and Sungmoon Kim, have pointed out the numerous shortcomings of liberal elections, and they have sought for remedies in the Confucian sources for the East Asian context.[227] To illustrate, invoking contemporary political scientists, Chan identifies a number of deficiencies of electoral democracy. He restates an empirical survey[228] by a group of American political scientists, which indicates that citizens' trust of politicians in 12 of 13 trilateral nations (including Japan, Europe, and North America) declined from 1974 to 1996, with increasing an number of citizens believing that their politicians were interested in votes rather than the well-being of the people, and that elected representatives have lost touch with constituents.[229]

In addition, Chan points out that elections through the process of party politics are not the best means to select the best people to serve in politics because,

> those who rise high in party organizations may not be the most capable, upright, and fair minded, or those most genuinely interested in working for the common good, but those who have learned to play the power games in party politics.[230]

Furthermore, Chan indicates that: "The fact that electoral campaigns require extremely high levels of financing and are increasingly influenced by corporations also contributes to the popular belief that parties serve only the interests of the powerful."[231] Chan continues: "Although democracy is generally effective in exposing corruption and administrative blunders, it is not always the best method of promoting quality deliberations and the politics of common good."[232] As far as the party politicians are concerned, they "are often seen as opportunists who exploit or exaggerate their opponents' weaknesses for partisan gains, sometimes going to such extremes as to risk the good of the country for the good of their party."[233] In terms of citizens, many of them "are apathetic and have lost interest in voting. If they do vote, many are ill informed and some vote irresponsibly, pursuing narrow self-interests at the expense of the common good."[234]

In seeking remedies for the drawbacks of liberal elections in the East Asian context, some Confucian democrats, such as Chan and Kim, draw theoretical inspiration from Western political scientists' new formulation of a *selection model* of political representation in contrast to the prevailing *sanction model.*[235] The sanction model rests on the metaphor of "principal–agent relations" in which the interests of the principals (the constituents) are assumed to conflict with the interests of the agents (the representatives). Periodic elections are therefore used as a mechanism to hold the agents accountable to the principals by monitoring the agents closely, rewarding the good behavior and punishing the bad.[236]

In the selection model, elections are a mechanism for the voters to select "a representative who is honest, competent, and already has policy goals much like the constituents."[237] Mansbridge underlines that: "This model works only when a potential agent already has self-motivated, exogenous reasons for doing what the principal wants. The principal and agent thus have similar objectives even in the absence of the principal's sanctions."[238] Different from accountability based on monitoring and sanctions, accountability in the selection model will take the form of "*narrative* and even *deliberative* accountability," which means that "the representative explains the reasons for her actions and even (ideally) engages in two-way communication with constituents, particularly when deviating from the constituents' preferences."[239]

The selection model seems more attractive to Confucian democrats. Joseph Chan states that behind the sanction model of elections "is the notion that politicians are opportunistic agents motivated solely by self-interest. Periodic elections and other accountability mechanisms are therefore necessary to monitor elected officials and induce them to do what the voters want."[240] To Chan, the sanctions model "is thus based on distrust and control," and this "goes deeply against the Confucian ideal conception of political relationship, which takes trustworthiness, sincerity, and mutual commitment of rulers and the ruled as an aspiration."[241] He also criticizes that:

> A political constitution designed on the basis of the sanctions model not only fails to express the ideal political relationship; it also has highly undesirable consequences. In the real world, not all politicians or people who seek to enter professional politics are motivated purely by private interests. Many people may have both public- and private-interest motivations.[242]

Chan believes that Confucianism can provide an "alternative understanding" of democratic elections, drawing from Confucian meritocracy. Confucian meritocracy "suggests a principle: to select the virtuous and competent to assume leadership, so that they can work for the public interest and cultivate trust and harmony with the people."[243] Chan then suggests that the meaning or point of elections can be understood in the light of the Confucian ideal of meritocracy, according to which,

> elections should not primarily be about monitoring or control, nor should they be seen as an accountability device to induce self-interested politicians to work for voters; they should rather be seen as a method for selecting people who have integrity, ability, and commitment to public service and who will cultivate trust and harmony with the people.[244]

Chan additionally comments that this Confucian understanding of elections is consistent with the selection model adumbrated by American framers like James Madison and developed by political scientists like Mansbridge and others.[245]

Sungmoon Kim also supports the selection model, equally drawing from Confucian meritocracy. Kim explains that political meritocracy is by no means opposed to democracy and political equality, since individuals as public citizens will choose the virtuous to take leadership positions through free and equal elections.[246] So, for Confucians, the concern is not to refute western representative democracy but to find a way to deal with "the predominance of the sanction model of political representation in the actually existing representative democracies including some East Asian democracies."[247] Like Chan, Kim believes that the Confucian tradition of meritocracy can support the selection model. But different from Chan, Kim gives the sanction model a peripheral position while taking the selection model as the core in democratic politics:

> Political sanction is necessary because we are living in a nonideal world where there are more knaves than people of moral integrity but, nevertheless, political sanction should be at the periphery of democratic politics, not its core. The mainstay of democratic politics must be filled with virtuous leaders who are genuinely committed to the moral and material well-being of the citizenry, particularly those citizens who deserve it.[248]

The theory of mixed constitutionalism in East Asia has good reasons to support the selection model. From a constitutionalist perspective, elections as accountability mechanisms of monitoring and sanctions are mainly concerned with limiting abuses of power.[249] They are the institutional manifestations of negative constitutionalism. Elections as a sanction model fail to promote proper exercise of the power for the common good or positive constitutionalism.

From a Confucian perspective, I agree that the tradition of meritocracy can support the selection model, but I would suggest that the main Confucian source to support the selection model should be tracked back to the Confucian principle of *minben* or people as basis, as elaborated in Chapter 1. A summary of its meaning here is useful. The Confucian principle of *minben* is the manifestation of the Confucian central principle of *ren* in the political sphere. While the principle of *ren* teaches the concern and care for others, its political embodiment is the ruler's concern and care for the people. A legitimate government is therefore the government that takes the people as base and works for their moral and material well-being. In Confucianism, meritocracy is derivative to *minben*. A government working for the people should be administrated by the "gentlemen" or the virtuous and wise persons.

The essence of the selection model lies in "the congruence between the principal's desires and the agent's behaviour."[250] The Confucian concept of *minben* supports this argument well. In the East Asian context, elections can be understood under the light of *minben*. Accordingly, elections are employed as a mechanism to principally select the persons who can take the people as basis and work for their benefits. Elections are therefore understood in a positive sense. Elections are mainly mechanisms of positive constitutionalism to promote the proper use of public power for public interests.

In the context of positive constitutionalism with elections as a selection model, political accountability will take a constructive form, namely *narrative* and *deliberative*. Confucianism has rich sources to support the narrative and deliberative accountability. As Sangjin Han has pointed out, "Confucianism is emphatically communicative. Human subjectivity as well as social relationships is understood as shaped through discourse and communication."[251] For Confucians, "comparative evaluations, persuasion, and consensual agreement are pursued and take place. No direct coercion, no violation, no economic incentives are presupposed for this learning."[252] To continue this tradition in contemporary East Asia, when elected politicians depart from the people's interests the chief accountability mechanism will not be their direct sanction by the people via elections but that they will explain the reasons for their actions and engage in constructive dialogues with the people.

However, in the context of mixed constitutionalism, the sanction model is by no means dismissed. As Mansbridge demonstrates:

> In practice both selection and sanctions are always at work. Selection and sanctions map directly onto the two commonly cited motivations of representatives, the desire to make good public policy and the desire to be reelected. These two motivations are almost always mixed. The alignment of principals' and agents' objectives will also never be perfect. Thus constituents will always have some reason to monitor their representatives in order either to try to induce new behaviour through the threat of sanction or simply to replace those representatives in the next election. Nor is the sanctions model ever pure. It is hard to imagine a representative with no intrinsic motivation to work for the policies he or she thinks good for the polity and hard to imagine any constituent voting for a representative whose preferences the constituent thought were always induced.[253]

Mansbridge then argues that "because both the sanction and the selection models are always mixed, it helps to think of the selection model as having selection at its core and sanctions at its periphery."[254] To follow Mansbridge, I submit that the Confucian *minben* understanding of elections as a selection model can be mixed with the conventional understanding of elections as a sanction model. In the mixed configuration, the selection model plays the central role while the sanction model plays the peripheral role. Elections are chiefly a mechanism to select the persons who can take the people as the basis and best serve the people. In case political leaders' egoist interests substantially depart from the public interests, elections can be used as a sanction mechanism.

So understood, I find Kim's construction of the selection model in a Confucian context to be more tenable than Chan's. Although I agree with Chan that Confucianism can support the selection model, I do not think that Confucianism can provide an "alternative" to sanction-based elections. It seems that Chan does not take the sanction mechanism seriously. The sanction model has no place in his Confucian perfectionist construction of democratic elections. As Chan states, many politicians may have both public- and private-interest motivations. So, while the selection mechanisms can be employed as the principal mechanisms to promote the public interest motivations, the sanction mechanisms can also be used as the supplementary mechanisms to ensure that private-interest motivations would not induce the political leaders to outrun the public interests.

Furthermore, viewed from a Confucian perspective, Chan's dismissal of the sanction model is problematic. Although Confucianism is emphatically communicative and persuasive, it does not completely deny sanction in the case the ruler betrays the interests of the people and communicative and persuasive solutions fail to rectify him. Recall Mencius' position on this point. Mencius suggests if the prince has great faults, the high ministers who are noble and relatives of the prince ought to remonstrate with him, and if he does not listen to them after they have done so again and again, they ought to dethrone him.[255] Now, when the sovereignty belongs to the people, this statement can be read anew in this way: when the politicians deviate from the public interests, and communicative and persuasive solutions fail, elections can serve as the sanction mechanism for the people to remove them.

Constitutional law and constitutional ethics

The fourth distinctive feature of the proposed East Asian constitutionalism concerns the rule of law. The normative theory of East Asian constitutionalism endeavors to mix the western concept of the rule of law with the Confucian concept of the rule of *li* (ritual propriety). Accordingly, the use of public power is bound by not only constitutional law but also constitutional ethics.

Western liberal constitutionalism is mainly concerned with rules, and this has connections with constitutional neutralism and democratic proceduralism. The preoccupation of liberal constitutionalism is to design and interpret rules and institutions as a neutral framework for limiting the public power and protecting individual rights. Its scholarly consequence is that contemporary constitutional studies have been dominated by the concerns of "constitution-making," "constitutional design," and "constitutional interpretation." What have been largely ignored in the contemporary constitutional studies are normative inquiries into how constitutional rules are properly used.

Constitutionalism cannot be equated to "constitution-making," "constitutional design," and "constitutional interpretation." It must also be concerned with how constitutional rules are properly used. Drawing from empirical evidence in Hungary, Egypt, and Venezuela, David Landau's recent study of "abusive constitutionalism" demonstrates that mechanisms of constitutional change have been constitutionally used by would-be autocrats to undermine democracy with relative ease.[256] Even in the liberal constitutional state like the United States, as Wittington argues, "Even if political actors are willing to respect the rules established by the Constitution, as interpreted and enforced by the courts, their actions may still be damaging to the constitutional system as a whole and contrary to important constitutional values."[257] Liberal constitutionalism virtually has nothing to do with constitutional but Machiavellian use of the public power for the private purpose.

That drawback of liberal constitutionalism gives rise to scholarly concern of constitutional ethics as additional to constitutional law.[258] Wittington is instructive in this regard. He laments that contemporary constitutional theory focuses too much on identifying constitutional rules and "ignores important aspects of our constitutional practice and necessary components of any viable constitutional system."[259] These aspects relate to constitutional ethics. Wittington therefore suggests broadening the concerns of constitutional theory. Accordingly, constitutional theory must be concerned with not only producing interpretive methodologies for judges so as to guide the production of the corpus of constitutional law, but also elaborating principles of constitutional ethics for politicians to guide political practice.[260] This, however, does not suggest that constitutional theory should abandon its traditional concern of constitutional law; instead, this suggests the necessary supplementation of a theory of constitutional ethics to the existing theories of constitutional law.[261]

To elaborate the need for a theory of constitutional ethics, Wittington first draws attention to what is called "constitutional fidelity." Constitutional fidelity involves the constitutional ethics of both citizens and politicians. Ethics of constitutional citizenship require citizens to have "an ethical obligation to enter directly and/or indirectly into an ongoing and continuing constitutional dialogue" and "seek to determine the possible consistency between a referred policy option and a referred constitutional structure."[262] Apart from the ethics of constitutional citizenship, constitutional fidelity "is a problem of building political support for both obeying and nurturing limits on political power."[263] Constitutional fidelity is a matter of building and nurturing an "ingrained habit" that requires the political actors (not only judges) to be willing "to be bound by inherited constitutional constraints and the possibility of being faithful to constitutionalism."[264]

Yet, constitutional fidelity is not sufficient, since even political actors are willing to be bound by constitutional rules, their behaviors may also be detrimental to constitutionalism as a whole.[265] This observation leads Wittington to formulate another principle of constitutional ethics, namely "constitutional propriety." The formulation of constitutional propriety draws attention to "a set of convention, norms, and custom deriving from constitutional consideration that should constrain political actors but nonetheless not judicially enforceable for any of a large number of reasons."[266] This set of unwritten constitutional values impose restraints on political actors with "a sense of responsibility" deriving from their constitutional offices that they "are obliged to advance and not simply avoid violating."[267] Wittington concludes:

> Issues of constitutional propriety suggest that government officials are not free to strategize so as to maximize their interests within an environment of legal restraints. The Constitution cannot be viewed simply as an obstacle to be overcome or circumvented. It also imposes possible duties that should be recognized in political practice.[268]

Wittington then points out two possible combined approaches to constitutional ethics, namely universalistic and contextualistic. In the first instance, constitutional ethics derive from "the consideration of the empirical and normative preconditions of a thriving constitutional order."[269] For example, any viable constitutionalist regime requires political actors to accept responsibility for maintaining that regime and understanding its precepts. In the second contextualistic approach, constitutional ethics derive from the consideration of a particular constitutional context. Wittington elaborates this approach as follows:

> Such an internal approach to constitutional ethics would be concerned with interpreting existing social practices.... The goal would be to identify the purposes, aspirations, available justifications and dominant practices inherent in the existing political system. A theory of constitutional ethics would be concerned with making the normative commitments embedded in those practices more explicit, while challenging political actors to better realize the possibilities of their own traditions and to grapple with the contradictions and competition with and across those traditions.[270]

Wittington provides powerful guidance for theorizing about constitutional ethics. Constitutionalism in East Asia, where a long tradition of emphasis on political ethics deriving from Confucian influences exists, would have good reasons to pay attention to constitutional ethics. East Asian constitutionalism would be concerned with articulating not only constitutional rules, but also ethical constitutional principles which guide how the rules are properly followed in political practices. East Asian constitutionalism would accept the universalist idea that any viable constitutionalist regime requires political actors to accept responsibility for maintaining that regime and understanding its precepts. As far as contextualism is concerned, East Asian constitutionalism derives from the consideration of Confucian *li* (ritual propriety) as distinctive local constitutional ethics, supplementary to constitutional law.

The reason to focus on *li* is that *li* presents "aspirations, available justifications and dominant practices" inherent in the existing East Asian constitutional systems. *Li* constitutes the "ingrained habits" that have guided the political behaviors in traditional Confucian East Asian societies and have continued to influence political realities in contemporary East Asian societies. To be sure, the concept of *li* is not often explicitly used in the public discourse in contemporary East Asia. However, Hahm Chaihark points out:

> The matter of *li* still remains a very "public" concern. People learn to relate to one another and define one's place in family and society in terms of *li*. As such, *li* represents East Asians what Cover called nomos, a normative universe, or a structure of meaning.[271]

Li is a maneuverable concept which possesses various nuances of connotation in different periods of time. The evolution of the concept of *li* has been elaborated at length in Chapter 1.[272] To summarize, *li* embraces institutions, social and moral norms, which regulate all dimensions of the people's lives, ranging from personal behavior and familial relationships, to socio-political functions and structures. In the political meaning, the concept of *li* is derivative of the central doctrine of *zheng ming* government. The *zheng ming* government requires the political institutions to function in concordance with the established standards, which defines the limitations of their authorities and duties together with the inherent virtues. *Li* is the articulation of such standards. First, *li* consists of institutions which define the scope of the authorities and duties of different governmental institutions. Second, *li* defines the positive moral norms inherent in government officials.

Stephen C. Angle distinguishes two roles that *li* plays in Confucianism, namely maximal and minimal.[273] The maximal role of *li* is expressed in Confucius' dictum in the *Analects* 12:1: "To subdue one's self and return to propriety [*li*] is perfect virtue [*ren*]." *Li* in this maximal role is the internal part of one's entire being, constitutive to one's achievement of the *ren* as "the pinnacle of ethic achievement."[274] The one who is fully ritualized would become a sage and would have nothing to do. It is in this maximal sense that Tu Wei-ming comments that, for Confucians, humanization substantially involves ritualization.[275] Yet, *li* also has the minimal role as expressed in this statement in the *Analects*:

> If the people be led by laws, and uniformity sought to be given them by punishments, they will try to avoid the punishment, but have no sense of shame. If they be led by virtue, and uniformity sought to be given them by rules of propriety [*li*] they will have the sense of shame and moreover will become good.[276]

Angle comments that

> Far from presenting the acme of ethic achievement as something that the mass can be taught. It has a positive effect on them, but no one will be tempted to conclude that as a result of the ritual teachings they have received, all the people now count as sages.[277]

Hahm is correct in drawing attention to the possible constitutional role of *li* in the prospects of constitutionalism in East Asia. Yet, he has misled when referring to *li*'s maximal role. Hahm's ritualist constitutionalism largely relies on the cited statement, *keiji fuli*, in the *Analects* 12:1, which he translated as "disciplining oneself and returning to ritual propriety."[278] Hahm opines that: "the idea of discipline is very helpful for understanding both the educative and constitutional aspects of *li*."[279] On this ground, Hahm suggests citizens in East Asia should discipline themselves according to the *li* and by that they spontaneously ensure that their political leaders will be similarly disciplined. He elaborates this idea in these words:

> From the perspective of the citizens, this means that in order to have a legitimate government, a regime that is accountable to the people, they must make sure that their chosen rulers are properly disciplined with *li*. Ideally, a democratic citizenry that has been properly educated through *li* will be one that has acquired the habits and beliefs – civic virtues – that enable it to "work through spontaneous coordination" toward ensuring that elected officials will be so disciplined. Of course, this ideal may seldom be realized. Thus, in the event that citizens cannot elect a person who is already so disciplined, they must at least institute measures which will ensure that occupants of the higher offices will be appropriately disciplined.[280]

Even though Hahm does not make clear that he advocates for the maximal role of *li*, the fact that he refers to *keiji fuli* implies this. In his vision of the prospects of constitutionalism in East Asia, both citizens and politicians are strictly disciplined according to the *li*. The implied consequence of this ritual discipline process tends to be the Confucian idealized personality of gentlemen or even sages.[281]

I believe that Hahm's proposal is not only ideal, as he admits, but also insensible in contemporary East Asia if one takes the empirical reality of value plurality here seriously. In this regard, I concur with Kim that:

> To impose *li* of this kind [*keiji fuli*] on members of a democratic civil society, where they belong to different religious and (sub-)cultural associations and thus are committed to different moral values, critically violates value pluralism. Indeed, in the modern context, it makes no sense to regard a person (say, a Korean Muslim) who does not subscribe to the comprehensive (or monistic) Confucian moral notion of ritual propriety as less authentic or less authoritative (according to Hall and Rosemont's translation of *ren*) as a human being.[282]

I contend that for *li* to play a constitutional role in contemporary pluralist East Asian societies, its minimal role is more relevant.[283] In the modern construction, *li*, which may include social and moral norms, habits, and customs, presents a kind of public constitutional ethics guiding people's proper behaviors in the public political life, irrelevant to personal moral perfection. Understood in this sense, *li* can be reconstructed as a form of constitutional fidelity and constitutional propriety.

To begin, *li* as constitutional fidelity concerns the constitutional ethics of both citizens and politicians. Citizens need to be educated with ritualist norms, positive social and moral norms, habits and customs, as public civic values for constitutional purposes, not as private moral values for personal moral perfection. These norms are instrumental to citizens' active engagement in constitutional development. Confucian classics are replete with ritualist norms. For example, recall Mencius' formulation of social and moral norms of "great men":

> To dwell in the wide house of the world, to stand in the correct seat of the world, and to walk in the great path of the world; when he obtains his desire for office, to practice his principles for the good of the people; and when that desire is disappointed, to practice them alone; to be above the power of riches and honours to make dissipated, of poverty and mean condition to make swerve from the principle, and of power and force to make bend.[284]

We do not expect that every citizen should achieve such norms to become "great men." Yet, these norms can be disconnected from the perfectionist aspiration to "great men" so as to be selectively and creatively transformed into public ethical norms of constitutional citizenship. For example, citizens need the spirit of uprightness, caring for the common good, and transcending the bending to power and force to engage in active discourse for constitutional development and combat against despotic power. Modern Confucianst such as Kang Youwei, Liang Qichao, Phan Bội Châu, and Phan Châu Trinh, who have actively fought for modern constitutionalism in China and Vietnam, can be partially explained by their adherence to these social and moral norms. Apart from citizens, political actors also need a commitment to *li* so that they will willingly observe constitutional restraints as a constitutional culture rather than as a political strategy. This correlates with the ethics of constitutional citizenship. When the citizenry is instilled with *li* as public civic culture, this will condition the political behaviors of political actors and induce them to commit to this culture, which stems from the logics of the sociological foundation of political legitimacy. Simply speaking, politicians who fail to commit to public political culture would not receive much social acceptance.

Apart from constitutional fidelity, *li* or ritual propriety can be transformed into "constitutional propriety." In this sense, *li* includes a set of conventions, norms, and custom which impose a sense of responsibility on the political actors inherent to their constitutional offices. Recall the Confucian doctrine of rectification of names from which *li* derives. To rectify the government names like "prince" or "ministers" means that those who occupy these offices must act consistently with not only the institutionally defined authorities, but also virtues inherent to these names or offices. *Li* includes both institutions which define the authorities and moral norms which define the inherent virtues. In the modern states of East Asia, the written constitutions play the role of defining institutional authorities. Yet, the written constitutions have little to do with elaborating the inherent virtues which impose a sense of responsibility on political actors. *Li* as the moral code of conduct is now still relevant in guiding the behaviors of political actors so that they will use their power not only constitutionally but also properly. In this regard, rectification of names is reconstructed to fit the modern context. Now, to rectify the names means to rectify the modern constitutional names, like "president," "premier," "ministers," "legislators," and "judges" in the sense that those who occupy these constitutional offices must act consistently with not only constitutionally defined authorities but also moral norms inherent to these constitutional offices or names. The consequence is that they will be bound by not only constitutional law but also constitutional *li* or propriety. This may be the Confucian resolution to prevent the phenomenon of "abusive constitutionalism" from happening in East Asia.

Let me now focus more on the Confucian ritualist justification of constitutional propriety in the East Asian context. From a Confucian ritualist perspective, humans' actions should be guided by positive education, persuasion, advice, and discourse rather than by negative coercion or punishment. This famous apophthegm in the *Analects* should be remembered:

> If the people be led by laws, and uniformity sought to be given them by punishments, they will try to avoid the punishment, but have no sense of shame. If they be led by virtue, and uniformity sought to be given them by rules of propriety [*li*] they will have the sense of shame and moreover will become good.[285]

By "the people," Confucius means the ordinary people. His idea is that political leaders should lead ordinary people by virtue and rules of propriety, which requires education, persuasion, and communication, not penal laws. The Confucians do not totally negate coercion, but they do not consider it ideal because coercion can only make the people try to avoid punishment and cannot make them have "the sense of shame" and will create better persons in the future.

Notably, the classical Confucians underline the importance of "the sense of shame" (*chi*) for being a good governor and a good person in general rather than exclusively for leading the plebeians. When asked about the qualities that a man must possess to entitle him to be called a true officer, Confucius says: "He who in his conduct of himself maintains a sense of shame, and when sent to any quarter will not disgrace his prince's commission, deserves to be called an officer."[286] Similarly, Mencius states: "A man may not be without shame. When one is ashamed of having been without shame, he will afterwards not have occasion to be ashamed."[287] For him, "the sense of shame is to a man of great importance."[288] He also questions: "When one differs from other men in not having this sense of shame, what will he have in common with them?"[289]

I submit that the Confucian idea of "the sense of shame" can be applied in the constitutional domain to produce a kind of constitutional propriety. The political leaders might have "the sense of shame," an unpleasant emotion, because of the discrepancy between their real actions with the virtues inherent to their offices. The discrepancy might result in the social disdain of the political leaders, which makes them shameful. Alternatively, the discrepancy might induce them to self-recognize that their characters are ethically flawed, which in turn makes them shameful.[290] Arguing in a parallel line with the Confucians, I contend that a constitutionalism that focuses mainly on constitutional rules may just make political actors try to avoid constitutional violations and sanctions, but may not make them "have the sense of shame" and even become better leaders who can use their powers for proper purposes and in the proper manner, not merely constitutionally. In contrast, more positive education, persuasion, advice, and discourse can induce the politicians to "have the sense of shame," which in turn has the effect of not only limiting the unconstitutional actions but also encouraging the constitutional actions and proper political behaviors. Simply demanding coercive actions (through, for example, sanctions by elections or judicial review power) might not make the leaders feel shameful of their deviation from the virtues inherent to their offices. Instead, directing their actions by education, persuasion, advice, and communication can make them feel shameful of their ignorance of constitutional values, which makes them self-conscious of the constitutional values and therefore encourages them to perform their work constitutionally and properly for the common good in a cultural rather than strategic manner.

Confucianism is replete with ritualist moral norms which impose the sense of responsibility on the ruler, including: residing over people with gravity; being final and kind to all; advancing the good and teaching the incompetent; honoring the talented and virtuous, and bearing with all; praising the good, and pitying the incompetent; loving propriety, righteousness, and good faith; paying reverent attention to business; being sincere; being economic in expenditure; loving for men; and employing the people at the proper seasons.[291] If these ritualist moral norms are disconnected from the perfectionist aspiration to a sage king, they can be selectively and creatively transformed into public ethical-political norms guiding the constitutional propriety of the political actors in the context of East Asia.

To promote constitutional propriety, some explicit constitutional references to ritualist moral norms may be necessary. Yet, I do not propose inscribing "the way of Yao, Shun, Confucius, and Mencius" into written constitutions as Jiang Qing does with the Chinese constitution.[292] Qing proposes this idea in the context where Confucianism is established as a state religion and as a comprehensive doctrine for building a new Confucian state. This proposal is insensible in the context where value plurality is appreciated and Confucianism is partially promoted as a public political culture disconnected from its moral perfectionism. For constitutional propriety, the constitution may need some explicit references to some Confucian political-ethic norms as public political virtues, but must not comprehensively include "the Way of Yao, Shun, Confucius, and Mencius." For example, from a reconstructionist perspective of the rectification of names, the name "president" suggests not only constitutionally allowed authorities, but also positive moral types of behavior, such as uprightness, trustworthiness, and integrity, that a physical president is expected to perform. To promote the constitutional propriety in his behavior, it is possible for the constitution to make clear such expected moral norms of behavior that he or she must advance.

Beyond judicial review

The last but not least distinctive feature of East Asian constitutionalism relates to constitutional enforcement. East Asian constitutionalism attempts to mix the western institution of judicial review with the Confucian means of constitutional rectification. Accordingly, constitutional norms are not merely enforced through judicial review mechanisms but are also upheld by constitutional self-rectification, popular constitutional moral discourse, constitutional remonstrance, constitutional lecture, and constitutional record.

Liberal constitutionalism features the existence of some form of judicial review, which allows ordinary courts (in the American decentralized model) or a specialist constitutional court (in the European centralized model) to implement fundamental human rights protected by a constitution.[293] At the beginning of the twenty-first century, constitutional review by the judicial mechanism or "judicial constitutionalism" is a widespread phenomenon.[294] The global wave of judicial review has spread to East Asia. South Korea and Taiwan have practiced the specialist constitutional courts,[295] while Japan[296] accords to the ordinary judiciary the power of judicial review. Notably, judicial constitutionalism is even becoming more attractive in socialist East Asian nations, namely China and Vietnam.

Judicial review, however, is not a sine qua non of a true constitutionalist state. Even in mature constitutionalist states in the modern era, judicial review is not essential. As Stéphanie Balme and Michael W. Dowdle point out, in the most effective constitutional systems, such as the United Kingdom, Netherlands, Switzerland, Italy, and Japan, "significant aspects of constitutional structure are invariably nonjusticiable."[297]

In addition, judicial review, albeit being prevalently practiced in the world, is by no means the best alternative for constitutional enforcement. In fact, some Western scholars have challenged the theoretical foundations of judicial review.[298] Practical problems of judicial review have been also identified. In the case of the United States, the so-called "counter-majoritarian difficulty"[299] is the perennial problem of judicial review. The legitimacy of judicial review is questionable because judicial review allows unelected judges to overturn the laws made by democratically elected representatives. Consequently, from a populist perspective, some American scholars, such as Mark Tushnet[300] and Larry D. Kramer,[301] have argued against the practice of judicial review in favor of the people's interpretation of the Constitution's meanings. In the case of the centralized judicial review, Allan R. Brewer-Carias recently revealed that legitimacy of the constitutional courts is questionable as these courts are no longer limited to merely practicing the traditional function of invalidating unconstitutional statutes, but have actively interfered with the constituent power and the legislative power, and their constitutional jurisdiction is not subjected to checks and balances or control.[302]

I do not wish to enter the ongoing debate over the limitations of the theory of judicial review, but for the purposes of this study I wish to add one point, namely the negative emphasis on controlling unconstitutional state actions and the lack of sufficient concern for encouraging constitutional state actions and promoting constitutional ethics. The focus on judicial review is the consequence of a constitutionalism that focuses mainly on constitutional rules. Judicial constitutionalism may just allow political actors to circumvent constitutional violations, but would not be helpful in promoting constitutional ethics. So, the business of constitutionalism must involve something more than judicial review, if constitutional ethics is taken seriously. This does not mean to deny judicial review completely. My true contention is that judicial review must be supplemented with other positive things which can be learned from Confucian tradition, as elaborated below.

Self-rectification

In Confucianism, the ruler is required to self-rectify their conduct in accordance with the requirements of *li*, by which his use of power is limited to the common good of the people. This teaching may have some contemporary relevance. To promote constitutional ethics in contemporary East Asia, self-rectification is still useful. The requirement of constitutional fidelity and constitutional propriety may need self-rectification of the political actors. Accordingly, they would willingly submit themselves to constitutional restraints, be self-conscious of ethic-political norms inherent to their constitutional offices, and subjectively act and behave in accordance with these norms. Yet, self-rectification in this sense is not a mission to become the Confucian idealized authoritative persons, such as a superior man or even a sage king. Self-rectification is disconnected from the moral perfectionist aspiration to become a political culture observed by political actors.

Self-rectification is highly ideal in the contemporary world where there are more knaves than upright persons, but it is not impossible. There are reasonable incentives for political actors to rectify themselves constitutionally and ethically. As Stephen Holmes points out, limited power has a paradox that "limited power can be more powerful than unlimited power," which explains "why elites have sometimes, if not invariably, submitted themselves to constitutional restraints even when no popular movement or deadly urban riot has been looming on the horizon."[303] To illustrate further, Homes states that: "social elites impose restraints upon themselves, when they do, to gain something they want, such as more security, more wealth, more territory, more cooperation, or more power."[304] Like

> celebrated athletes, musicians, inventors, and other popular idols" who "have invariably subjected themselves year after year to relentless physical and mental discipline to hone their skills and achieve a professional excellence unattainable by anyone who lounges about hedonistically, living day to day,[305]

political actors have reasonable incentives to rectify themselves to gain more acceptance. So, self-rectification is not an impossible idea, although there may be a mixture of public and private interests in attaining more sociological and moral legitimacy by self-rectification.

Popular constitutionalism

In classical Confucian constitutionalism, apart from internal effort, the ruler is constrained by external forces. One of the possible external constraints is the discourse of the wise and virtuous scholars by their social intellectual authority. I have called this "scholastic constitutionalism." In pre-modern East Asia, the social intellectual authority was limited to a group of the learned, hence the name "scholastic constitutionalism." In the contemporary societies of East Asia, Confucian scholastic constitutionalism can be transformed into popular constitutionalism in which the people would play the active role in advancing constitutional arguments. Yet, the distinctive feature of popular constitutionalism in the East Asian Confucian context would be the popular moral discourse. Rather than merely legalist reasoning, East Asian popular constitutionalism seeks to encourage the public to advance ethical arguments to promote constitutional ethics in political behavior. In this context, citizens would discuss not only the constitutionality of political actions, but also the morality of political behaviors. The former is similar to the liberal practice of popular political constitutionalism, while the latter illustrates a distinctive practice of "popular moral constitutionalism."

In this regard, Confucius' *Spring and Autumn Annals* provides useful guidance. One should be reminded that Confucius composed the *Spring and Autumn Annals* as a free scholar in the later stage of his life. Confucius' free scholarship, however, can serve the constitutionalist purpose because, as Mencius says, 'Confucius completed the *Spring and Autumn Annals*, and rebellious ministers and villainous sons are struck with terror."[306] The *Spring and Autumn Annals* establish the Confucian tradition of *pao-pien* ("praise and censure"). This tradition can be revived for constitutional purposes. Citizens can praise moral political behaviors and censure the immoral ones. Consequently, constitutional fidelity and constitutional propriety are promoted by the public moral discourse. Those who are censured by the people would have "the sense of shame" and may become better persons. Apart from the tradition of *pao-pien*, the *Spring and Autumn Annals* also establish the tradition of *qingyi* ("pure discussion"), which means that it is a forum for the individuals who are not in policy-making positions to express their opinion.[307] In the modern age, the tradition of *qingyi* can be developed for constitutional purposes. Free scholars and ordinary citizens, those who are not in policy-making positions, can advance "pure discussions" on the constitutionality of political actions and the morality of political behaviors. In short, "praise and censure" and "pure discussion" are the distinctive forms of popular constitutionalism in the East Asian context. Yet, they can only be practiced effectively with the maximum respect of freedom of speech and without the obstacle of statutes that make it a criminal offense to "insult" the honor or dignity of public officials.[308]

Constitutional review and constitutional remonstrance

As I elaborated in Chapter 1, Confucius, by composing the *Chunqiu*, operated as a de facto constitutional judge. Confucius produced this work not simply to record the historical facts of the Lu, but to rectify the names to deal with the problem of arbitrary power. By means of accurate terminology, Confucius' *Chunqiu* implicitly interprets the meaning of the political actions, defines the fundamental principles of organization and operation of the government, and passes critical judgment ("praise-and-censure") upon the state's actions.[309] In Chapter 2, I have also demonstrated that, following Confucius, the historian offices in the imperial government in East Asia composed the "veritable records" of the dynasties not to merely record the historical facts but, like their master, to interpret the meaning of the political actions, define principles of the polity, and pass critical judgments upon actions of the emperor and the court.[310]

East Asian democracies have created a system of constitutional review. This creation can be considered as the continuity of the Confucian tradition of rational judgment. Like Confucius and the imperial historian offices, the modern institutions of constitutional review can interpret the meaning of the political actions, define the fundamental principles of organization and operation of the government, and pass critical judgment on the state's actions, not explicitly by historical records but explicitly by constitutional review. The implicit traditional activities of interpretation of political actions and principles of the polity and judgment of the rightness and wrongness of state actions have been now transformed into explicit constitutional interpretation and constitutional adjudication. Justifying constitutional review in East Asia in that way can make the practice become a more natural and autogenic process.

Let us proceed to consider the effects of constitutional judgments. Systems of constitutional review vary in the effects of constitutional judgments. In the American decentralized system, courts reject the application of the law which they find unconstitutional in the concrete case, but do not void it. However, that law is void in practice, albeit remaining in books, due to the binding rule of *stare decisis*: decisions in subsequent similar cases must comply with the antecedent decision. In contrast, in the centralized system of constitutional review, where a tradition of *state decisis* is absent, constitutional courts have the authority to declare a law unconstitutional and void it immediately with *erga omnes* effects, meaning that these declarations are binding for all subsequent cases.[311]

Germany's experience presents a variation of two alternatives in rendering a constitutional adjudication. The German Federal Constitutional Court may declare laws or regulations that it finds unconstitutional either null and void (*nichtig*) or incompatible (*unvereinbar*) with the Basic Law. A statute held to be *nichtig* terminates its binding force immediately; a stature or legal norm declared to be *unvereinbar* is unconstitutional but not void, and its force remains during a transition period pending its correction by the legislature.[312] According to Donald P. Kommers, the latter version of declaration of unconstitutionality is one of two strategies adopted by the court to soften the political impact of its decisions.[313] The first strategy uses admonitory decisions (*Appellentscheidung*) to tender advice to the parliament on the unconstitutionality of the statutes. "The Court usually sets up a deadline for corrective legislative action and occasionally directs parliament to adopt a specific solution. More often, the court lays down the general guidelines within which parliament is required to legislate."[314] By the second strategy, "the court actually sustains a challenged statute but warns the legislature that it will void it in the future unless the legislature acts to amend or repeal the law."[315]

The German Federal Constitutional Court's second version of constitutional adjudication seems to be attractive in the East Asian context. To begin with, to render advisory and admonitory decisions to the legislature on the unconstitutionality of the statute is consistent with the Confucian tradition of remonstrance. The classical Confucians suggest that the ruler has to rule his kingdom with the advice, criticism, and remonstrance of the wise and virtuous scholars.[316] In imperial government in East Asia, in principle, every scholar-official could give advice to and admonish the ruler. However, the government created the Censorate as the centralized institution for the scholar-officials to remonstrate against the misconduct of the emperor and the court. To be sure, the Censorate did not and could not aggressively strike down acts but could remonstrate both *ex ante* and *ex post* against the bad policies and laws of the emperor and the court. This practice, nonetheless, could achieve to a certain extent the purpose of preventing and even excluding the bad policies and laws.[317]

The Confucian tradition of remonstrance can now be transformed into modern "constitutional remonstrance" practiced by the institutions of constitutional review in a way similar to the second version of constitutional adjudication of the German Federal Constitutional Court. Like its German counterpart, with the modern constitutional remonstrance, the institutions of constitutional review can have the authority to render a statute unconstitutional but not immediately nullify it; rather, they can issue remonstrative decisions which set up a deadline for the legislature to revise or abolish the challenged statute, provide general guidelines for the revision and abolition, and warn the legislature that the challenged statute is likely to be voided after the deadline if the legislature fails to make the statute constitutional.

The practice of constitutional review in the remonstrating manner is also justifiable because it is consistent with the Confucian emphasis on harmony. For Confucianism, humanization requires proper social relationships. Conflicts are inevitable in social relationships, and the propriety of interpersonal relations requires the conflicts to be handled in a harmonious manner. Constitutional remonstrance resolves constitutional questions in such a harmonious way. From the Confucian perspective, immediately nullifying the unconstitutional laws seems to be aggressive and hence less conducive to a harmonious political order.

In addition, constitutional remonstrance reflects the communicative nature of the Confucian tradition. To deal with social and political conflicts, the ideal way, for Confucians, is through mutual discourse, debate, advice, criticism, and learning rather than definitive negation. Constitutional remonstrance, which encourages active constitutional dialogues between the institutions of constitutional review and the legislature or other challenged political institutions, allows the resolution of constitutional questions in such a communicative manner. As Mark Tushnet states, "every constitution's terms are subject to reasonable disagreement among the interpreters."[318] Therefore, the handling of constitutional questions requires constitutional dialogues. Immediately voiding the arguably unconstitutional laws, which denies such necessary constitutional dialogues, seem less attractive for the practice of constitutional review in the East Asian Confucian context, which stresses the communicativity of social and political relationships.

Interestingly, empirical studies demonstrate that some constitutional courts in modern East Asia do practice constitutional review in the remonstrating manner. As Tom Ginsburg pointed out, the constitutional courts in South Korea and Taiwan have actually performed the judicial review function in the fashion of remonstrance similar to that of the imperial magistrates, despite their structures emulating the Kelsenian model. Ginsburg states that:

> In Korea and Taiwan, as presidential regimes, the president is sometimes characterized in political commentary as the modern-day equivalent of the emperor.... The courts have been more reluctant to directly challenge the interests of the emperors themselves. When confronted with questions involving the personal authority of the president, they play a role similar to magistrates remonstrating the emperor, sometimes suggesting or advising, but not demanding action.[319]

Ginsburg illustrates this argument by the remonstrative decisions of the respective constitutional courts in the Korean cases of prosecutions of former presidents Roh Tae-woo and Chun Doo-hwan in South Korea, and the Taiwanese case of president Lee Teng-hui's failure to renominate his designated successor, Lien Chan, as premier, after presidential elections.[320] He eventually characterizes judicial review in the East Asian Confucian context as remonstrance.[321] South Korea and Taiwan's constitutional courts' practice of judicial review presents the indigenization of the transplanted western institution. The two East Asian jurisdictions borrow the western institution of constitutional review, but have adapted it to the local context. "Judicial review has been in some sense localized or domesticated by its interaction with local political culture and conditions."[322] As the resonances of the idea and practice of remonstrance and the concerns for harmonious and communicative relations in the Confucian tradition, the modern constitutional courts have exercised the constitutional review power in the remonstrating manner. However, the practices of constitutional remonstrance may be inadvertent and may potentially be a political compromise. East Asian constitutionalism as a distinctive model of constitutionalism seeks to make constitutional remonstrance principled.

Constitutional lecture[323]

Modern institutions of judicial review tend to focus on negatively checking the unconstitutional state actions. One of their deficiencies is the lack of the function to encourage the political leaders to perform their work constitutionally and properly. As I have suggested previously, an institution responsible for ensuring the constitutionality of the state actions should not exclusively involve negatively checking the unconstitutional actions, but should carry out something more positive to encourage constitutional performances by the politicians. I believe that the Confucian tradition of imperial lectures can be adopted and transformed for this purpose.

For the classical Confucians, the wise and virtuous scholars on the ground of their sui generis merits are the best men to uphold fundamental values of a polity and therefore should be treated as the friends or even the teachers of the rulers.[324] In imperial East Asia, the Confucian idea of teaching the rulers by the scholars was practiced by the institution of the imperial lecture.[325] Following the tradition of imperial lectures, the seventeenth-century Chinese neo-Confucian Huang Zongxi (1610–1695) designed his Academy with the teaching function: the libationers of the Academy discuss openly public affairs, while the emperor sits among the rank of students.[326] Hahm also calls for the revival of the Confucian notion of lecturing to the political leaders.[327]

To fix the deficiencies of the modern institution of judicial review, I concur with Hahm's suggestion that we need a modern analogy of the imperial lecture. The imperial lectures can be transformed into modern constitutional lectures carried out by a constitutional academy as an independent constitutional institution consisting of scholars in the fields of constitutional law and theory, political science, philosophy, history, and ethics. They will employ their scholarship to promote constitutionality, constitutional fidelity, and constitutional propriety in the politicians' actions and behaviors. Members of the constitutional academy as a constitutional institution may need a democratic source. This not only satisfies the modern democratic requisite but also is consistent with the Confucian principle of *minben* (people-as-base), which highlights the popular source of a legitimate government. On that ground, members of the constitutional academy can be selected by the legislature. However, a pure political procedure (even democratically) of formulating the personnel of the constitutional academy may not guarantee the academic nature of the institution. The deputies coming from different backgrounds may not select the most distinguished academics appropriate for the business of constitutional promotion by means of scholarship.

To select the most qualified members of the constitutional academy, a scholarly procedure can be supplemented prior to the democratic parliamentary procedure. This scholarly procedure can be described as follows. First, universities, research institutes, and academic associations may recommend suitable candidates on the basis of the candidates' academic achievements and conduct. Subsequently, these candidates will attend a constitutional examination analogous to the imperial examination of the past, which is created and regulated by an act.

The constitutional examination is meant to evaluate deeply the candidates' capacity to analyze and handle constitutionalist issues from the perspective of their corresponding disciplines or from a multidisciplinary perspective. The questions should be general enough for possible responses from various disciplines mentioned. The responses will be anonymously examined. The formulation of the questions and the examination of the responses can be conducted by the most prestigious relevant universities of the nation.

The National Assembly then selects the constitutional academicians for a fixed term on the ground of the candidates' academic achievements, conduct, and performance in the constitutional examination. This combination of democratic and scholarly procedures of the selection of the constitutional academy's members can both enhance the legitimacy of the institution and ensure its independence from political pressure and its scholastic identity, which is the essential condition for the practice of constitutional guarantee by means of scholarship.

The Constitutional Academy will conduct constitutional lectures. Constitutional lectures can be defined as the doctrinal sessions in which the Constitutional Academicians and other wise and virtuous men teach the politicians principles of constitutional government and good governance while explicating constitutional and moral theories and practices and overtly discussing public affairs and the politicians' actions and behaviors from the constitutional and moral perspectives.

Like the past imperial lectures, the prospective constitutional lectures must be formally institutionalized and regularly organized, and regular attendance is mandatory rather than recommended. Who should be the attendants or "the students"? In the past imperial lectures, the attendants normally included the emperor, royals, and key ministers. In the modern constitutional lectures, the attendants might include the top leaders of the three branches of the state, the legislators, and the ministers. Who should be the lecturers? They should mainly include the constitutional academicians, but might extend to others. National constitutional judges and distinguished scholars in the fields of constitutional law and theory, philosophy, and ethics can be invited to give lectures in the constitutional academy. Moreover, in the age of global constitutionalism, there might be the invited guest speakers who are prominent international constitutional law experts and constitutional judges.

Let us consider next the contents of the constitutional lectures. Certainly, what will be considered in constitutional lectures are no longer the *Five Classics* and the *Four Books*, but modern constitutional and moral knowledge, notwithstanding that some Confucian wisdom can be discussed. To begin with, the constitutional lectures can examine the constitutional theories and practices. The constitutional academicians and others can lecture to and discuss with the politicians on fundamental principles of a constitutional government, the constitutional history of the nation, the meaning of the current constitution of the nation, the constitutional structure of the nation, the constitutional rights of the citizens, the constitutional cases of both the nation and other nations, and basic constitutional systems in the world. The constitutional lectures on these issues can arouse the politicians' constitutionalist self-conscience, which is in turn instrumental to guiding them on how to avoid unconstitutional actions and how to perform their political duties and authorities constitutionally and properly, and ultimately to encourage them to conduct constitutional actions for the public good.

Apart from that, the contents of the constitutional lectures may also include theories and practices of political morality. The constitutional academicians and other wise and virtuous persons can lecture and discuss with the politicians on moral principles of a constitutional government and fundamental virtues of constitutional citizens and constitutional leaders that are instrumental to constitutional fidelity and constitutional propriety.

In the imperial lectures, the scholar-officials not only taught the emperor and key ministers the Confucian principles of good government expressed in the classical works, but also discussed the national affairs on that basis. Similarly, scholars of the constitutional academy might not only lecture on the constitutional and moral theories and practices, but can also overtly discuss issues of constitutionality and morality in the conduct of the politicians and national affairs. The "students" may not be keen on that. However, if such a practice is carried out not by vituperative words but in a constructive and elegant manner (the typical manner of the Confucian scholars), this makes the politicians "have the sense of shame" and therefore in the long run is instrumental to their self-rectification and their positive constitutional performance.

Apart from the political leaders, the constitutional academy should also educate the citizens. A constitutionalist community needs both constitutionalist leaders and constitutionalist citizens. Hence, the constitutional academy should educate not only the political leaders but also the ordinary citizens.[328] Citizens of a constitutionalist community need to be educated with constitutional knowledge and instilled with fundamental moral values. It is, however, unlikely that the constitutional academy can regularly organize the constitutional lectures for the citizens. Instead, a more appropriate method for constitutional education of the public is to widely publicize the constitutional lectures delivered to the political leaders.[329] By this, the ordinary citizens can benefit from and be educated by the constitutional lectures.

Constitutional record

Another function that the constitutional academy can perform to both negatively prevent unconstitutional state actions and positively encourage constitutional actions and constitutional ethics is what can be called the "constitutional record," drawing from the traditional historical records institutions in imperial East Asia. In this regard, I concur with Hahm and Qing that the Confucian tradition of historical records can be transformed in the modern age for the constitutionalist purpose: to produce political leaders accountable to their time, to history, and to future generations.[330]

To begin with, the constitutional academy can install the analogy to the *qijuzhu* (Chinese), the two historiographers responsible for recording all words and actions of the emperor. The modern analogy can be named as "constitutional historiographers" responsible for recording verbal transactions and physical movements of the top political leaders. By this, they operate as the routine watchdogs of the practice of public power.

The records by the constitutional historiographers, however, are just the raw materials. In the past, the raw records were sent monthly to the historian office to compose the "veritable records" of the dynasty which were more systematic and judgmental. Similarly, the raw materials by the constitutional historiographers can be sent to the "constitutional historians" of the Constitutional Academy to compose "the constitutional veritable records" of the nation. The constitutional veritable records document systematically and judgmentally the work and conduct of the individual political leaders, constitutional events, constitutional cases, and important activities of the central institutions of the nation.

The constitutional historians of the constitutional academy, by composing the constitutional veritable records, will not simply record the facts, but will pass critical judgments on the state's actions. As the members of the independent constitutional academy of a constitutional government, they can be more explicit in their judgments, compared with their imperial counterparts. However, to make the political leaders have "the sense of shame," the traditional method of accurate terminology (or rectification of names in the narrow meaning) advanced by Confucius in his *Spring and Autumn Annals* can still be effective. This method of record has the constitutional effects of "praise-and-censure."[331] Rectification of names in that way can make the leaders "have the sense of shame," warning them to refrain from unconstitutional actions and improper behaviors and encouraging their constitutional actions and their consideration of constitutional fidelity and constitutional propriety so as to be reverentially memorized by the future generations.

Constitutional records are also useful to "constitutional integrity," the term coined by Dworkin. Constitutional records provide historical materials for the people, judges, and other political actors to recognize the dominant lines of past constitutional evolution. On that ground, they can advance constitutional and political-ethical arguments consistent with the general trend of the whole polity. By this, constitutional law and constitutional ethics are anchored to history, practice, and integrity, preventing the arbitrary constitutional interpretations and mistaken constitutional considerations.

Quis custodies ipso custodiem?

There are certainly limits inherently associated with academics and their scholarship, such as egoism, personal ambition, jealousy, and ongoing conflict in constitutional discourse, which may be destructive to constitutional justice. Hence, it is legitimate to worry about the risks for the arbitrary practice of different powers vested in the constitutional academy. To deal with these limits, several democratic checks in the practice of the constitutional academy's powers can be employed. Ordinary people may be aware of the limits of the academics better than the academics themselves. Therefore, it is necessary to establish mechanisms for the people to check on the actions of the constitutional academy. For example, the people can be allowed to propose topics for constitutional lectures. The constitutional lectures can be televised live and then published online or in print so that people can be involved in the public debates.

Apart from this popular mechanism, a political mechanism could be instrumental in holding the constitutional academy's members accountable for their activities. There may be a constitutional requirement for the legal articulation of "good behavior" of the academics. Serious misbehavior could be subject to legislative impeachment, which could lead to the removal of the academics before the expiration of their term. The third mechanism for restraining the powers of the constitutional academy is scholastic. The constitutional academy's constitutional jurisprudence is developed on the ground of the collective advanced understandings of constitutional justice, appropriate policy, and political morality shared among the scholarly community. Thus, to guard the guardians, what is necessary is a vibrant scholarly community, to which the constitutional academics belong and with which they constantly remain connected.

Conclusion

This chapter introduces a normative theory of mixed constitutionalism in East Asia. East Asian constitutionalism is defined by the axiological, ideational mixtures of ingredients of Confucianism and ingredients of western liberal constitutionalism. This theory has implications for the development of both established constitutionalist polities (Japan, South Korea, and Taiwan) and transforming constitutional systems (China and Vietnam) in East Asia. Particularly, as far as China is concerned, there is the normative theory of "state-party constitutionalism" based on socialist ideology.[332] This is a controversial proposal and needs more debate. At least, proponents of "state-party constitutionalism" must grapple with the ironic fact that the state-party was inhospitable to the discourse on constitutionalism.[333] Mixed constitutionalism is among alternative constitutional possibilities for constitutional development in China. In any case, western liberal constitutionalism may not be the final destination of constitutional development in East Asia. There are a variety of possibilities for the development of constitutionalism in East Asia.

I conclude this chapter by pointing out some implications for the study of global constitutionalism. The burgeoning studies of global constitutionalism argue for the global constitutional convergence, which implicitly or explicitly assumes the convergence of liberal constitutional practices, such as written constitution, the separation of powers, human rights, and judicial review. However, this study of experiences and possibilities of constitutionalism in a Confucian context suggests that western liberal constitutionalism may not be the end of humans' constitutional history, to paraphrase Francis Fukuyama.[334] The thinking of liberal constitutionalism as the final end is bound by the fallacious "*presupposition of exhausted possibilities*," as David Sciulli argues.[335] Michael W. Dowdle also writes that: "the human project of constitutionalism will always contain possibilities that exceed our current constitutional imagination."[336] There is a plurality of constitutional practices in different corners of the globe. Accordingly, a more nuanced approach to global constitutionalism is to take global plurality seriously. Empirically, pluralist global constitutionalism would acknowledge and explore the diversity of constitutional experiences in different sites of the globe.

There is also the normative dimension of pluralist global constitutionalism. Liberal constitutionalism is the conflation of liberalism and constitutionalism. In the west, western liberalism has been called into question by recent scholarship of western communitarianism, and western liberal constitutionalism has been challenged accordingly. The integration of some communitarian values may be the response to the deficiencies of liberal constitutionalism. Mixed constitutionalism or a form of constitutionalism in which western liberal and communitarian values are married is not an impossible imagination in the western context.

However, in the age of globalization, the line between west and east blurs and mutual learning and respect is always necessary. Communitarians, communitarian constitutionalists, libertarians, liberal constitutionalists, mixed constitutionalists, regardless of their western or Confucian backgrounds, should engage in global dialogues for world constitutional justice.

Notes

1 See Chapters 1 and 2.
2 Louis Henkin, "New Birth of Constitutionalism: Genetic Influences and Genetic Defects," *Cardozo Law Review* 14 (1992–1993): 533.
3 Dieter Grimm, "The Achievement of Constitutionalism and Its Prospects in a Changed World," in *The Twilight of Constitutionalism?* ed. Petra Dobner and Martin Loughlin (Oxford: Oxford University Press, 2010).
4 Jiunn-Rong Yeh and Wen-chen Chang "The Emergence of East Asian Constitutionalism: Features in Comparison," *American Journal of Comparative Law* 59(3) (2011): 805–839; Albert H. Chen, "Pathways of Western Liberal Constitutional Development in Asia: A Comparative Study of Five Major Nations," *International Journal of Constitutional Law* 8 (2010): 849–850.
5 For a comprehensive study of Meiji Constitutionalism, see: G. Akita, *Foundations of Constitutional Government in Modern Japan: 1868–1900* (Cambridge, MA: Harvard University Press, 1967)
6 Chen, "Western Liberal Constitutional Development in Asia," 854.
7 See, generally, Kyoko Inoue, *MacArthur's Japanese Constitution: A Linguistic and Cultural Study of Its Making* (Chicago, IL: University of Chicago Press, 1991).
8 Shigenori Matsui, *The Constitution of Japan: A Contextual Analysis* (Oxford: Hart Publishing, 2011), 29–32.
9 Lawrence W. Beer and Hiroshi Itoh, *The Constitutional Case Law of Japan, 1970 through 1990* (Seattle, WA: University of Washington Press, 1996), 12–18.
10 Ibid., 12 ("Some survey data have suggested the Constitution is the most respected and trusted of all Japan's national institutions.")
11 Yeh and Chang "East Asian Constitutionalism," 807.
12 We put aside North Korea for a moment. See, generally, Dae-Kyu Yoon, "The Constitution of North Korea: Its Changes and Implications," *Fordham International Law Journal* 27 (2003): 1289.
13 Chen, "Western Liberal Constitutional Development in Asia," 867.

14 Ibid.; Kyong Whan Ahn, "The Influence of American Constitutionalism on South Korea," *Southern Illinois University Law Journal* 22 (1997): 71.

15 See, generally, Han-Key Lee, "Constitutional Developments in South Korea," *Hong Kong Law Journal* 4 (1974): 41; Dae-Kyu Yoon, "New Developments in Korean Constitutionalism: Changes and Prospects," *Pacific Rim Law and Policy Journal* 4 (1995): 395.

16 Yeh and Chang "East Asian Constitutionalism," 807.

17 Tom Ginsburg, *Judicial Review in New Democracies: Constitutional Courts in Asian Cases* (New York: Cambridge University Press, 2003), 206–246.

18 Chen, "Western Liberal Constitutional Development in Asia," 870–871; Tom Ginsburg, "The Constitutional Court and the Judicialization of Korean Politics," in *New Courts in Asia*, ed. Andrew Harding and Penelope Nicholson (New York: Routledge, 2010), 145–157; Chaihark Hahm, "Beyond 'Law vs. Politics' in Constitutional Adjudication: Lessons from South Korea," *International Journal of Constitutional Law* 10 (2012): 6; Hahm Chaihark and Sung Ho Kim, "Constitutionalism on Trial in South Korea," *Journal of Democracy* 16 (2005): 28; Youngjae Lee, "Law, Politics, and Impeachment: The Impeachment of Roh Moo-hyun from a Comparative Constitutional Perspective," *American Journal of Comparative Law* 53 (2005): 403.

19 Chen, "Western Liberal Constitutional Development in Asia," 871.

20 Albert Chen, "A Tale of Two Islands: Comparative Reflections on Constitutionalism in Hong Kong and Taiwan," *Hong Kong Law Journal* 37 (2007): 653.

21 See Chapter 3.

22 Chen, "Constitutionalism in Hong Kong and Taiwan," 653.

23 Ibid., 666.

24 Ibid., 668–670.

25 Yeh Jiunn Rong, "Constitutional Reform and Democratization in Taiwan, 1945–2000," in *Taiwan's Modernization in Global Perspective*, ed. Peter C.Y. Chow (Westport, CT: Praeger, 2002).

26 Chen, "Western Liberal Constitutional Development in Asia," 876.

27 Wen-Chen Chang, "The Role of Judicial Review in Consolidating Democracy: The Case of Taiwan," *Asia Law Review* 2 (2005): 73. See also Ginsburg, *Judicial Review in New Democracies*, 106–157.

28 See Xiaohong Xiao-Plannes, "Of Constitution and Constitutionalism: Trying to Build a New Political Order in China, 1908–1949," in *Building Constitutionalism in China*, ed. Stéphanie Balme and Michael W. Dowdle (New York: Palgrave Macmillan, 2010), 56; Phan Đăng Thanh, *Tư tưởng Lập hiến Việt Nam nửa đầu Thế kỷ 20* [*Vietnamese Constitutional Thoughts in the First Half of the Twentieth Century*] (Hanoi: Judicial Publishing House, 2006).

29 See, generally, Mo Jihong, "The Constitutional Law of People's Republic of China and Its Development," *Columbia Journal of Asian Law* 23 (2009): 137.

30 Dingjian Cai, "The Development of Constitutionalism in the Transition of China," *Columbia Journal of Asian Law* 19 (2005–2006): 1.

31 Thomas E. Kellogg, "Constitutionalism with Chinese Characteristics? Constitutional Development and Civil Litigation in China," *International Journal of Constitutional Law* 7 (2009): 218.

32 For a collection of essays discussing the content and the political meaning of Charter 08, see Jean-Philippe Beja, Fu Hualing, and Eva Pils, eds., *Liu Xiaobo, Charter 08, and the Challenges of Political Reform in China* (Hong Kong: Hong Kong University Press, 2012). See also, Pitman Potter, "International and Domestic Selective Adaptation: The Case of Charter 08," in *Law and Development and the Global Discourses of Legal Transfers*, ed. John Gillespie and Pip Nicholson (Cambridge: Cambridge University Press, 2012).

33 For an analysis of this debate, see Rogier Creemers, "China's Constitutionalism Debate: Content, Context and Implications," *The China Journal* 74 (2015): 91. Note

that since the use of the term "constitutionalism" (*xianzhing)* has been discouraged in mainland China's official publications, pro-constitutionalist arguments are expressed mainly via intellectual websites, blogs, and channels like Weibo. Ibid.

34 Ibid.

35 Bui Ngoc Son, "Petition 72: The Struggle for Constitutional Reforms in Vietnam," *International Journal of Constitutional Law Blog*, March 28, 2013, available at www.iconnectblog.com/2013/03/petition-72-the-struggle-for-constitutional-reforms-in-vietnam.

36 Bui Ngoc Son, "Vietnam's New Constitution: A Charter for Comprehensive Renovation?" *ConstitutionalNet*, available at: www.constitutionnet.org/news/vietnams-new-constitution-charter-comprehensive-renovation

37 Yeh and Chang, "East Asian Constitutionalism."

38 Ibid., 816.

39 Ibid., 809–916.

40 For detailed elaboration, see ibid., 816–833.

41 For detailed comparison, see ibid., 833–839.

42 Ibid., 839.

43 Chen, "Western Liberal Constitutional Development in Asia," 883.

44 Albert H.Y. Chen, "Constitutions, Constitutional Practice and Constitutionalism in East Asia," in *Routledge Handbook of Asian Law*, ed. Christoph Antons (Routledge, 2016 – forthcoming).

45 Ibid.

46 Ibid.

47 Ibid.

48 Ibid.

49 Ibid.

50 Ibid.

51 Ibid.

52 For discussion of contextualism, see the Introduction.

53 Tom Ginsburg, "Confucian Constitutionalism? The Emergence of Constitutional Review in Korea and Taiwan" *Law & Social Inquiry* 27(4) (2002): 793.

54 See, generally, Vicki Jackson, *Constitutional Engagement in a Transnational Era* (Oxford and New York: Oxford University Press, 2009).

55 See, generally, Saïd Amir Arjomand, ed., *Constitutionalism and Political Reconstruction* (Leiden and Boston, MA: Brill, 2007) (a collection of essays examining the relations of constitutionalism to political reconstruction in Southern and Central Europe, the Middle East, Africa, Asia, and Australasia); Joanne Wallis, *Constitution Making During State Building* (Cambridge: Cambridge University Press, 2014) (examining the positive role of participatory "constituent process" in state building in Timor-Leste and Bougainville); Sofía Sebastián Aparicio, *Post-War Statebuilding and Constitutional Reform* (Basingstoke: Palgrave Macmillan, 2014) (considering the relationship between post-conflict constitution-making and statebuiding in Bosnia and Herzegovina); David S. Law and Mila Versteeg, "The Evolution and Ideology of Global Constitutionalism," *California Law Review* 99 (2011): 1176–1177 (arguing that constitutionalist institutions have been instrumentally used to attract foreign investments and to gain international acceptance).

56 US Constitution, Preamble.

57 See, generally, Bruce Ackerman, *The Future of Liberal Revolution* (New Haven, CT: Yale University Press, 1992); Ulrich K. Preuss, *Constitutional Revolution: The Link Between Constitutionalism and Progress*, trans. Deborah Lucas Schneider (Amherst, MA: Prometheus Books, 1995).

58 Hannnah Arendt, *Between Past and Future* (New York: Penguin Classics, 2006).

59 Hannnah Arendt, *On Revolution* (New York: Viking Press, 1963).

60 Kim Lane Scheppele, "A Constitution Between Past and Future," *William and Mary Law Review* 49 (2008): 1377.

61 Ibid., 1381.
62 Ibid., 1379 (italic in original).
63 Ibid., 1380.
64 Ibid.
65 Ibid., 1388.
66 Ibid., 1389.
67 Ibid., 1402.
68 Jed Rubenfeld, *Freedom and Time: A Theory of Constitutional Self-Government* (New Haven, CT: Yale University Press, 2001), 154.
69 Ruti Teitel, "Transitional Jurisprudence: The Role of Law in Political Transformation," *The Yale Law Journal* 106 (1997): 2071.
70 Yeh and Chang, "East Asian Constitutionalism," 839.
71 Graham Walker, "The Mixed Constitution After Liberalism," *Cardozo Journal of International and Comparative Law* 4 (1996): 313.
72 Vietnam Constitution, Preamble; China Constitution, Preamble.
73 China Constitution, Preamble; Vietnam Constitution, Article 4.
74 On China, see Stéphanie Balme and Michael W. Dowdle, eds., *Building Constitutionalism in China* (New York: Palgrave Macmillan, 2009). On Vietnam, see Bui Ngoc Son, "Constitutional Developments in Vietnam in the First Decade of the Twenty First Century," in *Constitutionalism in Asia in the Twenty First Century*, ed. Albert Chen (Cambridge: Cambridge University Press, 2014).
75 Tom Ginsburg, "East Asian Constitutionalism in Comparative Perspective," in *Constitutionalism in Asia in the Early Twenty-First Century*, ed. Albert H.Y. Chen (Cambridge: Cambridge University Press, 2014).
76 Michel Rosenfeld and András Sajó, eds., *The Oxford Handbook of Comparative Constitutional Law* (Oxford: Oxford University Press, 2012); Tom Ginsburg and Rosalind Dixon, eds., *Comparative Constitutional Law* (Cheltenham: Edward Elgar, 2011).
77 Rosalind Dixon and Tom Ginsburg, *Comparative Constitutional Law in Asia* (Cheltenham: Edward Elgar, 2014); Wen-Chen Chang, Li-ann Thio, Kevin Y.L. Tan, and Jiunn-rong Yeh, *Constitutionalism in Asia: Cases and Materials* (Oxford: Hart, 2014), 5. ("What this book does is to show how constitutionalism is practiced in Asia. It attempts to paint a picture of what is *actually going on*, rather than normatively suggest what should be done, or if an act or device qualitied as 'constitutional'.... There is nothing prescriptive in the book") (italic in original).
78 Keith E. Whittington, "Constitutionalism," in *The Oxford Handbook of Law and Politics*, ed. Keith E. Whittington, R. Daniel Kelemen, and Gregory A. Caldeira (Oxford and New York: Oxford University Press, 2008), 282–289.
79 See, for example, Herbert Wechsler, "Toward Neutral Principles of Constitutional Law," *Harvard Law Review* 73 (1959): 1.
80 See, generally, John Hart Ely, *Democracy and Distrust: A Theory of Judicial Review* (Cambridge, MA: Harvard University Press, 1980).
81 See, generally, John Rawls, *A Theory of Justice* (Cambridge, MA: Belknap Press of Harvard University Press, 1999).
82 I borrow this phrase from Graham Walker, *Moral Foundations of Constitutional Thought: Current Problems, Augustinian Prospects* (Princeton, NJ: Princeton University Press, 1990), 13.
83 Ibid., 9.
84 For normative moral theories of American constitutionalism, see: Jefferson Powell, *The Moral Tradition of American Constitutionalism: A Theological Interpretation* (Durham, NC: Duke University Press Books, 1993); Robert Lowry Clinton, *God and Man in the Law: The Foundations of Anglo-American Constitutionalism* (Lawrence, KS: University of Kansas Press, 1997).

85 For the argument on law as including principles, see Ronald Dworkin, *Law's Empire* (Cambridge, MA: Harvard University Press, 1986), 87–113. For the application of this argument in the sphere of constitutional law, see Ronald Dworkin, *Freedom's Law: The Moral Reading of the American Constitution* (Cambridge, MA: Harvard University Press, 1996).
86 Dworkin, *Freedom's Law*, 2.
87 Ibid., 8.
88 US Constitution, Preamble.
89 For a comprehensive study of the US Constitution from a welfare perspective, see Sotirios A. Barber, *Welfare and the Constitution* (Princeton, NJ: Princeton University Press, 2003).
90 French 1958 Constitution, Preamble.
91 Montesquieu, *The Spirit of Laws* (Berkeley, CA: University of California, 1977), 200.
92 James M. Buchanan, *The Logical Foundations of Constitutional Liberty* (Indianapolis, IN: Liberty Fund, 1999), 371.
93 Ibid., 368.
94 Ibid., 371.
95 Ibid.
96 Ibid.
97 Ibid.
98 Ibid., 372.
99 For an example of the worry of normative moral inquiry of constitutional law for the rule of law reason, see, Robert H. Bork, "Neutral Principles and Some First Amendment Problems," *Indiana Law Journal* 47 (1971): 30–35.
100 Dworkin, *Freedom's Law*, 10.
101 Ibid., 11.
102 Gary J. Jacobsohn, *Constitutional Identity* (Cambridge, MA: Harvard University Press, 2010), 108–109. See also, Alec Stone-Sweet, *Governing with Judges* (Oxford: Oxford University Press, 2000).
103 See, for example, Matthew Søberg Shugart, "Semi-Presidential Systems: Dual Executive and Mixed Authority Patterns," *French Politics* 3 (2005): 323.
104 Walker, "The Mixed Constitution After Liberalism," 313.
105 Ibid. See also, Graham Walker, "The New Mixed Constitution: A Response to Liberal Debility & Constitutional Deadlock in Eastern Europe," *Polity* 26 (1994): 503.
106 Walker, "The Mixed Constitution After Liberalism," 313.
107 Andrew Lintott, "Aristotle and the Mixed Constitution," in *Alternatives to Athens: Varieties of Political Organization and Community in Ancient Greece*, ed. Roger Brock and Stephen Hodkinson (Oxford and New York: Oxford University Press, 2003), 152; Kurt Von Fritz, *The Theory of the Mixed Constitution in Antiquity: A Critical Analysis of Polybius' Political Ideas* (New York: Columbia University Press, 1954).
108 Walker, "The Mixed Constitution After Liberalism," 314.
109 Ibid., 316. Walker elaborates in detail the possibility of nonliberal constitutionalism in Craham Walker, "The Idea of Nonliberal Constitutionalism," in *Nomos XXXIX: Ethnicity and Group Rights*, ed. Ian Shapiro and Will Kymlicka (New York and London: New York University Press, 1997), 154. Walker's idea of nonliberal constitutionalism informs the work of Beau Breslin and Li-ann Thio. See Beau Breslin, *The Communitarian Constitution* (Baltimore, MD: Johns Hopkins University Press, 2004); Li-ann Thio, "Constitutionalism in Illiberal Polities," in *The Oxford Handbook of Comparative Constitutional Law*, ed. Michel Rosefeld and András Sajó (Oxford: Oxford University Press, 2012).
110 Walker, "The Mixed Constitution After Liberalism," 316.

111 Ibid., 317.
112 Ibid.
113 Ibid., 317.
114 Ibid., 318.
115 Ibid.
116 Ibid.
117 Ibid., 319–320.
118 Ibid., 322.
119 Ibid.
120 Ibid., 322–324.
121 Ibid., 328.
122 Ibid., 325.
123 Ibid., 327.
124 Ibid., 328.
125 Ibid.
126 Mark Tushnet, *Advanced Introduction to Comparative Constitutional Law* (Cheltenham: Edward Elgar, 2014), 114–115.
127 Mark Tushnet, "Authoritarian Constitutionalism," *Cornell Law Review* 100 (2015): 391.
128 Tushnet's theory of "authoritarian constitutionalism" is a sort of institutional mixed constitutionalism. It attempts to mix institutions of constitutionalism with institutions of authoritarianism.
129 William A. Galston, "Pluralist Constitutionalism," *Social Philosophy and Policy*, 28 (2011): 228.
130 See, generally, Isaiah Berlin, *Four Essays on Liberty* (Oxford: Oxford University Press, 1969), 167–172.
131 For Galston's comprehensive elaboration of the theory and the practice of value pluralism, see William A. Galston, *The Practice of Liberal Pluralism* (New York: Cambridge University Press, 2004); William A. Galston, *Liberal Pluralism: The Implications of Value Pluralism for Political Theory and Practice* (Cambridge and New York: Cambridge University Press, 2002).
132 Galston, "Pluralist Constitutionalism," 324.
133 Ibid.
134 Ibid.
135 Ibid.
136 Ibid., 234–235.
137 Ibid., 236.
138 The rule of law in this context is likely understood in procedural rather than substantial sense. It includes eight formal standards, namely publicity, prospectivity, generality, clarity, consistence, reality, stability, and enforceability, as elaborated by Lon Fuller. Lon L. Fuller, *The Morality of Law* (New Haven, CT: Yale University Press, 1963).
139 Galston, "Pluralist Constitutionalism," 236.
140 Ibid.
141 Ibid., 238 (emphasis added).
142 Ibid., 239.
143 Ibid., 238.
144 Walker, "The Mixed Constitution After Liberalism," 327.
145 Stephen C. Angle, "Contemporary Confucian and Islamic Approaches to Democracy and Human Rights," *Comparative Philosophy* 4 (2013): 3.
146 Ibid.; Sungmoon Kim, *Confucian Democracy in East Asia: Theory and Practice* (New York: Cambridge University Press, 2014); Joseph Chan, *Confucian Perfectionism: A Political Philosophy for Modern Times* (Princeton, NJ: Princeton University Press, 2013).

147 Yash Ghai, "The Theory of the State in the Third World and the Problem of Constitutionalism," *Connecticut Journal of International Law* 6 (1990–1991): 411; David T. Butler Ritchie, "Critiquing Modern Constitutionalism," *Appalachian Journal of Law* 3 (2004): 37; Louis Henkin, "A New Birth of Constitutionalism: Genetic Influences and Genetic Defects," *Cardozo Law Review* 14 (1993): 533; Li-ann Thio, "Constitutionalism in Illiberal Polities," in *The Oxford Handbook of Comparative Constitutional Law*, ed. Michel Rosefeld and András Sajó (Oxford: Oxford University Press, 2012).
148 Thio, "Constitutionalism in Illiberal Polities."
149 Evan Ramstad, "Seoul Media Bills Pass After Brawl," *Wall Street Journal*, July 23, 2009, accessed July 8, 2015, www.wsj.com/articles/SB124825738778771665; "Taiwanese MPs in Parliament Brawl," *BBC News*, Tuesday, May 8, 2007, accessed July 8, 2015, http://news.bbc.co.uk/2/hi/asia-pacific/6636237.stm
150 See the Introduction.
151 Ibid.
152 David S. Law and Mila Versteeg, "The Evolution and Ideology of Global Constitutionalism," *California Law Review* 99 (2011): 1173.
153 James Legge, *The Chinese Classics with Translations, Critical and Exegetical Notes, Prolegomena, and Copious Indexes, Volume I., Confucian Analects, The Great Learning, The Doctrine of the Mean* (Hong Kong: Hong Kong University Press, 1960), 66.
154 Chan, *Confucian Perfectionism*, 2.
155 Ibid., 118–119.
156 Ibid., 118.
157 Cited in Stephen C. Angle, *Contemporary Confucian Political Philosophy* (Cambridge, MA: Polity, 2012), 53.
158 See Chapter 1.
159 See Chapter 2.
160 Tom Ginsburg, "Confucian Constitutionalism," 763; Albert H.Y. Chen, "Is Confucianism Compatible with Liberal Constitutional Democracy?" *Journal of Chinese Philosophy* 34(2) (2007): 195.
161 Jacobsohn, *Constitutional Identity*, 15.
162 See, generally, William L. Tung, *The Political Institutions of Modern China* (The Hague: M. Nijhoff, 1964).
163 Judgment of October 15, 1998 (98 H6n-Ma 168).
164 Chaihark Hahm, "Law, Culture, and the Politics of Confucianism," *Columbia Journal of Asian Law* 16(2) (2003): 287.
165 2013 Constitution of Vietnam, Preamble, Para. 1.
166 2013 Constitution of Vietnam, Art. 8.
167 1982 Constitution of People's Republic of China, Art. 3
168 1982 Constitution of People's Republic of China, Art 49. The 1992 Constitution of Vietnam had similar provision (Art. 64), stipulating that: "The family is the cell of society.... Parents are duty bound to bring up and educate their children into useful citizens of society. Children have an obligation to respect and care for their grandparents and parents." However, this provision is removed in the current 2013 Constitution.
169 Walker, "The Mixed Constitution After Liberalism," 322.
170 Galston, "Pluralist Constitutionalism," 240.
171 Ibid., 241.
172 Jiang Qing, *A Confucian Constitutional Order: How China's Ancient Past Can Shape Its Political Future*, ed. Daniel A. Bell and Ruiping Fan, trans. Edmund Ryden (Princeton, NJ: Princeton University Press, 2013).
173 Galston, "Pluralist Constitutionalism," 235.
174 Ibid.

175 The doctrine is principally expressed in the work entitled *Doctrine of the Mean*, one of the *Four Books*, reportedly authorized by Zisi, a grandson of Confucius. Legge, *The Chinese Classics with Translations*.
176 For "Hundred Schools of Thought," see Benjamin I. Schwartz, *The World of Thought in Ancient China* (Cambridge, MA: Harvard University Press, 1985).
177 Wm. Theodore de Bary, ed., *Sources of Chinese Tradition* (New York: Columbia University Press, 1060), 154–155.
178 See, generally, John Makeham, *New Confucianism: A Critical Examination* (New York: Palgrave MacMillan, 2003).
179 Galston, "Pluralist Constitutionalism," 236–237.
180 Thomas Hobbes, *Leviathan*, ed. Richard E. Flathman and David Johnston (New York and London: W.W. Norton & Company, 1997), 55 (speaking of "a general inclination of all mankind a perpetual and restless desire of power after power, that ceaseth only in death").
181 Jean-Jacques Rousseau, *The Social Contract*, trans. Christopher Betts (Oxford: Oxford University Press, 1994), 102 ("If there were a nation of gods, it would be governed democratically. So perfect government is not suitable for men.")
182 W.B. Allen, ed., *George Washington: A Collection* (Indianapolis, IN: Liberty Classics, 1988), 521 (speaking of "that love of power, and proneness to abuse it, which predominates in the human heart").
183 See, generally, *James Madison and the Future of Limited Government*, ed. John Samples (Washington, DC: Cato Institute, 2002).
184 Barbarra B. Oberg, ed., *The Papers of Thomas Jefferson, Volume 30* (Princeton, NJ: Princeton University Press, 2003), 541. ("In questions of power, then, let no more be heard of confidence in man, but bind him down from mischief by the chains of the Constitution.")
185 Leslie Lipson, *The Great Issues of Politics: An Introduction to Political Science* (Englewood Cliffs, NJ: Prentice-Hall, 1960), 236.
186 Stephen Holmes, *Passions and Constraint: On the Theory of Liberal Democracy* (Chicago, IL: University of Chicago Press, 1995).
187 Ibid., 7.
188 Ibid.
189 Ibid., 101 (italic in original).
190 Ibid., 163.
191 Lipson, *The Great Issues of Politics*, 236.
192 See Chapter 1.
193 Michael J. Sandel, *Democracy's Discontent* (Cambridge, MA: Harvard University Press, 1996), 4.
194 Keith E. Whittington, "On the Need for a Theory of Constitutional Ethics," *The Good Society* 9 (2000): 61.
195 Michael J. Sandel, *Justice: What's the Right Thing To Do* (New York: Farrar, Straus and Giroux, 2009), 251–260.
196 Whittington, "Constitutional Ethics," 61.
197 Galston, "Pluralist Constitutionalism," 230.
198 Ibid.,, 263–269.
199 Alasdair MacIntyre, *Whose Justice? Which Rationality?* (Notre Dame, IN: University of Notre Dame Press, 1988); Alasdair MacIntyre, *After Virtue* (Notre-Dame, IN: University of Notre Dame Press, 1984).
200 Charles Taylor, *Sources of the Self: The Making of the Modern Identity* (Cambridge: Cambridge University Press, 1989); Charles Taylor, *Philosophy and the Human Sciences: Philosophical Papers 2* (Cambridge: Cambridge University Press, 1985).
201 Michael Walzer, *Thick and Thin* (Notre-Dame, IN: University of Notre Dame Press, 1994); Michael Walzer, *Interpretation and Social Criticism* (Cambridge, MA:

Harvard University Press, 1987); Michael Walzer, *Spheres of Justice* (Oxford: Blackwell, 1983).

202 Sandel, *Democracy's Discontent*; Sandel, *Liberalism and the Limits of Justice*; Michael J. Sandel, *Public Philosophy: Essays on Morality in Politics* (Cambridge, MA: Harvard University Press, 2006); Sandel, *Justice.*

203 See Chapter 1.

204 See, generally, Wm. Theodore de Bary and Tu Weiming, eds., *Confucianism and Human rights* (New York: Colombia University Press, 1998).

205 This worry is traced back to Chen Duxiu (1879–1942), a leading figure of the May Fourth Movement, who was highly critical of Confucianism and strongly supportive of western democracy and science. Chan, *Confucian Perfectionism*, 133.

206 Seung-Hwan Lee, "Was there a Concept of Rights in Confucian Virtue-Based Morality?" *Journal of Chinese Philosophy* 19 (1992): 256.

207 Wm. Theodore de Bary, "Introduction," in *Confucianism and Human rights*, ed. Wm. Theodore De Bary and Tu Weiming (New York: Colombia University Press, 1998), 5–6.

208 Ibid.

209 Ibid., 122.

210 Ibid., 125.

211 Fan Ruiping, *Reconstructionist Confucianism: Rethinking Morality After the West* (Dordrecht: Springer, 2010), 58.

212 Angle, *Contemporary Confucian Political Philosophy*, 85.

213 Julian Rivers, "A Theory of Constitutional Rights and the British Constitution," in Robert Alexy, *A Theory of Constitutional Rights*, trans. Julian Rivers (New York: Oxford University Press, 2002), xix.

214 Justin Tiward, "Confucianism and Human Rights," in *The Routledge Handbook of Human Rights*, ed. Thomas Cushman (New York: Routledge, 2011), 251.

215 Angle, *Contemporary Confucian Political Philosophy*, 83.

216 Hahm, "Constitutionalism, Confucian Civic Virtue, and Ritual Propriety," 53.

217 Stephen Macedo, *Liberal Values: Citizenship, Virtue, and Community in Liberal Constitutionalism* (Oxford: Clarendon Press, 1990); William Galston, *Liberal Purposes: Goods, Virtues, and Diversity in the Liberal State* (New York: Cambridge University Press, 1991); Joseph Raz, *The Morality of Freedom* (Oxford: Oxford University Press, 1986).

218 Sungmoon Kim, *Confucian Democracy in East Asia*, 50.

219 This particular constitutional argument is inspired by Michael J. Meyer's general argument of marrying rights and virtues. See Michael J. Meyer, "When Not to Claim Your Rights: The Abuse and Virtuous Use of Rights," *The Journal of Political Philosophy* 5 (1997): 149.

220 For general argument on combining rights with Confucian virtues, see Seung-Hwan Lee, "Liberal Rights or/and Confucian Virtues," *Philosophy East and West* 46 (1996): 367.

221 Meyer, "When Not to Claim Your Rights."

222 Ibid., 158.

223 Differently, Joseph Chan tries to tie these Confucian virtues to perfectionist goals; see Chan, *Confucian Perfectionism*, 97.

224 See Chapter 3.

225 Walker, "The Idea of Nonliberal Constitutionalism," 175.

226 Ibid., 176.

227 Daniel A. Bell, *Beyond Liberal Democracy: Political Thinking for an East Asian Context* (Princeton, NJ: Princeton University Press, 2006); Chan, *Confucian Perfectionism*; Kim, *Confucian Democracy.*

228 Susan J. Pharr and Robert D. Putnam, eds., *Disaffected Democracies: What's Troubling the Trilateral Countries?* (Princeton, NJ: Princeton University Press, 2000), 13–16.

229 Chan, *Confucian Perfectionism*, 70.
230 Ibid., 87–88.
231 Ibid., 88.
232 Ibid.
233 Ibid.
234 Ibid.
235 Jane Mansbridge, "A 'Selection Model' of Political Representation," *The Journal of Political Philosophy* 17 (2009): 369.
236 Ibid.
237 Mansbridge, "A 'Selection Model'" 370.
238 Ibid., 369.
239 Ibid., 371.
240 Chan, *Confucian Perfectionism*, 372.
241 Ibid.
242 Ibid., 72.
243 Ibid.
244 Ibid., 374.
245 Ibid., 374–376.
246 Kim, *Confucian Democracy*, 187.
247 Ibid., 187.
248 Ibid., 189–190.
249 Ruth W. Grant and Robert O. Keohane, "Accountability and Abuses of Power in World Politics," *American Political Science Review* 99 (2005): 29.
250 Mansbridge, "A 'Selection Model,'" 370.
251 Han, "Confucianism and Human Rights," 136. For a similar argument, see Antonio Cua, "The Status of Principles in Confucian Ethics," *Journal of Chinese Philosophy* 16 (1989): 281; David B. Wong, "Rights and Community in Confucianism," in *Confucian Ethics*, edited by Kwong-lon Shun and David B. Wong (Cambridge: Cambridge University Press, 2004), 45.
252 Han, "Confucianism and Human Rights," 136.
253 Ibid.
254 Ibid.
255 See Chapter 1.
256 David Landau, "Abusive Constitutionalism," *UC Davis Law Review* 47 (2013): 189.
257 Wittington, "Constitutional Ethics," 62.
258 Wittington, "Constitutional Ethics"; "Symposium: Fidelity in Constitutional Theory," *Fordham Law Review* 65 (1997): 1247; James M. Buchanan, *The Economics and the Ethics of Constitutional Order* (Ann Arbor, MI: University of Michigan Press, 1991).
259 Wittington, "Constitutional Ethics," 65.
260 Ibid., 65.
261 Ibid., 61.
262 Ibid., 62. See also, Buchanan, *The Economics and the Ethics of Constitutional Order*, 154–156.
263 Wittington, "Constitutional Ethics," 62.
264 Ibid.
265 Ibid.
266 Ibid.
267 Ibid., 62–63.
268 Ibid., 64.
269 Ibid., 65.
270 Ibid., 65.
271 Hahm, "Constitutionalism, Confucian Civic Virtue, and Ritual Propriety," 46–47.
272 See Chapter 1.

273 Angle, *Contemporary Confucian Political Philosophy*, 93.
274 Ibid.
275 Tu Wei-ming, "Li as the Process of Humanization," *Philosophy East and West* 22 (1972): 187.
276 James Legge, *The Chinese Classics with Translations* (Hong Kong: Hong Kong University Press, 1960), 146.
277 Angle, *Contemporary Confucian Political Philosophy*, 93.
278 Hahm, "Constitutionalism, Confucian Civic Virtue, and Ritual Propriety," 43.
279 Ibid.
280 Ibid., 50.
281 This sort of ritual maximalism can also be found at: Fan Ruiping, *Reconstructionist Confucianism*; Roger T. Ames, *Confucian Role Ethics: A Vocabulary* (Hong Kong: Chinese University Press, 2011).
282 Kim, "A Pluralist Reconstruction of Confucian Democracy," *Dao* 11 (2012): 326–327.
283 For similar adoption of the minimal role of *li*, see: ibid.; Angle, *Contemporary Confucian Political Philosophy*, 102.
284 James Legge, *The Chinese Classics with Translations, Critical and Exegetical Notes, Prolegomena, and Copious Indexes, Volume II., The Works of Mencius* (Hong Kong: Hong Kong University Press, 1960), 265.
285 Legge, *Analects*, 146.
286 Legge, *Analects*, 135.
287 Legge, *Volume II, The Work of Mencius*, 327.
288 Ibid.
289 Ibid., 328.
290 Bryan W. Van Norden distinguishes between "conventional shame" and "ethical shame." Accordingly, conventional shame "is a sort of unpleasant feeling we have when we believe those whose views matter to us look down on us (or on those with whom we identify) on the basis of standard of appearance we share." In contrast, ethical shame "is a sort of unpleasant feeling we have when we believe that we (or those with whom we identify) have significant character flaws." Nordern demonstrates that classical Confucians are more emphatic on the significance of ethical shame than the conventional one. However, he also notes that the two sorts of shame are closely connected because, for the Confucians, human beings are social beings, and hence "our understanding of what is shameful is, and ought to be, informed by the views of others about what is shameful." Bryan W. Van Norden, "The Virtue of Righteousness in Mencius," in *Confucian Ethics*, ed. Kwong-lon Shun and David B. Wong (Cambridge and New York: Cambridge University Press, 2004), 161–162, 168, 174.
291 See Chapter 3.
292 Qing, *Confucian Constitutional Order*, 68.
293 Mauro Cappelletti, *Judicial Review in the Contemporary World* (New York: Bobbs-Merill Company, 1971); Allan R. Brewer-Carias, *Judicial Review in Comparative Law* (Cambridge and New York: Cambridge University Press, 1989).
294 Francisco Ramos Romeu, "The Establishment of Constitutional Courts: A Study of 128 Democratic Constitutions," *Review of Law and Economics* 2 (1) (2006): 103.
295 Tom Ginsburg, *Judicial Review in New Democracies: Constitutional Courts in Asian Cases* (New York: Cambridge University Press, 2003); Wen-Chen Chang, "Transition to Democracy, Constitutionalism and Judicial Activism: Taiwan in Comparative Constitutional Perspective" (JSD dissertation, Yale Law School, 2001).
296 Jun-ichi Satoh, "Judicial Review in Japan: An Overview of the Case Law and an Examination of Trends in the Japanese Supreme Court's Constitutional Oversight," *Loyola of Los Angeles Law Review* 41 (2008): 603–627.

297 Stéphanie Balme and Michael W. Dowdle, "Introduction," in *Building Constitutionalism in China*, ed. Stéphanie Balme and Michael W. Dowdle (New York: Palgrave Macmillan, 2009), 2.
298 Carlos Santiago Nino, "A Philosophical Reconstruction of Judicial Review," in *Constitutionalism, Identity, Difference, and Legitimacy: Theoretical Perspectives*, ed. Michel Rosenfeld (Durham, NC: Duke University Press, 1994), 285–334; Michel Troper, "Logic of Justification of Judicial Review," *International Journal of Constitutional Law* 1 (1) (2003): 99–121.
299 Alexander Bicker, *The Least Dangerous Branch* (New Haven, CT: Yale University Press, 1962).
300 Mark Tushnet, *Taking the Constitution Away from the Courts* (Princeton, NJ: Princeton University Press, 1999).
301 Larry D. Kramer, *The People Themselves: Popular Constitutionalism and Judicial Review* (Oxford and New York: Oxford University Press, 2004).
302 Allan R. Brewer-Carias, *Constitutional Courts as Positive Legislators: A Comparative Law Study* (Cambridge and New York: Cambridge University Press, 2011), 38.
303 Stephen Holmes, "Constitutions and Constitutionalism," in *The Oxford Handbook of Comparative Constitutional Law*, ed. Michel Rosenfeld and András Sajó (Oxford: Oxford University Press, 2012), 198.
304 Ibid.
305 Ibid.
306 Legge, *Volume II, The Work of Mencius*, 283.
307 Hyunyi Cho, "Public Opinion as Personal Cultivation: A Normative Notion and a Source of Social Control in Traditional China," *International Journal of Public Opinion Research* 12(3) (2000): 306.
308 Kim, *Confucian Democracy*, 198.
309 Chapter 1.
310 Chapter 2.
311 Ginsburg, *Judicial Review*, 40; Cappelletti, *Judicial Review*, 85–88.
312 Donald P. Kommers, *The Constitutional Jurisprudence of the Federal Republic of Germany* (Durham, NC and London: Duke University Press, 1997), 52–53.
313 Ibid., 53.
314 Ibid.
315 Ibid.
316 Chapter 2.
317 Chapter 2.
318 Tushnet, "The Rise of Weak-Form Judicial Review," 322.
319 Ginsburg, "Confucian Constitutionalism," 792.
320 Ibid., 792–793.
321 Ibid., 793.
322 Ibid. Korean Constitutional Court is even considered the "venue through which people can engage in a cultural debate on the relevance of Confucian tradition for modern Korean identity." Chaikark Hahm, "Law, Culture, and the Politics of Confucianism," 300.
323 This section and the next section on constitutional record are modified from my previous article, "Beyond Judicial Review: The Proposal of the Constitutional Academy," 2(1) *Chinese Journal of Comparative Law* 2 (2013): 43–77. In that article I have proposed the creation of a constitutional academy as a model of constitutional enforcement in China and Vietnam, where a system of constitutional review is now lacking. It has three functions, namely constitutional review practiced in the manner of constitutional remonstrance, constitutional lecture, and constitutional record. In the context of East Asian democracies (Japan, Taiwan, and South Korea), where a system of constitutional review has already been established, the

constitutional academy can be created as an additional institution with the two functions of constitutional lecture and constitutional record.

324 See Chapter 1.

325 See Chapter 2.

326 Huang Zongxi, *Waiting for the Dawn: A Plan for the Prince*, trans. Wm. Theodore de Bary (New York: Columbia University Press, 1993), 107.

327 Hahm, "Constitutionalism, Confucian Civic Culture, and Ritual Propriety," 52.

328 I thank Professor William Alford at Harvard Law School for his drawing my attention to the idea of constitutional education of the citizens.

329 This can be conducted conveniently and effectively thanks to advanced technology. The constitutional lectures can be reported live on TV. The delivered lectures can then be published both in the traditional print form and on the internet.

330 Hahm, "Constitutionalism, Confucian Civic Culture, and Ritual Propriety," 52; Qing, *A Confucian Constitutional Order*, 58.

331 For example, Mr. A, a president of the state who often acts unconstitutionally and behaves like a knave, can be only rendered as A, not President A, in the records. In contrast, if he acts as a constitutionalist president with constitutional considerations of fidelity and propriety, he can be rendered in the records as President A. The simple rendering of A implicitly censures the recorded: the recorded does not deserve the name of president because he did not act in concordance with the meanings (the defined authorities and duties and the expected virtues) that the name president stands for. This can make the leader have the sense of shame. In contrast, the respectful rendering of President A implicitly praises the recorded: the recorded is a constitutionalist leader who deserved to be recalled and memorized by later generations as president.

332 Larry Cata Backer, "The Party as Polity, the Communist Party, and the Chinese Constitutional State: A Theory of State-Party Constitutionalism," *Journal of Chinese and Comparative Law* 16 (2009): 101.

333 See, generally, Creemers, "China's Constitutionalism Debate."

334 Francis Fukuyama, *The End of History and the Last Man* (London: Penguin Books, 1992).

335 David Sciulli, *Theory of Societal Constitutionalism: Foundations of a Non-Marxist Critical Theory* (Cambridge: Cambridge University Press, 1992), 9–10.

336 Michael W. Dowdle, "Constitutional Listening," *Kent-Chicago Law Review* 88(1) (2012): 119.

Index

FSC
www.fsc.org
MIX
Papier | Fördert
gute Waldnutzung
FSC® C083411

Kolibri 360 GmbH
Ferdinand-Jühlke-Straße 7
99095 Erfurt, Deutschland
produktsicherheit@kolibri360.de